Minnesota's Criminal Justice System

CAROLINA ACADEMIC PRESS

State-Specific Criminal Justice Series

Criminal Justice Basics and Concerns
William G. Doerner, ed.

Alabama's Criminal Justice System
Vicki Lindsay and Jeffrey P. Rush, eds.

Arkansas's Criminal Justice System
Edward Powers and Janet K. Wilson

California's Criminal Justice System
Second Edition
Christine L. Gardiner and Pamela Fiber-Ostrow, eds.

Florida's Criminal Justice System
Second Edition
William G. Doerner

Georgia's Criminal Justice System
Deborah Mitchell Robinson

Illinois's Criminal Justice System
Jill Joline Myers and Todd Lough, eds.

Minnesota's Criminal Justice System
Jeff Bumgarner, Susan Hilal, and James Densley

Missouri's Criminal Justice System
Frances P. Reddington, ed.

Minnesota's Criminal Justice System

Jeff Bumgarner
PROFESSOR OF CRIMINAL JUSTICE
NORTH DAKOTA STATE UNIVERSITY

Susan Hilal
PROFESSOR OF CRIMINAL JUSTICE
METROPOLITAN STATE UNIVERSITY

James Densley
ASSOCIATE PROFESSOR OF CRIMINAL JUSTICE
METROPOLITAN STATE UNIVERSITY

CAROLINA ACADEMIC PRESS
Durham, North Carolina

Library of Congress Cataloging-in-Publication Data

Names: Bumgarner, Jeffrey B., author. | Hilal, Susan M., author. | Densley,
James A. (James Andrew), 1982- author.
Title: Minnesota's criminal justice system / Jeff Bumgarner, Susan Hilal, and
James Densley.
Description: Durham, North Carolina : Carolina Academic Press, [2016] |
Series: State-specific criminal justice series | Includes bibliographical
references and index.
Identifiers: LCCN 2016002518 | ISBN 9781611631777 (alk. paper)
Subjects: LCSH: Criminal justice, Administration of--Minnesota. | Law
enforcement--Minnesota.
Classification: LCC HV9955.M6 .B87 2016 | DDC 364.776--dc23
LC record available at http://lccn.loc.gov/2016002518

CAROLINA ACADEMIC PRESS, LLC
700 Kent Street
Durham, North Carolina 27701
Telephone (919) 489-7486
Fax (919) 493-5668
www.cap-press.com

Printed in the United States of America

*This book is dedicated to our students—past, present, and future—
and their efforts to improve the criminal justice system we write about.*

Contents

List of Figures and Tables

Series Note

Carolina Academic Press' state-specific criminal justice series fills a gap in the field of criminal justice education. One drawback with many current introduction to criminal justice texts is that they pertain to the essentially non-existent "American" criminal justice system and ignore the local landscape. Each state has its unique legislature, executive branch, law enforcement system, court and appellate review system, state supreme court, correctional system, and juvenile justice apparatus. Since many criminal justice students embark upon careers in their home states, they are better served by being exposed to their own states' criminal justice systems. Texts in this series are designed to be used as primary texts or as supplements to more general introductory criminal justice texts.

Acknowledgments

The authors wish to thank the following individuals for contributions large and small during this project:

Colleen Clarke
Mary Clifford
Deborah Eckberg
John Harrington
Paul Iovino
David Squier Jones
Kelly Kalla
John Kirkwood
Sheila Lambie
Bryan Litsey
Kyle Loven
Hugo McPhee
Staff at Minnesota POST Board
Sara Morell
Scott Nadeau
Jillian Peterson
Greg Rye
Nancy Sabin
Ellen Sackrison
Raj Sethuraju
Wade Setter
Dana Swayze

Thanks also to our families and friends for continued enthusiasm and encouragement and Beth Hall and the team at Carolina Academic Press for helping bring this book to fruition.

A special thanks to Michael C. Flynn, who is responsible for the artistic illustrations at the beginning of several chapters.

Introduction

Welcome to Minnesota. Clear blue water. Star of the North. Gopher State. Flyover country. The land of 10,000 lakes (technically 11,842, but who's counting) and 5 million people, 60 percent of whom live in the Twin Cities of Minneapolis and Saint Paul. Some of the largest Hmong, Karen, Somali, and Native American minority populations in the country call Minnesota home. So, too, do 50 different species of mosquitoes, which is not so good. The state is the source of the mighty Mississippi River and site of some of the coldest places in the contiguous United States. It is also home to some of the oldest rocks found on earth and some of the most famous rock stars, including Bob Dylan, Eddie Cochran, and the man who made Minnesota purple with pride, the late Prince Rogers Nelson. Legend has it, the Rolling Stones' hit, "You Can't Always Get What You Want," was inspired by a passing remark to Mick Jagger in an Excelsior drugstore.

Other Minnesota VIPs include one of the greatest writers of all time, F. Scott Fitzgerald, author of *The Great Gatsby*, and one of world's best cartoonists, Charles Shultz, creator of the comic strip *Peanuts*. Minnesotans have elected a former Saturday Night Live writer to the U.S. Senate, and a former prowrestler to the state Governor's Residence. Minnesotans can also claim one former vice president of the United States and one former chief justice. Additionally, a Minnesotan is the associate justice of the Supreme Court responsible for writing the landmark *Roe v. Wade* opinion.

Minnesota is home to the largest Sherlock Homes archive in the world, which is housed on the Minneapolis campus of the University of Minnesota. Aviator Charles Lindbergh grew up in Minnesota. *The Mary Tyler Moore Show*, Garrison Keillor's *A Prairie Home Companion*, Judy Garland ("There's no place like home!"), and the Academy Award-winning sibling filmmakers, the Coen Brothers, also claim Minnesota origins. The state further celebrates Greg LeMond, America's only *official* Tour de France winner (sorry, Lance)!

Food features prominently in Minnesota life. Both General Mills, one of the largest food makers in the world, and Hormel Foods, maker of the iconic Spam, are headquartered in the state. And every year, during one of the nation's largest state fairs, over 1,000,000 people "Get-Together" to consume any and all food on a stick. Shopping is big too. Minnesota birthed the nation's first indoor shopping mall, Southdale Center in Edina, and still hosts its largest, the modestly named "Mall of America" in Bloomington.

Eighteen Fortune 500 companies (more per capita than any other state) and the largest privately owned company in the United States also comprise the Minnesota landscape. Inline skating became a popular activity because two Minnesotans created Rollerblade Inc. Several Minnesota cities have appeared in *Money Magazine's* Top 10 list of "Best Places to Live" in the United States, and one has even garnered the top spot. Other Minnesota cities have earned number one rankings in the country for being the most literate, most bike friendly, even the healthiest. One city, Lake City, is the birthplace of water skiing and 45 minutes south (Minnesotans define distance by how far it takes to drive) is Rochester, home of one of the world's best hospitals, the Mayo Clinic.

As you can tell, we're proud of this state. And while a list of all of Minnesota's cultural, historical, and social fun facts could go on and on, this state is also known for its criminal justice system and rich crime history—the subjects of this book. *Minnesota's Criminal Justice System* is part of Carolina Academic Press's State-Specific Criminal Justice Series and is designed to be a primary text or supplement to a general introduction to criminal justice textbook. Why do we need another intro textbook, you may ask? The answer is that every state *does* criminal justice differently. Our Constitution grants us this authority. Likewise, every state *teaches* criminal justice differently. There are no initial-entry police academies in Minnesota independent of higher education, for instance; instead, colleges and universities administer our professional peace officer education programs. This is but one example of why a book examining the local criminal justice landscape for the benefit of students embarking upon careers in their home state is so important. Further, current practitioners and residents alike should know how this state administers justice to ensure it is being served. In the end, all Minnesotans should find something of interest in this book.

Preview of *Minnesota's Criminal Justice System*

This book is organized over ten chapters. Some chapter titles are a bit satirical, even peculiar, but they link aspects of the criminal justice system to all things Minnesotan.

Chapter One, "Not-So-Minnesota-Nice," offers an overview of crime and crime trends in Minnesota, including key definitions, exploration of some of the state's most famous crimes and criminals, and celebration of some of the best known criminal justice policies, practices, and innovations with Minnesota roots. Chapter Two, "What the Movie *Fargo* Didn't Teach You," outlines how policing is structured in Minnesota at the state and local levels, with special attention paid to Minnesota's one-of-a-kind education and training standards for entry into the law enforcement field. Chapter Three, "Warren Burger Was Born Here," describes how Minnesota's court system is organized and how cases progress through the system, with additional focus on crime victims. Chapter Four, "The Land of 10,000 Lakes and 10,000 Prisoners," discusses the administration of corrections in Minnesota, both in confinement and the community. Attention then shifts to Chapter Five, "Involuntarily Committed," and those Minnesotans in need of acute inpatient psychiatric services or committed by the court as sexual psychopathic personalities, sexually dangerous persons, or mentally ill and dangerous. Chapter Six, "Meet Me at the Mall of America," explores juvenile delinquency and the juvenile justice apparatus in Minnesota. Chapter Seven, "The Shame of the Cities," discusses Minnesota's gangs and gangsters, outlining why the Twin Cities will be forever linked to some of the most notorious criminals (and infamous policies) in history. Minnesota does not police crime and administer justice in isolation, thus Chapter Eight, "The State and District of Minnesota," outlines the role of the federal system in Minnesota. Chapter Nine, "The Death of the Death Penalty," examines the controversial story of capital punishment in Minnesota, which was once a sentencing option and still deserves special attention in this state. The tenth and final chapter, "The Times They Are A-Changin'," evokes the Bob Dylan classic to explain emerging crime and justice concerns in Minnesota, with implications and predictions for the future.

Minnesota's Criminal Justice System

Chapter One

Not-So-Minnesota-Nice: An Overview of Crime in Minnesota

Learning Objectives

- Explore the criminal justice process
- Define crime and understand how it is measured in Minnesota
- Understand the calculation of crime rates and clearance rates
- Distinguish between crime types and categories
- Explore historical "true crime" cases unique to Minnesota
- Examine statistical crime trends in Minnesota compared to other states
- Identify Minnesota innovations in criminal justice policy and practice

The Criminal Justice Process

In simple terms, the criminal justice system is the set of institutions developed as the state response to crime and criminals. The main elements of the American criminal justice system are the police, courts, corrections (including probation, parole, jails, and prisons), and, to a lesser extent, victims' services. The popular *systems* perspective of interrelated justice agencies originated with the American Bar Foundation's landmark *Survey of the Administration of Justice* (Remington, 1956). The fact criminal justice agencies are largely independent bodies that set their own policies, take their authority and budgets from different sources, and at times fail to coordinate their activities, however, has led to criticism the criminal justice *system* is not a system at all (Walker, 1992). Still, most criminal justice functions in the U.S. are performed at the state and local levels, hence why this book is crucial for students and scholars of criminal justice in Minnesota and beyond.

We have a system of dual sovereignty. The federal criminal justice system handles only violations of federal law or crimes that cross state boundaries. When there are conflicting state laws, the *preemption doctrine* applies, meaning the federal law overrides state law because the Constitution (under Article VI) defines federal law as the "Supreme Law of the Land." There are some state laws that do diverge from federal law in our federalist system. For example, some states have de-criminalized marijuana while it remains an illegal substance under federal law. *Concurrent jurisdiction* means an individual who violates both state and federal law can be separately charged and tried in each jurisdiction. So too can someone be charged both criminally and civilly at the same time. *Criminal law* includes two types: (a) *procedural law*, which is how people are treated in the system, and (b) *substantive law*, which defines what conduct is considered criminal. *Civil law* deals with private rights between individuals or organizations.

Justice is the general principal that individuals should get what they deserve—a common sense idea that has received many philosophical formulations from Aristotle to Kant (Russell, 1945). But when we think of *criminal* justice, we are generally referring to the application of the law and the administration of legal institutions, which in Minnesota are mainly operated by trained legal professionals. Here conceptions of formal or procedural fairness are paramount, namely the operation or *rule of law* according to prescribed "principals" of "due process" (Rawls, 1971). Every country around the world has its own rules of law, and in the U.S. every state does, but there are four key principles that should be associated with the concept, which include:

1) The government and its officials and agents as well as individuals and private entities are accountable under the law.
2) The laws are clear, publicized, stable, and just; are applied evenly; and protect fundamental rights, including the security of persons and property.
3) The process by which the laws are enacted, administered, and enforced is accessible, fair, and efficient.
4) Justice is delivered in a timely way by competent, ethical, and independent representatives and neutrals who are of sufficient number, have adequate resources, and reflect the makeup of the communities they serve.

(World Justice Project, 2015)

Figure 1.1 outlines the main steps in the criminal justice process in Minnesota for crimes that are punishable by at least one year and one day in a state prison (adult felonies; for the juvenile justice process, see **Chapter Six**). This assembly-line process is like a funnel, wide at the top and narrow at the bottom. Early in the criminal justice process, there are many cases, but the number of cases dwindles as decision makers remove cases from the process (see President's Commission on Law Enforcement and Administration of Justice, 1967).

Crime in Minnesota

The most basic definition of crime is an infraction of criminal law, or conduct proscribed by the law and liable to attract punishment (see Farmer, 2008). Since publication of Sir William Blackstone's (1765) seminal treatise on English common law, it is ordinary to think of some crimes, murder for example, as *mala in se* (Latin for "evil unto itself") or morally wrong, and other crimes, such as speeding, as *mala prohibita*, or criminal simply because law prohibits them. *Social constructionists* argue, however, crime is merely a classification of behavior defined by individuals with the power and authority to make such a classification (Henry, 2009). They remind us that crime is diverse. Crime is defined into being. Crime is time, space, and culture bound. Hence, "one man's deviation may be another's custom" (Matza, 1969, p. 11).

In Minnesota, an act is not classified as a crime unless there is the possibility of imprisonment. There are four levels of offenses in Minnesota: felony, gross misdemeanor, misdemeanor, and petty misdemeanor. As defined by Minnesota Statutes §609.02:

- *Felony* is a crime for which a sentence of imprisonment for more than one year may be imposed.
- *Gross Misdemeanor* is any crime which is not a felony or misdemeanor. The maximum fine which may be imposed is $3,000.
- *Misdemeanor* is a crime for which a sentence of not more than 90 days or a fine of not more than $1,000, or both, may be imposed.
- *Petty Misdemeanor* is a petty offense which is prohibited by statute, which does not constitute a crime and for which a sentence of a fine of not more than $300 may be imposed.

In general, crimes are often categorized into three types: (1) violent/personal crime; (2) property crime; and (3) public order crime. However, the Federal Bureau of Investigation's (FBI) Uniform Crime Reporting (UCR) program defines official crime classifications. The FBI has been responsible for

Figure 1.1. The Criminal Justice Process for Felony Crimes in Minnesota

Crime Occurs and Is Reported
Police witness a crime or suspicious activity or some-one reports it, typically by calling 911.

Police Investigate
The police respond to, and investigate, re-ported incidents to determine whether what happened could be considered a crime and if there is enough evidence to present the case for possible prosecution.

Criminal Complaint
When there is enough evidence to charge a crime, pros-ecutors will issue a criminal complaint (a formal written statement of the charges against a defendant). A judge must approve and sign the complaint. There are three types of complaint: (1) *Detention*, issued when the de-fendant is in custody. If someone is arrested without a warrant, prosecutors have 36 hours to either charge the case or release the individual; (2) *Warrant*, a court order authorizing police officers to arrest and jail the defen-dant before the defendant's first appearance in court; and (3) *Summons*, a court order that requires the de-fendant to appear in court on a specific day.

Criminal Charge
Prosecutors review the police report to de-termine if there is enough evidence to charge a crime. Charges are filed when there is enough evidence that a conviction at trial is likely. If there is not enough evidence, the prosecutor will either refer the case back to law enforcement for more investigation or will not file charges.

Indictment
Crimes that carry a potential life sentence must be heard by an independent grand jury of up to 23 randomly se-lected citizens. If the grand jury determines there is prob-able cause to believe that the crime has been committed and that the defendant has committed it, the grand jury issues charges in a document called an indictment. If the grand jury finds that there is not enough evidence to support criminal charges, then there is a "no bill."

Arraignment or "First Appearance" in Court
The defendant is informed of the charges and his or her rights, including the right to an at-torney. If the defendant cannot afford to pay for an attorney, the court will appoint a pub-lic defender to represent the defendant. The defendant may enter a plea, usually "guilty" or "not guilty." The judge sets bail and/or con-ditions of release.

Trial
A defendant has a right to a jury trial for any offense punishable by jail or prison time. Juries of 12 people hear felonies, and juries of six people hear gross mis-demeanors. The judge and attorneys for both sides ques-tion potential jurors to determine who should serve on the jury. This process is called jury selection or *voir dire*.

The prosecution must present enough evidence to prove *beyond a reasonable doubt* that a crime happened and that the defendant committed it. The jury must reach a unanimous verdict for a defendant to be convicted of a crime. A defendant may also choose to have the trial heard by a judge rather than a jury.

Omnibus Hearing
At a pre-trial conference the prosecutor and defense attorney determine whether the case can be resolved without trial, as follows: (1) plead guilty as charged; (2) plead guilty to an amended charge; (3) diversion; (4) dismissal. If the case does not resolve and is going to trial, the pre-trial hearing also addresses is-sues such as matters of evidence, constitu-tional issues, and other issues related to trial.

Sentencing
The judge determines the sentence, taking into account the sentence recommended by state guidelines, other information in the pre-sentence investigation, victim impact statements, and suggestions from the prosecu-tion and defense. Sentences can include: (1) prison time at a state facility; (2) jail time at a local facility; (3) money paid to the victim for expenses related to the crime (restitution); (4) labor performed to benefit the com-munity (community service); (5) probation; or (6) other penalties as recommended or negotiated.

Source: Author created from Hennepin County Attorney (2015).

"collecting, publishing, and archiving" U.S. crime statistics since 1930. The agency tracks crimes known to police, which of course is limiting both because some people choose not to report crime to the police, while others commit crime, but go undetected. Despite these limitations, the UCR is the most widely used measure of crime in the United States.

The FBI classification system divides offenses into two groups, Part I and Part II crimes. Within Part I offenses, there are two categories: violent and property. The eight Part I offenses (see **Figure 1.2**) collectively make what is referred to as the *crime index*. See **Table 1.1** for Minnesota State Statute definitions. In order for meaningful comparisons to be made, crime statistics often are provided as a *rate* that controls for the variance in population sizes. Crime rates usually are presented as X number of crimes reported per 100,000 people. In 2012, for example, Minneapolis had approximately 390,000 residents and 39 homicides. In the same year, St. Paul had approximately 290,000 residents and 12 homicides. If we "plug in" the numbers, we have the following 2012 homicide victimization rates:

Minneapolis: (39 / 390,000) × 100,000 = 10 per 100,000
St. Paul: (13 / 290,000) × 100,000 = 4.5 per 100,000

The rate thus reveals a tale of two cities—the homicide risk for someone living in Minneapolis is over double that of someone living on the other side of the Mississippi River in St. Paul. Keep in mind, however, the numbers only tell us *what*, not *why*.

Figure 1.2. FBI Uniform Crime Report Part I Crimes

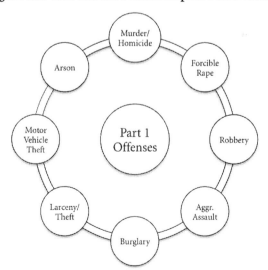

Source: Author created from Federal Bureau of Investigation (2013).

Table 1.1. Minnesota Statutory Definitions of Part 1 Offenses

Part 1 Offenses	Degree of Offense (All Felony Level)	Minnesota Statutory Reference	Definition
Criminal Homicide	Murder in the First Degree	§609.185 Subd. A(1)	Causes the death of a human being with premeditation and with intent to effect the death of the person or of another.
Forcible Rape	Criminal Sexual Conduct in the First Degree	§609.342 Subd. 1	A person who engages in sexual penetration with another person, or in sexual contact with a person under 13 years of age.
Robbery	Aggravated Robbery in the First Degree	§609.245 Subd. 1	Whoever, while committing a robbery, is armed with a dangerous weapon or any article used or fashioned in a manner to lead the victim to reasonably believe it to be a dangerous weapon, or inflicts bodily harm upon another.
Aggravated Assault	Assault in the First Degree	§609.221 Subd. 1	Whoever assaults another and inflicts great bodily harm.
Burglary (Breaking or Entering)	Burglary in the First Degree	§609.582 Subd. 1	Whoever enters a building without consent and with intent to commit a crime, or enters a building without consent and commits a crime while in the building, either directly or as an accomplice.
Larceny-Theft (Except Motor Vehicle Theft)	Theft	§609.52 Subd. 2(a)	Intentionally and without claim of right takes, uses, transfers, conceals, or retains possession of movable property of another without the other's consent and with intent to deprive the owner permanently of possession of the property.
Motor Vehicle Theft	Theft	§609.52 Subd. 2(17)	Takes or drives a motor vehicle without the consent of the owner or an authorized agent of the owner, knowing or having reason to know that the owner or an authorized agent of the owner did not give consent.
Arson	Arson in the First Degree	§609.561 Subd. 1	Whoever unlawfully by means of fire or explosives, intentionally destroys or damages any building that is used as a dwelling at the time the act is committed, whether the inhabitant is present therein at the time of the act or not, or any building appurtenant to or connected with a dwelling whether the property of the actor or of another.

Note: Only the first degree (if applicable) of each offense is highlighted for illustration purposes.
Source: Author created from Minnesota Revisor of Statutes.

The FBI selected the Part I crimes "because they are serious crimes, they occur with regularity in all areas of the country, and they are likely to be reported to police" (Federal Bureau of Investigation, 2004). For Part I crimes, the FBI includes clearance statistics. In order for a crime to be considered cleared by arrest, at least one person must have been: "1) arrested, 2) charged with the commission of the offense, and 3) turned over to the court for prosecution" (Federal Bureau of Investigation, 2013). If a person is not arrested, a case can still be cleared by exceptional means when investigators have met the following four criteria:

1) Identified the offender;
2) Gathered enough evidence to support an arrest, make a charge, and turn over the offender to the court for prosecution;
3) Identified the offender's exact location so that the suspect could be taken into custody immediately;
4) Encountered a circumstance outside the control of law enforcement that prohibits the agency from arresting, charging, and prosecuting the offender.

(Federal Bureau of Investigation, 2013)

Figure 1.3. Criteria for Exceptional Clearance Classification in Minnesota, Involving Circumstances Outside of the Control of Law Enforcement

1. The offender commits suicide.
2. A double murder occurs (two people kill each other).
3. The offender dies after making a confession.
4. The offender is killed by a law enforcement officer.
5. Offender admits to committing a crime while already in custody for another offense.
6. The offender is prosecuted in another city for a different crime by federal, state, or local authorities and the other jurisdiction refuses to release the offender.
7. Another jurisdiction refuses to cooperate with the prosecution.
8. Victim of crime refuses to cooperate with the prosecution.
9. The offender is prosecuted for a less serious charge than the one for which he is arrested.
10. The offender is a juvenile who is handled by a verbal or written notice to the parents in instances involving minor offenses.

Source: Author created from Minnesota Department of Public Safety UCR Report (2013).

Part II offenses are less serious offenses for which only arrest data is collected, and includes crimes such as driving under the influence, forgery, prostitution, gambling, disorderly conduct, drunkenness, and drug offenses. The FBI also keeps track of and disseminates hate crimes statistics (see **Chapter Seven**) committed throughout the United States, as well as the number of officers killed in the line of duty. Furthermore, for some crimes, namely homicide, the FBI provides additional information (expanded data), including victim data, weapons used, and the circumstances related to the homicide.

The Federal Bureau of Investigation is responsible for national-level crime data collection. The Minnesota Bureau of Criminal Apprehension (BCA) is responsible for data collection at the state level, per Minnesota Statutes § 299C. The BCA has compiled arrest data from law enforcement agencies in the state since 1972 using the same data repository: The Criminal Justice Reporting System (CJRS). The BCA publishes arrest data annually in the *Minnesota Crime Information Report*, also known as the state UCR. Minnesota data are then submitted to the FBI for inclusion in the federal UCR. Close to 94% of law enforcement agencies in the state report to the BCA, representing 99% of the total population (Department of Public Safety, 2013). The summary includes information on: "offenses, clearances and arrests, as well as the number of law enforcement officers killed or assaulted, firearms discharges by law enforcement, missing children reports, police pursuits and bias offenses" (Minnesota Department of Public Safety, BCA, 2015).

It is important to mention that while the UCR is the official crime record for crimes *known* to police, there are other methods to measure crime, including the hidden or "dark figure" of unreported and undiscovered crime (Biderman & Reiss, 1967). The National Crime Victimization Survey (NCVS), administered by the Bureau of Justice Statistics, is one such mechanism. The NCVS is an annual survey of about 50,000 to 80,000 households twice a year that relies on victims' memories and honesty to explore the "frequency, characteristics, and consequences" of crime victimization nationwide (Bureau of Justice Statistics, 2013). Self-report surveys are other means, which provide information on the profiles and motivations of (typically incarcerated) offenders. Surveys that invite respondents to disclose the nature and extent of any prior drug use are one example. All crime data collection methods have strengths and weaknesses, discussion of which is beyond the scope of this chapter (see Birdman & Lynch, 1991). Suffice it to say, each method contributes in its own way to our understanding of crime in Minnesota and beyond.

A Brief History of Crime in Minnesota

Minnesota has a long, at times unflattering, crime history (MinnPost, 2008). Below is a snapshot of some of the most notorious cases and criminals from the past 100 years, in chronological order:

1920

Elias Clayton, Elmer Jackson, and Isaac McGhie, three black circus workers, are attacked and lynched by a mob in Duluth following unsubstantiated rumors they had raped and robbed a teenage girl (Fedo, 2000). The killings shocked the country, particularly for their occurrence in the northern United States. In 2003, the city of Duluth erected a memorial to the murdered workers.

1931

In *Near v. Minnesota*, 283 U.S. 697 (1931), the U.S. Supreme Court rules that prior restraint on publications is a violation of free speech and free press. In so doing, the Court struck down a state law that allowed the police to confiscate publications that were "malicious," "scandalous," or "obscene." The case involved a virulently anti-Semitic pamphlet.

1933

William Hamm Jr. of Hamm's Brewery is kidnapped by the Barker-Karpis Gang and held for a $100,000 ransom. The ransom was paid and Hamm was set free. However, the FBI, using new technology for the time, "latent fingerprint identification" with the silver nitrate method, were able for the first time ever to lift the prints off the ransom notes linking the notorious gangsters to the ransom (Federal Bureau of Investigation, 2003). The FBI eventually apprehended the Barker-Karpis Gang following another kidnap, this time of banker Edward Bremer Jr. **Chapter Seven** provides more details of gangsters and their crimes.

1934

On July 20, one month into the three-month-long, bloody, history-changing Minneapolis Teamsters strike, police open fire on unarmed strikers, killing two and injuring fifty. Many of those injured were shot in the back as they tried to flee the scene. The incident is now known as "Bloody Friday" (Teamsters, 2013).

1963

One of St. Paul's most notorious crime cases is the murder of 34-year-old homemaker Carol Thompson (Swanson, 2007). T. Eugene Thompson paid a hit man $3,000 to kill his wife in their upper-middle-class Highland Park home. The motive? To collect more than $1 million in life insurance and free himself for another woman. On the morning of March 6, the hit man surprised Mrs. Thompson in her bedroom, knocked her out with a rubber hose and tried to drown her in the bathtub. When she came to and escaped, the hit man's pistol misfired, so he beat her with the gun's butt, then stabbed her in the neck. Thinking she was dead, he went to wash up—only to find she had fled out the door to a neighbor's house. "I never saw anyone who wanted to live so hard in all my life," the hit man was later quoted as saying (Duchschere, 2013). But Mrs. Thompson died four hours later at Ancker Hospital in St. Paul. The Coen brothers' movie *Fargo* is based in part on the botched nature of the crime, which at the time inspired a year-long media frenzy and, eventually, a life sentence for the husband, who took the stand in his own defense.

1972

The abduction of Virginia Piper from her Orono home still is the largest kidnap-for-ransom crime in FBI history. Masked men demanded $1 million for her return and retired investment banker Harry C. Piper Jr. obliged (Swanson, 2014). Mrs. Piper is soon found alive, chained to a tree in Jay Cooke State Park near Duluth. Five years later, Kenneth Callahan and Donald Larson are arrested and charged with the kidnapping. A court convicts them, but the verdict is overturned on appeal and the men win acquittal in a second trial. The kidnapping remains unsolved and just $4,000 of the ransom money was ever recovered.

1977

Glensheen, a Duluth mansion with 39 rooms and the look of an English manor, is the scene of an infamous unsolved crime (Feichtinger, DeStanto, & Waller, 2009). Elisabeth Congdon, 83, is discovered smothered with a pink pillow; her night nurse, Velma Pietila, is found bludgeoned to death with a candlestick. Suspicion falls on Congdon's daughter, Marjorie, and her husband, Roger Caldwell, who stand to gain $8 million from the Congdon estate. Roger is convicted of the crime. Marjorie is later accused of planning the murders, but is acquitted. Five years after Caldwell's suicide in 1993, however, Marjorie is imprisoned in Arizona for arson and insurance fraud. Glensheen is now one of northern Minnesota's top tourist attractions.

1988

Lois E. Jenson v. Eveleth Taconite Co. was the first class-action sexual harassment lawsuit in the United States, filed on behalf of Lois Jenson and other female workers at the EVTAC mine in Eveleth, on the state's northern Iron Range. Jenson and other women endured over a decade of hostile behavior from male employees, including sexual harassment, abusive language, threats, stalking, and intimidation (Bingham & Ganslet, 2003). During the trial, lawyers from the mine company were controversially allowed to obtain lifetime medical records of all of the women. Ahead of the trial, the plaintiffs endured long depositions that explored their personal lives in great detail. On December 23, 1998, however, just before a second jury trial on damages was set to begin, fifteen women settled for a total of $3.5 million.

1989

One of America's most infamous child-abduction cases begins with a trip by three boys to a convenience store in St. Joseph. As the kids make their way home, a masked and armed man snatches 11-year-old Jacob Wetterling. The other boys run for help and police quickly arrive to comb the area. They find few clues other than the discarded bikes and a faint tire track. Thousands of man-hours and some 50,000 leads later, Jacob's fate remains a mystery. But the crime leads to federal legislation requiring states to establish sex-offender registries, and a foundation is established in Jacob's name to prevent child exploitation.

1989

Billy Glaze, a convicted serial killer, is sentenced to three life terms for killing three Native American women in Minneapolis. Despite his conviction, Glaze maintained his innocence and sought the assistance of the Innocence Project. Since the conviction, strides were made in DNA testing, and as such, some of the physical evidence at the scene was tested. The DNA tested belonged to another offender. Glaze asked for a new trial and the Hennepin County attorney denied it, stating that "new evidence is inconclusive and unpersuasive, does not meet the clear and convincing standard required for a new trial and already was heard by the original jury" (Hennepin County Attorney, 2014). Glaze died in prison on December 22, 2015.

1997

Andrew Cunanan kills two men in Minnesota, one in Chicago, and another in New Jersey, before shooting fashion designer Gianni Versace to death two months later in Miami. Cunanan later committed suicide after being cornered by police on a houseboat.

1999

The past catches up with Kathleen Soliah, 23 years after she went underground to avoid an indictment for attempted murder in connection with police car bombings in California. On her way to teach English as a second language, the former Symbionese Liberation Army member—known in the Twin Cities as Sara Jane Olson—is arrested in St. Paul. In 2002, she is convicted and sentenced to two consecutive terms of 10 years to life. "She's led a good life," observes *America's Most Wanted* host John Walsh, "but if you have tried to kill cops, you're going to be in trouble."

2001

Almost a month before the deadly September 11, 2001, terrorist attacks in which 19 al-Qaeda operatives hijacked and then crashed four passenger airliners into the World Trade Center complex in New York City, New York, the Pentagon in Arlington County, Virginia, and into a field near Shanksville, Pennsylvania, killing 2,977 people, FBI agents based in Minneapolis are unable to get approval from higher echelons elsewhere to obtain a criminal search warrant for the laptop of Zacarias Moussaoui, who had aroused the suspicions of his instructors at a commercial flight training school in Eagan, Minnesota (Office of the Inspector General, 2006).

2003

Dru Sjodin is abducted from the Columbia Mall parking lot in Grand Forks, North Dakota, by 50-year-old registered level-3 sex offender Alfonso Rodriguez Jr. Approximately five months later her body was discovered near Crookston, Minnesota, with evidence that she was raped and murdered. Her death prompted the creation of the Dru Sjodin National Sex Offender Public Website. The registry is coordinated by the United States Department of Justice (n.d.) and operates a website search tool allowing the public to submit a single query to obtain information about sex offenders throughout the United States. Alfonso Rodriguez Jr. was tried in federal court in 2006 due to the interstate nature of the crime. He was convicted and sentenced to death, a possibility not allowed under North Dakota or Minnesota law (see **Chapter Nine**). He is still on death row appealing his conviction.

2003

Fifteen-year-old John Jason McLaughlin shoots two of his classmates at Rocori High School in Cold Springs, Minnesota (see **Chapter Six**). One dies the same day, another a few days later. McLaughlin claimed one of his victims, Seth Bartell, "teased him all the time." He tried to claim he was not competent to stand trial, but the Minnesota Supreme Court declined this motion (*State of Minnesota vs. John Jason McLaughlin*, 2007). McLaughlin was sentenced to life in prison.

2005

Sixteen-year-old Jeff Weise goes on a bloody rampage on the Red Lake Indian Reservation, killing his grandfather, his grandfather's companion, a teacher, a school security guard, and five students at Red Lake High School before turning the gun on himself (Enger, 2015). A dozen others are wounded in what was, at the time, the deadliest school shooting since 15 people were killed at Columbine High School near Littleton, Colorado, in 1999 (see **Chapter Six**).

2007

Koua Fong Lee is wrongfully convicted of vehicular homicide after his 1996 Toyota Camry accelerated uncontrollably at the end of a St. Paul freeway exit ramp and crashed into two vehicles, killing one man and two children, and injuring two other people. Lee maintained his innocence and two years later, Toyota admitted some of their vehicles were experiencing acceleration issues. After serving almost three years in prison, Lee was exonerated on August 5, 2010 (Minnesota Innocence Project, 2015). A jury ultimately ruled that Toyota was 60% responsible for the deadly crash. Toyota was ordered to pay $11 million in damages to the victims and $2 million to the Lee family (Furst, 2015).

2007

Police work at the Minneapolis-St. Paul (MSP) International Airport became national news when then U.S. Senator Larry Craig (R-Idaho) was charged with lewd conduct in a public bathroom. There had been an undercover operation by law enforcement to respond to complaints of sexual activity occurring in the men's bathroom. Craig pled guilty, but a long battle ensued. In 2014 Craig was ordered to pay back nearly $250,000 in campaign funds he misappropriated to cover up the MSP bathroom scandal (Krusei, 2014).

2007

Michael John Anderson, 19, murders Katherine Ann Olson, 24, in Savage, Minnesota, after she responds to his fake advertisement for a babysitter on Craigslist, a popular classified advertising website (Michels, 2009). Anderson, in turn, becomes the first "Craigslist Killer," a generic term for murderers who find their victims by placing or responding to ads in Craigslist (Associated Press, 2009).

2008

Businessman Tom Petters is caught masterminding a 13-year, $3.65 billion Ponzi scheme, the largest business fraud in Minnesota history and third largest in U.S. history (Phelps, 2013). Ponzi schemes, named after Charles Ponzi, who first used the technique in 1920 (Zuckoff, 2006), are fraudulent investment operations that pay returns to separate investors from their own money or money paid by subsequent investors, rather than from any actual profits earned (U.S Securities and Exchange Commission, 2013). Petters was found guilty in the U.S. District Court in St. Paul on 20 counts of mail fraud, wire fraud, and money laundering, and sentenced to 50 years in federal prison. He was forced to forfeit his assets and his companies, Petters Company Inc. and Petters Company Worldwide, went bankrupt.

2011

Denny Hecker, a prominent auto mogul in the Twin Cities, is sentenced to 10 years in prison for bankruptcy and wire fraud. He schemed to defraud financial lenders, such as Chrysler Financial and others, out of millions of dollars by using fraudulent documents (U.S. Attorney, 2011). He was ordered to pay $31 million in restitution and hundreds of millions more in bankruptcy debt (U.S. Attorney, 2011). Within the first two years of his prison sentence he was moved to nine different prison facilities throughout the country. While moving inmates to various facilities is not uncommon, the sheer number in a short period of time had the news media speculating why this might be, ranging from behavior problems to access to health facilities or special programing (CBS Minnesota, 2013).

2012

Andrew J. Engeldinger commits one of the deadliest workplace shootings in Minnesota's history. After being brought into his supervisor's office and told he was being fired from Accent Signage, Engeldinger pulls out a gun and begins a shooting spree, where he killed the company founder, three other employees, and a UPS driver before killing himself (Williams, 2013).

2014

Adrian Peterson, a Minnesota Viking and top-ranked running back in the NFL, is charged in Texas for child abuse for disciplining his son with a "switch." The case drew national headlines, sparked a debate about the use of corporal punishment for disciplining children, sidelined the Vikings player for an entire season, and, on account of this and other high-profile incidents of intimate partner violence within the league, forced the NFL to revisit their policy on the handling of such cases (see **Chapter Six**).

2015

The Vatican announces that they accepted the resignations of Minnesota Archbishop John Nienstedt and Auxiliary Bishop Lee Piche. Nienstedt and Piche resigned on the heels of the archdiocese being *criminally* charged after years of revelations that the Catholic Church in the Twin Cities covered up sexual crimes and failed to protect children from clergy sexual abuse. See **Chapter Ten** for more information.

Crime Trends in Minnesota

As shown in **Figure 1.4**, the crime rate in Minnesota and its neighboring states is less than the national average. The violent crime rate encompasses homicide, rape, aggravated assault, and robbery. The property crime rate includes burglary, theft, and motor vehicle theft. Arson, although a Part I crime, is not included. The FBI provides a separate table for arson statistics because of the wide variance of reporting by agencies (Federal Bureau of Investigation, 2014a). It should also be noted there were 167 hate crimes in Minnesota in 2013, of which 63 were classified as intimidation, 38 as simple assault, 32 as destruction/vandalism, and 25 as aggravated assaults. The rest of the crimes were rape (revised definition), robbery, larceny, and burglary (Federal Bureau of Investigation, 2014b) (see **Chapter Seven** for more information on hate crimes). When looking at crime rates in multiple jurisdictions, the FBI provides an official warning about rankings, and strongly discourages using them to evaluate the effectiveness of police departments, in part because myriad factors contribute to the volume and scope of reported crime, including "cultural factors and educational, recreational, and religious characteristics, administrative and investigative emphases on law enforcement, citizens' attitudes toward crime, and crime reporting practices of the citizenry" (Federal Bureau of Investigation, 2011).

Figure 1.4. UCR Crime Rates in Minnesota and Surrounding States, 2013

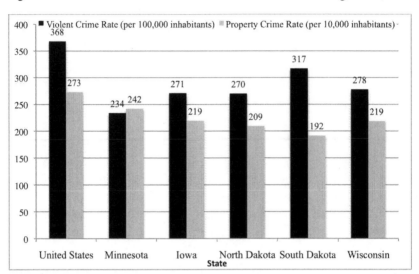

Source: Author created from Federal Bureau of Investigation Uniform Crime Report (2015).
* Noticeably absent from the table is Minnesota's northern border, Canada. While Canada also has a uniform crime reporting system, the focus of this book will remain on the United States.

Figure 1.5 provides a review of Minnesota crime rates over a ten-year time span. As shown, crime decreased about 25% over the decade (Part I=21% and Part II=29%). While encouraging, this only mirrors a general trend in a decrease in reported crime throughout the United States since the mid-1990s. Explanations for this great crime drop are controversial and varied (see Levitt, 2004), including (a) criminal justice factors, such as enactment of right-to-carry gun laws, increased incarceration, increased police numbers, and the introduction of data-driven policing; (b) economic factors, such as lower unemployment; and (c) social and environmental factors, such as decreased alcohol consumption, decreased crack cocaine use, an aging population, legalization of abortion, and decreased atmospheric lead density (Roeder, Eisen, & Bowling, 2015). The evidence suggests the introduction of CompStat, a data-driven policing technique, played a significant role in reducing crime in cities that introduced it, but various social, economic, and environmental factors also contributed (Roeder, et al., 2015).

Whatever the precise mechanism, the fact remains that as a whole, people living in United States in general, and Minnesota in particular, are far less likely to be victims of crime today than in previous years.

Figure 1.5. The Statewide Crime Rate in Minnesota (per 100,000 inhabitants), 2004–2013

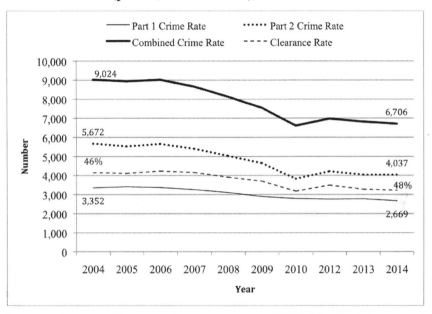

Source: Author created from annual summary reports of UCR Crime Statistics prepared by the BCA.

While crime is decreasing, there is still crime that occurs that the federal and state criminal justice systems work 24 hours a day, 365 days a year to respond to. In looking at violent crime in Minnesota, from 2004–2013, on average, 101 people were murdered, 2,261 were raped, 4,044 were robbed, and 7,384 were assaulted per year. On the property side, there were 26,326 victims of burglary, 108,874 victims of theft, 10,356 victims of motor vehicle theft, and 905 victims of arson. In the largest city in the state, Minneapolis, there were 32 homicides, 411 rapes, 1,880 robberies, 4,130 burglaries, 13,551 thefts, 1,555 motor vehicle thefts, and 118 arsons reported in 2014. Minneapolis reported a 1% decrease in crime between 2013 and 2014, which was an improvement from a 1% increase between 2012 and 2013, and a 2% increase from 2011 to 2012 (Minneapolis Police Department, 2015). The city of Minneapolis provides access to daily interactive crime maps through the use of RAIDS Online. They also provide weekly reports of shootings, shots fired, and ShotSpotter (a technology used to detect gunfire) activations. In addition, they provide a monthly report of Part I crimes, broken down by neighborhood. Most police departments in the state do not provide this same level of crime data on their agency's webpage.

Table 1.2. UCR Part I Arrests in Minnesota, 2004–2013

Year	Murder	Rape	Robbery	Aggravated Assault	Burglary	Theft/ Larceny	Motor Vehicle Theft	Arson	Total Arrests (Adult Arrests)
2004	110	2,373	4,049	7,396	27,754	113,433	13,410	1,050	209,127 (156,861)
2005	125	2,442	4,714	8,255	29,564	113,307	14,249	1,304	210,955 (160,013)
2006	120	2,562	5,390	8,655	29,496	112,516	12,961	1,093	224,287 (169,903)
2007	111	2,341	4,695	8,081	28,790	111,216	12,179	858	213,350 (168,735)
2008	109	2,292	4,148	7,536	26,063	110,372	9,948	908	209,080 (161,851)
2009	69	2,229	3,607	7,131	25,165	103,695	8,379	809	197,890 (154,720)
2010	90	2,230	3,363	6,978	23,947	101,616	8,398	675	186,378 (147,585)
2011	73	2,080	3,359	6,364	25,153	100,636	7,927	657	178,469 (142,277)
2012	92	2,090	3,450	6,721	24,829	102,154	8,251	773	171,132 (138,376)
2013	111	1,971	3,661	6,726	22,500	99,794	7,873	930	160,797 (134,017)

Source: Author created from annual summary reports of UCR Crime Statistics prepared by the BCA.

Homicide

The BCA, like the FBI, publishes supplemental homicide crime data. In looking at the 111 homicides committed in 2013, 76 or 68% were cleared by arrest. *Clearance* does not equal *conviction*, which means *at least* one third of all homicides in Minnesota go unsolved, leaving victims' families and friends without justice. We can also infer from this that it is likely police have come face-to-face with multiple un-apprehended murderers, possibly serial killers (i.e., responsible for three or more murders, see Hickey, 2012), while going about their business. Homicide clearance rates reflect law enforcement priorities and resources, but also higher standards of evidence than in years past. Some police complain prosecutors demand "open-and-shut cases" that lead to quick plea bargains (Kaste, 2015). New technologies and tools such as DNA analysis help, but they are offset by worsening relationships between police and the public and a growing "stop snitching" culture among potential witnesses, especially in minority communities where homicide is highest (Kaste, 2015).

Minnesota's homicide clearance rate is no worse than the 2013 national clearance rate of 64%. Homicides have the highest clearance rate of all crimes, followed by aggravated assault at 57.7%. Burglary is at the bottom at 13.1% (Federal Bureau of Investigations, 2014). Of the 111 homicide victims in Minnesota, 20 were stranger killings, an immediate family member perpetrated 20, 56 were a non-nuclear family or acquaintance, and for the rest the relationship was unknown. The victims had about a 50/50 of chance of being killed with a firearm or some other weapon (knife, personal weapon, fire, by asphyxiation, etc.). Furthermore, in two-thirds of the cases there was only one victim and one offender.

Drugs and Crime

Drug use is an important issue in Minnesota and elsewhere. To determine the scope of drug use there are several data sources, including police and arrest records, hospital records, death records, and self-report data. The main self-report drug surveys include the National Survey on Drug Use and Health (NSDUH), the Minnesota Survey of Adult Substance Use (MNSASU), the Minnesota Student Survey, and Monitoring the Future. EpiMachine, LLC (2015) prepares a summary of all of these self-report data sources to give to the Minnesota Department of Health and Human Services, Alcohol and Drug Division information for grant funding purposes and for monitoring of programs in the community. Their work provides the following summary statements on marijuana use in Minnesota (see also **Chapter Ten**):

- Since 2005–2006 Minnesota's rates of marijuana use have remained relatively flat, decreasing slightly compared to national rates (NSDUH).
- Males, young adults, American Indians, and individuals reporting more than one race reported higher levels of past 30-day marijuana use (MNSASU).
- The use of marijuana by 9th-grade students decreased from 14% in 2001 to 9.4% in 2013.

- Almost 17% of 11th graders reported past 30-day marijuana use in 2013. Twenty-five percent reported past-year usage.

(EpiMachine, LLC, 2015)

For other illicit drugs, they report the following:

- Current illicit drug use in Minnesota has remained stable in recent years and is below national rates.
- Current illicit drug use is most common among adults age 18–25, compared to other age groups.
- There has been an overall decrease in reported use of inhalants, methamphetamine, MDMA/Ecstasy, crack/cocaine, and psychedelics since 2001.
- The largest decline is for inhalants, from 9% in 1995 to 1% in 2013.

(EpiMachine, LLC, 2015)

There are over 100 Minnesota addresses listed on the National Clandestine Laboratory Registry (Drug Enforcement Agency, 2015). In 2014, the National Institute on Drug Abuse reported that in Minneapolis and St. Paul there was an increase in heroin and methamphetamine indicators (Falkowski, 2014). This is the same year the legislature passed "Steve's Law" (Minnesota Statutes §144E.101), named for Steve Rummler, who died from a heroin overdose in July 2011. Steve's Law enables first responders to administer an opiate antagonist to reverse the effects of an overdose (National Institute of Health, 2015). The law also has a "Good Samaritan" provision, which essentially provides those who assist someone experiencing an overdose some immunity from prosecution. See **Chapter Ten** for further discussion.

In looking at a national level, of all drug arrests, only about 20% are for sale and distribution, the rest are for drug use (Bureau of Justice Statistics, 2012). This means when examining criminal justice responses, addiction is a central concern. One way Minnesota is addressing this issue is through the use of drug courts. This type of specialty court provides drug and alcohol treatment services while using a range of intermediate sanctions and monitoring to help offenders with their addiction (see **Chapter Four** for more details).

Minnesota Innovations in Criminal Justice

Minnesota Sentencing Guidelines

In 1980, Minnesota became the first state to adopt sentencing guidelines to provide "uniform and proportional sentences" to convicted felony offenders in the state. The guidelines were developed by an independent sentencing commission and are reviewed annually and updated when necessary (Minnesota Sentencing Guidelines Commission, 2015). Having an independent sentencing commission was also innovative as no other state utilized one to make sentencing recommendations (Frase, 2015). Since its creation, other states and the federal government have followed suit, developing their own guidelines to ensure sentences are not based on factors like gender or race. When a judge departs from the stated guidelines, he/she must provide a rationale for the departure and the prosecution or defense attorneys have the right to appeal the departure. The guideline also "makes it easier for states to foresee and prevent overcrowded prisons, and set priorities in the use of limited prison space" (Frase, 2015). A further discussion of the sentencing guidelines is provided in **Chapter Nine.**

The 1984 Minneapolis Domestic Violence Experiment

The Minneapolis Domestic Violence Experiment provided the first statistically significant evidence for the effectiveness of police policy. Sherman and Berk's (1984) classic study, funded by a grant from the National Institute of Justice, was the first to use a randomized, controlled field experiment to test the impact of arrest on crime. The experiment was set up such that a police officer responding to a misdemeanor domestic assault call would select one of three possible outcomes at random: (1) arrest; (2) counsel/mediation; and (3) separation. Minnesota law at the time meant any of these three responses was viable. The research team tracked offenders for six months and found arrest, which meant spending a night in jail, had the strongest deterrent effect on recidivism.

Subsequent trials in Omaha, Nebraska, Charlotte, North Carolina, Milwaukee, Wisconsin, Miami-Dade County, Florida, and Colorado Springs, Colorado, funded by the National Institute of Justice, commonly known as the Spousal Assault Replication Program (SARP), failed to replicate the Minneapolis findings (Berk et al., 1992; Sherman, 1992). Nevertheless, the original results received national media attention and informed the creation of a slew of mandatory arrest policies throughout the country, many of which are still in use today.

The Duluth Model or Domestic Abuse Intervention Project

Established in the early 1980s in Duluth, Minnesota, the Duluth Model is a community approach and initiative that works towards protecting victims of domestic abuse and providing programs for abusers in order to come to a collective solution on how to end domestic violence in Minnesota. The Duluth Model, including the famous "Power and Control" wheel (see **Figure 1.6**), informs the public on policies that hold offenders accountable, eases the stigma a victim of domestic abuse feels when reporting the abuse, and provides communities with the resources it needs to end domestic violence. The model also provides court-ordered alternatives for offenders to receive treatment through their select program (Domestic Abuse Intervention Programs, 2011).

The Minnesota Twin Family Study

The Minnesota Twin Family Study is a longitudinal study of twins conducted by researchers at the University of Minnesota, which seeks to explore fundamental questions of *nature versus nurture* by separating genetic and environmental influences on the development of psychological traits (Iacono & McGue, 2002). Twin studies are valuable to researchers because identical twins share 100% of their genes (fraternal twins share, on average, 50% of their genes) *and* certain aspects of their environment (e.g., being raised in the same household). As such, researchers can estimate the heritability of certain traits of interest to criminal justice practitioners, such as the prevalence of psychopathology or substance abuse.

DNA Evidence

The Minnesota Bureau of Criminal Apprehension was one of the first DNA laboratories in the nation in 1990, and shortly afterward became the first in the nation to identify a suspect based solely on DNA (Department of Public Safety, BCA, 2015). In 2004, the BCA became one of four laboratories in the nation selected by the FBI to serve as a regional mitochondrial DNA laboratory. The BCA was also first in the nation to implement an Automated Fingerprint Identification System, allowing the submission of fingerprints via computer.

Figure 1.6. The Power and Control Wheel

Source: Domestic Abuse Intervention Programs (2011). Reprinted with permission.

Restorative Justice

Minnesota is in many ways the capital of restorative justice in the United States. In contrast to retributive justice, which is focused on determining guilt and delivering appropriate punishment through an adversarial process, restorative justice emphasizes repairing the harm caused or revealed by crime and managing the relationship between offender, victim, and community (Bazemore & Umbreit, 1994). In 1990, several community groups and a not-for-profit criminal justice agency sponsored a conference on restorative justice and introduced the idea to some key practitioners in Minnesota (Pranis, 1997). Subsequently, the Minnesota Department of Corrections began exploring ways that principles of restorative justice could be applied in law enforcement, courts, corrections, schools, and communities. Mark Umbreit and colleagues founded the Center for Restorative Justice and Peacemaking (2015; formerly Center for Restorative Justice and Mediation) at the University of Minnesota School of Social Work, and organizations such as the Minnesota Restorative Services Coalition (MRSC, 2015) emerged to provide technical assistance, training, and research to support restorative justice practices and principles. As the field grows, and the interest in restorative work expands across a variety of settings, Minnesota has become home base for many restorative justice initiatives.

Court Monitoring

In 1992 Minnesota became home to the nation's first court monitoring organization. Women at the Courthouse, or WATCH, was created "to make the justice system more effective and responsive in handling cases of violence against women and children, and to create a more informed and involved public" (WATCH, 2015). It has become a national model for other court monitoring groups around the United States. It was founded in response to a murder committed by an assailant who had a record of seven felony arrests in three states for rape, assault, and burglary. The assailant was imprisoned in Minnesota for second-degree criminal sexual conduct in 1984 and was on parole for that offense when he committed murder. In 1991, a small group of women met to discuss the issues of lenient sentencing, ways to reduce violence against women and children, and the dismal success rate in treating pedophiles and other sex offenders. In researching the issues, it became apparent that although there were many victim support services, there were no organizations regularly present in the courtroom to monitor the justice system and hold it accountable for its actions, and so WATCH was created.

Concluding Remarks

This chapter has provided a brief introduction to Minnesota's criminal justice system and crime history and trends. In the pages that follow we develop this outline to paint a detailed picture of Minnesota's criminal justice landscape, from police to courts, corrections to community. Crime is a genuine concern for Minnesotans, although as the data in this chapter show, crime is in decline and our "fear" of being a victim of crime is likely greater than our actual probability of being a victim of crime (Glassner, 2000). So often crime is glamorized or mythologized by media sources, which, in an effort to keep us reading and watching, focus only on the most sensational stories or stories that are not nearly as relevant to our lives as portrayed (Kappeler & Potter, 2005). Not true here. This book aims to provide a more nuanced, measured response to criminal justice issues in Minnesota, for the benefit of all Minnesotans.

Key Terms

Arraignment
Bureau of Criminal Apprehension
Civil law
Clearance Rate
Concurrent jurisdiction
Crime as Social Construct
Crime Index
Criminal Justice Process
Dark Figure of Crime
DNA Evidence
Drugs
Duluth Model
Indictment
Justice
Level of Offenses
Mala in se
Mala prohibita
Minneapolis Domestic Violence
    Experiment

Minnesota Twin Family Study
National Crime Victimization Survey
Omnibus Hearing
Part I Offenses
Part II Offenses
Ponzi Scheme
Power and Control Wheel
Procedural Law
Restorative Justice
Rule of Law
Sentencing Guidelines
ShotSpotter
Steve's Law
Substantive Law
Summons
Uniform Crime Report
Voir dire
Warrant
WATCH

Selected Internet Sites

Bureau of Justice Statistics
http://www.bjs.gov

Center for Restorative Justice and Peacemaking
http://www.cehd.umn.edu/ssw/rjp/

Council on Crime and Justice
http://www.aclu-mn.org/issues/criminaljustice/

The Duluth Model
http://www.theduluthmodel.org

FBI Uniform Crime Reporting
http://www.fbi.gov/about-us/cjis/ucr/ucr

Minnesota Alliance on Crime
http://www.mnallianceoncrime.org

Minnesota Association of County Administrators
http://www.maca-mn.org

Minnesota Association of County Social Service Administrators
http://www.macssa.org

Minnesota Department of Public Safety
https://dps.mn.gov/Pages/default.aspx

Minnesota Legislative Reference Library
http://www.leg.state.mn.us/lrl/links/links.aspx?links=criminal

Minnesota Revisor of Statutes
https://www.revisor.leg.state.mn.us

Minnesota Social Service Association
https://www.mnssa.org

WATCH
http://www.watchmn.org

World Justice Project
http://worldjusticeproject.org

Discussion Questions

1. How would you define crime in your own terms? How would you define justice?
2. What are the main steps in the criminal justice process? Do you think other steps are needed?
3. How do we measure crime in the United States?
4. What are the various types of criminal complaints?
5. What situations would allow for an *exceptional clearance* in crime reporting?
6. What is the difference between Part I offenses and Part II offenses?
7. What do you think are the main reasons why crime, in general, is decreasing?
8. What can be said about illicit drug use in Minnesota?
9. Choose one of the snapshots in time and discuss why the case is (in)famous.
10. Describe the experiment that led to mandatory arrests in Minnesota. If you had to conduct your own experiment to measure some police policy,

how would you set it up? Identify the policy and then explain how you would measure it.

11. For what type of offenders do you think restorative justice practices should be used? Why?

References

Associated Press (2009, April 3). "Craigslist killer" Michael John Anderson gets life in murder of Katherine Olson. *New York Daily News*. Retrieved from http://www.nydailynews.com/news/world/craigslist-killer-michael-john-anderson-life-murder-katherine-olson-article-1.361506

Bazemore, G., & Umbreit, M. (1994). *Balanced and restorative justice*. Washington, DC: U.S. Department of Justice, Office of Juvenile Justice and Delinquency Prevention.

Berk, R., Campbell, A., Klap, R., & Western, B. (1992). The deterrent effect of arrest in incidents of domestic violence: A Bayesian analysis of four field experiments. *American Sociological Review*, 57, 698–708.

Biderman, A., & Lynch, J. (1991). *Understanding crime incidence statistics: Why the UCR diverges from the NCS*. New York, NY: Springer.

Biderman, A., & Reiss, A. (1967). On exploring the 'dark figure' of crime. *The Annals of the American Academy of Political and Social Science*, 374, 1–15.

Bingham, C., & Gansler, L. (2003). *Class action: The landmark case that changed sexual harassment law*. New York: Anchor.

Blackstone, W. (1765). *Commentaries on the laws of England*. Oxford: Clarendon Press.

Bureau of Justice Statistics. (2012). *Sourcebook of criminal justice statistics online*. Retrieved from http://www.albany.edu/sourcebook/pdf/t42920 12.pdf

Bureau of Justice Statistics. (2013). *National crime victimization survey*. Retrieved from http://www.bjs.gov/index.cfm?ty=dcdetail&iid=245

CBS Minnesota. (2013, March 29). Denny Hecker moves to 9th prison. Retrieved from http://minnesota.cbslocal.com/2013/03/29/denny-hecker-moves-to-his-9th-prison/

Center for Restorative Justice and Peacemaking (2015). *About us*. Retrieved from http://www.cehd.umn.edu/ssw/RJP/About/default.html

Domestic Abuse Intervention Programs (2011). *What is the Duluth model?* Retrieved from http://www.theduluthmodel.org/about/index.html

Drug Enforcement Agency. (2015). National clandestine laboratory register. Retrieved from http://www.dea.gov/clan-lab/mn.pdf

Duchschere, K. (2013, December 2). Thompson case unforgettable, even after 50 years. *Star Tribune*. Retrieved from http://www.startribune.com/even-after-50-years-st-paul-wrestles-with-thompson-murder-for-hire/233885361/

Enger, J. (2015, March 18). The shooting at Red Lake: What happened. *MPR News*. Retrieved from http://www.mprnews.org/story/2015/03/18/red-lake-shooting-explained

EpiMachine, LLC. (2015). Substance abuse in Minnesota. A state epidemiological profile. Retrieved from http://www.sumn.org/~/media/181/Drugs%202015.pdf

Falkoski, C. (2014). *Drug abuse trends in Minneapolis and St. Paul*. Retrieved from http://www.drugabuse.gov/about-nida/organization/workgroups-interest-groups-consortia/community-epidemiology-work-group-cewg/highlights-summaries-january-2014-reports/minneapolis-st-paul-minnesota

Farmer, L. (2008). Crime, definitions of. In P. Cane & J. Conoghan (eds.), *The new Oxford companion to law*. Oxford: Oxford University Press.

Federal Bureau of Investigation. (2003). *A byte out of history: Latent prints in the 1933 Hamm Kidnapping*. Retrieved from http://www.fbi.gov/news/stories/2003/september/hamm090803

Federal Bureau of Investigation. (2004). *Appendix II: Offenses in Uniform Crime Reporting*. Retrieved from https://www2.fbi.gov/ucr/cius_04/appendices/appendix_02.html

Federal Bureau of Investigation. (2011). *Uniform Crime Reporting statistics: Their proper use*. Retrieved from http://www.fbi.gov/about-us/cjis/ucr/ucr-statistics-their-proper-use

Federal Bureau of Investigation. (2014a). *Crime in the United States, 2013*. Retrieved from http://www.fbi.gov/about-us/cjis/ucr/crime-in-the-u.s/2013/crime-in-the-u.s.-2013/cius-home

Federal Bureau of Investigation (2014b). *2013 Hate crimes statistics*. Retrieved from http://www.fbi.gov/about-us/cjis/ucr/hate-crime/2013/tables/11tabledatadecpdf/table_11_offenses_offense_type_by_participating_state_2013.xls

Fedo, M. (2000). *Lynching in Duluth*. St. Paul, MN: Borealis Books.

Feichtinger, G., DeStanto, J., & Waller, G. (2009). *Will to murder: The true story behind the crimes and trials surrounding the Glensheen killings* (4th ed.). Duluth, MN: Zenith City Press.

Frase, R. (2015). *Sentencing policies and criminal justice in Minnesota: Past, present, and future*. Minneapolis, MN: Council on Crime and Justice. Retrieved from http://www.crimeandjustice.org/councilinfo.cfm?pID=52

Furst, R. (2015, February 6). Jury divides responsibility of fatal crash: 60% Toyota; 40% driver. *Star Tribune*. Retrieved from http://www.startribune.com/local/stpaul/290700041.html

Glassner, B. (2000). *The culture of fear: Why Americans are afraid of the wrong things*. New York: Basic Books.

Hennepin County Attorney. (2014). Prosecutors detail why serial killer should not get a new trial. Retrieved from http://www.hennepinattorney.org/news/news/2014/october/glaze-postconviction-answer

Hennepin County Attorney. (2015). *Criminal justice process*. Retrieved from http://www.hennepinattorney.org/get-help/crime/criminal-justice-process

Henry, S. (2009). Social construction of crime. In J. Miller (ed.). *21st Century criminology: A reference handbook* (pp. 296–305). Thousand Oaks, CA: Sage.

Hickey, E. (2012). *Serial murderers and their victims* (6th ed.). Belmont, CA: Wadsworth.

Iacono, W., & McGue, M. (2002). Minnesota twin family study. *Twin Research*, 5, 482–487.

Kappeler, V., & Potter, G. (2005). *The mythology of crime and criminal justice* (4th ed.). Long Grove, IL: Waveland Press.

Kaste, M. (2015, March 30). Open cases: Why one-third of murders in America go unresolved. Retrieved from http://www.npr.org/2015/03/30/395069137/open-cases-why-one-third-of-murders-in-america-go-unresolved

Levitt, S. (2004). Understanding why crime fell in the 1990s: Four factors that explain the decline and six that do not. *Journal of Economic Perspectives*, 18, 163–190.

Matza, D. (1969). *Becoming deviant*. Englewood Cliffs, NJ: Prentice-Hall.

Michels, S. (2009). Craigslist Killer lured victim with baby sitter ad. *ABC News*, April 1. Retrieved from http://abcnews.go.com/Technology/story?id=7227285&page=1

Minneapolis Police Department. (2015). *Uniform Crime Reports*. Retrieved from http://www.minneapolismn.gov/police/statistics/WCMS1P-104396

Minnesota Department of Public Safety. (2015). *Criminal justice data reporting*. Retrieved from https://dps.mn.gov/divisions/bca/bca-divisions/mnjis/Pages/uniform-crime-reports.aspx

Minnesota Innocence Project. (2015). *Koua Fong Lee*. Retrieved from http://ipmn.org/koua-fong-lee-wrongful-conviction/

Minnesota Restorative Services Coalition (2015). *History*. Retrieved from http://www.mnmrsc.org/about-mrsc/mrsc-history/

Minnesota Revisor of Statutes. (2015). Statutes. Retrieved from https://www.revisor.leg.state.mn.us

Minnesota Sentencing Guidelines Commission. (2015). *About the guidelines.* Retrieved from http://mn.gov/sentencing-guidelines/guidelines/about/

MinnPost. (2008, July 2). 150 Minnesota moments we'd just as soon forget. *MinnPost.* Retrieved from http://www.minnpost.com/politics-policy/2008/07/150-minnesota-moments-wed-just-soon-forget

National Institute of Health. (2015). *Naloxone injection.* Retrieved from http://www.nlm.nih.gov/medlineplus/druginfo/meds/a612022.html

Office of the Inspector General. (2006). *A review of the FBI's handling of intelligence information related to the September 11 attacks.* Washington DC: U.S. Department of Justice.

Phelps, D. (2013, September 23). Five years later: Tom Peters Ponzi Scheme. *Star Tribune.* Retrieved from 224430151.html

Pranis, K. (1997). The Minnesota restorative justice initiative: A model experience. *The Crime Victims Report,* May/June. Retrieved from http://www.nij.gov/topics/courts/restorative-justice/perspectives/pages/minnesota.aspx.

President's Commission on Law Enforcement and Administration of Justice. (1967). The Challenge of crime in a free society. Washington DC: U.S. Government Printing Office.

Rawls, J. (1971). *A theory of justice.* Oxford: Oxford University Press.

Remington, F. (1956). Survey of the administration of justice. *National Probation and Parole Association Journal,* 2, 260–265.

Roeder, O., Eisen, L-B., & Bowling, J. (2015). *What caused the crime decline?* New York: Brennan Center for Justice. Retrieved from https://www.brennancenter.org/publication/what-caused-crime-decline

Russell, B. (1945). *History of western philosophy.* New York: Simon & Schuster.

Sherman, L. (1992). The influence of criminology on criminal law: Evaluating arrests for misdemeanor domestic violence. *Journal of Criminal Law and Criminology,* 83, 1–45.

Sherman, L., & Berk, R. (1984). The specific deterrent effects of arrest for domestic assault. *American Sociological Review,* 49, 261.

State of Minnesota v. John Jason McLaughlin, 2007. A05-2327

Swanson, W. (2014a). *Dial M: The murder of Carol Thompson.* Saint Paul, MN: Borealis Books.

Swanson, W. (2014b). *Stolen from the garden: The kidnapping of Virginia Piper.* Saint Paul, MN: Borealis Books.

Teamsters. (2013). *1934 Minnesota strike.* Retrieved from http://teamster.org/about/teamster-history/1934

U.S. Attorney. (2011, Feb. 11). Denny Hecker sentenced tor bankruptcy fraud and conspiracy to commit wire fraud. *FBI.* Retrieved from https://www.fbi.gov/minneapolis/press-releases/2011/mp021111.htm

U.S. Department of Justice. (n.d.). *National sex offender public website*. Retrieved from http://www.nsopw.gov

U.S. Securities and Exchange Commission. (2013). *Ponzi schemes*. Retrieved from http://www.sec.gov/answers/ponzi.htm

Walker, S. (1992). Origins of the contemporary criminal justice paradigm: The American Bar Foundation Survey, 1953–1969. *Justice Quarterly*, 9, 47–76.

Williams, B. (2013, September 29). A year after Accent Signage shootings, debate shifts from gun control to mental health. Retrieved from http://www.mprnews.org/story/2013/09/27/news/accent-signage-shooting-one-year

WATCH (2015). WATCH MN. Retrieved from http://www.watchmn.org/initiatives/court-monitoring/

World Justice Project. (2015). What is the rule of law. Retrieved from http://worldjusticeproject.org

Zuckoff, M. (2006). *Ponzi's scheme: The true story of a financial legend*. New York: Random House.

Chapter Two

What the Movie *Fargo* Didn't Teach You: Law Enforcement in Minnesota

Learning Objectives

- Articulate how to become a peace officer in Minnesota
- Define the responsibilities of the Minnesota POST Board
- Describe the demographics of Minnesota Peace Officers
- List the disqualifiers that prevent someone from being a peace officer
- Describe the role of the Bureau of Criminal Apprehension
- List the largest law enforcement agencies in Minnesota
- Identify the agencies responsible for protecting the natural resources of Minnesota
- Describe the roles and functions of task forces in Minnesota
- Identify the law enforcement leaders in Minnesota
- Identify and articulate the functions of some of the more unique law enforcement agencies in Minnesota
- Appreciate major law enforcement responses in Minnesota

Minnesota has been in the business of policing longer than it has been a state. The St. Paul Police Department has the distinction of being the first to protect and serve the community, beginning in 1854 under the command of City Marshall William Miller (St. Paul Police Historical Society, 2015). Four years later, Minnesota became the 32nd state on May 11, 1858 (Library of Congress, 2015), and almost 10 years after this, St. Paul's "twin," Minneapolis, started their police force in 1867. Since these early beginnings, more than 450 agencies have been developed in the state to protect and serve a population of 5.4 million (Minnesota State Demographic Center, 2014).

Like elsewhere, in Minnesota the formal reference to a police office is a *peace* officer. As defined in Minnesota Statutes § 626.05, subdivision 2, a peace officer is one

> who serves as a sheriff, deputy sheriff, police officer, conservation officer, agent of the Bureau of Criminal Apprehension, agent of the Division of Alcohol and Gambling Enforcement, University of Minnesota peace officer, Metropolitan Transit police officer, Minnesota Department of Corrections Fugitive Apprehension Unit member, or State Patrol trooper.

There are approximately 10,500 full-time and 190 part-time peace officers in Minnesota, including city, county, tribe, university, and state agencies (Minnesota POST, 2014). Federal law enforcement agents also work in Minnesota (see **Chapter Eight** for a discussion). Residents and visitors should know officers in Minnesota are held to the highest education entrance requirements in the country. Minnesota police are more formally educated than police in any other state and more degreed than the general population they serve (Hilal & Densley, 2013).

Becoming a Peace Officer in Minnesota

There are several ways to become a peace officer in Minnesota. The most common route is through a degree program. To become *eligible* for a Minnesota Peace Officer License, candidates must earn at least a two-year degree from a regionally accredited college or university and successfully complete a program of Professional Peace Officer Education (PPOE) from one of approximately 30 colleges and universities certified by the Minnesota Board of Peace Officer Standards and Training (POST) (Minnesota POST, 2014). Colleges and universities granted authority to deliver police-related education for licensure are reaccredited every five years and required to employ a designated "POST Co-ordinator," whose job it is to ensure compliance with POST-approved learning objectives (Minnesota Administrative Rule 6700.0300). The POST Coordinator is a school's liaison with the Minnesota POST Board.

In addition to traditional classroom learning, PPOE programs include a hands-on police academy, known colloquially as "Skills." During Skills, students learn the daily functions of law enforcement and practice in things like firearms, defensive tactics, traffic stops, responding to domestic assaults, driving, and searches and seizures. Only students who have a valid driver's license, have submitted a copy of their criminal history (to ensure there are no statutory disqualifiers), and have passed a psychological and medical exam are allowed to attend Skills. Sometime during their academic preparation, students must also obtain Emergency Medical Responder certification (formerly known as First Responder), which prepares students to provide pre-hospital care in medical emergencies.

Once the POST Coordinator has "signed-off" with the state that a student has met the educational requirements outlined above, the student can take the Minnesota Peace Officer Licensing Examination (Minnesota Department of Public Safety, 2014b). Students who pass the licensing examination are considered *license-eligible*. License-eligible individuals become *licensed* only after they are appointed by a specific law enforcement agency and can satisfy the minimum selection standards (see below). If a license-eligible candidate is not licensed within three years of passing the exam, they must retake the exam. In order to maintain their license, moreover, a *licensed* officer must complete at least 48 continuing education credits each three-year period, some of which must include use of force training.

In many states, a person only has to secure employment with a law enforcement agency to become a police officer. During their initial year of employment, they attend a basic training course or police academy at the expense of the employer. Not so in Minnesota. Minnesotans pay out-of-pocket for their police officer education and training, without any guarantee they will be hired and licensed. The up-front costs are significant, as Skills alone in 2015 cost approximately $4,500 (Metropolitan State University, 2014). On the upside, Minnesotans typically self-select into law enforcement and are highly motivated to succeed. On the downside, high achieving disadvantaged students and students of color may be excluded from the process (see **Chapter Ten**).

A certificate program is the second way someone can become a peace officer in Minnesota. Certificate programs service aspiring peace officers that already have earned a degree in an area other than law enforcement or criminal justice by providing the minimum coursework and Skills training necessary for them to meet POST learning objectives.

Minnesota's reciprocity licensing exam is the third and final route into law enforcement in the state. Peace officers who have worked in another state for at least three years and persons who have performed military police service in the U.S. military can qualify, the latter contingent on cumulative experience, time of service, and level of education.

Regardless of the pathway chosen, Minnesota Administrative Rule 6700.0700 sets the "minimum selection standards" that must be met to become a licensed peace officer in Minnesota. The minimum requirements mirror what most states do, including requirements like being a U.S. citizen, having a valid driver license, and submitting to a thorough background investigation, including fingerprinting. The Administrative Rules also outline the statutory disqualifiers to being a peace officer, as outlined in **Table 2.1**. These pertain to acts committed as an adult.

Table. 2.1. Automatic Disqualifiers to Be a Peace Officer in Minnesota (Minnesota Rules, Chapter 6700.0300, subp 5B)

Felony in Minnesota or any other state	Failure to report (maltreatment of vulnerable adult)
Assault in 5th degree	Other prohibited acts (prostitution related)
Domestic assault	Presenting false claims
Mistreatment of persons confined	Medical assistance fraud
Mistreatment of residents or patients	Theft
Criminal abuse (vulnerable adult)	Disorderly conduct regarding vulnerable adults
Criminal neglect (vulnerable adult)	Registration as a predatory offender
Financial exploitation (vulnerable adult)	Registration under the predatory offender registration law for other offenses

Individual police agencies are responsible for their own hiring methodologies and selection standards. There is no uniform or "correct" way to screen and select applicants. What works for one agency may not be best suited to another, not least because agencies vary in terms of size, philosophy, and populations served (see Hilal, Densley, & Jones, 2015 for more discussion of various screening processes used in Minnesota). However, all agencies are required to conduct a thorough background investigation of a candidate they are looking to hire, per Minnesota Statutes §626.87, subd. 5. The applicant must also complete a physical and psychological exam. Minnesota POST has created a mechanism for agencies to track applicants and share information with other agencies interesting in hiring them, called the Background Pointer System.

Once hired by an agency, an officer is given a license number, which stays with them throughout their law enforcement career, regardless of where they work in the state. Like elsewhere, after securing employment, officers receive agency-specific instruction from an experienced Field Training Officer (FTO), whose job it is to best prepare new hires to protect and serve their jurisdiction. While not required under Minnesota law, many departments also have what is referred to as a "Swearing In" ceremony, where new officers take a symbolic Law Enforcement Oath of Honor (International Association of Police, 2015).

Figure 2.1. How to Become a Peace Officer in Minnesota

Education/Experience Requirements		
2/4 year approved LE degree + Skills or	Degree + Certificate + Skills or	Military or Prior Law Enforcement Experience

⬇

Exam Requirements
Successfully pass Minnesota POST licensing exam to become license eligible

⬇

Application Process
Apply for full-time employment as a peace officer at city, county, or state law enforcement agency

⬇

Testing at Agency
Can include a written, physical agility, simulation, panel interview, or some other type of assessment

⬇

Agency Hiring Process
Thorough background check, chief interview, conditional offer, and medical and psychological tests

⬇

Hired
License activated, swearing-in ceremony (in some agencies) and start FTO

Source: Author created from information obtained through the Minnesota POST.

This process is unique to Minnesota. While it provides for a more educated police force (see Hilal & Densley, 2013), it does create some challenges. Because the training to be a peace officer is entrusted to higher education, there is an inherent conflict. Higher education relies on student enrollment to do their job. For state colleges and universities, the number of students they enroll becomes part of a funding formula, which then dictates how much funding they receive from the state. Schools need large numbers of Full-Time Equivalent (FTE) students in their programs in order to continue to offer them. Law enforcement is an especially expensive program for colleges and universities to maintain. Skills in particular has unique costs, such as purchasing squad cars, firearms and ammunition, and Tasers, while also employing role players, the POST Coordinator, and instructors.

In addition to the business aspect of higher education, most PPOE programs are housed in open-access colleges and universities that exist to provide education and training to *anyone* and *everyone* who wants it. The problem is not *anyone* can become a police officer and certainly not *everyone* can be good at it (see Hilal, Densley, & Jones, 2015). Unless a student has a disqualifier that would clearly prevent them from being a peace officer, however, there is nothing a PPOE school can do to stop them enrolling in the program. While the POST Coordinator at the institution can advise the student against it, they cannot bar them outright, for to do so would violate the school's anti-discrimination policy.

Hiring agencies invest significant resources on the back end of the education and training process to separate high quality law enforcement graduates from their low quality counterparts. But this is two or fours years removed from the front end of the process, when students declare a major. This means that in Minnesota, there are people who have spent the time and paid the money necessary to become a peace officer, who are *license eligible*, but likely never will be *licensed*. The one saving grace is they will have earned a college degree and perhaps can use it for a different career path.

POST Board

The POST Board regulates law enforcement in Minnesota. The board is an independent oversight body, answerable directly to the governor. It was legislatively formed in 1967 and since then has adopted several changes, the most significant occurring in 1977 when it adopted the statewide two-year degree requirement for officers outlined above (Minnesota POST, 2014).

The POST Board is made up of 15 voting members who are tasked with establishing and maintaining policies for all licensed officers in the state. Among their products are model policies for law enforcement agencies in use of force, vehicle pursuit, and domestic abuse, which are mandated by state statute. Each agency must have written policies in these areas (Minnesota POST, 2014). The board meets quarterly throughout the year and their meetings are open to the public. It has authority to suspend or revoke a peace officer license, if necessary (this portion of the meeting is closed to the public). It does not, however, deal with individual use of force complaints or most other issues concerning individual officers. This happens at the agency level. It only has jurisdiction over licensing issues. Since it has jurisdiction over licensing, it also creates and administers the state's Peace Officer Licensing Exam. The exam costs $105 to take and is administered multiple times a year at various locations throughout the state.

Peace Officer Demographics

From 2005–2014, there were 4,863 new officers in the state of Minnesota. In any given year, approximately 10% of all officers are newly licensed in the state. The POST Board does not track the number of officers who retire or leave the profession, so it is not clear how many new positions are created versus replacements. The POST Board tracks limited data, including demographic characteristics of gender, age, geographic distribution, and level of education.

Table 2.2. Number of Officers from 2006–2014

As of ...	Total number of officers	Newly Licensed
June 30, 2006	11,518	1,115
June 30, 2008	11,726	1,179
June 30, 2010	12,135	766
June 30, 2012	11,738	751
June 30, 2014	10,458	1,052

Source: Author created from information obtained through the Minnesota POST Board (2015).

Gender

Only 11% of all officers are female (Minnesota POST, 2014). This is consistent with national trends (Bureau of Justice Statistics, 2010). Among the largest agencies in Minnesota, in 2013 women constituted 128 (15%) of the 844 sworn officers in Minneapolis, 104 (18%) out of 587 in St. Paul, 22 (14%) out of 153 in Duluth, 13 (10%) out of the 133 in Rochester, and 11 (10%) out of 111 in Bloomington (Minnesota Department of Public Safety, Uniform Crime Report, 2014).

The top law enforcement job in the state of Minnesota is the public safety commissioner, who is appointed by the governor. Since 2011, a female, Mona Dohman, has held this position (Minnesota Department of Public Safety, 2014). In looking at other law enforcement leaders, the largest police department in the state, Minneapolis, hired its first female police chief, Janee Harteau, in 2012 (City of Minneapolis, 2014). The St. Paul Police Department, the second largest and oldest in the state, has not yet had a female police chief (St. Paul Police Historical Society, 2014), but women do hold the rank of assistant chief. Among sheriffs, there are only a handful of female sheriffs. Teresa Amazi was the first female sheriff and was elected in 2002 in Mower County (Doetkott, 2014).

The Minnesota Association of Women Police (MAWP) was created in 1955 with a mission to create equality for women in the criminal justice field. They are affiliated with the International Association of Women Police. Every year they hold a training conference, provide scholarships for female recruits, and recognize women who have made outstanding contributions to the community, among various other activities (MAWP, 2014).

Race

The Bureau of Justice Statistics (2014) reports that in 2007, 25% of local officers in the United States were of a racial or ethnic minority. Since the Minnesota POST Board does not collect information on race and ethnicity, there is no official state-level data on minority officers. We do know that in 2013, 86.2% of Minnesota's total population was white, 5.7% was black or African American, 5% was Hispanic or Latino, 4.5% was Asian, and the rest were Native American, Native Hawaiian, or Pacific Islander, and two or more races (U.S. Census, 2014). A study conducted in 2008 of a random sample of police officers in the state showed that 6.8% were non-white (Hilal & Erickson, 2009).

The largest agency in the state, Minneapolis, is made up of about 9% minority officers (Williams, 2014). Minneapolis is actively trying to recruit more minorities into their department and have stated that increasing diversity is one of their top priorities (see **Chapter Ten**). Some Minnesota agencies are part of a Joint Community Police Partnership to offer a Cadet Program that seeks recruits who have "exceptional diversity [of] skills, knowledge, and connections" (Brooklyn Park Police Department Cadet Program, 2014). They offer recruits scholarships, mentoring, compensation, practice, and promotional opportunities (Brooklyn Park Police Department Cadet Program, 2014). Considering that in Minnesota most recruits must pay for their own education (classroom and Skills) prior to being hired, this is a significant benefit for those recruits who can offer diversity to an agency.

James Burrell has the distinction of being the first documented police officer in the St. Paul Police Department who was black. He was hired on October 25, 1892 (Griffin, 1975). Almost 100 years later, St. Paul appointed its first black police chief, William Finney, on July 14, 1992 (St. Paul Police Historical Society, 2014). Finney's successor, J. Mark Harrington, was also black.

There are certain races and ethnicities that have their own professional associations. For example, the Minnesota Asian Peace Officer Association (MNAPOA) was formed in 2008 in order to

> ... build a successful recruitment and retention of talented multilingual and educated Asian law enforcement professionals, create a stronger working relationship between the Asian community and law enforcement, establish a networking system among Asian peace officers, and promote awareness and understanding of the many rich Asian ethnic cultures into law enforcement (MNAPOA, 2014).

Partnered with the MNAPOA is the National Latino Peace Officer's Association (NLPOA), Minnesota Chapter. This chapter was founded in 2002 by two St. Paul police officers. The organization hosts yearly events, including a 5K run, a soccer game, and an Adopt-A-Family program. Their mission is to

> ... ensure opportunity in the administration of justice for our members and the communities we serve through leadership, mentoring, and charitable giving, and the creation of professional association that provides support, advocacy, personal and professional development to its members and the diverse communities we serve (NLPOA, 2015).

In 2014, the Minnesota chapter of the National Black Police Association (NBPA) was created. The mission of this association is "To increase the awareness of the community, to be the conscience of the Criminal Justice System, and to enhance the quality of life in the African-American community" (NBPA, 2014). The Minnesota chapter is focusing on recruiting African Americans into the profession and supporting those already hired (Norfleet, 2014).

Still another organization is the Somali-American Police Association (SAPA). Although a national organization, the SAPA is especially relevant to the Minnesota policing community as the state is home to over 30,000 Somalis, which is the largest concentration of Somalis in the United States (Koumpilova, 2014). The SAPA provides a mechanism for police officers of Somali descent to network with each other and to improve the relationship between the police and the broader Somali-American community (SAPA, 2015).

Law Enforcement Opportunities (LEO) is an organization in Minnesota designed to help provide scholarships, education, networking, and employment for minorities and women looking to enter the law enforcement profession. Each year they provide scholarships and hold a widely attended career fair to help bring agencies and recruits together (LEO, 2014).

Education

Because of the two-year degree requirement for licensure in the state, Minnesota has a very educated police force. While a few officers have been "grandfathered" in since the education mandate took effect in 1977, 96% of officers have at least a two-year degree, which is significantly higher than the U.S. adult population as a whole, of which only 40.6% hold an associate's degree or more (U.S. Census Bureau, 2012). As it relates to police in particular, at a national level, only 9% of all agencies require a two-year degree and 1% require a four-year degree (Hickman & Reeves, 2006). In a random sample of police officers in Minnesota in 2008, the specific educational breakdown of officers included what is shown in Figure 2.2.

Figure 2.2. Highest Degree Peace Officer Has Earned in Minnesota
Percentage of Officers (N=622)

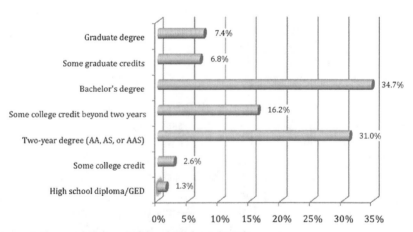

Source: Author created from Hilal and Erickson (2009).

There is no shortage of literature that discusses the benefits of education in general, however, when it comes to policing specifically, the benefits are not as clearly identified, especially when drilled down to the two-year degree versus four-year degree level. However, some evidence exists in support of degreed officers, for example, higher education and promotion are associated in law enforcement (Polk & Armstrong, 2001; Whetstone, 2000) and there is less use of force when officers have at least some college experience (Paoline & Terrill, 2007), including deadly force (McElvain & Kposowa, 2008). The pioneer of education in policing is August Vollmer, whose reports in the 1930s to the Wickersham Commission called for an increase in education in policing (Vollmer, 1932). Since then there have been many federal commissions, reports, and debates about education, but Minnesota still remains the only state in the country that requires the two-year degree as a minimum requirement (Hilal & Erickson, 2009), although most federal agents are held to this standard. When officers were asked in this state if a four-year degree should be the minimum requirement, almost one-third of them thought it should be and when asked if the four-year degree requirement were in place would they have still pursued law enforcement, 71% answered in the affirmative (Hilal, Densley, & Zhao, 2013).

Age

Unlike in federal law enforcement, there is not a state mandatory retirement age. However, as seen in **Figure 2.3**, a vast majority of officers in Minnesota are below the age of 44.

Figure 2.3. Age of Minnesota Peace Officers in May 2015

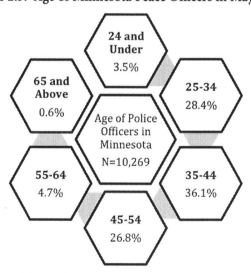

Source: Author created from information obtained through the Minnesota POST (2015).

Law Enforcement Agencies

Minnesota Statutes § 626.84 defines a "law enforcement agency" as

> a unit of state or local government that is authorized by law to grant
> full powers of arrest and to charge a person with the duties of pre-
> venting and detecting crime and enforcing the general criminal laws
> of the state; and subject to the limitations in section 626.93, a law en-
> forcement agency of a federally recognized tribe, as defined in United
> States Code, title 25, section 450b(e).

The Minnesota law enforcement community is highly decentralized. Moreover, 405 (91%) of agencies in Minnesota have fewer than 50 full-time officers. Twenty-two departments have only one officer, six have two officers, 13
have three officers, and 23 have only four officers (Minnesota POST, 2014).
One full-time chief and one or two part-time officers comprise some of these
smaller agencies. The Minnesota Legislature voted to eliminate part-time licenses
as of July 1, 2014 (Minnesota POST, 2014). Only those individuals (~180) already holding a part-time license and currently employed on this date were allowed to continue to hold and renew their part-time license until they changed
employment status, at which time their part-time licenses will also be voided.
In short, no new part-time licenses will be granted. Prior to 2014, only some
agencies were allowed to hire part-time officers and the state had set a quota
for how many part-time licenses were granted.

The size and scope of law enforcement agencies in Minnesota is like others
in the United States. Of the 17,985 agencies in existence throughout the United
States, for example, 15,498 (86%) have fewer than 50 officers (Reaves, 2011).
The top 10 largest police departments in the state, defined by the number of
officers, are provided in **Figure 2.4** (Minnesota POST, 2014).

Minnesota Department of Public Safety

The Minnesota Department of Public Safety is made of 15 different divisions
that are tasked with enforcement, licensing, and to provide services to the state.
Minnesota Statutes § 299A outlines the duties and functions of this department. The commissioner of public safety appoints each division leader. All divisions perform critical state functions. Two such divisions are highlighted
below: the Bureau of Criminal Apprehension and the State Patrol.

Figure 2.4. The Ten Largest Law Enforcement Agencies in
Minnesota in 2014 by Number of Officers

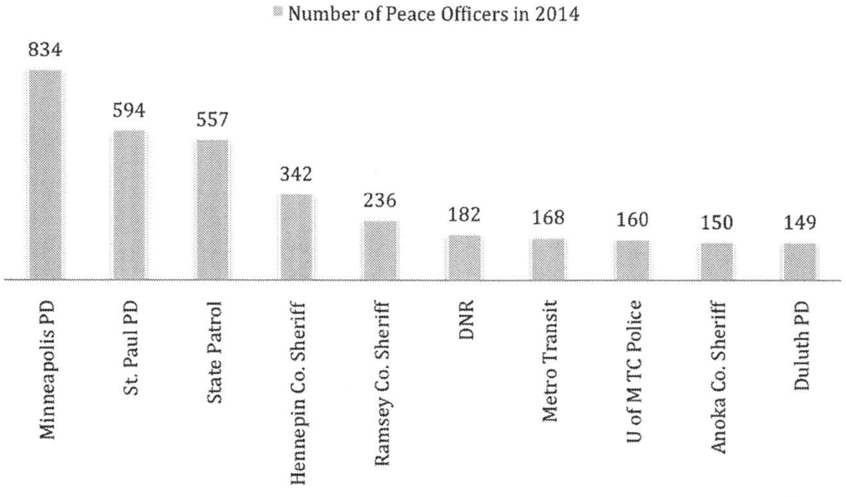

▒ Number of Peace Officers in 2014

Agency	Number
Minneapolis PD	834
St. Paul PD	594
State Patrol	557
Hennepin Co. Sheriff	342
Ramsey Co. Sheriff	236
DNR	182
Metro Transit	168
U of M TC Police	160
Anoka Co. Sheriff	150
Duluth PD	149

Source: Author created from information obtained from the Minnesota POST (2014).

Bureau of Criminal Apprehension

The Bureau of Criminal Apprehension (BCA) was legislatively created in 1929 to provide assistance in solving crime and criminal apprehension to all peace officers in the state (Department of Public Safety, BCA, 2014). The BCA has ten field offices, three crime labs, and is headquartered in St. Paul. Minnesota Statutes § 299C.03 outlines the rules of the bureau:

> … The bureau shall cooperate with the respective sheriffs, police, and other peace officers of the state in the detection of crime and the apprehension of criminals throughout the state, and shall have the power to conduct such investigations as the superintendent, with the approval of the commissioner of public safety, may deem necessary to secure evidence which may be essential to the apprehension and conviction of alleged violators of the criminal laws of the state. The various members of the bureau shall have and may exercise throughout the state the same powers of arrest possessed by a sheriff, but they shall not be employed to render police service in connection with strikes and other industrial disputes.…

There are four main divisions within the BCA:

1) *Administrative Division* is responsible for training programs offered to Minnesota peace officers on a variety of topics. This division is also in charge of public outreach for programs like AMBER Alert (a child abduction alert system) and Drug Abuse Resistance Education (D.A.R.E., see Ennett et al., 1994).

2) *Forensic Science Division* provides "quality forensic science services for the criminal justice community and fosters partnerships that promote research, education and overall forensic science laboratory improvement." The BCA's crime lab has been in existence for over 65 years and, as noted in Chapter 1, was the first in the country to use only DNA to identify a suspect. The lab was also first in the nation to use an automated fingerprint identification system and first in the Midwest to receive international accreditation for their calibration laboratory.

3) *Investigations Division* has agents located throughout Minnesota, assisting other agencies as needed, for "investigative, analytical and crime scene responses, as well as long-term assistance with complex investigations." They also assist with cold cases, internet crimes against children, predatory offender registry, technical support, and operations.

4) *Minnesota Justice Information Services Division* is the largest division within the BCA and provides services both to the public (e.g., criminal history database, fingerprinting, and predatory offender registry) and to criminal justice agencies (e.g., access and exchange of crime data and information between agencies). They have a Criminal Justice Data Communication Network (CJDC) to assist with information management. (Department of Public Safety, BCA, 2014)

The BCA is also home to Minnesota's Fusion Center. There are 78 state and local Fusion Centers throughout the United States, which are supported by the Department of Homeland Security. Created after the September 11, 2001, terror attacks, its mission is to "collect, evaluate, analyze and disseminate information regarding organized criminal, terrorist and all-hazards activity in Minnesota, while complying with state and federal law to ensure the rights and privacy of all" (Department of Public Safety, BCA, 2014). The center is made up of approximately 20 personnel representing 11 different agencies. In addition, there are 330 Threat Liaison Officers (TLOs) throughout Minnesota who work for local agencies and serve as the "information bridge" to the Fusion Center. The Minnesota Fusion Center created the Intelligence Communications Enterprise for Information Sharing and Exchange (ICEFISHX) which is an intelligence sharing initiative and alert network that is internet-based and available to law enforcement, the government, and a select portion of the private sector.

State Patrol

The Minnesota State Patrol was created in 1929, but until 1974 it was known as the Minnesota Highway Patrol (Department of Public Safety, Minnesota State Patrol, 2014). This is understandable given one of the main functions of the State Patrol is to provide for safe roadways in Minnesota. They also:

- educate Minnesotans about the importance of traffic safety;
- investigate and reconstruct serious crashes;
- conduct flight patrols and search and rescue missions;
- assist other law enforcement agencies; and
- serve as a vital component of the state's homeland security efforts.

(Department of Public Safety, Minnesota State Patrol, 2014)

These functions necessitate specialized training and assignments for the troopers, some of which include: aviation, special response teams, crash reconstructions, drug recognition experts, capitol security, communications, canine units, and public information officers. They do all of this while maintaining their core values of "respect, integrity, courage, and honor."

Troopers have been recognized locally and nationally for their work. In September 2014, for example, Brian Beuning was awarded the Officer of the Month, an honor given to one officer in the country by the National Law Enforcement Officers Memorial Fund. Trooper Beuning helped rescue a woman from flood waters (Norfleet, 2014).

The State Patrol is able to hire individuals with a two- or four-year degree from an accredited school in any major and put them through a licensing certification provided by an approved POST certified school. This means the State Patrol pays the cost of Skills while also compensating the trainee at 70% of his or her base salary to attend. Applicants who accept a position with the State Patrol, therefore, are required to sign a two-year work commitment contract (Minnesota State Patrol LETO program, 2014).

Hennepin and Ramsey County Sheriff's Departments

The two most populated counties in Minnesota are Hennepin and Ramsey; as such they also make up two of the largest law enforcement agencies in the state. These sheriff departments have many responsibilities, including such important tasks as operating each county's jail facility (see **Chapter**

Four), maintaining court security, providing patrol and investigation services (including water and park patrol), issuing warrants, issuing civil processes (e.g., subpoenas, orders for protection, mortgage foreclosures, evictions, and judgment collections), emergency management, notification of predatory offenders, managing permits to carry handguns, and providing crime lab services (in Hennepin County). The Hennepin County sheriff's crime laboratory is busy. A majority of the crimes they focus on are property-related, but they have services in five main areas: biology, crime scene, evidence, firearms and tool mark examination, and latent prints (Hennepin County Sheriff's Office, 2015).

Minneapolis Police Department and Minneapolis Park Patrol

The largest police department in the state, and one of the oldest, is the Minneapolis Police Department (MPD). H. H. Bracket was the first police chief and was appointed in 1867 (City of Minneapolis Police Department, 2015). As the population increased, so did the number of full-time officers and civilian personnel who worked in one of five precincts in the city. MPD is one of the only police departments in the state to have its own crime laboratory, offering film and digital photo processing; computer, video, and author forensics; firearms and tool mark examination; a forensic garage; fingerprinting; and crime scene process and examination. MPD has its own academy for new recruits and many specialty divisions and outreach programs, including school resource officers, canine unit, police band, mounted patrol, juvenile outreach, and diversion. The city also has its own citizen advisory council, created in 2013 to help facilitate "community outreach and engagement, recruitment, hiring and promotion, training, and accountability" (Minneapolis Police Department, 2015).

The Minneapolis Park Patrol is a separate law enforcement entity created 20 years after the Minneapolis Police Department was created, in 1887. While they work closely with the Minneapolis Police Department, they are responsible for parklands in the city. While both Park Police Officers and Minneapolis Police Officers have jurisdiction throughout the city, including the parks, they are governed by separate elected officials. They are a busy law enforcement agency with only thirty full-time and twenty part-time officers; they respond to about 13,000 calls for service each year (Minneapolis Park and Recreation Board, 2015).

St. Paul Police Department

Located in the state's capital, the St. Paul Police Department is the state's oldest police department. Responding to over a quarter million calls per year this agency is also one of the busiest in the state (Saint Paul, Minnesota, 2015). To help respond to these calls, the department has a major crimes division, which is separated into seven units: family and sexual violence, property crimes, gangs (see **Chapter Seven** for a discussion of gangs in St. Paul), homicide and robbery, youth services, special investigations, narcotics and vice, and safe streets task force (Saint Paul, Minnesota, 2015). With St. Paul's rich history, leadership, diversity, training opportunities and professional development, an array of specialty duty assignments, location, and other local attractions, employment as a St. Paul police officer is competitive. Recruitment to their cadet academy happens once a year or once every several years. In addition to the standard application process, like other major agencies, this police department requires applicants to complete a physical fitness assessment, which includes body composition, flexibility, muscular endurance and strength, and anaerobic and explosive power. Once hired, their recruits also complete an internal academy (13+ weeks) beyond Skills to further refine driving, shooting, and defensive tactics skills, as well as learning department-specific expectations.

St. Paul police have done a great job of tracking their department's history by having their own museum. Their museum is on the second floor of the headquarters building. The museum is possible in part because of a group of committed volunteers who form The St. Paul Police Historical Society. The society is "committed to preserving and promotion the history of the St. Paul Police Department" (St. Paul Police Historical Society, 2014). They have collected artifacts, documents, and oral histories of important happenings in their agency.

Special Types of Law Enforcement Agencies in the State

While every law enforcement agency performs a critical function, below highlights a few of those agencies that are tasked with some of the more unique types of law enforcement. See **Chapter Eight** for a review of federal law enforcement.

University of Minnesota Police Department

The University of Minnesota Twin Cities is Minnesota's largest university campus, with 52,500 students (University of Minnesota, 2014). With this large student body there is a need for a dedicated police force. The University of Minnesota Police Department (UMPD) is the only university police in the state that is a licensed agency with a variety of functions, as shown in **Figure 2.5.**

Figure 2.5. The Main Functions of University of Minnesota
Police Department

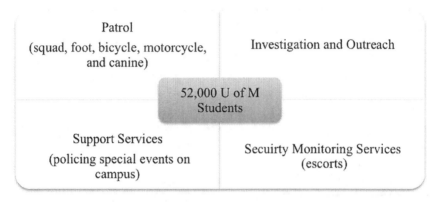

Source: Author created from University of Minnesota Police Department (2014).

The University of Minnesota Police maintains strong partnerships with the Minneapolis Police Department, the St. Paul Police Department, and the St. Anthony Police Department (University of Minnesota Police Department, 2014). The campus is also home to TCF Bank Stadium, which holds football games for the University of Minnesota Division 1 team and, for the 2014 and 2015 seasons, the Minnesota Vikings National Football League team.

Department of Natural Resources

Minnesota is the "Land of 10,000 Lakes" (the motto on state license plates for passenger vehicles) and home to a myriad of multi-use state trails, state parks, and recreation areas; forest campgrounds and day use areas; fishing piers and shore-fishing sites; and waterways (Minnesota Department of Natural Resources, 2014). Combining these natural resources with Minnesotans who are avid hunters and fishermen, the Department of Natural Resources in Minnesota is the 21st largest natural resource agency in the country (Reaves, 2011). According to the U.S. Fish and Wildlife Service 2011 Census (2013), there were 1,562,000 anglers, 477,000 hunters, and 1,577,000 wildlife watchers, totaling about 2.5 million participants, in Minnesota. This is big business in Minnesota, where anglers spend $2.4 billion and hunters spend $725 million on trips, equipment, and other related expenses (U.S. Fish and Wildlife Service 2011 Census, 2013). In Minnesota, "state wildlife management areas (WMA), state forests, national forests, and federal waterfowl production areas (WPAs)" are the most common places to hunt (Minnesota Department of Natural Resources, 2014). Fishing happens in many lakes throughout Minnesota. To aid in the process of finding where to fish, the Minnesota Department of Natural Resources has a searchable database on their webpage to include detailed information on things like quality, clarity, and depth of the water.

Conservation officers (CO) are fully licensed by the Minnesota POST Board. COs are responsible for law enforcement related duties as well as to be a resource for the protection of natural resources. COs are given a take-home squad car, boat, snowmobile, and ATV to help them do their job (Minnesota Department of Natural Resources, 2014). As such, this often is a highly competitive, sought after law enforcement position.

Three Rivers Park District Department of Public Safety

While the Department of Natural Resources patrols the state parks, Three Rivers Park District Department of Public Safety patrols some of the regional parks, trails, and special use facilities (totaling over 27,000 acres) located in some of the most populated, largest counties in Minnesota, including Hennepin, Dakota, Anoka, and Carver Counties (Three Rivers Park District Department of Public Safety, 2014). This full-fledged law enforcement agency, with 21 licensed peace officers (three of them female), has been in existence since 1971 (Department of Public Safety, Uniform Crime Report, 2013). Like state conservation officers they serve a niche type of law enforcement to include search and rescue operations, land use, and dealing with conservation-related statutes. They also provide education—teaching patrons how to properly use the natural resources with the goal of "cooperative compliance" (Three Rivers Park District Department of Public Safety, 2014). Officers patrol using a variety of methods, including snowmobiles, ATVs, boats, cross-country skis, and bikes, and are all trained to render emergency medical care. They have been recognized by the International Association of Chiefs of Police for using GPS to combat environmental crime and make the parks more accessible to certain populations. For example, in 2014, Three Rivers Park District introduced free of charge a new GPS tracking system called PAL (Protect And Locate) for vulnerable people who tend to wander (e.g., people with Alzheimer's, autism, or dementia) so they and their families can use and enjoy the parks (Slavik, 2014).

Airport Police Department

The Minneapolis-St. Paul International Airport (MSP) is one of the busiest airports in the United States and is a Delta Airlines hub. The Airport Police is a licensed agency. They have jurisdiction to patrol all of MSP and work in close collaboration with the Transport Security Administration (TSA), which is a federal agency tasked with securing the U.S. transportation system (MSP Airport Police, 2014). As in airports throughout the world, enforcement at MSP is incredibly important because of the emerging threat of terrorism. There have been several former MSP employees who have links to terrorism, including Shirwa Ahmed, who was one of the first American suicide bombers (Lyden, 2014). In 2009, the U.S. Attorney General released a press statement regarding Ahmed, which said he attended an al-Shabaab training camp and became one of five simultaneous suicide attackers who drove explosives into an office of the Puntland Intelligence Service in Bossasso, Puntland (a region of Somalia) (U.S. Attorney's Office, 2009).

Public Safety Departments

Public safety departments are integrated agencies where emergency services such as police, fire, and/or paramedics are combined. Woodbury Public Safety Department is one example in the state as officers here hold the dual role of police/paramedic or police/firefighter. This means the police officers, firefighters, and paramedics train and work together (City of Woodbury Public Safety, 2014). Integration models like this, while not new, are estimated to represent a very small percentage of law enforcement agencies throughout the country (Hilal & Jones, 2014). More research is being done and provided by Michigan State University's Program on Police Consolidation and Shared Service to help better understand the strengths, weaknesses, and best practices for implementation that is evidence-based.

Joint Powers Agencies

Minnesota State Statutes § 471.59 permits joint power agreements whereby

> two or more governmental units, by agreement entered into through action of their governing bodies, may jointly or cooperatively exercise any power common to the contracting parties or any similar powers, including those which are the same except for the territorial limits within which they may be exercised....

An example of one such agreement is South Lake Minnetonka Police Department. This department was created in 1973 and includes four cities: Excelsior, Greenwood, Shorewood, and Tonka Bay to serve approximately 12,000 residents combined (U.S. Census Bureau, 2014). Shorewood is the largest at 7,500 and Greenwood is the smallest with 700. There are some real benefits for smaller cities to consider joint powers. Litsey (2006) highlights that it affords cities more police and related resources in a cost-effective manner, while still allowing some measure of local control. The local control is possible because there is a coordinating committee whereby the mayor of each city is represented equally (regardless of size of city) to make police-related policies and decisions. This also means the chief of this agency must report to the coordinating committee (all four mayors, which is essentially four supervisors).

Metro Transit Police

The Metro Transit Police Department (MTPD) has been in existence since 1994 to protect over 300,000 transit riders a day and over 84 million riders per year (Metropolitan Council, 2014). Their jurisdiction is very large, covering 8 counties and over 90 cities and working in partnership with many agencies. It is the youngest and fastest growing policing agency in Minnesota. It is also one of the most diverse departments in Minnesota, with over 30% of staff consisting of people of color and women.

MTPD ascribes to core values of innovation, partnerships, ethics, diversity, and education (Metro Transit Police, 2014). They operate very much under a "neighborhood and problem solving philosophy." They patrol (both in uniform and plainclothes) the buses and trains and along the transportation routes in the metropolitan area. They are also aided by technology as every bus and train has multiple digital onboard cameras (Metro Transit Police, 2014). The Metro Transit Police is part of the Metropolitan Council, which is tasked with planning, policy creation, and serving the metropolitan area and transit users.

Task Forces

While not specific agencies, task forces provide an important function in Minnesota law enforcement. Throughout the state there are task forces set up to help work on specific criminal problems, including drugs, gangs, financial crimes, violent crimes, and human trafficking. The benefits of task forces can be significant, including:

1. Increased levels of knowledge and expertise.
2. Access to training not readily available to officers on other assignments.
3. Returning officers taking that experience, training, and their resources back to their departments.
4. Co-location providing for constant communication between task force members and helping to build rapport, trust, and solid relationships.

5. Frequently providing assistance and resources to other law enforcement agencies during other non-drug investigations. (Office of Justice Programs—Minnesota Department of Public Safety, 2012, pp. 8–9)

The Minnesota Department of Public Safety Office of Justice Programs has provided funding for task forces since 1988 (Office of Justice Programs–Minnesota Department of Public Safety, 2012). A legislative council oversees these task forces. In 2005, the Minnesota Gang and Drug Oversight Council was created to help guide investigations and prosecutions of drugs and gang crimes (Minnesota Drug and Gang Oversight Council, 2010). In 2010, the council was replaced with the Violent Crimes Coordinating Council (VCCC). The VCCC is tasked to "develop an overall strategy to ameliorate the harm caused to the public by gang and drug crimes within the state of Minnesota" (Office of Justice Programs–Minnesota Department of Public Safety, 2012, p.2). Twenty-three task forces throughout Minnesota help respond to narcotics-related crimes and the harmful consequences of these crimes, as well as provide education to the community. In 2011, they were responsible for 3,522 narcotics-related arrests (including 40% for methamphetamine, 38% for marijuana, 15% for crack/cocaine, and 14% for prescription drugs), and seized drugs and 687 firearms valued at $14 million (Office of Justice Programs—Minnesota Department of Public Safety, 2012).

Like drug task forces, the Minnesota Financial Crime Task Force (MFCTC) pools resources with municipal, county, state, and federal agencies to help respond to financial crimes.

Figure 2.6. Crimes the Minnesota Financial Crime Task Force Investigates

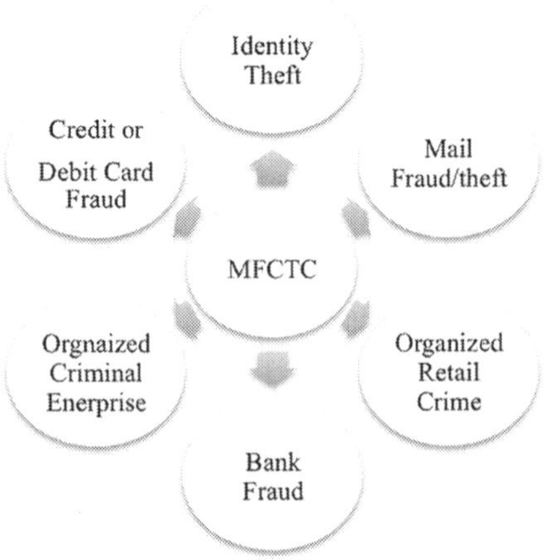

Source: Author created from information provided by Department of Public Safety, MFCTC, 2014.

The Minnesota Human Trafficking Task Force (MNHTTF) consists of 13 government and non-government agencies with the goal to "end human trafficking and other forms of sexual exploitation in Minnesota through a coordinated, multidisciplinary, statewide response." See **Chapter Ten** for more discussion of human trafficking in Minnesota. Other task forces that Minnesota law enforcement agents are involved with include the North Star Fugitive Task Force, Joint Terrorism Task Force, Internet Crimes Against Children Task Force, and U.S. Immigration Customs and Enforcement Agents Task Force.

Tribal Police

Minnesota is home to tribal land, and as such, there are eight tribal law enforcement agencies in the state. In 1953, Minnesota was one of the original six states, including Alaska, California, Nebraska, Oregon, and Wisconsin to "have jurisdiction over offenses committed by or against Indians in the areas of Indian country listed opposite the name of the State or Territory to the same extent that such State or Territory has jurisdiction over offenses committed elsewhere within the State or Territory, and the criminal laws of such State or Territory shall have the same force and effect within such Indian country as they have elsewhere within the State or Territory" (18 U.S.C. §1162, United States Department of Justice, 2015). This law, referred to as Public Law 83-280, (1) "Eliminated most federal Indian country criminal jurisdiction," (2) "Authorized state criminal jurisdiction, a broader scope than previous federal jurisdiction," and (3) "Opened state civil courts to suits against Indians" (Tribal Court Clearing House, 2015). Minnesota Statutes §626.90–626.94 further provide the legal basis for enforcement on tribal land, " ... the tribe's governing body has authorized its peace officers to enforce criminal laws within the boundaries of the tribe's reservation...." Officers who work for a tribal agency governed by the POST Board must still follow the same licensing procedures as any other peace officer in the state.

Minnesota Department of Commerce, Commerce Fraud Bureau

The Commerce Fraud Bureau's mission is "to protect Minnesotans from fraud by conducting aggressive criminal investigations in the pursuit of justice." In 2004, Minnesota became the 41st state to have a state-wide law enforcement agency dedicated to conducting criminal investigations and providing assistance with the criminal prosecution of insurance fraud and related offenses. These cases are brought to the attention of the Bureau by: (1) the general public, (2) insurance companies, (3) law enforcement agencies, and/or (4) other regulatory agencies (Minnesota Department of Commerce, 2012).

While their agency is small (11 licensed peace officers and four analysts), their specific duties are large as outlined by Minnesota Statutes § 45.0135, which include: review notices and reports of insurance fraud submitted by authorized insurers, their employees, and agents or producers; respond to notifications or complaints of suspected insurance fraud generated by other law enforcement agencies, state or federal governmental units, or any other person; initiate inquiries and conduct investigations when the bureau has reason to believe that insurance fraud has been or is being committed; and report incidents of alleged insurance fraud disclosed by its investigations to appropriate law enforcement agencies. According to statistics maintained by the Bureau, in 2014 they received 1,834 cases for investigation. These investigations resulted in the filing of 192 state and federal criminal charges, with an economic impact of $59,586,222 to Minnesotans. In recent years, some of the most prevalent types of insurance fraud include those dealing with automobile, healthcare, and homeowner insurance.

Salaries of Peace Officers

Officers in Minnesota make close to the median *household* income for the state overall. According to the U.S. Census (2014), the Minnesota median household income (2009–2013) was $59,836, which is more than the U.S. average of $53,046. The Bureau of Labor Statistics (2014) report 2013 Minnesota's median salary of police officers and sheriff's deputies was $51,900–$59,100. This is the same for the neighboring states of Wisconsin and Iowa, but more than North Dakota, which was $42,800–$51,110 and South Dakota which was $29,960–$42,030. An entry-level officer in the largest municipality, Minneapolis, makes between $54,504 and $69,565 (City of Minneapolis, 2015). An entry-level sheriff in the largest county, Hennepin, has a salary range of $50,034–$68,506 (Hennepin County, 2015).

Law Enforcement Leaders

Sheriffs

Sheriffs hold the distinction of being the "oldest" law enforcement position in the country (Scott, 2011). There are 87 sheriffs in Minnesota, one for each of Minnesota's 87 counties. Sheriffs are elected to four-year terms with no term limits. Minnesota Statutes § 387.01 sets the qualifications to be a sheriff, which include the following:

> Every person who files as a candidate for county sheriff must be licensed as a peace officer in this state. Every person appointed to the office of sheriff must become licensed as a peace officer before entering upon the duties of the office. Before entering upon duties every sheriff shall give bond to the state in a sum not less than $25,000 in counties whose population exceeds 150,000, and not less than $5,000 in all other counties, to be approved by the county board, conditioned that the sheriff will well and faithfully in all things perform and execute the duties of office, without fraud, deceit, or oppression, which bond, with an oath of office, shall be recorded with the county recorder.

Like in other states, the sheriffs' main responsibilities as outlined in Minnesota Statutes § 387.03 include:

- Keep and preserve the peace of the county
- Pursue and apprehend all felons
- Execute all processes, writs, precepts, and orders issued or made by lawful authority
- Perform all of the duties pertaining to the office, including investigating recreational vehicle accidents involving personal injury or death that occur outside the boundaries of a municipality, searching and dragging for drowned bodies, and searching and looking for lost persons.

In 1885, the Minnesota Sheriff's Association was formed to provide training and education for the 87 sheriffs and their deputies in Minnesota.

Chiefs of Police

Like the sheriffs, the chiefs of police throughout the state are instrumental in helping shape what law enforcement is in Minnesota. There is a five-day Chief and Command Academy offered by the Minnesota Police Chiefs Association to help chiefs and their command staff do their jobs effectively (Minnesota Police Chiefs Association, 2014). Some chiefs and command staff have also attended the FBI National Academy. This is a selective training program that is by *invitation only* for law enforcement leaders throughout the United States and internationally (Federal Bureau of Investigation, 2014). It is held at the FBI's training facility in Quantico, Virginia. In addition to the leadership training it offers, it provides an excellent opportunity to network with other law enforcement leaders throughout the United Stated and abroad (Federal Bureau of Investigation, 2014).

The requirements to be a chief vary from agency to agency. In 2014, an option to be certified as a Chief Law Enforcement Officer (CLEO) became a reality in Minnesota. CLEO certification is a voluntary program for any senior law enforcement officer that reviews applicants in seven areas, including:

> (1) Operations management, (2) Personnel, (3) Personal development, (4) Finance and budgets, (5) Technology, (6) Ethics, (7) Additional electives, such as diversity enhancement and emergency management, are also identified as key educational areas (Minnesota Police Chiefs Association, 2014).

By going through certification, leaders can compare and build towards the established "gold standard" for executive police leadership.

Officers Killed in Line of Duty

Two hundred and thirty-six Minnesota peace officers have been killed in the line of duty (Officer Down Memorial Page, 2014). More officers have been killed in Minnesota than in the neighboring states of North Dakota (50), South Dakota (52), and Iowa (164), but slightly fewer than in Wisconsin (261) (National Law Enforcement Officers Memorial Fund, 2014). If we look at population statistics this matches with Wisconsin and Minnesota being the most populated, followed by Iowa and then South Dakota and North Dakota. Between 2007 and 2014, a total of 10 officers were killed (Nelson, 2014). The Minneapolis Police Department has lost the most officers in the line of duty at 47, followed by the St. Paul Police Department at 32, the Minnesota Department of Natural Resources at 14, and the State Patrol at 8 (Officer Down Memorial Page, 2014). A majority of officers were killed by gunfire in the month of August (Officer Down Memorial Page, 2014).

Anyone who causes the death of a peace officer while the officer is performing his/her duties is guilty of murder in the first degree and is sentenced to imprisonment for life, as defined by Minnesota Statutes §609.185, subdivision 4. Minnesota does not have the death penalty (see **Chapter Nine** for more details). In addition to the officers killed, there have been four K-9 line of duty deaths (Officer Down Memorial Page, 2014). Minnesota Statutes §609.596 makes it a felony-level crime for the killing of or causing great bodily harm to a police dog.

The Minnesota Law Enforcement Memorial Association (LEMA) has created a peace officer memorial on the grounds of the Minnesota State Capital. This granite memorial was originally located at the Minneapolis-St. Paul International Airport, but was later moved to the state capital. Every year during National Police Week (which falls the calendar week of May 15, the day congress designated as National Peace Officer Memorial Day), LEMA holds a memorial service to honor all the fallen officers in the state (LEMA, 2014). LEMA also raises money to pay for college scholarships to the immediate family members of fallen officers (LEMA, 2014).

Major Law Enforcement Responses in Minnesota

Minnesota law enforcement agencies rely on each other, as well as other emergency and first responders to help protect and serve the people of this state. When major events occur, cooperation is vital.

35-W Bridge Collapse

A good example of multi-jurisdiction cooperation happened when a major eight-lane bridge, I-35W in the city of Minneapolis, collapsed while carrying over 100 vehicles (including a school bus) on August 1, 2007, killing 13 people and injuring 120. The emergency response, involving all jurisdiction levels, including municipal, county, state, and federal agencies, was well orchestrated and helped with the rescue and recovery efforts. This was in part because of the amount of planning and preparation that took place prior to the incident. A case study analysis by the Federal Communications Commission (2008) reported that prior to the disaster the public safety community had taken the following steps:

- Deployed an 800 MHz Protocol Project 25 (P25) trunked LMR radio system that was shared across local, county, and state agencies.
- Invested in a $5.2M dollar computer-aided dispatch system capable of mapping all emergency response vehicles with global positioning service (GPS).
- Extended National Incident Management System (NIMS) training to all employee levels to help ensure that all emergency responders understood their respective roles during a disaster, acted as a collective team, and shared necessary information with designated decision makers.

- Invested in the development of Special Operations Teams at a cost of $8M, which included the development of hazardous materials, collapsed structures, and bomb teams.
- Held inter-agency disaster training exercises in advance of an actual event to determine the effectiveness of their overall strategies, which allowed the public safety community to identify problems prior to the disaster. (Federal Communications Commission, 2008, p.10)

Since this disaster, the *Star Tribune* newspaper created an interactive webpage called "13 Seconds in August: The 35W Bridge Collapse" which allows viewers to see images and learn more information about the disaster (Star Tribune, 2015). ABC's *In an Instant* also produced a two-hour episode (*Rush Hour Disaster*) to illustrate the bridge collapse.

Republican National Convention

In 2008, Minnesota hosted the Republican National Convention (RNC). The Republican nominees for president and vice president in 2008, U.S. Senator John McCain from Arizona and Governor Sarah Palin from Alaska, respectively, attended the event. President George W. Bush and Vice President Dick Cheney were supposed to attend the event, but were unable to because of Hurricane Gustav. Rudy Giuliani, Joe Lieberman, Mike Huckabee, Mitt Romney, and John Boehner were among many other notable Republicans in attendance, along with First Lady Laura Bush.

From a law enforcement perspective, hosting such an event was an enormous undertaking. The I-35W bridge collapse had happened the year before, and provided useful practice in inter-agency cooperation and command.

Planning for the RNC began in 2006. According to Presidential Decision Directive 62 (1998) issued by the National Security Council, for a National Specialty Security Event (NSSE), there is shared lead responsibility. The Secret Service is the designated lead agency for "security design/planning and implementation and will identify and coordinate the appropriate secret service and anti-terrorism measures and counter-terrorism assets that will be needed to effect the overall security requirements." The FBI is the designated lead agency for "intelligence, crisis management, hostage rescue, and its statutory federal criminal investigation." The Federal Emergency Managment Agency (FEMA) is designated the lead agency for "consequence planning and management coordination" (White House, 1998).

In addition to federal agencies, state and local law enforcement provided critical support, including the St. Paul Police Department (who was the lead local law enforcement agency because the RNC was held in the City of St.

Paul), the Ramsey County Sheriff's Department (the county in which St. Paul is located), and the Minnesota Department of Public Safety, which includes the State Patrol and BCA. Altogether over 2,000 law enforcement officers helped ensure the RNC would be secure. Anticipating large protests against the war in Iraq, so-called "strategic incapacitation" was the approach. Strategic incapacitation comprises use of: (1) surveillance and information sharing to assess and monitor risks; (2) pre-emptive arrests and non-lethal weapons to target actual or potential disruptive protesters; and (3) space control to isolate and contain disruptive actual or potential disruptive protesters (Gillham, 2011).

Before the RNC began, police executed a number of controversial "no-knock" search warrants on potential disruptive protestors, which set a hostile tone for events to come. During the convention, police used tear gas, smoke bombs, pepper spray, "flash" grenades, paint marker rounds, and rubber bullets to prevent a march that would have been in violation of court-approved march permits (Hilal & Densley, 2012). More than 30 journalists were arrested and detained, at times without probable cause or reasonable suspicion. Three of the journalists later filed a federal lawsuit that resulted in a $100,000 settlement to compensate for medical expenses and damaged property. The St. Paul Police Department was later court-ordered to implement a training program to educate officers regarding First Amendment rights and procedures on dealing with the press at demonstrations (POV, 2011).

Despite the protests, arrests, lawsuits, injuries, and property damage, it was clear that Minnesota law enforcement was able to safely host large-scale events. The city used technology such as closed-circuit cameras to good effect. This was demonstrated again during the Major League Baseball All-Star Game in 2014 and will be highlighted again when Minnesota hosts the Super Bowl in 2018.

Concluding Remarks

As this chapter has highlighted, law enforcement in Minnesota is a vast network of agencies and individual officers all working to control crime and maintain order for the people of Minnesota. Law enforcement does not work alone and is aided by the community, technology (see **Chapter Ten**), and countless other organizations and individuals with a common mission to ensure justice. Law enforcement is also not static. With the recent release of the President's 21st Century Policing Report (see **Chapter Ten**) changes will likely occur in law enforcement in Minnesota and elsewhere, with the goal to help improve the profession for the future.

Key Terms

Automatic Disqualifiers

BCA

CLEO

Crime Laboratory

DNR

Fusion Center

ICEFISHX

Joint Powers Association

LEMA

LEO

License Eligible

Peace Officer

POST Board

Professional Peace Officer Education

Public Law 83-280

RNC

Sheriff

Skills

State Patrol

Strategic Incapacitation

Task Forces

Selected Internet Sites

Law Enforcement Opportunities
http://www.laweo.org

Minneapolis Police Department
http://www.ci.minneapolis.mn.us/police/

Minnesota Association of Women Police
http://www.mnwomenpolice.org/index.html

Minnesota Bureau of Criminal Apprehension
https://dps.mn.gov/divisions/bca/Pages/default.aspx

Minnesota Chiefs of Police Association
http://www.mnchiefs.org

Minnesota Department of Natural Resources
http://www.dnr.state.mn.us/parks_trails/index.html

Minnesota Department of Public Safety
https://dps.mn.gov/Pages/default.aspx

Minnesota Joint Analysis Center
https://icefishx.org/default.aspx/MenuItemID/412/MenuGroup/_Public.htm

Minnesota POST Board
https://dps.mn.gov/entity/post/Pages/default.aspx

Minnesota Office of Revisor of Statutes
https://www.revisor.leg.state.mn.us

Minnesota Sheriff's Association
https://netforum.avectra.com/eWeb/StartPage.aspx?Site=MSA&WebCode=
HomePage

Minnesota State Patrol
https://dps.mn.gov/divisions/msp/Pages/default.aspx

St. Paul Police Department
http://www.stpaul.gov/index.aspx?nid=461

Discussion Questions

1. What makes Minnesota law enforcement unique compared to other states?
2. What is noteworthy about the Minnesota Bureau of Criminal Apprehension Crime Laboratory and why is this significant?
3. What are task forces and what value do they add?
4. When we say a law enforcement community is decentralized, what does this mean? Do you think this is positive or negative and why?
5. How do you think being a Metro Transit peace officer is both different and similar to being a peace officer in a municipality?
6. What do you think Minnesota should do to help recruit women and minorities into law enforcement?
7. What are the roles and responsibilities of (a) state trooper, (b) conservation officer, and (c) university peace officer?

References

Brooklyn Park Police Department. (2014). *Police cadets.* Retrieved from http://www.brooklynpark.org/city-government/public-safety/police-cadets/

Bureau of Justice Statistics. (2010). *Women in law enforcement, 1987–2008.* NCJ23051. Retrieved from http://www.bjs.gov/content/pub/pdf/wle8708.pdf

Bureau of Justice Statistics. (2014). *Local police: Summary findings.* Retrieved from http://www.bjs.gov/index.cfm?ty=tp&tid=71

Bureau of Labor Statistics. (2014). Occupational employment and wages: Police and sheriff patrol officers. Retrieved from http://www.bls.gov/oes/current/oes333051.htm

City of Minneapolis. (2014). *Police administration.* Retrieved from http://www.ci.minneapolis.mn.us/police/precincts/police_about_administration

City of Minneapolis. (2015). *Inside the Minneapolis Police Department*. Retrieved from http://www.ci.minneapolis.mn.us/police/about/index.htm

City of Woodbury Public Safety. (2014). Retrieved from http://www.ci.wood bury.mn.us/police-department

Doetkott, J. (2014). Advocates call for more female police officers. *ABC 6 News.* Retrieved from: http://www.kaaltv.com/article/stories/s3651689 .shtml.

Ennett, S., Tobler, N., Ringwalt, C., & Flewelling, R. (1994). Resistance education? A meta-analysis of Project D.A.R.E. outcome evaluations. *American Journal of Public Health,* 84, 1394–1401.

Federal Bureau of Investigation. (2014). *The national academy.* Retrieved from http://www.fbi.gov/about-us/training/national-academy

Federal Communications Commission. (2008). Emergency communication during the Minneapolis bridge disaster: A technical case study by the Federal Communications Commission's Public Safety and Homeland Security Bureau's Communications Systems Analysis Division. Retrieved from https://tran sition.fcc.gov/pshs/docs/clearinghouse/references/minneapolis-bridge-report.pdf

Gillham, P. (2011). Securitizing America: Strategic incapacitation and the policing of protest since the 11 September 2001 terrorist attacks. *Sociology Compass,* 5, 636–652.

Griffin, J. (1975). *Blacks in the St. Paul Police Department: An eighty year survey.* St. Paul, MN: Minnesota Historical Society. Retrieved from http:// collections.mnhs.org/MNHistoryMagazine/articles/44/v44i07p255-265.pdf

Hennepin County. (2015). Job announcement for Sheriff, Deputy. Retrieved from https://www.governmentjobs.com/jobs/1095876/sheriff-deputy

Hickman, M., & Reaves, B. (2006). *Local police departments, 2003.* Washington, DC: U.S. Department of Justice, Bureau of Justice Statistics. Retrieved from http://bjs.ojp.usdoj.gov/index.cfm?ty=pbdetail&iid=1045

Hilal, S., & Densley, J. (2012). Is law enforcement prepared for the new normal of protest? *Minnesota Police Chief,* 32, 19–22.

Hilal, S., & Densley, J. (2013). Higher education and local law enforcement. *FBI Law Enforcement Bulletin,* 82(5).

Hilal, S., Densley, J., & Jones, D. (2015). A signaling theory of law enforcement hiring. *Policing and Society.* doi: 10.1080/10439463.2015.1081388.

Hilal, S., Densley, J., & Zhao, R. (2013). Cops in college: Police officers' perceptions on formal education. *Journal of Criminal Justice Education,* 24, 461–477.

Hilal, S., & Erickson, T. (2009). College education as a state-wide licensing requirement: An analysis of the Minnesota model 30 years later. *Critical Issues in Justice and Politics,* 2, 1–19.

Hilal, S., & Jones, D. (2014, September). A package deal: Police, fire, and EMS all in one. *The Police Chief.* Retrieved from http://www.policechief magazine.org/magazine/index.cfm?fuseaction=display_arch&article_id= 3466&issue_id=92014

International Association of Police (2015). *What is the law enforcement oath of honor?* Retrieved from http://www.theiacp.org/What-is-the-Law-Enforcement-Oath-of-Honor

Koumpilova, M. (2014, November 1). New Somali refugee arrivals in Minnesota are increasing. *Star Tribune.* Retrieved from http://www.startribune.com/ new-somali-refugee-arrivals-in-minnesota-are-increasing/281197521/

Law Enforcement Memorial Association (LEMA) (2014). MN State Memorial. http://www.mnlema.org/index.php/layout/history

Law Enforcement Opportunities. (2014). *About us.* Retrieved from http:// www.laweo.org/about_us.html

Library of Congress. (2015). *America's story.* Retrieved from http://www.amer icaslibrary.gov/jb/reform/jb_reform_minnesota_2.html

Litsey, B. (2006). *About the South Lake Minnetonka Police Department.* Retrieved from http://www.southlakepd.com/about.asp

Lyden, T. (2014, November 16). Insider threat: Side-by-side with a future terrorist at MSP Airport. *Fox9.* Retrieved from http://www.myfoxtwin cities.com/story/27399922/insider-threat-side-by-side-with-a-future-terrorist-at-msp-airport

McElvain, J., & Kposowa, A. (2008). Police officer characteristics and the likelihood of using deadly force. *Criminal Justice and Behavior, 35,* 505–521.

Metropolitan Council. (2014). *What we do.* Retrieved from http://www.metro council.org/About-Us/Organization.aspx

Metropolitan Transit Police (2014). *Who we are.* Retrieved from http://www .metrotransit.org/who-we-are.aspx

Minneapolis Park and Recreation Board. (2015). *About Minneapolis park police.* Retrieved from http://minneapolisparks.org/default.asp?PageID=641

Minneapolis-St. Paul International Airport Police. (2014). Retrieved from https:// www.mspairport.com/security-and-public-safety/police-department.aspx

Minnesota Asian Peace Officer Association. (2014). Retrieved from www.mnapoa.org/

Minnesota Association of Women Police. (2014). Retrieved from http:// www.mnwomenpolice.org/index.html

Minnesota Department of Commerce. (2012). *Division of insurance fraud and prevention, Minnesota Department of Commerce, annual report 2012.* Retrieved from http://mn.gov/commerce/images/IFD-2012-Report.pdf

Minnesota Department of Natural Resources. (2014). *Parks and trail division.* Retrieved from http://www.dnr.state.mn.us/parks_trails/index.html

Minnesota Department of Public Safety. (2014a). Bureau of Criminal Apprehension. Retrieved from https://dps.mn.gov/divisions/bca/Pages/default.aspx

Minnesota Department of Public Safety. (2014b). *How to become a peace officer in Minnesota.* Retrieved from https://dps.mn.gov/entity/post/becoming-a-peace-officer/Pages/peace-officer-how-to-become.aspx

Minnesota Department of Public Safety. (2014c). *Minnesota State Patrol.* Retrieved from https://dps.mn.gov/divisions/msp/about/Pages/history.aspx

Minnesota Department of Public Safety. (2014d). *Uniform Crime Report.* Retrieved from https://dps.mn.gov/divisions/bca/bca-divisions/mnjis/Documents/2013%20Crime%20Book.pdf

Minnesota Department of Public Safety. (2015). *Minnesota financial crime task force.* Retrieved from https://dps.mn.gov/divisions/bca/bca-divisions/investigations/Pages/mn-financial-crimes-task-force.aspx

Minnesota Drug and Gang Oversight Council. (2010). *Minnesota gang and drug oversight council 2010 annual report to legislature.* Retrieved from http://www.house.leg.state.mn.us/comm/docs/2010GDOCAnnualReport.pdf

Minnesota Human Trafficking Task Force. (2014). *About MNHTTF.* Retrieved from http://mnhttf.org/our-role-purpose/about/

Minnesota Office of Revisor of Statutes. (2014). Retrieved from https://www.revisor.leg.state.mn.us

Minnesota Peace Officer Standards and Training. (POST). (2014). Retrieved from https://dps.mn.gov/entity/post/Pages/default.aspx

Minnesota Police Chiefs Association (2014). *Cleo and command academy.* Retrieved from http://www.mnchiefs.org/cleo-and-command-academy

Minnesota State Demographic Center. (2014). *Population data, key findings.* Retrieved from http://mn.gov/admin/demography/data-by-topic/population-data/our-estimates/index.jsp

Minnesota State Patrol. (2014). *Law enforcement trainee opportunity trainee 1 program.* Retrieved from https://dps.mn.gov/divisions/msp/forms-reports/Documents/2014%20LETO%20Posting.pdf

National Black Police Association. (2014). Retrieved from http://www.blackpolice.org/about.html

National Latino Peace Officer Association, Minnesota Chapter. (2015). Retrieved from http://www.nlpoamn.org/

National Law Enforcement Officers Memorial Fund. (2014). *Officers death by states.* Retrieved from http://www.nleomf.org/facts/officer-fatalities-data/state.html

Nelson, T. (2014, July 31). Recent Minnesota police officers who have died in the line of duty. *MPR News.* Retrieved from http://www.mprnews.org/story/2014/07/31/recent-minnesota-police-officers-died-in-the-line-of-duty

Norfleet, N. (2014, April 25). Minnesota police form black officer chapter. *Star Tribune.* Retrieved from http://www.startribune.com/local/east/256787941.html

Norfleet, N. (2014, September 22). Minnesota state trooper given national award for flood rescue. *Star Tribune.* Retrieved from http://www.startribune.com/local/276405401.html

Officer Down Memorial Page. (2014). Minnesota line of duty deaths. Retrieved from http://www.odmp.org/search/browse/MN

Office of Justice Programs, Minnesota Department of Public Safety. (2012). *Drug and violent crime task force annual report, 2012.* Retrieved from https://www.stlouiscountymn.gov/Portals/0/Departments/Sheriff/Documents%20-%20Sheriffs%20Office/2012%20Task%20Force%20Report.pdf

Paoline, E., & Terrill, W. (2007). Police education, experience, and the use of force. *Criminal Justice and Behavior, 34,* 179–196.

Polk, E., & Armstrong, D. (2001). Higher education and law enforcement career paths: Is the road to success paved by degree. *Journal of Criminal Justice Education, 12,* 77–102.

POV (2011, September 6). *Timeline: Protests at the 2008 RNC.* Retrieved from http://www.pbs.org/pov/betterthisworld/photo_gallery_timeline-protests-2008-rnc.php#.VXKW5rq1hUs

Reaves, B. (2011). Census of state and local law enforcement agencies. *Bureau of Justice Statistics. NCJ 233982.* Retrieved from http://www.bjs.gov/content/pub/pdf/csllea08.pdf

Scott, R. (2011). Roots: An historical perspective on the office of the sheriff. *National Sheriff's Association.* Retrieved from http://www.sheriffs.org/content/office-sheriff

Slavik, R. (2014). Three River Park District unveils GPS tracker for vulnerable adults. *CBS Minnesota.* Retrieved from http://minnesota.cbslocal.com/2014/07/12/three-rivers-park-debuts-gps-tracker-for-vulnerable-guests/

Somali-American Police Association. (2015). Retrieved from http://somaliamericanpa.org/

Star Tribune. (2007). 13 seconds in August: The 35W Bridge Collapse. Retrieved from http://www.startribune.com/local/minneapolis/12166286.html

St. Paul, Minnesota. (2015). Retrieved from http://www.stpaul.gov/index.aspx?nid=461

St. Paul Police Historical Society. (2014). *Chiefs of police.* Retrieved from http://www.spphs.com/origins.php

Three River Park District. (2014). *Public safety*. Retrieved from http://www.threeriversparks.org/about/public-safety/patrol-methods.aspx

Tribal Court Clearing House. (2015). *Public Law 280*. Retrieved from http://www.tribal-institute.org/lists/pl280.htm

United States Attorney's Office. (2009). Terror charges unsealed against eight defendants, Justice Department announces. Retrieved from http://www.fbi.gov/minneapolis/press-releases/2009/mp112309.htm

United States Census Bureau. (2012). Educational attainment in the United States. Retrieved from http://www.census.gov/hhes/socdemo/education/data/cps/2012/tables.html

United States Census Bureau. (2014). Minnesota state and county quick facts. Retrieved from http://quickfacts.census.gov/qfd/states/27000.html

United States Department of Justice. (2015). What is Public Law 280. Retrieved from http://www.justice.gov/usao/mn/PL-280%20FAQ.html

United States Fish and Wildlife Service 2011 Census. (2013). *2011 national survey of fishing, hunting, and wildlife-associated recreation in Minnesota*. Retrieved from http://www.census.gov/prod/2013pubs/fhw11-mn.pdf

University of Minnesota Police Department. (2014). Retrieved from http://police.umn.edu

Vollmer, A. (1932). Abstract of the Wickersham police report. *Journal of Criminal Law and Criminology*, 22, 716–723.

Whetstone, T. (2000). Getting stripes: Educational achievement and study strategies used by sergeants. *American Journal of Criminal Justice*, 24, 247–257.

White House. (1998). Presidential Decision Directive/NSC-62. #20365. Retrieved from http://www.fas.org/irp/offdocs/pdd/pdd-62.pdf

Williams, B. (2014, September 3). Minneapolis police make an effort to hire more minority officers. *National Public Radio*. Retrieved from http://www.npr.org/2014/09/03/345308385/minneapolis-pd-makes-an-effort-to-hire-more-minority-officers

Chapter Three

Warren Burger Was Born Here: Minnesota's Judicial System

Learning Objectives

- Identify the three levels of court of the Minnesota Judicial Branch
- Describe the budgetary resources devoted to the Minnesota Judicial Branch annually
- Describe the jurisdictions of the Minnesota Court of Appeals and Supreme Court
- Explain the role and function of Minnesota district courts
- Describe judicial selection and election in Minnesota
- Identify agencies responsible for oversight of Minnesota's judicial and legal communities
- Identify the sources of legal education in Minnesota
- Explain the various problem-solving courts in Minnesota
- Describe factors influencing prosecutorial decisions regarding charges and plea bargains
- Articulate the rights of crime victims in Minnesota

As the chapter title suggests, one of Minnesota's judicial claims to fame is the fact that Warren Burger, Chief Justice of the United States Supreme Court from 1969 to 1986, came from the state. Burger was born in St. Paul, Minnesota, in 1907. He attended the University of Minnesota prior to law school. He then attended the St. Paul College of Law (the Mitchell Hamline School of Law today) part-time at night, graduating in 1931. In the two decades after graduating, he worked in private practice in the Twin Cities, as well as serving as a part-time faculty member at the St. Paul College of Law (Supreme Court Historical Society, 2015).

Burger was active in Minnesota's Republican Party. He played a leadership role in the successful gubernatorial campaigns of Harold Stassen, as well as Stassen's losing bid to secure the Republican Party's presidential nomination in 1948 and 1952. Burger and the Minnesota delegation to the 1952 Republican National Convention got behind Dwight Eisenhower when it was clear that Stassen wasn't going to win the nomination. Burger delivered to Eisenhower Minnesota's delegates — something for which Eisenhower remained grateful upon being elected President (Biography, 2015).

In 1953, President Eisenhower appointed Burger to be Assistant Attorney General of the United States. He was placed in charge of the Justice Department's Civil Division. In 1955, President Eisenhower appointed Burger to the Circuit Court of Appeals for Washington DC. This appellate court is widely regarded as the most powerful and influential court in the United States short of the U.S. Supreme Court. However, Burger did not have to settle for the second most powerful court. In 1969, President Richard Nixon nominated Burger to be Chief Justice of the United States Supreme Court. The Senate confirmed the nomination and he took his seat on the Court in June of 1969 — a position he held for 17 years until his retirement in 1986 (Biography, 2015).

As proud as the juridical community in Minnesota is of its favorite son, Chief Justice Burger never served in the judiciary at the state or local level. His career took him from private practice to federal executive service in Washington DC, and from there to the federal judiciary.

Minnesota's Judicial Branch

As with every other state and the federal government, Minnesota's government consists of three branches: the executive branch, led by the governor, a bi-cameral legislature, and the state judiciary. The judicial branch of government includes the Minnesota Supreme Court, the appellate courts, and the district courts, which include specialized courts. The judicial branch also includes the administrative and bureaucratic apparatus to operate the judiciary, including court administrators and court services personnel. In total, the Minnesota judicial branch employs over 2,500 people and has an annual budget in excess of $300,000,000 (Minnesota Judicial Branch, 2014).

The published mission statement of the Minnesota judicial branch is: "To provide justice through a system that assures equal access for the fair and timely resolution of cases and controversies" (Minnesota Judicial Branch, 2014a, p. 4). Access to justice is a fundamental goal for the judiciary in Minnesota and in every other state. Indeed, in addition to being a central piece of the mission statement, access to justice is the first goal among three key goals in the Minnesota judiciary's strategic plan in FY 2015. The plan states that the judicial branch seeks to deliver to the people of Minnesota a justice system that is "open, affordable, understandable, and provides appropriate levels of service to all users" (Minnesota Judicial Branch, 2014a, p. 5).

The two remaining stated goals for the judiciary include: administering justice for effective results (which is accomplished by adopting processes which enhance outcomes for participants in the system) and bolstering public trust, accountability, and impartiality. Notably, all of these stated goals of the Minnesota judicial branch are focused on citizenry—particularly those who use or become participants in the judicial system. Certainly, access to justice is a laudable end worthy to be pursued in and of itself. However, the 2nd and 3rd goals have more of a consumerist tone. Lofty goals such as finding the truth in conflict, or reducing crime, give way to customer service. Philosophically and politically, Minnesota is known for pragmatism and populism, so perhaps this orientation of the judiciary should come as no surprise.

Table 3.1. Minnesota's Judicial Branch

FY2015 Budget:
    $256,1622,000—District (Trial) Courts
    $11,035,000—Court of Appeals
    $32,925,000—Supreme Court/State Court Administration/State Law Library
    $300,582,000—Total
Judicial Branch Members:
    Approximately 2,500 permanent employees
    Number of authorized judgeships—315
    Supreme Court—7
    Court of Appeals—19
    District (Trial) Courts—289
Judicial Districts and Facilities:
    10 judicial districts statewide
    106 judicial branch hearing facilities
    Oldest Courthouse: Washington County Courthouse (Stillwater) built in 1869
    62 Minnesota courthouses on the National Register of Historic Places

Source: 2014 Annual Report, Minnesota Judicial Branch

Minnesota Supreme Court

The court system in Minnesota is established in Article VI of the Minnesota Constitution. Similar to the U.S. Constitution, which establishes the U.S. Supreme Court but leaves the appellate and lower courts to be established by Congress, the Minnesota Constitution only requires that there shall be a Supreme Court; the court of appeals, district courts, and courts inferior to district courts are to be established by the legislature. The Constitution nevertheless anticipates district courts to be established as it speaks to the jurisdiction, number and boundaries of judicial districts and district judges, and qualifications and compensation of district judges. Interestingly, for most of Minnesota's state history (beginning in 1858), there were only district courts and the Supreme Court. The Court of Appeals was not created by the legislature until 1983.

Of the composition of the Supreme Court, the Constitution specifies that there shall be a chief judge and no fewer than six, and no more than eight, associate Supreme Court judges. Today, the Minnesota Supreme Court has a chief judge and six associate judges.

The Minnesota Supreme Court serves as a court of appeals and well a court of original jurisdiction in certain cases. As an appellate court, it hears appeals from:

- Minnesota Court of Appeals decisions;
- District court decisions when the Supreme Court chooses to bypass the Court of Appeals;
- Tax court decisions; and
- Workers' Compensation Court of Appeals decisions.

The Minnesota Supreme Court takes original action regarding (Minnesota Judicial Branch, 2012b):

- automatic review of all first degree murder convictions (which require life without parole);
- writs of prohibition (which seek to prevent the government from taking some action);
- writs of habeas corpus (which require the government to justify why someone is in custody);
- writs of mandamus (which seek to compel the government to perform some act);
- disputes involving legislative elections; and
- attorney and judge disciplinary cases brought by the Lawyers Professional Responsibility Board and the Board on Judicial Standards, respectively.

Figure 3.1. How a Case Gets to the Supreme Court
and What Happens to It

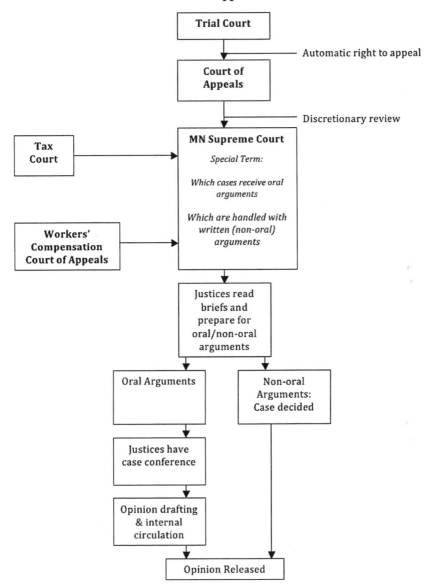

Source: Minnesota Judicial Branch, 2012

Each year, the Minnesota Supreme Court receives about 900 petitions for review. Prior to the creation of the Court of Appeals in 1983, the number was over 1,800 petitions annually. Petitioners must file a "petition for review" for their cases to be considered by the Supreme Court. This is akin to petitioning to the U.S. Supreme Court for a writ of certiorari. Only about 5% of the cases petitioned to the Minnesota Supreme Court come from the Court of Appeals. Most of the cases come to the Supreme Court from the Tax Court, the Workers' Compensation Court of Appeals, and from petitioners requesting that the Supreme Court act under its original jurisdiction authority. Of the 900 cases on average for which the Supreme Court is petitioned, it actually accepts about 1 in 8 for review (Minnesota Judicial Branch, 2015d). The Supreme Court tends to focus on the most contentious constitutional and public policy issues.

The Supreme Court also possesses regulatory and administrative functions. The Supreme Court is the body responsible for regulating the practice of law in Minnesota, as well as enforcing standards of conduct for attorneys and judges in the state. The Court develops and implements rules and procedures for the practice of law in Minnesota. The Supreme Court is also tasked, through its administrative personnel, with overseeing the operations of the Minnesota court system state-wide.

The Minnesota Judicial Branch employs approximately 2,500 people, only a fraction of whom are judges. The annual budget for the entire Minnesota judicial branch totaled in excess of $290 million in Fiscal Year 2014. This includes $32,282,000 appropriated for the Supreme Court and the State Court Administration Office. In FY 2014, the salary for the Chief Judge of the Supreme Court was set at $167,002. Salary for each associate judge was set at $151,820.

Court of Appeals

The Minnesota Court of Appeals first began to operate on November 1, 1983. The Court of Appeals was created to relieve the case load of the Supreme Court by providing a prompt review of all final legal decisions of the district courts, as well as administrative and regulatory decisions of state and local government agencies. The Court of Appeals exists to correct legal errors committed at the district court level and handles 95% of all appeals in the state. The Court of Appeals hears or considers in conference approximately 2,400 cases each year.

The Court of Appeals in Minnesota has the quickest turn-around time on accepted cases in the United States. By law, the Court of Appeals must issue a decision within 90 days of oral arguments or 90 days of a case's scheduled conference date. No other appeals court in the country operates under a shorter imposed deadline for decisions. District judges in Minnesota operate under similar deadlines. Minnesota's computerized case management system alerts court system officials, as well as oversight bodies such as the Board on Judicial Standards, when judges fail to render decisions in a timely manner.

The Minnesota Court of Appeals consists of 19 judges. The judges rotate into three-judge panels and travel throughout the state to hear oral arguments. The traveling nature of the Court of Appeals is intended to make access to appellate review less expensive and more broadly available to the citizens of Minnesota (Minnesota Judicial Branch, 2015a). The entire appellate court is housed, however, in St. Paul at the Minnesota Judicial Center.

The appropriated budget in Fiscal Year 2014 for the Court of Appeals in Minnesota was $10,641,000. The Chief Judge of the Court of Appeals had an annual salary of $150,206. The remaining 18 appellate judges earned $143,054 per year.

District Courts

In Minnesota, there are 10 judicial districts encompassing the state's 87 counties. Presiding over trials in these districts are 289 judges. There is at least one judge in each county. Every district is made up of two or more counties, with the exception of the two most populated counties in Minnesota—Hennepin and Ramsey Counties (which include the cities of Minneapolis and St. Paul, respectively). The Fourth Judicial District consists of Hennepin County and the Second Judicial District consists of Ramsey County.

District courts, or trial courts, are primarily courts of original jurisdiction. That is to say, cases are first heard, or originally heard, in district court. The kinds of cases heard in Minnesota district courts include: civil cases, criminal cases, family disputes, juvenile delinquency cases, probate cases, and violations of municipal and county ordinances. District courts serve as an appellate court for cases originating in housing court, probate/mental health court, and conciliation court, although such cases technically amount to a new trial rather than strictly an appeal on issues of law.

The administration of judicial districts is state administrative function. Each district is managed by the district's chief judge and assistant chief judge. Each district is also assigned a judicial district administrator. Additionally, the courthouse in each county is managed by a court administrator. Judicial district administrators and court administrators are Minnesota state employees of the State Court Administrator's Office. They are responsible for the day-to-day operation of the courts, including scheduling, filing legal documents, processing charges, human resources, budgeting, and other administrative functions.

By state law, all district courts are funded by the state rather than at the local level. This is to ensure equitable and quality jurisprudence state-wide. In

Fiscal Year 2014, the budget for the district courts collectively in Minnesota was $247,459,000. This includes an annual set salary of $141,003 for each of the 10 district chief judges, as well as an annual salary of $134,289 for the remaining 279 district judges.

Figure 3.2. Minnesota Judicial Districts

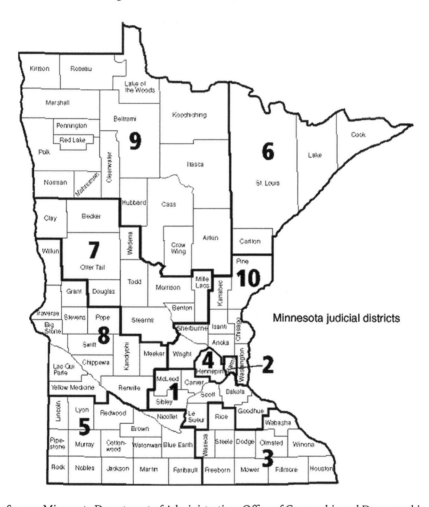

Source: Minnesota Department of Administration, Office of Geographic and Demographic Analysis

Figure 3.3. Minnesota Courts Structure

District Court
Civil Actions Criminal actions Family Juvenile Probate Ordinance Violations Trial de novo—Conciliation Court* --- * Conciliation Division (Civil disputes up to $10,000)

Court of Appeals
Administrative agency decisions except Tax Court and Workers Compensation All trial court decisions except first-degree murder Decisions of Commissioner of Economic Security *Original Actions:* Writs of mandamus or prohibition which order a trial judge or public official to perform a specified act

Minnesota Supreme Court
Appeals from: Court of Appeals Trial court decisions in all first degree murder convictions and other decisions if Supreme Court chooses to bypass the Court of Appeals Tax Court and Workers Compensation Court of Appeals *Original Actions:* Writs of prohibition, habeas corpus, and mandamus Legislative election contests

Source: Minnesota Judicial Branch, 2012

Problem-Solving Courts

Minnesota, like many other states, have created specialized problem-solving courts to deal with certain offenses therapeutically rather than punitively. Problem-solving courts target specific constituencies and attempt to get at the root causes of criminal behavior associated with issues to which the specialized courts are tasked with addressing (Merchandani, 2008). The proliferation of problem-solving courts in the United States mirrors a broader court reform movement that has taken hold in England, Australia, and Canada (Berman & Feinblatt, 2005).

Minnesota's problem-solving courts include drug courts, DWI courts, domestic violence courts, veterans courts, community courts, and mental health courts. These courts are organized under the auspices of district courts. Chief among the specialized problem-solving courts in Minnesota are the drug courts. The first drug court in Minnesota was established in 1996 in Hennepin County (Minneapolis). By 2007, the number of drug courts had expanded to 27 (Minnesota Judicial Branch, 2012a). In 2015, Minnesota had 50 drug courts in operation.

Drug courts in Minnesota are designed to provide a coordinated response to criminal offenders who are dependent on drugs and alcohol. The coordination involves judges, prosecutors, defense attorneys, probation officers, the police, treatment providers, and drug court case managers. Offenders must undergo what is known as a Rule 25 assessment to determine eligibility for participation in a drug court program when public funding is to be used for chemical dependency treatment. A Rule 25 assessment results in a determination of treatment needs and strategies. At an individual level, the goal of these courts is to reduce recidivism among drug and alcohol offenders through sustained treatment and supervision. More broadly, the expressed goals of drug courts in Minnesota is to (Minnesota Judicial Branch, 2014b):

1. Enhance public safety;
2. Ensure participant accountability; and
3. Reduce costs to society.

Over the years, Minnesota has had ample time to refine the structure and practices associated with its drug courts. The Minnesota Judicial Council, which is made up of leaders in the judiciary and constitutes the policy-making authority with the Minnesota judicial branch of government, has adopted 12 key standards by which all drug courts in Minnesota must operate. The standards have been derived from years of observation and evaluation of drug courts in the state and around the country, as well as from guidelines published by the U.S. Department of Justice. The standards for the operation of drug courts in Minnesota follows (Minnesota Judicial Branch, 2014b):

1. Drug courts must utilize a comprehensive and inclusive collaborative planning process;
2. Drug courts must incorporate a non-adversarial approach;

3. Drug courts must have published eligibility and termination criteria that have been collaboratively developed, reviewed, and agreed upon by members of the drug court team;
4. A coordinated strategy shall govern responses of the drug court team to each participant's performance and progress;
5. Drug courts must promptly assess individuals and refer them to the appropriate services;
6. A drug court must incorporate ongoing judicial interaction with each participant as an essential component of the court;
7. Abstinence must be monitored by random, frequent, and observed alcohol and other drug testing protocols;
8. Drug courts must provide prompt access to a continuum of approved alcohol, drug other related treatment and rehabilitation services, particularly ongoing mental health assessments, based on a standardized assessment of the individual's treatment needs;
9. The drug court must have a plan to provide services that are individualized to meet the needs of each participant and incorporate evidence-based strategies for the participant population. Such plans must take into consideration services that are gender-responsive and culturally appropriate and that effectively address co-occurring disorders while promoting public safety;
10. Immediate, graduated, and individualized sanctions and incentives must govern the responses of the drug court to each participant's compliance or noncompliance;
11. Drug courts must assure continuing interdisciplinary education of its team members to promote effective drug court planning, implementation, and ongoing operations; and
12. Drug courts must evaluate effectiveness.

The last standard emphasizes the need for program evaluation. When public monies and human resources are involved, it is not enough to engage in programs that are well-intentioned or merely seem like good ideas. Public programs and practices must be evidence-based. On this score, Minnesota drug courts appear to do quite well. In 2012, a study was conducted comparing over 500 drug court participants to approximately 650 offenders with similar profiles, but who did not enter a drug program. According to the study's findings, drug court participants (Minnesota Judicial Branch, 2014a):

- had lower rates of recidivism in the two years that followed;
- spent fewer days behind bars (which saved the state on average $3,200 per participant);

- showed gains in employment, educational achievement, home rental or ownership; and
- increased payment of child support over the run of the program.

Of course, a single study is not definitive. With program evaluations, there are always concerns about the adequacy of measures. This is for no fault of researchers; it is difficult to secure truly experimental conditions, samples, and measurements when dealing with real people in real programs.

For example, in the study above, it may be that the people selected for drug court as opposed to criminal court were so selected precisely because of their likelihood to succeed. It would be no surprise, then for these offenders to perform better than others who were not selected for drug court. While the offender profiles between participants and non-participants were similar, the only way to establish true cause and effect regarding drug courts is through experimental controls. But that would mean randomly selecting some people who might benefit from the drug court program to not go into the program, and randomly selecting others who likely would not benefit, to be placed into the drug court program. However, some would argue that doing so would be unethical. So, researchers are potentially left with only post-intervention observations of non-randomly identified participants and non-participants. Some social scientists researching Minnesota courts have largely overcome this methodological problem by comparing specialty court participants with matched samples from time periods before the specialty courts existed. The evidence we do have, in the form of aforementioned study and others conducted in Minnesota and around the country, is that there appears to be beneficial outcomes associated with participation in drug court for drug offenders.

A variant of Minnesota's drug courts are DWI courts. These courts, as with traditional drug courts, recognize the illness of addiction and the role it plays in recidivism if left untreated. Also, like traditional drug courts, DWI courts require a collaborative effort on the part of judges, prosecutors, defense attorneys, law enforcement, social services, and treatment providers. However, repeat DWI offenders pose a unique and substantial public safety concern that other addictions often do not entail. Consequently, DWI courts must also address transportation issues for offenders (which often challenge the ability of offenders to remain compliant) and rely on a regime of frequent alcohol-testing (NPC Research, 2014). To this end, the Minnesota Ignition Interlock Device Program was established in 2011 and is managed by the Minnesota Department of Public Safety. The optional program allows aggravated DWI offenders who are facing revocation or cancellation of their driver's licenses to retain their driving privileges provided they submit to the program protocols. The chief element of the program is that offending drivers must have a device installed on their motor vehicles which require a successful breath test through a blow tube for the vehicle to start (Minnesota DVS, 2015).

While drug courts and DWI courts are the most prolific among Minnesota's specialized problem-solving courts, there are other such courts which have been established in various judicial districts around the state. Domestic violence courts in Minnesota are intended to counter typical problems associated with intimate partner and family violence. Such problems include low reporting, withdrawn charges, threats of retaliation made against victims, and high recidivism. Domestic violence courts overcome these problems by directing a high level of judicial scrutiny toward the offender and by close cooperation between the judicial branch and social service agencies (Minnesota Judicial Branch, 2015b). Offenders are customarily subjected to intense monitoring and strict compliance requirements, e.g. obeying protective orders, completing anger management and substance abuse counseling, etc. Court-appointed case managers are assigned to monitor the offender's compliance, but also work with the offender's attorney to ensure due process rights are preserved (Minnesota Judicial Branch, 2015b).

Minnesota has also embraced the strategy of specialized courts to confront domestic violence. In particular, the domestic violence courts throughout Minnesota exist to apply intense judicial supervision of repeat and dangerous domestic violence offenders in an effort to overcome traditional problems in these cases, namely (Minnesota Judicial Branch 2015e):

- infrequent reports
- withdrawn charges
- threats to victim
- lack of defendant accountability
- high recidivism

Steans County, seated in St. Cloud, provides a good example of how Minnesota's domestic violence courts are organized. Eleven different agencies and organizations participate in the program; these include city and county law enforcement agencies, the 7th Judicial District Court, the county attorney's office, community corrections, the local public defender's office, and various social service governmental and non-profit organizations. The domestic violence court in Stearns County, as in other counties around the state, focus on felony level offenders. In Minnesota, domestic violence is generally a misdemeanor offense akin to simple assault. However, repeat offenders, or offenders engaging domestic violence involving serious injuries or weapons, will face felony-level charges. It is this type of offender, particularly recidivists, who are heavily scrutinized through this program. The stated goals of Minnesota's domestic violence court programs are bifurcated between offenders and victims. For offenders, the goals are (Stearns County, n.d.):

- reduction in violations of court ordered conditions of release and probation;
- increased compliance with treatment;
- elimination of violent behavior; and
- increased accountability (through sanctions) for continuing violence.

For the victims of domestic violence, the goals of the program are (Stearns County, n.d.):

- increased provision of support services for victims and families;
- increased safety for victims and families; and
- provision of a viable pathway to end the cycle of violence

Certainly, these are laudable goals of the district courts in partnership with other agencies and organizations. The actual effectiveness of these programs in reducing chronic domestic abuse continues to be evaluated at academic and public policy levels. However, many studies which have been conducted around the country do suggest some promise in the intensive intervention directed toward offenders and victims which these programs provide.

Minnesota's mental health courts specialize in dealing with individuals who have one or more psychiatric disabilities and who have been charged criminally. The intention in using mental health courts in certain cases is to focus on the alleged offender's mental health condition rather than the criminal behavior, given that the mental health condition is thought to be the precipitating cause of the criminal behavior. As with the other problem-solving courts, mental health courts create a structure by which judges, law enforcement, social services, and the medical and psychological service communities can partner together to strategically address an offender's underlying condition (Minnesota Judicial Branch, 2015c). Veterans courts, which are a relatively new iteration of mental health courts, expand on the strategies of mental health courts by recognizing the unique circumstances of veterans dealing with mental illness and who are have had trouble reintegrating into society after returning home from war-related deployment.

Judicial Selection and Elections

Judges at every level in Minnesota stand for election every six years. The elections are non-partisan. While elections have allowed for a system in which judges are accountable to the people in the communities they serve, the fact that there is no political party identification attached to the candidates has made it difficult for some candidates to distinguish themselves from others. Historically, voters don't follow the rulings to judges very carefully. Unless a judge makes a highly publicized and unpopular ruling, most incumbents benefit from an easy path to re-election.

In recent years, judicial candidates have attempted to explain in some detail their legal philosophies and distinguish those philosophies from their opponents. For example, some candidates might wish to explain how tough on criminals they would be. Other candidates might wish to express their belief in judicial restraint—emphasizing the view that judges should be very reluctant to overrule the will of the people who act through their legislators, and whose will is reflected in the passage of laws.

While these kinds of statements are helpful to voters in delineating one judicial candidate from another, the Minnesota Supreme Court had promulgated rules making it improper for candidates to explain their legal perspectives so vividly—particularly if the position taken relates to issues which could come before the judge at some point in the future. Of course, virtually any issue falls into that category. This point eventually made its way to the United States Supreme Court. In *Republican Party of Minnesota v. White* (2002), the U.S. Supreme Court said that candidates running for judicial office should not be barred from explaining their views about legal issues before the courts. In a 5–4 decision, Justice Antonin Scalia wrote for the majority:

> There is an obvious tension between the article of Minnesota's popularly approved Constitution which provides that judges shall be elected, and the Minnesota Supreme Court's announce clause which places most subjects of interest to the voters off limits.

The U.S. Supreme Court decided that elections imply messaging. You can't impede one's ability to cast himself or herself in a particular light, and his or her opposition in a different light, and still expect an election to be meaningful.

Minnesota Commission on Judicial Selection

When a judge retires from the bench, dies in office, or for some other reason must step down and a vacancy occurs during a judge's term, the governor of Minnesota will appoint a replacement to serve until the next election cycle. The Minnesota Commission on Judicial Selection exists to help the governor make a merit-based selection in such cases. When a vacancy occurs, the commission will seek and collect applications and nominations of attorneys and sitting judges (for appellate court vacancies). The commission, which consists of 49 members—27 appointed by the governor and 22 appointed by the Supreme Court—will examine applications and nominations for qualities, such as knowledge of the law, judicial temperament, integrity, and a record of community service. An example of a solicitation of candidates for a judicial vacancy is provided below.

Figure 3.4. Solicitation of Candidates for a Judicial Vacancy

Commission on Judicial Selection Announces Vacancy in the Third Judicial District

April 20, 2015

ST. PAUL, MN –The Commission on Judicial Selection announced today that a judgeship vacancy is occurring in Minnesota's Third Judicial District Court. This vacancy was created upon the retirement of the Honorable Robert Birnbaum, and will be chambered at Rochester in Olmsted County.

The Commission is searching for fair, experienced, and civic-minded individuals to serve on the bench and offer their talents and services to Minnesota's judicial system. The following qualities will be considered for judicial office: integrity, maturity, health (if job related), judicial temperament, legal knowledge, ability, experience, and community service. The application process is now open for this vacancy.

An individual wishing to apply may request an application by writing to Lee E. Sheehy, Chair of the Commission on Judicial Selection, at 116 Veterans Service Building, 20 West 12th Street, St. Paul, MN 55155, or by contacting Andrew Olson, Deputy Director of Appointments, via e-mail at andrew.c.olson@state.mn.us. A cover letter and resume should also be submitted with the application. **Application materials are due by close of business on Monday, May 11, 2015. Interviews are scheduled to be held on Monday, June 1, 2015 in Rochester, MN.**

For inquiries concerning the application process, please contact Andrew Olson at andrew.c.olson@state.mn.us or at (651) 201-3413.

Once the commission identifies top candidates, based on judicial and employment records of the candidates and the recommendation letters received, the leading names will be submitted to the governor for his or her consideration and an appointment will be made.

Board on Judicial Standards

In 1972, Minnesota legislation was enacted to create the Board on Judicial Standards. This is a state board whose purpose is to enforce standards of conduct among the Minnesota judiciary. The board consists of 10 gubernatorial appointees: four judges, two lawyers, and four public members (who are not lawyers or judges). The Board also employs an executive secretary to handle the day-to-day operations of the board.

The Board receives and investigates complaints of judicial misconduct. The Board does not assess or address alleged legal errors committed by judges. That is the role of appellate courts. Rather, the Board investigates allegations such as improper courtroom demeanor, improper or unprofessional treatment of parties; witnesses, court staff, jurors, attorneys, etc.; failing to dispose of judicial business in a timely manner; conflicts of interest; substance abuse; engaging in improper political and campaign activities; and other issues.

When the Board receives an allegation of judicial misconduct, it evaluates the complaint for merit. If the complaint appears to be worthy of further exploration, the Board will investigate the complaint (including interviewing relevant parties) and conduct hearings. If the allegation against a judge is sustained, the Board has a range of sanctions available to it that can be meted out to the offending judge. The possible sanctions include: issuing private letters of caution or reprimand, requiring training or other remedial action, or recommending suspensions or removals to the Supreme Court.

In 2013, the Board on Judicial Standards received a total of 108 written allegations of misconduct. Most complaints each year are dismissed by the Board without investigation because they are deemed to be frivolous or they do not allege an actual violation of the Code of Judicial Conduct. Many of these instead alleged an error of law, which is the purview of the appellate courts. In most cases, complaints are found to be without merit or outside the jurisdiction of the Board and therefore are dismissed. In 2013, a total of 16 complaints were fully investigated, and seven resulted in a public reprimand, private admonition, or a letter of caution (Minnesota Board on Judicial Standards, 2013).

Attorneys at Work in Minnesota's Judicial System

Minnesota Lawyers Professional Responsibility Board

A sister oversight organization of the Board on Judicial Standards is the Lawyers Professional Responsibility Board. While the Board on Judicial Standards polices the conduct of judges, the Lawyers Professional Responsibility Board polices the conduct of attorneys licensed to practice law in the State of

Minnesota. This board consists of lawyers and non-lawyer public members appointed by the Minnesota Supreme Court. The Board, in conjunction with the Office of Lawyers Professional Responsibility, receives and investigates complaints of unethical conduct alleged against practicing attorneys in Minnesota. The Lawyers Professional Responsibility Board may take action against an attorney's license to practice law in the state. Of course, if an attorney is suspended or disbarred in Minnesota for unethical conduct, he or she may still practice law in other states where the attorney is bar certified. It is not uncommon, however, for the Board to pass on information about the disposition of complaints and sanctions to other jurisdictions in which an attorney practices law.

In 2013, the Lawyers Professional Responsibility Board received 1,253 complaints. Of those, 43% were dismissed without an investigation and another 29% were dismissed after an investigation. Only 9% received some form of public discipline. The remaining cases resulted in private admonitions or became moot through attrition, i.e., death of the attorney being investigated, resignation, etc. (Lawyers Professional Responsibility Board, 2014).

Minnesota's Law Schools

Minnesota has three law schools within its borders. Most of the state's 24,000 practicing attorneys attended one of these schools. The only public Minnesota law school is operated by the University of Minnesota. The two private law schools are the Mitchell Hamline School of Law and the University of St. Thomas School of Law. All three of Minnesota's law schools are located in Minneapolis or St. Paul.

The University of Minnesota is the state's flagship university and the lone land grant university. The University of Minnesota was founded in 1851, seven years before the Territory of Minnesota became a state. The law school was founded in 1888, enrolling at the time 32 students in the day school and 35 in night school. Today, the University of Minnesota School of Law enrolls 855 students, including 732 in its traditional Juris Doctor (J.D.) program. The balance of students are enrolled in international and Master of Laws (LL.M.) programs. The school is Minnesota's top-ranked law school (ranked #20 nationwide by U.S. News and World Report). It is also the most expensive, despite being a public institution, with tuition topping $40,000 per year for state residents. About one-third of its students are Minnesota residents. Nearly 60% are men. Racial and ethnic minorities make up 19% of the student body.

The University of Minnesota School of Law boasts over 12,000 living alumni. These former students no doubt are primarily responsible for the law school

$95 million endowment. Despite the surplus of law graduates nationwide, the majority of graduates from the University of Minnesota School of Law find related employment. According to the National Association for Law Placement, less than 40% of law school graduates are employed as attorneys in permanent positions within 9 months of graduating. By contrast, over 98% of the 2012 University of Minnesota law school graduates were known to be permanently employed in 2013. The median starting salary for graduating attorneys from the University of Minnesota who sought positions in the private sector (which comprised 61% of graduates) was $102,000 in 2012 (University of Minnesota, 2015).

The second largest law school in Minnesota is the Mitchell Hamline School of Law. This law school was established in 2015 by the merger of the William Mitchell College of Law and the Hamline University School of Law. A little background on both schools is provided below.

The William Mitchell College of Law was founded in 1900 as the St. Paul College of Law. It was founded exclusively as a night law school for working students. The William Mitchell College of Law has many notable alums, including Supreme Court Chief Justice Warren Burger, several state Supreme Court justices (in Minnesota and other states), many federal district and appellate judges, governors, and members of Congress. William Mitchell has over 11,000 living alumni and was often viewed as Minnesota's other great law school. However, its overall ranking by U.S. News and World Report placed the College of Law at #135 leading up to the merger, which was the lowest ranking among Minnesota schools. As at its founding, William Mitchell provided legal education for students who were only able to attend at night and part-time. Its part-time option was always viewed as one of its great strengths. Indeed, U.S. News and World Report ranked the college #1 in the region for part-time legal education. The William Mitchell College of Law always emphasized the practice of law and applied lawyering skills (William Mitchell College of Law, 2015).

While there have been many William Mitchell Law graduates who have gone on to the federal bench and federal elected positions, much of the backbone of Minnesota's legal and political systems at the state level is made up of William Mitchell graduates as well. Currently, the college's graduates include 111 of the state's current district judges, six state senators, six state house members, nine state appellate court judges, 32 elected county attorneys, and Minnesota's elected Attorney General (William Mitchell College of Law, 2015).

Hamline University, located in St. Paul, Minnesota, is the oldest university in Minnesota, having started in 1854—four years prior to Minnesota joining the Union as a state. The Hamline University School of Law was founded in 1972 as an independent law school in Minnesota. In 1976, the school was acquired by Hamline University. *U.S. News and World Report* ranked Hamline

University's law school as the top private law school in Minnesota in 2015. The Hamline Law School placed considerable emphasis on experiential learning for its students, requiring 15 experiential credits to be completed by third year students. The school operated eight different law clinics which serve as conduits for gaining practitioner experience for students (Hamline School of Law, 2015).

In 2014, Hamline Law School enrolled 90 first-year law students, including 24 part-time students. A little under half of the matriculating students were women. Students came from 17 states and 10 different countries (Hamline School of Law, 2015). According to the Minnesota State Board of Law Examiners, Hamline Law graduates consistently performed well on the Minnesota Bar Exam. The pass rates for Hamline graduates from 2007 to 2012 ranged from a low of 88% to a high of 93%. Despite the favorable measures for these students, only about half of Hamline graduates found full-time employment practicing law within 9 months of graduation. The abundance of Hamline law graduates relative to the number of legal positions is consistent with law graduate employment trends generally. In fact, leading up to the merger, Hamline's placement trailed slightly the national average. According to the National Association for Law Placement (NALP), there were 46,776 new law school graduates nationwide in 2013. Roughly 58% of law school graduates were known to be employed in non-temporary attorney jobs nine months after graduation (NALP, 2014).

The third law school in Minnesota is the University of St. Thomas School of Law. Although the University of St. Thomas is located in St. Paul, the law school is located in downtown Minneapolis. The University of St. Thomas is Minnesota's largest private university and one of the largest and oldest Catholic universities in the country, having been founded in 1885. The present law school was constituted in 1999 and offered its first classes in 2001 and received its full accreditation from the American Bar Association in 2006. Interestingly, this is the second go-around for the St. Thomas School of Law. The university operated its law school from 1923 to 1933. That law school was shuttered in the wake of the Great Depression (St. Thomas School of Law, 2015a).

As with every law school in Minnesota, St. Thomas has a number of accolades it can point to which signifies its quality relative to other law schools around the country. For example, the publication *National Jurist* ranked St. Thomas School of Law the number one school in the country for practical training. This is significant as competitor Mitchell Hamline also touts its experiential bona fides. Additionally, the faculty at St. Thomas School of Law ranked 30th among the faculty of over 200 law schools nationwide for scholarly impact. In fact, the Princeton Review ranked the St. Thomas law faculty 8th on its 2014 "Best Professors" list (St. Thomas School of Law, 2015b).

The state of Minnesota, with recently four and now three law schools, has a population of 5.4 million people. In today's climate, with so many more law graduates than law positions available to them, many have come to believe that Minnesota has too many law schools given the state's size. Adam Wahlberg (2015) noted that the states of Maryland, Wisconsin, and Colorado—each with a similarly sized population as Minnesota—have only two law schools a piece.

The over-abundance of legal education options in the relatively small state of Minnesota, all of which are located in the same metropolitan area, and the competition for prospective law students from the region who did not get into the University of Minnesota, helps explain why the William Mitchell College of Law and the Hamline University Law School announced in February of 2015 that they would be merging into a single institution. The fact is, both schools saw a decline since 2011 of first-year enrollment near or above 50% (Weissmann, 2015). The merger, which might better be coined an "absorption" (Hamline into William Mitchell), was effective fall of 2015, after the American Bar Association approved the merger plan. There is also pending legal action because of the merger process. Two tenured law professors at William Mitchell College of Law filed a lawsuit over faculty layoffs stemming from the merger, which plaintiffs claimed amounted to a breach of contract.

Minnesota's Prosecutors

There are 87 county attorneys in Minnesota. The county attorney is an elected official who serves as the chief criminal prosecutor for a given county. He or she also provides legal counsel to the county board, pursues civil enforcement action for non-criminal cases, and represents the county in legal action concerning areas such as asset forfeiture, land use, zoning, and other public policy matters. Assistant county attorneys are staff attorneys of the County Attorney offices. They are non-elected civil servants who carry out the legal duties of the county attorney's office at the behest of the elected county attorney, just as deputy sheriffs carry out the duties of an elected county sheriff.

County attorneys and their assistants are responsible for determining appropriate charges in criminal cases, filing those charges by way of a criminal complaint or by securing a grand jury indictment, and prosecuting the cases once charges are formalized. The county prosecutor's first court appearance in a criminal case is the initial appearance. For petty misdemeanor and misdemeanor offenses, the initial appearance for the defendant is the arraignment. It is during this hearing that the defendant will be asked to enter a plea of guilty or not guilty to the charge(s). In more serious cases (gross misdemeanors and felonies), the initial appearance before the judge, known as a Rule 5 hearing, does not result in a plea. Rather, the judge will explain to the defendant what his or her rights are and is notified of the formal charges (Washington County, 2015).

As is the case with prosecuting offices all around the country, there is a strong preference among Minnesota county prosecutors for resolving cases through plea bargaining before they ever make it to trial. Prosecutors along with defense attorneys and judges make up the courtroom workgroup. Although the criminal justice system in the United States is ostensibly adversarial, in reality these individuals often work together to resolve criminal cases to a degree that is mutually satisfying. Neubauer and Meinhold (2013) note that there are different types of plea bargains. Charge bargaining is when the defendant is afforded an opportunity to plead guilty to less serious charges than the one originally specified. Count bargaining is when a defendant pleads guilty to fewer criminal charges than originally specified. Finally, sentence bargaining involves the defendant pleading guilty on the basis of the promise of a specific sentence. Ultimately, however, a promised sentence is really only a promised recommended sentence to the judge. A judge may always choose to disregard a plea agreement—particularly when the assigned punishment is a part of the deal. Prosecutors in Minnesota and around the country regularly use all three types of plea bargaining to facilitate the resolution of criminal cases in one's county.

Criminologist Samuel Walker identified a number of prosecutorial decision points which serve to highlight the amount of discretion prosecutors have in deciding who gets charged with what, regardless of what the police may recommend. These decision points include (Walker, 1993):

- decision to charge or dismiss
- decision on the top charge
- decision on the number of charges
- decision on using or deferring to a grand jury (see Appendix 3.1)
- decision to plea bargain

While factors such as available time and resources and the law enforcement priorities of the day will influence prosecutors at the decision point junctures, a key factor is simply the strength of one's case. Joan Jacoby (1979) identified the importance of case qualities in discretionary making prosecutorial decisions. She offered three models to explain the variance in the attractiveness of criminal cases. The Legal Sufficiency Model requires only minimum level of legal elements necessary to prove a case. Many of these cases will eventually be dismissed because of substandard evidence, witness problems, and other issues. The System Efficiency Model involves screening out weak cases. However, the majority of the cases which are left are disposed of outside of court. Emphasis on the use of plea bargains to make the system (or some would say, the assembly line) continue to operate smoothly. The final model identified by Jacoby—the Trial Sufficiency Model—involves the most stringent approach to case screening. Prosecutors operating under this model (often federal prosecutors) will only accept cases that would clearly win at trial. While plea bargains may still be considered, prosecutors who have determined a case to be trial sufficient have less incentive to consider significant reductions in the number or type of charges or probably prison time.

In addition to county attorneys, the State of Minnesota Office of the Attorney General participates in the criminal justice process. The Attorney General's office represents the State of Minnesota in state and federal court much like the county attorney's office represents county governments in court. The Attorney General is the chief source of legal advice for state agencies and provides education and legal opinions to local prosecutors on various criminal matters which have a statewide impact. The Office of Attorney General takes the lead on most criminal appeals in the state. The office also plays a significant role in combating consumer fraud by going after fraudulent businesses civilly and criminally.

Finally, city attorneys also play a significant prosecutorial role in Minnesota. In larger cities, such as Minneapolis and St. Paul, city attorneys are staff municipal employees; in smaller towns, city attorneys are often private practice lawyers in the community with whom the municipality contracts to act as the city attorney. City attorneys in Minnesota are responsible for prosecuting most petty misdemeanor and misdemeanor state-level offenses (especially traffic violations and DWIs) and city ordinance violations (such as nuisance offenses).

Minnesota's Public Defenders

Just as there is a network of prosecutors around the state to levy criminal charges as appropriate, so too are there public defenders in all 10 judicial districts poised to provide legal counsel to accused offenders who are unable to afford procuring legal assistance themselves. The work of public defenders across the state is coordinated by the Minnesota Board of Public Defense. The Board oversees a statewide staff of attorneys who work fulltime as publicly funded defense attorneys. The state's public defender needs are supplemented by private, non-profit public defense corporations. These organizations are funded through grants and donations and provide indigent defendants, often persons of color, with legal and paralegal assistance.

Victims' Rights in Minnesota

In many states, services provided to crime victims to help them navigate the criminal justice system and to recover from their victimization are provided through court services offices. In the state of Minnesota, victims' rights, counseling, and advocacy services come from a myriad of sources, including the courts, police department, prosecutors' offices, and social service agencies. State statute defines crime victims as " … persons who incur loss or harm as a result of a crime, including a good faith effort to prevent a crime" (Minnesota Statutes § 611A.01b). Crime victims in Minnesota have many rights under state law. Minnesota Statutes § 611A.02 requires law enforcement officers to notify alleged victims of their many rights under the law, including and particularly the availability of victim support services and counseling and concerning the right of victims to seek victim compensation from the state.

Victims are often thought to be victimized twice when they fall prey to criminal activity. They are first victimized by the crime itself. This harm manifests itself in physical injury, lost wages due to injury, property loss through damage or theft, and financial loss. But then many victims are victimized a second time through their participation in the criminal justice process. This is known as double victimization. Costs to a victim because of their cooperation with criminal justice authorities in an effort to secure justice include (Doerner & Lab, 2014):

- Time loss (due to court delays and cancelled proceedings)
- Lost wages (do to court appearances)
- Transportation and parking costs
- Intimidation by offenders, their families, and their friends

Through victim services an effort is made to mitigate the prospect of being victimized twice by a criminal episode.

Of course, one of the chief concerns for any victim is financial loss. Being victimized by crime—especially violent crime resulting in the death or sidelining of a family income earner—can devastate a family. The emotional toll is easy to imagine. But that toll is compounded when the bills, expected and unexpected, begin to mount. There are different remedies a crime victim might pursue to be made whole again financially. In some cases, insurance payouts provide relief (for those who have it). A civil suit against the offender is another option; but in many cases, criminal offenders and their families do not have deep pockets. Lawsuits are expensive and a civil judgment on paper against an indigent defendant goes very little distance toward paying the bills. Further, this all assumes the offender is known and identifiable. A third mechanism for a victim to be made whole financially is restitution. Restitution is court ordered as part of a convicted offender's punishment. However, restitution is no more a panacea than are civil judgments as it requires a perpetrator to be identified and further, for him or her to have financial means (Doerner & Lab, 2011).

The fourth mechanism to help make victims whole by restoring them to pre-victim conditions is victim compensation. To this end, the Minnesota Crime Victims Reparations Board exists to provide victims with financial support. The board is not a part of the Minnesota Judicial Branch, but instead is located in the Department of Public Safety's Office of Justice Programs. Different public policy arguments exist for a government agency to provide direct monetary compensation for criminal victimization. On a broader level, there is the argument that the state has a social contract with its citizens and delivering assistance after the fact of crime is an extension of its obligation to protect citizens from the criminal elements. A more acute public policy rationale is that crime victims are just another class of citizens in need, and government in the United States has a long history of providing welfare benefits to people in times of need (Doerner & Lab, 2011).

It is not clear which, if either, rationale Minnesota relied upon when the Minnesota Crime Victims Reparations Board was created in 1974, but its goal has always been to reduce the economic impact of violent crime on victims and their families (Office of Justice Programs, 2015). Today, if you are a victim of certain violent crimes in Minnesota, you are eligible to apply for financial assistance. Of course, completing the application form is no small task (see Appendix 3.2). Crimes which make for eligible victims are: homicide, assault, child abuse, sexual assault, robbery, kidnapping, domestic abuse, stalking, and criminal vehicular operation and drunk driving resulting in injury or death. Property crimes alone are not eligible triggers for reparations. In order to receive reparations, which in Minnesota can total as much as $50,000, one must have reported the crime to police within 30 days of the incident, the offender must not be unjustly enriched by the reparations (as is sometimes the case in domestic violence cases), and the victim must cooperate fully with law enforcement (Office of Justice Programs, 2015). This last requirement is key to securing the participation of victims in the criminal justice process despite the looming prospect of "double victimization." Covered expenses include (Office of Justice Programs, 2015):

- medical and dental expenses
- counseling
- lost wages
- funeral/burial expenses
- survivor's benefits
- miscellaneous other expenses

Crime victims in Minnesota also have many rights unrelated to financial loss; instead, certain rights are focused on their dignity and emotional wellbeing. These rights include being notified about the release of offenders from incarceration, having victim identities concealed from the public for certain types of crimes, being kept apprised of the criminal justice processes at work involving their case, and having an opportunity to provide victim impact statements to the court at the time of sentencing.

Victim impact statements are especially beneficial to victims as they are given voice through spoken word, written statement, or both in court. These statements allow victims to explain to judges and juries about how the criminal episode has affected them and their families. It gives victims a chance to address offenders in a face-to-face forum if the victims so choose. Victim impact statements are not evidence. They are not delivered to the court members until sentencing, which of course occurs after conviction. Statements relating to how victims have been impacted by the crime are strictly limited in court because they are so prejudicial and yet, in most cases, provide little evidentiary value to the case.

Although Minnesota uses sentencing guidelines in determining criminal sanctions for offenders (see **Chapter Nine**), the testimony of victims during the sentencing phase can indeed have an impact on the punishment handed down. Even within the sentencing guidelines, judges have available to them a sentencing range which permits a sentence above the guidelines' presumptive sentence for a given crime committed by an offender with a given criminal history. What's more, the judge may elect an upward departure from the guidelines' range if there are aggravating circumstances, many times of which emerge from the victim impact statements.

Concluding Remarks

This chapter has explored the structure, processes, and mechanisms of accountability of the judiciary in Minnesota. As is the case at the national level of government, the judiciary in Minnesota is constitutionally prescribed and exists in three layers: the district courts, the appellate court, and the Supreme Court. Additionally, the state's myriad of problem-solving courts which operate under the authority of the district courts was considered. The chapter also examined the legal community—particularly within the criminal justice context—which consumes the services of the judicial branch. This includes prosecutors at the state, county, and municipal level, and defense attorneys. Finally, the rights of crime victims who must navigate judicial processes to secure justice for themselves and family members were highlighted. It should be evident to readers of this chapter that Minnesota's judicial branch is a robust and essential element of Minnesota's government and criminal justice efforts.

Key Terms

Attorney General
Board on Judicial Standards
Charge Bargaining
Count Bargaining
County Attorney
Court of Appeals
District Court
Domestic Violence Court
Drug Court
DWI Court
Grand Jury
Minnesota Board of Public Defense

Minnesota Lawyers Professional
   Responsibility Board
Problem-Solving Courts
Republican Party of Minnesota v. White
Rule 25 Assessment
Sentence Bargaining
Supreme Court
Victim Compensation
Victim Impact Statements
Writ of Prohibition
Writ of Habeas Corpus
Writ of Mandamus

Selected Internet Sites

American Bar Association
www.americanbar.org

Minnesota Attorney General
www.ag.state.mn.us

Minnesota Board on Judicial Standards
www.bjs.state.mn.us

Minnesota County Attorneys Association
www.mcaa-mn.org

Minnesota Judicial Branch
www.mncourts.gov

Minnesota Lawyers Professional Responsibility Board
www.mncourts.gov/lprb

Minnesota Revisor of Statutes
www.revisor.leg.state.mn.us

Minnesota State Bar Association
www.mnbar.org

Discussion Questions

1. What qualities are desired for someone to become a judge?
2. Do we have too many lawyers in society? Why or why not?
3. What considerations should guide a prosecutor in deciding how to charge a case?
4. Are plea bargains fair to the accused offender? The victim? Society?
5. Are problem-solving courts, which depart from traditional court processes, a good thing? Explain.
6. Should the government pay crime victims money to help them out? What kind of crimes should qualify? What expenses should qualify?

References

Berman, G. & Feinblatt, J. (2005). *Good Courts: The case for problem-solving justice.* New York: New York Press.

Biography of Warren Burger. (2015). *Biography.* Retrieved from http://www.biography.com/people/warren-burger-9231479.

Doerner, W. & Lab, S. (2014). *Victimology.* Boston, MA: Anderson/Elsevier.

Hamline School of Law (2015). *About Hamline law.* Retrieved from http://www.hamline.edu/law/about/

Jacoby, J. (1979). The charging policies of prosecutors. In W. McDonald (ed.) *The Prosecutor.* Thousand Oaks, CA: SAGE.

Lawyers Professional Responsibility Board (2014). *Annual report of the Lawyers Professional Responsibility Board and the Office of Lawyers Professional Responsibility.* Retrieved from http://lprb.mncourts.gov/AboutUs/Documents/2014%20Annual%20Report.pdf

Merchandani, R. (2008). Beyond therapy: Problem-solving courts and the deliberative democratic state, *Law & Social Inquiry, 33*(4), 853–893.

Minnesota Board on Judicial Standards. (2013). *Annual report 2013.* Retrieved from http://www.bjs.state.mn.us/file/annual-reports/2013-annual-report-final.pdf

Minnesota Driver and Vehicle Services. (2015). *Minnesota ignition interlock device program.* https://dps.mn.gov/divisions/dvs/programs/mn-ignition-interlock/Pages/default.aspx

Minnesota Judicial Branch. (2015a). *Court of appeals factsheet.* Retrieved from http://www.mncourts.gov/?page=551

Minnesota Judicial Branch. (2015b). *Domestic violence courts.* Retrieved from http://www.mncourts.gov/?page=1737

Minnesota Judicial Branch. (2015c). *Mental health courts.* Retrieved from http://www.mncourts.gov/?page=1717

Minnesota Judicial Branch. (2015d). *Supreme court.* Retrieved from http://www.mncourts.gov/Documents/0/Public/Court_Information_Office/Informational%20Brochures/QF-_Supreme_Court2013.pdf

Minnesota Judicial Branch. (2015e). *Domestic violence courts.* Retrieved from http://mncourts.gov/?page=1737

Minnesota Judicial Branch. (2014). *Report to the community: The 2014 annual report of the Minnesota judicial branch.* Retrieved from http://www.mncourts.gov/Documents/0/Public/Court_Information_Office/2014_Annual_Report_to_the_Community.pdf

Minnesota Judicial Branch. (2014b). *Minnesota offender drug court standards: Policy 511.1.* St. Paul, MN: Minnesota Judicial Council.

Minnesota Judicial Branch. (2012a). *Minnesota statewide adult drug court evaluation.* Retrieved from http://www.mncourts.gov/Documents/0/Public/Drug_Court/2012%20Statewide%20Evaluation/MN_Statewide_Drug_Court_Evaluation_Report_-_Final_Public.pdf

Minnesota Judicial Branch. (2012b). *The Minnesota Supreme Court.* St. Paul, MN: Court Information Office.

Minnesota Revisor of Statutes. (2015). *Statutes.* Retrieved from www.revisor.leg.state.mn.us

Office of Justice Programs. (2015). *Minnesota crime victims reparations board.* Retrieved from https://dps.mn.gov/divisions/ojp/help-for-crime-victims/Pages/crime-victims-reparations.aspx

National Association of Law Placement. (2014). *Class of 2013 national summary report.* Retrieved from http://www.nalp.org/uploads/NatlSummaryChartClassof2013.pdf

Neubauer, D. & Meinhold, S. (2013). *Judicial process: Law, courts, and politics in the United States.* Boston, MA: Wadsworth.

NPC Research. (2014). *Minnesota DWI courts: A summary of evaluation findings in nine DWI court programs.* Retrieved from http://www.mncourts.gov/Documents/0/Public/Court_Information_Office/MN_DWI_All_Site_Summary_August_2014_FINAL_FOR_OTS.pdf

Republican Party of Minnesota v. White, 536 US 765 (2002).

Stearns County Domestic Violence Partnership. (n.d.). *Felony domestic violence court.* Retrieved from http://www.co.stearns.mn.us/Portals/0/docs/Department%20Files/Attorney/Domestic%20Violence%20Court/DVP%20Public%20Brochure%202013.pdf

Supreme Court Historical Society. (2015). *Timeline of the justices: Warren E. Burger, 1969–1986.* Retrieved from http://supremecourthistory.org/timeline_burger.html

St. Thomas School of Law. (2015a). *About St. Thomas school of law. History.* Retrieved from http://www.stthomas.edu/law/about/history

St. Thomas School of Law. (2015b). *About St. Thomas school of law. Rankings.* Retrieved from http://www.stthomas.edu/law/about/rankings

University of Minnesota. (2015). *Law school profile.* Retrieved from https://www.law.umn.edu/prospective/profile.html

Wahlberg, A. (2015, February 18). Why William Mitchell and Hamline law had to merge. *MinnPost.*

Walker, S. (1993). *Taming the system: The control of discretion in criminal justice, 1950-1990.* New York: Oxford University Press.

Washington County. (2015, February 18). *Initial court appearances.* Retrieved from http://www.co.washington.mn.us/index.aspx?NID=418

Weissmann, J. (2015). The great law school bust is about to claim its first victim. *Slate.*

William Mitchell College of Law. (2015). *About William Mitchell.* Retrieved from http://web.wmitchell.edu/about/

Appendix 3.1. The Important Role of Grand Juries in the Minnesota Criminal Justice System*

James C. Backstrom[1]
Dakota County Attorney

Grand juries have been front and center in the national news recently. While each state in our nation has different forms of grand juries, this legal forum has been a fundamental part of the criminal justice system in America since our nation was founded. Grand juries have their origin in English law (as much of our legal system does) and were initially created as a check upon the unrestricted power of the sovereign or government to decide who should be charged with a criminal offense.[2] Today, grand juries continue to provide a check and balance upon the discretion afforded American prosecutors in the criminal charging process. They also provide a forum for prosecutors to seek direction from the citizens of their community in other cases where the charging decision is a particularly difficult one given the nature of the case or the prosecutor otherwise wishes citizen involvement in the charging process.

A grand jury is an independent decision making body comprised of individuals unrelated to the parties brought before it. In some jurisdictions grand juries must approve all serious criminal charges either before the commencement of a case or before the matter proceeds to trial.[3] In Minnesota, a grand jury is convened by the court upon the request of the prosecutor and these proceedings are mandated by law to occur before any criminal case goes to trial where the ultimate sanction, if the suspect is convicted, is life in prison.[4] This includes charges of first degree murder, treason and some violent rapes under Minnesota law.[5] In these cases, where a person's liberty could be taken away for life, Minnesota's law appropriately requires an extra check upon a prosecutor's authority to initiate criminal charges without independent review.

By custom and practice, grand juries also often hear cases involving a shooting death caused by a police officer. This is to avoid any appearance of conflict

---

* Reprinted with permission.

1. James C. Backstrom has served as the elected prosecutor in Dakota County, Minnesota, since 1987 and is a member of the Board of Directors of the National District Attorneys Association and Minnesota County Attorneys Association.

2. *State v. Iosue*, 19 N.W.2d 735, 739-40 (Minn. 1945); *Costello v. U.S.*, 350 U.S. 359, 362 (1956).

3. 4 Crim. Proc. §15.1(d) (3d ed.).

4. Minn. R. Crim. P. 17.01, subd. 1.

5. Minn. Stat. §609.185 (Murder in the First Degree); Minn. Stat. §609.385 (Treason); and Minn. Stat. §609.3455 (Dangerous Sex Offender Sentences).

of interest due to the close working relationship between prosecutors and law enforcement agencies. It is also done to assure public confidence in the decision being made.

Grand jury proceedings are not public trials, but rather are private investigative inquiries which must be conducted with absolute fairness. There are specific reasons for maintaining the secrecy of the grand jury process. Unlike a jury trial where the determination by jurors is whether someone has been proven guilty of a crime, grand juries (like prosecutors in the vast majority of cases) are reviewing evidence gathered by law enforcement agencies to determine if someone should be charged with a crime. This important decision making process should not be one conducted in a public setting as doing so may jeopardize the integrity of an on-going criminal investigation.[6] In addition, the Minnesota Supreme Court has made it clear on two separate occasions that a grand jury may not issue a written investigation report to the public which could damage the reputation of individuals not formally charged by indictment with a crime.[7]

Secrecy of a grand jury proceeding also exists to encourage witnesses to come forward, to shield persons from public scrutiny of what the grand jury may determine are allegations which are either unfounded or insufficient to warrant prosecution, and to allow the citizen members of a grand jury to make these difficult decisions without threat of reprisal or public rebuke. Many cases presented to a grand jury are high profile in nature. It is not appropriate to place grand jurors in a situation where they could be publicly criticized if their decision is not a popular one in the eyes of some beholders. Prosecutors are elected officials who have willingly chosen to place themselves in the public eye for scrutiny of their decisions. Citizen members of a grand jury are not obligated to explain the basis for their decisions, nor should they be subject to public pressure to do so.

In some ways, a grand jury acts as a judge. The finding of probable cause is a judicial decision which in the vast majority of prosecutions is made by a judge, who determines whether the facts attested to under oath by a law enforcement officer in a document known in Minnesota as a criminal complaint constitutes probable cause for the charges being filed by the prosecutor. A grand jury makes the finding of probable cause in cases presented to it.[8]

---

6. *State v. Falcone*, 195 N.W.2d 572, 575 (Minn. 1972); *U.S. v. Procter & Gamble Co.*, 356 U.S. 677, 681-82 (1958).

7. *In re Grand Jury of Hennepin County Impaneled on November 24, 1975*, 271 N.W.2d 817 (1978); *In re Grand Jury of Wabasha County*, 244 N.W.2d 253 (1976).

8. *State v. Eibensteiner*, 690 N.W.2d 140, 150 (Minn. Ct. App. 2004); Minn. R. Crim. P. 18.05, subd. 2.

A grand jury, however, also acts as a prosecutor in making the determination of whether or not someone should be charged with a crime given the facts of the case. Prosecutors are known as "ministers of justice"[9] and have a higher ethical standard than simply finding probable cause exists to support a criminal charge.[10] In addition to finding probable cause, before filing criminal charges a prosecutor must make an independent judgment, based upon the available and admissible evidence, that there is a reasonable likelihood of proving a defendant guilty by proof beyond a reasonable doubt to the satisfaction of all twelve trial jurors when the case goes to trial.[11] Because grand jurors are in essence making a charging decision in lieu of the prosecutor, they too need to consider whether there is a reasonable likelihood of proving the defendant guilty at trial before finding that criminal charges are warranted.

In some states grand juries can conduct independent investigations without the presence or involvement of a prosecutor.[12] This does not occur in Minnesota, which is a good thing. The powers to investigate alleged criminal wrongdoing and to charge someone with a crime are two of the most significant actions a government can take against an individual and it is important to have a prosecutor, who is learned in the law, lead such inquiries.

Leading such inquiries, however, does not mean controlling them. Grand juries are not, as some claim, merely a rubber stamp for what a prosecutor wants to occur. A grand jury proceeding is not a forum for the prosecutor to argue why someone should be charged with or convicted of a crime. A grand jury operates independently of the prosecutor and grand jurors must base their decision upon all the evidence presented to them, along with the applicable law and the interests of justice. Prosecutors insure that only evidence that will be admissible at trial is heard and considered by a grand jury[13] and that the inquiry is conducted fairly and without bias in any form. Prosecutors are also

---

9. *See* Comment to Rule 3.8 of the American Bar Association's Model Rules of Professional Conduct and the Minnesota Rules of Professional Conduct.

10. Bennett L. Gershman, *A Moral Standard for the Prosecutor's Exercise of the Charging Discretion*, 20 Fordham Urb. L.J. 513 (1992); Minn. R. Prof'l Conduct 3.8(a); Model R. Prof'l Conduct 3.8(a).

11. Bennett L. Gershman, *A Moral Standard for the Prosecutor's Exercise of the Charging Discretion*, 20 Fordham Urb. L.J. 513 (1992); Minn. R. Prof'l Conduct 3.8(a); Model R. Prof'l Conduct 3.8(a).

12. *State v. Cosgrove*, 186 Conn. 476, 479–80, 442 A.2d 1320, 1322 (1982); *State v. Colson*, 262 N.C. 506, 512-13, 138 S.E.2d 121, 126 (1964); *Ex parte McLeod*, 272 S.C. 373, 377, 252 S.E.2d 126, 128 (1979).

13. Minn. R. Crim. P. 18.05, subd. 1; *State v. Roan*, 532 N.W.2d 563, 570 (Minn. 1995).

required to present to the grand jury evidence which may tend to exonerate a suspect.[14]

A charging decision by necessity involves discretion and reasonable minds can differ when weighing the facts, law, and interests of justice in determining what criminal charges, if any, are appropriate. Consequently, a grand jury need not be unanimous in its decision. In Minnesota grand juries consist of 16 to 23 jurors, at least 12 of whom must agree to return an indictment (the name given the criminal charging document in the grand jury process) or a "no bill" (the name given the document signifying that no criminal charges are appropriate).[15]

A weak grand jury which fails to charge those who should be charged with a crime, or a reckless grand jury which indicts those who should not be criminally charged, are equally problematic. The private and independent investigations and determinations of a grand jury are, and should remain, an important and integral part of criminal justice in our state and nation.

---

14. *State v. Morrow*, 834 N.W.2d 715, 721 (Minn. 2013).
15. Minn. R. Crim. P. 18.02, subd. 1; Minn. R. Crim. P. 18.06.

Appendix 3.2. Reparations Claim Form

Application

Minnesota Crime Victims Reparations Board

The Minnesota Crime Victims Reparations Board provides financial assistance to victims of violent crime and their family members for related expenses that cannot be reimbursed by insurance or other sources. Expenses for damaged/stolen property are not covered.

Instructions

If you need help completing this application form, contact our office or your local victim assistance program. Visit our website for a listing of victim assistance programs. Please read the following before completing the form:

- Print clearly and provide as much information as possible.
- Submit application as soon as possible. Additional bills/documents can be sent later.
- Complete a separate application form for each victim.
- A parent, guardian or relative must file the application on behalf of a minor, incapacitated or deceased victim.
- Include copies of all expenses (medical bills, receipts, insurance statements), if available.
- Complete the W9 form (page 5) for the person who may receive a direct payment.
- Sign and date the release form (page 6). The time period in Section 15 should cover from the crime date through the last expected treatment date.
- Mail, fax or email your completed application form. See below.

Eligibility Requirements

- Victim of a crime in Minnesota or a Minnesota resident victimized while traveling in another country
- Claim submitted within 3 years of the crime (some exceptions apply)
- Crime reported to police within 30 days (exceptions for child abuse and sexual assault)
- Victim/claimant cooperated fully with police and prosecution
- Victims who contributed through serious misconduct or criminal activity may be disqualified or receive reduced benefits.

*There are other factors not listed that might make you ineligible.

Expenses Covered

- Medical/Dental
- Counseling
- Lost Wages
- Funeral/Burial
- Survivor's benefits
- Miscellaneous expenses (see brochure)

*Caps/limits apply

Office of Justice Programs
Crime Victims Reparations Board
445 Minnesota Street, Suite 2300•St. Paul, MN 55101
651-201-7300•888-622-8799•Fax 651-296-5787•TTY 651-205-4827
dps.justiceprograms@state.mn.us
ojp.dps.mn.gov

MINNESOTA CRIME VICTIMS REPARATIONS APPLICATION FORM

Date Received:	Complete and submit to:	Claim Number:
	Minnesota Crime Victims Reparations Board 445 Minnesota Street, Suite 2300 St. Paul MN 55101-1515 651.201.7300 or 1.888.622.8799 (Toll-Free) 651.296.5787 (Fax) 651.205.4827 (TTY) dps.justiceprograms@state.mn.us	
		Claims Specialist:
(Office Use Only)		(Office Use Only)

SECTION 1. VICTIM INFORMATION — Name of person injured or killed as the result of the violent crime. Complete a separate application form for each victim.

Victim's Name (last, first, m.i.)		Date of Birth (MM/DD/YY)	Social Security Number None ❐
Gender ❐ Male ❐ Female	What is the language preference of the victim and/or claimant? ❐ English ❐ Spanish ❐ Other_____		Is Victim Deceased? ❐ No ❐ Yes
Address	City	State	Zip Code
Phone	Email Address		

SECTION 2. CLAIMANT INFORMATION — Complete **only** if the person(s) submitting the application is not the victim. This section must be completed by a parent, guardian or relative if the victim is a minor, deceased or incapacitated.

Claimant 1

Claimant's Name (last, first, m.i.)		Date of Birth (MM/DD/YY)	Social Security Number None ❐
Gender ❐ Male ❐ Female	Relationship to Victim ❐ Parent ❐ Spouse/Partner ❐ Former Spouse/Partner ❐ Child ❐ Sibling ❐ Grandparent ❐ Other _____		
Address	City	State	Zip Code
Phone	Email Address		

Claimant 2

Claimant's Name (last, first, m.i.)		Date of Birth (MM/DD/YY)	Social Security Number None ❐
Gender ❐ Male ❐ Female	Relationship to Victim ❐ Parent ❐ Spouse/Partner ❐ Former Spouse/Partner ❐ Child ❐ Sibling ❐ Grandparent ❐ Other _____		
Address	City	State	Zip Code
Phone	Email Address		

SECTION 3. REFERRAL SOURCE — How did you learn of the reparations program?

❐ County Attorney	❐ Hospital	❐ Sexual Assault Program	❐ Website
❐ Domestic Abuse Program	❐ Police	❐ Social Services, Cleric or School	❐ Other_____
❐ Funeral Home	❐ Probation	❐ Victim Assistance Program	

SECTION 4. CRIME INFORMATION	Date of Crime	Date Reported to Police	County Where Crime Occurred
Police Department	Police Case Number		Investigating Officer's Name

Did the crime involve? ❏ Domestic or Family Violence ❏ Bullying ❏ Elder Abuse ❏ Hate Crime ❏ Mass Violence

Type of Crime (check all that apply)			
❏ Assault	❏ Child Physical Abuse	❏ DWI	❏ Burglary
❏ Homicide	❏ Child Sexual Abuse	❏ Other Vehicular Crime	❏ Fraud/Financial Crime
❏ Robbery	❏ Child Pornography	❏ Stalking	❏ Terrorism
❏ Adult Sexual Assault	❏ Human Trafficking	❏ Arson	❏ Other
	❏ Kidnapping		

Briefly describe crime and injuries. Attach additional pages if necessary.

Name of Offender(s) (last, first, m.i.)	Gender ❏ Male ❏ Female	Date of Birth (MM/DD/YY)

SECTION 5. FEDERAL REPORTING INFORMATION	The following **voluntary** information is for the victim for whom this application was filed and is used for statistical purposes only to comply with federal regulations.			
Ethnicity ❏ American Indian/ Alaskan Native ❏ Asian	❏ Black/African American ❏ Hawaiian/Other Pacific Islander	❏ Hispanic/Latino ❏ Multi-Racial ❏ Other ❏ White	Country of Birth	Was the victim disabled prior to the crime? ❏ No ❏ Yes

SECTION 6. AUTHORIZED CONTACT INFORMATION	Your claim is confidential. If you would like the Board to be able to discuss your claim with anyone (parent, spouse, social worker) you must list their information below.		
Name	Relationship to you	Phone	
Name	Relationship to you	Phone	

SECTION 7. REPRESENTATION BY OTHERS	The Board is authorized to release private and confidential data about this claim to the representatives listed below.
ATTORNEY INFORMATION	**VICTIM ASSISTANCE PROGRAM INFORMATION**
Are you represented in this matter by a private attorney? ❏ No ❏ Yes	Are you working with an advocate? ❏ No ❏ Yes
Name of Attorney	Name of Advocate
Law Firm	Victim Assistance Program
Address	Address

City	State	Zip Code	City	State	Zip Code
Phone	Fax		Phone	Fax	

SECTION 8. OTHER SOURCES OF PAYMENT	All bills must first be submitted to your insurance company. The Board may deny payment if you fail to use other available sources.

Was there insurance or another source of payment to cover expenses related to the crime? ❏ No ❏ Yes

Check all that apply
❏ Automobile Insurance   ❏ Homeowner's Insurance   ❏ Medicare   ❏ Veteran's Benefits
❏ Dental Insurance   ❏ Long/short term Disability   ❏ MNSure   ❏ Worker's Compensation
❏ Health Insurance   ❏ Medical Assistance (MA)   ❏ Social Security Disability   ❏ Other_____

Complete for all other sources available to pay for crime related expenses, or attach a copy of insurance card.

Insurance company	Address	Phone	Policy	Group
Insurance company	Address	Phone	Policy	Group
Insurance company	Address	Phone	Policy	Group

ATTACH INSURANCE EXPLANATION OF BENEFITS FOR ALL PAYMENTS AND/OR DENIALS

SECTION 9. LOSS OF EARNINGS	Complete if the victim and/or claimant lost income due to the crime. All leave time (vacation/sick) or other benefits must be used first.

Victim Employment Information

Were you employed on date of crime? ❏ No ❏ Yes	Were you self-employed on the date of the crime? ❏ No ❏ Yes If yes, attach a copy of your most recent federal tax return	Your occupation/Job Title		
Employer's Business Name	Supervisor's Name	Phone	Fax	
Address		City	State	Zip Code
First Date Missed	Date Returned	Did the crime occur while you were on the job? ❏ No ❏ Yes		

Did you receive any benefits for time missed from work? ❏ No ❏ Yes

❏ Disability ❏ Workers Compensation ❏ Sick Leave ❏ Vacation Pay ❏ Other (explain)_____

Doctor/Counselor who can verify disability	Hospital/Clinic	Address

Claimant Employment Information (If more than 1, attach a separate sheet with all requested information.)

Claimant's Name	Were you self-employed on date of crime? ❏ No ❏ Yes If yes, attach a copy of your most recent federal tax return		
Employer's Business Name	Phone	Fax	Your Occupation/Job Title
Address		City	State	Zip Code
First Date Missed	Date Returned	Why did you miss work? ❏ To provide care to victim ❏ Medical/counseling appts. ❏ Emotional injury from crime	

Did you receive any benefits for time missed from work? ❏ No ❏ Yes

❏ Disability ❏ Workers Compensation ❏ Sick Leave ❏ Vacation Pay ❏ Bereavement ❏ Other (explain)_____

SECTION 10. MEDICAL AND DENTAL EXPENSES	List the healthcare providers who treated crime related injuries, including pharmacies. Attach itemized bills and receipts, if available. **Providers must also be listed on the release form on page 6.**	
Provider	Address	Phone
Provider	Address	Phone
Provider	Address	Phone
Provider	Address	Phone

SECTION 11. MENTAL HEALTH COUNSELING EXPENSES		List the mental health providers who treated the victim and/or claimant. Attach itemized bills if available. **Providers must also be listed on the release form on page 6.**	
Patient	Counselor/Clinic	Address	Phone
Patient	Counselor/Clinic	Address	Phone
Patient	Counselor/Clinic	Address	Phone

COMPLETE SECTIONS 12 & 13 ONLY IF THE VICTIM DIED AS A RESULT OF THE CRIME

SECTION 12. FUNERAL EXPENSES	List all funeral homes/cemeteries that provided services. Attach a copy of funeral and burial contracts, if available. Attach receipts if you had travel/lodging expenses to attend the funeral.	
Funeral Home/Cemetery	Address	Phone
Funeral Home/Cemetery	Address	Phone

SECTION 13. LOSS OF SUPPORT FOR DEPENDENTS OF DECEASED VICTIMS		Loss of support benefits are paid to dependents (spouse/partner, minor children) of the deceased victim. The legal guardian must file on the minor child's behalf.	
Was the victim providing support to a spouse/partner at the time of his/her death? ☐ No ☐ Yes			
Spouse/Partner	Address		Phone
Does the victim have dependent children under the age of 18? ☐ No ☐ Yes			
Child	Guardian	Address	Phone
Child	Guardian	Address	Phone
Child	Guardian	Address	Phone

SUBSTITUTE FORM W-9

Name (print your name clearly):   DATE:_____

_____

FROM: CRIME VICTIMS REPARATIONS BOARD_____

SUBJECT: Request for Taxpayer Information.

The purpose of this form is to obtain or confirm your correct taxpayer name and identification number.

Please complete items 1, 2, and 3 below.

1. Check your tax filing status below and enter your social security number or federal employer identification number. If you have been issued a separate Minnesota tax identification number, write it in the space provided.

    If you have recently applied for a taxpayer number, write "Applied For" in the space for the number.

☒ Individual: Use SSN ☐ Sole Proprietorship: Use SSN or FEIN ☐ Corporation: Use FEIN ☐ S Corporation ☐ Legal Partnership: Use FEIN ☐ Tax Exempt Organization: Use FEIN and list the section number of the IRS code under which you are claiming exemption: _____ ☐ Other: Please explain on reverse side and include a tax number.	(Fill in your social security number, or write "none".) _____ -- _____ -- _____ SOCIAL SECURITY NUMBER (SSN) _____ -- _____ FEDERAL EMPLOYER IDENTIFICATION (FEIN) _____ MINNESOTA TAX I.D. NUMBER (IF APPLICABLE)

2. Print the full name belonging to the social security number or employer identification number written above.

    _____

3. Certification. Under penalty of perjury, I certify the number shown on this form is my correct taxpayer identification number.

Signature_____Phone No.:_____Date_____

PRIVACY ACT NOTICE - Internal Revenue code Section 6109 requires you to furnish your correct taxpayer identification number to payers who must file information returns with IRS. IRS uses the numbers for identification purposes and to help verify the accuracy of your tax return.

FOR MMB USE ONLY	TYPE	IND	TIN	USED

COMPLETE SECTIONS 15 AND 18

SECTION 14. ASSIGNMENT OF SUBROGATION RIGHTS

I agree that the Board is subrogated to the extent of reparations awarded and to all my rights to recover benefits for economic loss from another source. I assign such rights to the Board so that they may protect their subrogation interest. I agree to inform the Board in writing if I pursue a civil suit or receive any restitution moneys related to the crime.

SECTION 15. INFORMED CONSENT TO RELEASE PATIENT INFORMATION

I consent to the release of all patient health care records for _____, Date of Birth_____/_____/_____, including reports of alcohol or drug abuse and psychiatric treatment, to the Minnesota Crime Victims Reparations Board from all providers of medical and mental health treatment services, including but not limited to the providers listed below. I authorize CVRB staff to complete this section on my behalf, if necessary.

1.	2.	3.	4.
5.	6.	7.	8.
9.	10.	11.	12.

The consent to release patient information covers the time period of: /   /   to: /   /

SECTION 16. AUTHORIZATION TO OBTAIN AND RELEASE INFORMATION

I authorize any law enforcement agency, employer, insurance company, social service agency, victim advocacy program, county, state or federal prosecutor's office, or any other federal, state or local government agency to release all records and information that the Board determines will help in deciding my eligibility or level of benefits in this claim. I specifically authorize the Minnesota Department of Revenue to release a copy of my tax returns to the Board for the purpose of determining my lost wages.

I authorize the Minnesota Crime Victims Reparations Board to release private and confidential data about my claim to the court administrator, prosecutor, and any officers of the court and probation and parole officials for the purpose of assessing the economic impact of the crime upon me and for determining the amount of restitution to be paid by the offender.

I authorize the Board to release private and confidential data about my claim to a local Emergency Fund administrator for the purpose of coordinating benefits.

SECTION 17. MISCELLANEOUS CONSENTS/AGREEMENTS

I agree that any reparations awarded may be paid directly to the provider of the service on my behalf.

I understand that authorizing the disclosure of health information is voluntary. I can refuse to sign this authorization. I need not sign this form in order to assure treatment by a health provider.

I understand that my refusal to provide information or not allow access to information needed to analyze my claim may result in the denial of reparations.

I understand that any disclosure of information carries with it the potential for an unauthorized redisclosure and the redisclosure of protected health information may not be protected by federal privacy rules.

This consent will remain in effect for one year from the date of my signature. I consent to the release of healthcare records created after the date of my signature below. I understand that I may revoke this authorization at any time by submitting a written notification to the Board. This revocation will not apply to information that has already been released in response to this authorization.

A photocopy of this consent form may be accepted as the original.

SECTION 18. VICTIM AND CLAIMANT SIGNATURES — The victim must sign and date the application form. If the victim is deceased, under the age of eighteen or an incapacitated adult victim, the claimant must sign and date the application form.

I have read and understand the statements in Sections 14-17 above. I hereby certify that the information contained in this application is true and correct to the best of my knowledge. I understand that it is a gross misdemeanor to knowingly file a false claim.

Victim/Patient Signature	Victim/Patient Printed Name	Date of Birth	Date Signed
Claimant 1 Signature	Claimant Printed Name	Date of Birth	Date Signed
Claimant 2 Signature	Claimant Printed Name	Date of Birth	Date Signed
Claimant 1's relationship to victim	Claimant 2's relationship to victim	Reason victim cannot sign claim form ☐ Deceased ☐ Minor ☐ Incapacitated Adult	

6 of 6

(Rev. 3/15)

Chapter Four

Land of 10,000 Lakes and 10,000 Prisoners: Minnesota's Correctional System

Learning Objectives

- Identify some of the causes and consequences of mass incarceration
- Describe the demographics of Minnesota's prison population
- Describe the structure of corrections in Minnesota (state and county)
- Describe the statistics as they relate to offenders under supervision
- Explain the different levels of correctional facilities in Minnesota
- Identify the use of probation in Minnesota
- Describe how Minnesota responds to pregnant inmates
- Articulate some of the issues associated with an aging prison population
- List the job duties of a probation officer and correction officer
- Identify intermediate sanctions used in Minnesota
- Define pardons and the role of the Pardon Board
- Explain what is PREA

Incarceration is one of the main forms of punishment to which lawbreakers in our society may be subjected. Punishment is an undesirable or unpleasant outcome, typically justified under the rubrics of deterrence, incapacitation, retribution, or rehabilitation. On deterrence, first articulated by Cesare Beccaria in 1764, we imprison people to prevent them from committing future crimes. Beyond *specific deterrence* for the offender, time behind bars also offers the possibility of *general deterrence* for the wider public, wherein the prisoner serves as a cautionary tale of expected consequences (see Stafford & Warr, 1993). Penal confinement also physically separates offenders from the community, thus removing or reducing their ability to carry out future crimes

(Zimring & Hawkins, 1995). Of course, prison also serves a retributive function, as a way of "getting even" with the offender; an idea often associated with the Biblical tenet of *lex talionis* or "an eye for an eye, a tooth for a tooth." Owing to the five "pains of imprisonment" (Sykes, 1958), including the deprivation of liberty, deprivation of goods and services, deprivation of heterosexual relationships, deprivation of autonomy, and deprivation of security, incarceration ensures offenders also receive their "just deserts" for wrongdoing (von Hirsch, 1976). Finally, prison time can also help reform and rehabilitate the offender so they will not commit the crime again.

Minnesota has been in the business of corrections since 1853, when the first adult territorial prison was established in Stillwater after Congress in 1850 allocated $20,000 to complete the six-cell, two-dungeon facility (Dunn, 1960). Prior to this time, criminals were held at two of the state's military posts, Camp Ripley and Fort Snelling. In the early days, the prison had problems with escapees, counties failing to pay for their prisoners to stay at the facility, contract prison labor disputes, fires, wardens with little training in penology, bed bugs, and poor air quality, among other issues. In 1905, Congress approved construction of new buildings close to the site in an effort to transform Stillwater into the "best penal structure in the country" (Dunn, 1960, p.151). Minnesota Correctional Facility–Stillwater in nearby Bayport, replaced the original prison in 1914. By the turn of the twentieth century Minnesota was well on its way to becoming a modern penal state.

Today, Minnesota has a wide range of adult and juvenile, male and female facilities and programs. The Department of Corrections (DOC) was legislatively created in 1959 to "Reduce recidivism by promoting offender change through proven strategies during safe and secure incarceration and effective community supervision." They work to achieve this mission through many policies, programs, and initiatives; however, the state is not the only one in the business of corrections. There are county-level jails and programs, as well as non-profit organizations that all work with offenders in a variety of capacities. This is because of the state's wide use of intermediate sanctions, which as defined by Minnesota Statutes § 609.135 subd b include:

> incarceration in a local jail or workhouse, home detention, electronic monitoring, intensive probation, sentencing to service, reporting to a day reporting center, chemical dependency or mental health treatment or counseling, restitution, fines, day-fines, community work service, work service in a restorative justice program, work in lieu of or to work off fines and, with the victim's consent, work in lieu of or to work off restitution.

This chapter provides an overview of corrections in Minnesota, with particular attention paid to how state, county, and community correction services are administered.

Prison Statistics

The United States incarcerates more people than any country in the world, both per capita and in terms of total people behind bars—approximately one in every 100 adults (Travis, Western, & Redburn, 2014). America's state and federal prison population has increased more than sixfold in 40 years from 200,000 inmates in the mid-1970s to approximately 1.5 million today, and if we include local jails, the total is closer to 2.3 million (Sentencing Project, 2015).

The *causes* of mass incarceration are legion: "zero tolerance" policing, the war on drugs, mandatory and longer sentencing, the trying of juveniles as adults, the prison-industrial complex, and the "New Jim Crow" (for a discussion, see Alexander, 2012). The *consequences* are serious (Stuntz, 2011): prisons are overcrowded, understaffed, and dangerous places; prison gangs have institutionalized (Skarbek, 2014); and ex-offenders struggle to access education, employment, and training or to find housing, transportation, and basic healthcare upon release.

Nationwide, including offenders supervised in the community, 6,899,000 people were under correctional control in 2013 (Glaze & Kaeble, 2014). This represents a decrease of .06% from 2012, which is in part attributable to a decline in the probation and jail populations. The federal prison population declined for the first time since 1980, but the state prison rate increased. Furthermore, since 2010, the female population grew by 3.4%, which is attributed to a growth in the total jail population (Glaze & Kaeble, 2014).

In 2013, 189 per 100,000 Minnesotans were incarcerated, which is the second lowest incarceration rate, behind Maine, in the country (National Institute of Corrections, 2015). The U.S. national average is 395 per 100,000 people, and the state with the highest incarceration rate is Louisiana with 847 per 100,000. While this may be encouraging to Minnesota, globally, a rate of 189 per 100,000 is still very high. For example, if we looked at Minnesota as a country it would be ranked the 12th highest out of 57 countries in Europe, 10th highest of 31 countries in Asia, 3rd highest out of 12 in the Middle East, and 10th highest out of 53 in Africa (International Center of Prison Studies, 2015).

The prison population in Minnesota on July 1, 2014, was 9,929 adult inmates, of which 456 inmates have a sentence of life *with* the possibility of parole and another 110 *without* the possibility of parole (Minnesota Department of Corrections, 2014). These sentences are given for the crime of murder in the first degree as defined by Minnesota Statutes § 609.185. Minnesota is currently a non-death penalty state, but did have the death penalty a century ago (for a discussion, see **Chapter Eight**). In addition to the above, another 299 offenders were juveniles certified as adults in the criminal justice system. Minnesota Statutes §260B.125 allows for certification "when a child is alleged to have committed, after becoming 14 years of age, an offense that would be a felony if committed by an adult, the juvenile court may enter an order certifying the proceeding for action under the laws and court procedures controlling adult criminal violations." Refer to **Chapter Six** for a more complete discussion of juvenile certification.

Offenders committed to the Commissioner of Corrections (sent to prison versus local jail) committed the crimes that are displayed in **Figure 4.1**. Since 2004, an average of 17.2% have been incarcerated for criminal sexual conduct, 13.9% for homicide, and 10.7% for assault. In addition, on average, 19.7% are incarcerated for drugs and another 7.2% for burglary (Minnesota Department of Corrections, 2015). In looking at felony-level crime, in 2013 there were 15,318 offenders sentenced. Thirty-two percent of these sentences were for person crimes, approximately 30% for property, and the remaining for other crimes, which include crimes like felony-level DWIs and non-person sex offenses (Minnesota Sentencing Guidelines Commission, 2014).

Figure 4.1. Number of Minnesota DOC Inmates by Offense Type on July 1, 2014

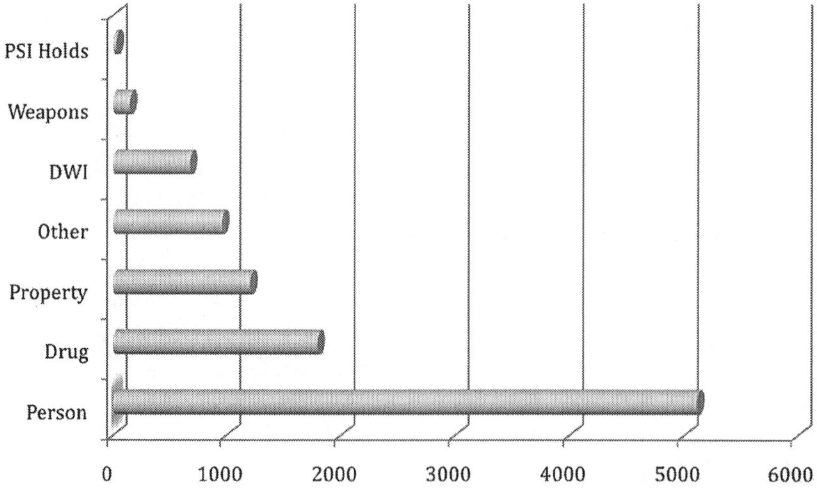

Source: Author created from Minnesota Department of Corrections (2015).

The length of time an inmate spends in prison is a very important variable as we look towards programming, costs, over-crowding, rehabilitation, and so on. A discussion of sentencing practices in Minnesota and the Minnesota Sentencing Guidelines is found in **Chapter Nine**. In should be noted that in 2013, almost three-quarters (72%) of felony offenders did receive a sentence per the guidelines, the remaining received mixed (1%), aggravated (4%), or mitigated departures (23%) (Minnesota Sentencing Guideline Commission, 2014). At the federal level, in March 2015, 53% of inmates were serving sentences 10 years or longer and the rest are fewer than 10 years as shown in **Figure 4.2**. In Minnesota, the average length of time an offender served in 2009 was 2.3 years. This number represents an increase of nearly 38% since 1990; however it is less than the national average of 2.9 years (PEW Charitable Trust, 2012).

Figure 4.2. Length of Sentences for Federal Inmates in March 2015

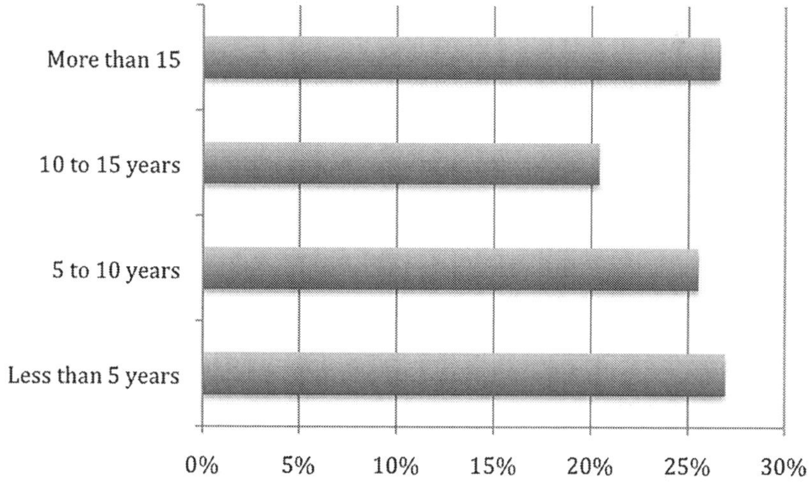

Source: Author created from Federal Bureau of Prison (2015b).

Jail Statistics

In 2012, the average daily jail population was 6,531 (Minnesota Department of Corrections, 2014). Hennepin County, home to the most populous city in the state, Minneapolis, also has the largest and busiest jail facility, which is operated by the Sheriff's Department. The facility includes two separate buildings, which together hold 839 beds. Each year the Hennepin County Sher-

iff's Office books 40,000 offenders into their jail, generally for pretrial or awaiting hearings (Hennepin County Sheriff Office, 2015). In addition, Hennepin
County has an Adult Corrections Facility to provide short-term (less than a
year) custody and programming for 477 adult offenders (Hennepin County,
2015c). In 2012, it was selected by the National Institute of Corrections and Urban
Institute as one of the six learning jail sites in the country to pilot Phase II of
the Transition from Jail to Community (TJC) initiative (Urban Institute, 2012).
This comprehensive model is designed to improve reintegration into the community from the jail, increase public safety, and reduce recidivism. Results
from Phase I show promise. Phase II results are not yet available.

The second largest jail facility is Ramsey County Jail, which has 500 beds (Ramsey County, 2015) and like Hennepin County, they also have an Adult Corrections Facility.

Figure 4.3. Rates of Correctional Population in Minnesota and Nationally

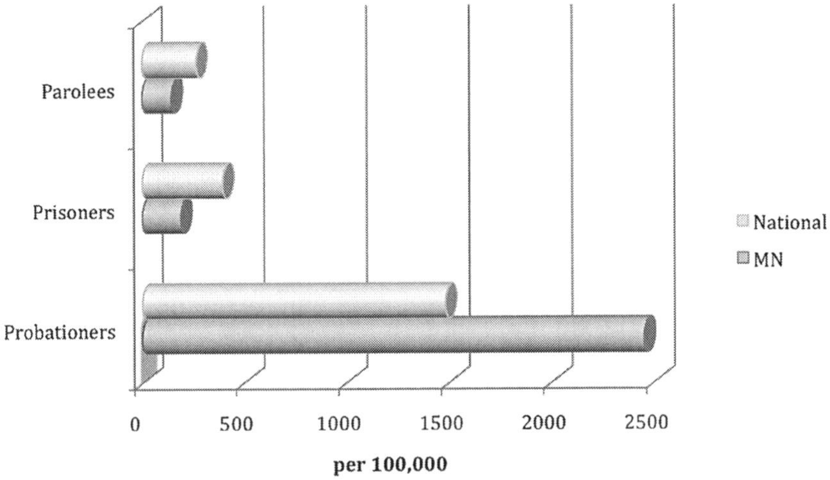

Source: Author created from National Institute of Corrections (2015).

Demographics of Minnesota's Prison Population

Gender

Consistent with national trends, men significantly outnumber women in
Minnesota prisons. Since 2004, men have consistently comprised between

93%–94% of the total prison population (Minnesota Department of Corrections, 2014c). Minnesota Department of Corrections Policy 202.045 (2014) provides guidelines for "evaluation, placement, and treatment of offenders who claim to be undergoing transgender treatment, or are identified as transgender or gender-variant, and to assure offender safety and access to appropriate medical/mental health care."

Education

Per Minnesota Department of Corrections Policy 204.040 (2010):

> The minimum educational standard for all DOC offenders is a verified high school or GED diploma. The educational goal for all DOC offenders is preparation for and/or completion of post-secondary training or education. Adult facilities will provide eligible incarcerated offenders with comprehensive educational programming including literacy, General Education Development (GED) and high school diploma, Special Education, transition to post-secondary, post-secondary, enrichment, and other programs designed to prepare offenders for successful reentry into society.

In short, if DOC inmates do not have a high school diploma or GED they are required to go to school. If they refuse, they are not eligible for other work assignments.

In looking at education levels, the percentage of prison inmates with at least a high school diploma/GED equivalent has doubled since 2004. In breaking down the percentages even more, in 2013, for example, 16.8% have a college degree or higher, 26.7% have a GED, 25.6% have a high school diploma, 25% have completed grades 9–11, and the rest have completed 0–8th grade, other, or unknown (Minnesota Department of Corrections, 2014c). In looking at state data as a whole, 92.1% of people ages 25 or older have a high school/GED equivalent, of which 32.6% have earned a bachelor's degree or higher (U.S. Census Bureau, 2015). In 2012, the DOC released a report that highlighted the following additional education statistics:

- 2,450 offenders are enrolled in education programs on any given day.
- 632 offenders earned a GED or high school diploma in fiscal year 2011.
- Education classes had over 9,000 offender enrollees during fiscal year 2011.

- 644 career/technical certificates and diplomas were completed in fiscal year 2011.
- The Minnesota Department of Corrections ranks second among the 52 state Adult Basic Education consortia in number of student instructional hours. (Minnesota Department of Corrections, 2012a)

Table 4.1. Minnesota Prison Population by Gender and
Education from 2004–2014

Year	Population	Males	Females	Education Level (High School/ GED & Up)
2004	8333	7843 (94%)	490 (6%)	2918 (35%)
2005	8708	8195 (94%)	513 (6%)	4000 (46%)
2006	9010	8466 (94%)	544 (6%)	4480 (50%)
2007	9214	8639 (94%)	575 (6%)	4355 (47%)
2008	9224	8630 (94%)	594 (6%)	5053 (55%)
2009	9353	8727 (93%)	626 (7%)	5848 (63%)
2010	9650	9027 (94%)	623 (6%)	6212 (64%)
2011	9338	8714 (93%)	624 (7%)	6285 (67%)
2012	9501	8844 (93%)	657 (7%)	6451 (68%)
2013	9772	9090 (93%)	682 (7%)	6754 (69%)
2014	9929	9228 (93%)	701 (7%)	6866 (69%)

Source: Author created from Minnesota Department of Corrections (2015).

Race

The issue of race and incarceration is an important topic in Minnesota and elsewhere. Since 2004 the percentage of those incarcerated has not been proportional to the racial make-up of the population as a whole. As can be observed in **Table 4.2**, whites are underrepresented in Minnesota prisons and jails, while Hispanics, blacks, and Native Americans are overrepresented (Sakala, 2014). According to the U.S. Census Bureau, for example, only 5% of the population in Minnesota is black, but one out of every three inmates is black. In looking at federal statistics, in March 2015, 38% of the inmates were black, 59% were white, 2% were Native American, and 2% were Asian. Furthermore, 34.2% of inmates were Hispanic (Federal Bureau of Prisons, 2015a).

Table 4.2. 2010 Minnesota Incarceration Rates by Race/Ethnicity

Race	Minnesota Population	State Incarcerated Population
White	83%	47%
Hispanic	5%	12%
Black	5%	31%
Native American	1%	8%

Source: Sakala (2014). The figures only reflect individuals in local, state, or federal custody, and do not include people on probation or parole.

In 2014, the American Civil Liberties Union issued a report highlighting disparities in sentencing to the Inter-American Commission on Human Rights. Some of the highlights of their report include: (1) Sentencing imposed on black males is 20% longer than those of whites for similar offenses in federal prison; (2) The odds for black and Latino offenders being sentenced to incarceration and for longer periods of times compared to whites is greater in some jurisdictions; (3) blacks disproportionately are sentenced to life without the possibility of parole (and it is even more pronounced for juveniles) and the death penalty.

In 2009, Minnesota legislators passed the Disproportionate Minority Contact Act (Minnesota Statutes § 260B.002), which states:

> It is the policy of the state of Minnesota to identify and eliminate barriers to racial, ethnic, and gender fairness within the criminal justice, juvenile justice, corrections, and judicial systems, in support of the fundamental principle of fair and equitable treatment under law.

Minnesota also has some of the "deepest economic disparities in the nation based on race and while the reasons are complicated, involvement in the criminal justice system is one important factor driving such disparities" (Minnesota Department of Human Rights, 2013). In Minnesota, the disparity between whites and blacks with criminal records is four times higher than the national average. This is perhaps one of the reasons why in 2014, Minnesota became the first state to enact a "Ban the Box" law prohibiting criminal history checkmark boxes on employment applications (Minnesota Department of Human Rights, 2013). Ban the Box laws aim to reduce the stigma attached to having a criminal record.

The Ban the Box requirement has been in effect for public employers in Minnesota since 2009 and is designed to provide job candidates with an arrest or conviction with more opportunities to be evaluated on their skills and experience when applying for positions with private employers. The law does not require an employer to hire any candidate with a criminal background, and employers may still conduct background checks. Ban the Box simply requires an employer to wait until later in the hiring process—at the interview stage or when a conditional job offer has been extended—before asking the applicant about their criminal record or conducting a criminal background check (Minnesota Department of Human Rights, 2013).

Age

Inmates in prison are getting older in both state and federal prisons, and elderly inmates represents one of the fastest growing populations in prisons. Sixteen percent of state and federal inmates are age 50 and older, with Minnesota having one of the smallest percentages (American Civil Liberty [ACLU], 2012). Mandatory minimums and longer sentences mean some prison facilities operate like nursing homes for some inmates. Elderly inmates impact how prisons do business, most notably on costs (see section later in chapter labeled **Costs of Corrections**), but also on programming, movement policies, structural design, and other related issues. In addition, according to the ACLU (2012), housing elderly inmates requires more staffing (and training) because of various reasons, including more assistance with day-to-day activities and protection from mental and physical abuse from younger inmates.

Table 4.3. Age of Inmates in Minnesota State Prisons

Year	Average Age	Age over 50	Total pop. on July 1	% of Total pop. over 50
2005	34.5	703	8,708	8.1%
2006	35.1	796	9,010	8.8%
2007	35.4	866	9,214	9.4%
2008	35.7	971	9,224	10.5%
2009	35.8	1,033	9,353	11.0%
2010	35.2	1,024	9,650	10.6%
2011	35.9	1,118	9,338	12.0%
2012	36.3	1,328	9,501	14.0%
2013	36.4	1,322	9,772	13.5%
2014	36.6	1,378	9,929	13.9%

Source: Author created from Minnesota Department of Corrections (2015).

Religion in Prison

Prisoners, like everyone else, have a right to believe in whatever religion they chose. Furthermore, a prison cannot coerce or force an inmate to participate in a religious practice or belief (*Lee v. Weisman*, 1992). There are two key pieces of legislation that provide for religious freedom in prisons and these include the Religious Land Use and Institutionalized Person's Act of 2000 (for state inmates) and the Religious Freedom Restoration Act of 1993 (for federal inmates). Refinement of what exact practices are permissible has occurred through legislation since these acts were passed. For example, in *Holt v. Hobbs* (2015), the U.S. Supreme Court ruled that it was wrong to force a Muslim inmate to shave his beard. In Minnesota, state law mandates that

> [f]acilities provide all offenders with reasonable opportunities to pursue individual religious beliefs and practices, within facility budgetary and security constraints. When considered necessary for the security and good order of the institution, the warden my limit attendance at or discontinue a religious activity. Attendance at or participation in religious activities may not be restricted on the basis of race, color, nationality, sex, sexual orientation, or creed. Offenders are not required to attend religious services. (Minnesota Statutes § 241.05)

Community items are stored by the facility, but offenders can designate personal religious items. Offenders also are allowed to purchase religious items, but all religious items must be approved and adhere to rules of the facility. For example, there is a designated time and place to use religious artifacts. Each correctional facility has a space designated for holding religious services and "a trained and qualified facility chaplain to oversee the reasonable delivery of religious services to all faith traditions." If an offender has a religious diet, moreover, it is adhered to as long as the facility has the budget and security restraints. Donated food is not allowed (Minnesota Department of Corrections, 2015c). Some facilities have also created policies as they relate to religious head coverings. The Federal Bureau of Prisons, under Policy 5360.09, also permits the wearing of head coverings (yarmulke, kufi, headband, crown, turban, etc.) and even identifies what colors each of the various types of head coverings can include (U.S. Department of Justice, 2004).

Minnesota facilities have several faith-based programs. InnerChange Freedom Initiative is one such example that has been a part of Minnesota's prison programming since 2002. This program helps offenders "prepare for re-entry through educational, values based programming that connects spiritual development with educational, vocational, and life skills programming" (Duwe & Johnson, 2013, p.4). Some of these programs include religion-specific elements, like Christian religious services and Bible study and prayers, as well as other types of programming, including substance abuse education, cognitive skill development, mentoring, and seminars. Research has shown this is effective at reducing recidivism and is cost-effective; it saved the Minnesota Department of Corrections $3 million over a six-year period (Duwe & Johnson, 2013).

Pregnant Inmates

Since 2004, approximately 6–7% of the total prison population in Minnesota has been women (Minnesota Department of Correction, 2015). Female inmates have different needs than male inmates, most notably as it relates to pregnancy and childbirth. Approximately 6–10% of females nationwide enter prison pregnant (Gerrity, 2013). Minnesota was the twentieth state to pass an anti-shackling law in regards to pregnant women and became the first state to pass legislation mandating that correctional facilities offer all pregnant women and women who have given birth in the past six weeks doula services. The legislation went into effect July 1, 2014, for state facilities and all other correctional facilities must be in compliance by July 1, 2015 (Office of the Revisor of Statutes, 2014). The law forbids the use of restraints (with strict exceptions) on women who are known to be pregnant or have given birth during transportation, labor, delivery, and three days postpartum.

In addition to banning the use of restraints and requiring doula services to be offered, the legislation mandates that all women be given pregnancy tests as well as testing for sexually transmitted diseases upon arrival to a correctional facility; additionally, educational materials regarding pregnancy, birth, breastfeeding, and parenting must be provided to all pregnant women and those who have given birth in the previous six weeks (Office of the Revisor of Statutes, 2014). Both of these allow women to not only become aware of a pregnancy, but also provide them with all the necessary information regarding what to expect.

The legislation also states requirements in regards to mental healthcare and treatment if it is needed; these provisions are in effect for all pregnant women and women who have given birth in the past six months. It allows for these women to receive mental health assessments and any treatments that may be necessary including medications and therapy (Office of the Revisor of Statutes, 2014).

Minnesota's Department of Corrections

The Minnesota Department of Corrections is one of the main components of the criminal justice system in this state. It provides a vast range of services in an effort to improve community safety, rehabilitate offenders, and ensure justice is served.

Structure

The governor appoints a commissioner of corrections to lead the Department of Corrections. The commissioner has a broad range of responsibilities, including the operation of adult and juvenile correctional facilities in the state, oversight of probation and parole, service on the Minnesota Sentencing Guidelines Commission, and administration of the Community Corrections Act. Upon entering office, the commissioner

> shall take and subscribe an oath and give a bond to the state of Minnesota, to be approved by the governor and filed with the secretary of state, in the sum of $25,000, conditioned for the faithful performance of the commissioner's duties. (Minnesota Statutes § 241.01)

Two deputy commissioners, one tasked with facilities and another tasked with community corrections, support the commissioner. In addition, there is an assistant commissioner who oversees operation support and another who assists the deputy commissioner of facilities. A chief executive officer (warden) leads each facility, while seven different division leaders direct community corrections.

The Department of Corrections also utilizes the services of four legislatively mandated advisory groups (Roy, 2013), which include:

1. *Advisory Task Force on Women and Juvenile Female Offenders in Corrections.* This task force is mandated by Minnesota Statutes § 241.71 to "promote and advocate gender and culturally responsive services for women and girls in the criminal and juvenile justice systems." They do so by "(1) suggesting model programs to receive funding, (2) reviewing and making recommendations on matters affecting female offenders, (3) identifying problem areas, and (4) assisting the Commissioner in seeking improved programming for female offenders" (Minnesota Department of Corrections, 2015).
2. *Interstate Adult Offender Advisory Council.* This council is mandated by Minnesota Statutes § 243.1606 to oversee the administration and operation of the interstate movement between compacting states for adult offenders. More information about interstate commissions for adult offenders can be located at http://www.interstatecompact.org.
3. *Interstate Compact for Juveniles, Advisory Council.* This council is mandated by Minnesota Statutes § 260.515 to oversee the administration

and operations of the interstate movement between compacting states for juvenile offenders.

4. *Health Care Peer Review Committee*. This committee is mandated by Minnesota Statutes § 241.021 "To review and evaluate the quality of on-site and off-site offender care and treatment, including deaths of offenders, in order to evaluate and improve the quality of care and reduce morbidity and mortality too."

Minnesota Correctional Facilities (MCF)

Minnesota Statutes § 241.021 defines licensing and supervision of facilities. As illustrated in **Figure 4.4**, Minnesota's correctional system has four levels of adult custody classification, ranging from two (minimum) to five (maximum). MCF–Oak Park Heights is the one and only maximum-security facility in the state, designed specifically to house people who pose extreme risks to the public. They are held in the Administrative Control Unit, which includes nearly 24-hour lockdown and complete isolation. Some prisons have solitary cells, but there is no indefinite solitary confinement in Minnesota. Likewise, Minnesota prisons track inmates who are members or associates of prison gangs (also known as Security Threat Groups or STGs), but do not segregate inmates from the general population due to their gang or STG status.

One of the minimum-security boot camp facilities is at MCF–Moose Lake, legislatively created in 1992 to provide early release to non-violent offenders who qualify. In addition, MCF–Willow River offers the Challenged Incarcerated Program (CIP) for adult males, an early release program option to those within 60 months of confinement release. The goals of the program are "(1) to punish and hold the offender accountable, (2) to protect the safety of the public, (3) to treat offenders who are chemically dependent, and (4) to prepare the offender for successful reintegration into society" (Minnesota Statutes § 244.171).

Each Minnesota Correctional Facility (MCF) meets the standards established by the American Correctional Association (Minnesota Department of Corrections, 2014) and many incorporate MINNCOR Industries sites, which provide employment and training for offenders and manufacturing goods and services to all government agencies, private non-profits, K–12 schools, universities, cities, and counties.

Figure 4.4. Custody Levels in Minnesota (Minnesota DOC, 2015)

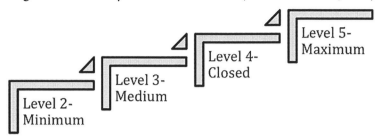

Source: Minnesota Department of Corrections, (2015).

Table 4.4. Minnesota Correctional Facilities at a Glance

Facility	Date	Population	Custody Level	Capacity	Did you know?
MCF–Faribault	1989	Adult male	2 Minimum/ 3 Medium	2,005	Largest facility in the Minnesota DOC system.
MCF–Lino Lakes	1963	Adult male	2 Minimum/ 3 Medium	1,310	Highest concentration of educational and treatment programs. Offenders often serve the final phase of their sentence at Lino Lakes.
MCF–Moose Lake	1988	Adult male	3 Medium	1,029	MINNCOR Industries operates a textile/garment plant that produces the clothing for all offenders in the DOC system.
MCF–Oak Park Heights	1982	Adult male	5 Maximum	438	Contains a modern medical infirmary designed to handle transitional health care needs for offenders transferred from other facilities. It also houses the only Supermax unit.
MCF–Red Wing	1889	Juvenile male	N/A	189	Served as the subject of "Walls of Red Wing," a protest song by Bob Dylan.
MCF–Red Wing Adult	1889	Adult male	2 Minimum	42	This separate community re-entry program is located adjacent to the main Red Wing campus.
MCF–Rush City	2000	Adult male	4 Closed	988	The DOC's newest facility.

Table 4.4. Minnesota Correctional Facilities at a Glance, *continued*

MCF–St. Cloud	1889	Adult male	4 Closed	1,010	Serves as the DOC intake facility. Also the oldest facility in the DOC system, surrounded by the longest granite wall in the world.
MCF–Shakopee	1911	Adult female	All	600	The only women's correctional facility in the nation to house maximum custody level offenders without a perimeter fence (until 2016).
MCF–Stillwater	1914	Adult male	2 Minimum/ 4 Closed	1,606	Home to *The Prison Mirror*, the nation's oldest offender newspaper.
CIP–Willow River	1992	Adult Male	2 Minimum	177	Challenge Incarceration Program (CIP), minimum-security boot camp.
MCF–Togo	1955	Adult Male (as of July 1, 2015)	2 Minimum	N/A	Challenge Incarceration Program (CIP), minimum security.

Source: Author created from Minnesota Department of Corrections (2015).

Women and Juvenile Correctional Facilities

In 1867, the House of Refuge first opened in Saint Paul to house young offenders. Technically the state's second prison after the Minnesota Territorial Prison in Stillwater, the House of Refuge was renamed to the Minnesota State Reform School in 1879, and it moved to Red Wing, Minnesota, in 1889. Later, in 1895, it was renamed the Minnesota State Training School and is now known as MCF–Red Wing. MCF–Red Wing is the only state-operated juvenile facility in Minnesota providing treatment, education, and transition services for males (Minnesota Department of Corrections, 2015). MCF–Red Wing's mission is to "Restore the offender, victim, and community; Promote public safety, offender accountability, and pro-social competency; Provide a premier continuum of services for juvenile offenders within a therapeutic environment." Up until July 1, 2015, MCF–Togo offered a 21-day Wilderness Endeavors treatment option for girls and boys, a three-month residential treatment program for boys, and a chemical dependency program for boys, however, this was discontinued. Counties have separate facilities for housing juveniles awaiting court dispositions/placement. For example, the Hennepin County Juvenile Detention Facility is a secure, 24-hour facility that holds 87 male and female juveniles for an average of seven days and provides programming that includes school (Hennepin County, 2015a). For more on juvenile corrections in Minnesota, see **Chapter Six.**

The state legislature created a reform school for girls in 1907. Thirteen years later, the state opened its first reformatory for women (Minnesota Department of Corrections, 2015). There is now one all-female prison in Minnesota, housing offenders of all levels. MCF–Shakopee is notable because it is the only facility in the United States to house maximum-security level prisoners without a fence. This, however, changes in 2016 when a fence will be added (Minnesota Department of Corrections, 2015).

Federal Prisons in Minnesota

Minnesota is home to two Federal Correctional Institutions (FCI), one Federal Prison Camp (FPC), and one Federal Medical Center (FMC). FCI–Sandstone is a minimum-level, dormitory-style facility for 1,350 male inmates. FCI–Waseca is a minimum-security facility for 1,000 female inmates. Programming in this facility provides an array of options, including GED preparatory courses, apprenticeship programs in landscape and HVAC, Silent No More for Change (for victims of domestic abuse), Prisoners Assisting with Support Dogs (PAWS), Chairs Ministry, and classes in a variety of subjects from yoga to history (Maranell, 2013). There is also FPC–Duluth which is a minimum-security federal prison camp for 800 inmates. In 2013, the prison made news headlines because two white-collar criminals escaped from the prison, only to be arrested less than a week later (Durkin, 2013). Lastly, Rochester is home to one of only six federal medical referral centers within the Federal Bureau of Prisons. FMC–Rochester houses 845 inmates (Federal Bureau of Prisons, 2015b). Any male inmate, regardless of classification, can be sent here for long-term medical or mental healthcare. On February 5, 2015, this facility made news headlines because it was releasing Minnesota's first offender to fight with Al-Shabaab in Somalia. Abdifatah Yusuf Isse was charged in 2007 with providing material support for terrorism abroad (Lyden, 2015). He ended up becoming a star witness and provided important insight to how Minnesota men were being radicalized for violent extremism (Yuen, 2015). For further discussion of federal corrections in Minnesota, see **Chapter Eight.**

Table 4.5. Federal Inmates' Rights and Responsibilities

Rights	Responsibilities
1. You have the right to expect that as a human being you will be treated respectfully, impartially, and fairly by all personnel.	1. You have the responsibility to treat others, both employees and inmates, in the same manner.
2. You have the right to be informed of the rules, procedures, and schedules concerning the operation of the institution.	2. You have the responsibility to treat others, both employees and inmates, in the same manner.
3. You have the right to freedom of religious affiliation and voluntary religious worship.	3. You have the responsibility to recognize and respect the rights of others in this regard.
4. You have the right to healthcare, which includes nutritious meals, proper bedding and clothing, and a laundry schedule for cleanliness of the same, an opportunity to shower regularly, proper ventilation for warmth and fresh air, a regular exercise period, toilet articles, and medical and dental treatment.	4. It is your responsibility not to waste food, to follow the laundry and shower schedule, maintain neat and clean living quarters, to keep your area free of contraband, and to seek medical and dental care as you may need it.
5. You have the right to visit and correspond with family members and friends, and correspond with members of the news media in keeping with Bureau rules and institution guidelines.	5. It is your responsibility to conduct yourself properly during visits, not to accept or pass contraband, and not to violate the law or Bureau rules and institution guidelines through your correspondence.
6. You have the right to unrestricted and confidential access to the courts by correspondence (on matters such as the legality of your conviction, civil matters, pending criminal cases, and conditions of your imprisonment).	6. You have the responsibility to present honestly and fairly your petitions, questions, and problems to the court.
7. You have the right to legal counsel from an attorney of your choice by interviews and correspondence.	7. It is your responsibility to use the services of an attorney honestly and fairly.
8. You have the right to participate in the use of law library reference materials to assist you in resolving legal problems. You also have the right to receive help when it is available through a legal assistance program.	8. It is your responsibility to use these resources in keeping with procedures and schedule prescribed and to respect the rights of other inmates to the use of the materials and assistance.
9. You have the right to a wide range of reading materials or materials for educational purposes and for your own enjoyment. These materials may include magazines and newspapers sent from the community, with certain restrictions.	9. It is your responsibility to use these resources in keeping with procedures and schedule prescribed and to respect the rights of other inmates to the use of the materials and assistance.

Table 4.5. Federal Inmates' Rights and Responsibilities, *continued*

10. You have the right to participate in education, vocational training, and employment as far as resources are available, and in keeping with your interests, needs, and abilities.	10. You have the responsibility to take advantage of activities that may help you live a successful and law abiding life within the institution and in the community. You will be expected to abide by the regulations governing the use of such activities.
11. You have the right to use your funds for Commissary and other purchases, consistent with institution security and good order, for opening bank and/or savings accounts, and for assisting your family.	11. You have the responsibility to meet your financial and legal obligations, including but not limited to, court imposed assessments, fines, and restitution. You also have the responsibility to make use of your funds in a manner consistent with your release plans, your family needs, and for other obligations that you may have.

Source: U.S. Department of Justice, Bureau of Prisons, 2012.

Private Prisons

From 1996–2010, Minnesota housed inmates at Prairie Correctional Facility, a private medium-security 1,700-bed capacity facility owned and operated by Correction Corporation of America (CCA). CCA began in the early 1980s as a public–private partnership to provide correction services to states and has grown into the largest private-prison operator in the United States. CCA is a publicly traded company that employs 14,000 people in 21 states and lobbies to keep their prisons full (CCA, 2015). Focused on shareholder value, CCA controversially highlights how its prisons comprise a "unique investment opportunity" thanks to limited competition, "high recidivism" among prisoners, and the potential for "accelerated growth in inmate populations following the recession" (Taub, 2010).

Prairie Correctional Facility was located in Appleton, a small city in west-central Minnesota, on the South Dakota border. The prison was not equipped to hold offenders 60 years or older, offenders who had special medical or mental health needs, or those classified higher than medium custody (Duwe & Clark, 2013). At its height in 2008, Prairie Facility held 13% of the state's total prison population (Duwe & Clark, 2013). However, shortly after this, with the downturn in the economy, renovations to two state-run facilities, and slow growth in the Minnesota prison population (partially due to leveling out of the methamphetamine problem and multiple felony-level DWI convictions) the need to send inmates to this facility dwindled and other states did not send their inmates there, forcing the prison to shut down (Duwe & Clark, 2013; Steil, 2010). Prairie Correctional Facility closed its doors on February 2, 2010, and now sits vacant. The closure had a huge economic impact on the small city, as tax revenues from the prison alone made up 60% of Appleton's budget (Steil, 2010).

Duwe and Clark (2013) examined the effectiveness of private prisons in reducing recidivism using a sample from Prairie Correctional Facility. Duwe and Clark (2013) compared 1,766 Minnesota prisoners from Prairie Correctional Facility to 7,769 prisoners released from other state-run facilities in Minnesota, controlling for a variety of variables. The focus was recidivism, defined as (1) re-arrest, (2) reconviction, (3) re-incarceration for a new sentence, or (4) revocation for a technical violation. Results showed that inmates housed in a private facility did not lead to improved recidivism rates. In fact, because this facility housed healthy and well-behaved inmates, the authors concluded, "private prisons produce slightly worse recidivism outcomes ... for the same amount of money" (Duwe & Clark, 2013, p.391).

Visitors in Prison

The Department of Corrections recognizes the importance of visitors as a way to help reduce recidivism, among other benefits, and therefore allows visitors to enter their facilities (Minnesota Department of Corrections, 2015). Any visitor 18 years of age or older must complete a visitor application and get approval prior to visiting the facility. There are two types of visits: (1) *contact*, which means the offender meets with the visitor in the visiting room; and (2) *no contact*, which means the offender and visitor are separated by glass and speak via phone/video. As in most states, there are no conjugal visits in Minnesota prisons. There also are strict rules surrounding a visit, controlling things like dress, contraband, seating arrangements, touching, child-care, photography, and other important considerations to maintain safety. In addition to family and friends who may visit, inmates can also receive visits from professionals such as lawyers, probation officers, and religious personnel.

One non-profit organization in Minnesota, Amicus, has a One-to-One Program that has been in existence for nearly half a century (Amicus, 2015). It is designed to give offenders an opportunity to develop positive relationships with people who live in the community who are matched to them by gender and characteristics that may be important to them, like religion or age. A volunteer agrees to meet with the offender for at least one year to hopefully develop skills, trust, and a feeling that someone cares. To date, over 8,000 inmates from four state facilities have been paired with a volunteer.

Employment in Prison and Jails

The Minnesota Department of Corrections is a major employer in the state. To become a correctional officer in a state prison, an applicant must apply for a six-week trainee program. To qualify, he/she must:

- be 18 (unless they work in juvenile facility, then it is 21 years of age),
- have a high school diploma or GED,
- have a valid driver's license,
- be eligible to possess a firearm, and
- pass a criminal history background check.

Throughout the training, the new recruit learns about a variety of topics, as listed in **Table 4.6.**

Table 4.6. Minimum Topics of Training New Correction Officers Receive during Their First Year

Security procedures	Fire, emergency, and safety procedures	Preventing sexual harassment and PREA
Supervision of offenders	Firearms training (for employees authorized to use firearms as part of their assignment)	Security threat groups (STGs)
Signs of suicide risk and precautions	Use and handling of access control devices	Needs of mentally ill offenders
Use of force regulations and tactics	Interpersonal relations	Counseling techniques (juvenile only)
Report writing	Social/cultural lifestyles of the offender population	Chemical exposure
Offender discipline rules and regulations	Communication skills	Radio skills
Offender rights and responsibilities	First aid/CPR	Avoiding setups and maintaining boundaries

Source: Author created from Minnesota Department of Corrections, Policy Number 103.420.

While in the trainee academy, the applicant is paid around $15 per hour. After completion of the program, the applicant becomes a correctional officer 1 for one year at a pay of around $16–$19 per hour and then is eligible for promotion to correction officer 2, with a pay range of around $18–$26 per hour (Minnesota Department of Corrections, 2015). The growth trajectory after this is one of a supervisory or investigative capacity, including positions as a correction officer 3, caseworker, corrections captain, and corrections lieutenant (Minnesota Department of Corrections, 2015). The captain (also known as the watch commander) is a senior-level management position and in the absence of the warden, the captain may serve as the officer in charge of the institution. The Commission of Corrections appoints the warden. In addition to the correction officers and their supervisors, the DOC employs individuals with a variety of other skill sets, which includes such professions as teachers, nurses, accountants, counselors, and therapists.

Figure 4.5. Work Duties of a Corrections Officer

Job Functions of a Correctional Officer in Hennepin County, Minnesota:

1. Observe and supervise residents from stations or by patrolling cell blocks, yard, grounds, corridors, dormitories, or work areas to maintain order, safety, and security and enforce Minnesota laws and American Correctional Association (A.C.A.) standards relating to the confinement of prisoners, security regulations, rules of conduct, and work rules.
2. Maintain counts of residents in assigned areas.
3. Search residents and inspect cells, recreation areas, grounds, work location, and other activity areas for unauthorized objects or materials.
4. Respond to resident concerns, medical emergencies, perform emergency first aid, operate emergency equipment, and report to medical staff.
5. Write reports (e.g., disciplinary reports, incident reports) and maintain records (e.g., records of residents' funds and personal property).
6. Escort individuals and groups of residents to work and other activities, supervise and instruct residents in work crew activities and the operation of equipment (i.e., laundry, kitchen, industrial production, stockroom, cleaning, and grounds maintenance equipment), and participate in work crew activities as needed.
7. Respond to safety and security incidents and other emergency situations, break up fights and physically restrain and control resisting and uncooperative residents.
8. Provide directions, safety and security instructions, and program-related information to residents, employers, other agencies, and the public.
9. Pursue residents attempting escape, search visitors, participate in administrative and disciplinary hearings, administer drug and alcohol testing, and transport and assist in the supervision of residents outside the facility (i.e., court appearances, medical appointments, transfers to other facilities).
10. Converse with residents to ensure an open atmosphere of staff and resident communication.
11. Provide peer instructions/or training as appropriate.

Source: Hennepin County Job Classification, Correctional Officer (2015).

In looking at county-level employment in the jails, qualification requirements may vary. For example, to be a correctional officer in the largest county in Minnesota, Hennepin, an applicant must have two years of college/vocational training, military experience, or two years of experience in criminal justice. The salary is approximately $18–$29 per hour (Hennepin County, 2015b). The duties of a correctional officer are found in **Figure 4.5**. A senior correctional officer requires a bachelor's degree or three years of experience. The salary range for this position is approximately $19–$31 per hour (Hennepin County, 2015b).

Community Corrections

Community corrections involve the supervision of offenders in the community. The most common types include probation and parole.

Probation and Parole

Probation and parole are both alternatives to incarceration. As defined by the Bureau of Justice Statistics (2015), probation is "a court-ordered period of correctional supervision in the community, generally as an alternative to incarceration. In some cases, probation can be a combined sentence of incarceration followed by a period of community supervision." Parole is defined as "a period of conditional supervised release in the community following a prison term. It includes parolees released through discretionary or mandatory supervised release from prison, those released through other types of post-custody conditional supervision, and those sentenced to a term of supervised release." In Minnesota, the term "parole" is synonymous with supervised release.

Nationally, one in 51 people, or 4.75 million offenders, were under some form of community supervision in 2013, which includes probation, parole, or other post-prison supervision (Herbeerman & Bonczar, 2015). Probationers made up a vast majority of these at 82% or 3.9 million offenders. As previously noted, the rate of individuals on probation in Minnesota significantly exceeds the national average. Minnesota's probation population is sixth highest in the country at 2,446 per 100,000 people. The national average is 1,479 per 100,000, with the lowest rate in New Hampshire (379 per 100,000) and highest rate in Georgia (6,829 per 100,000) (National Institute of Corrections, 2015). Women make up approximately 25% of the probation population (Glaze & Kaeble, 2014).

State agents and county probation officers supervise probationers. This is dependent on the county. Some counties are part of the Community Corrections Act. The Community Corrections Act (CCA) was enacted in 1973 to provide more community corrections service by the reallocation of corrections resources. This came about because of (1) lack of effective public protection, (2) high cost of state institutionalization, (3) duplication of services and their delivery and, (4) inappropriate correctional supervision (Minnesota Department of Corrections, 1973). Any county with a population greater than 30,000 can be part of the CCA. A little less than half (37) of all the counties in Minnesota participate (Minnesota Department of Corrections, 2014). Twenty-eight counties utilize state probation officers, and the remaining 27 utilize both county and state probation agents (generally divided by level of offense, with state taking the more serious adult offenders and the county taking the juveniles and the adult non-felons).

As for parolees, Minnesota has 144 per 100,000, in comparison with a national average of 267. Maine ranks the lowest at 2 per 100,000 and Pennsylvania the highest at 1,029 per 100,000 (National Institute of Corrections, 2015). There is no federal parole for inmates who have committed a crime after 1987 because of the Sentencing Reform Act. However, there are offenders who were sentenced prior to this date who are still eligible.

The Minnesota Department of Corrections supervises 18,456 of the approximately 122,000 offenders statewide. In the 1980s, Minnesota instituted a series of reforms to the state's correctional system, including *Determinant Sentencing*, which abolished the parole board and time off for good behavior. As a result of Determinate Sentencing, most offenders now serve two thirds of their prison sentence behind bars and the remaining third on supervised release. However, some crimes, like felony-level DWI, impose a mandatory five-year conditional release if the offender is sentenced to prison for first-degree DWI, instead of just one third of the sentence. If a violation occurs, the offender can go back to prison to serve out the remaining one third of the original sentence (Cleary & Pirius, 2008, p.8). In turn, the Minnesota Department of Corrections supervises two types of offenders:

1. Felony offenders who have served the mandatory two-thirds of their prison sentence who have been released from prison; and
2. Probationers who were not committed to the custody of the Commissioner of Corrections but reside in counties that do not find it practical to operate a local supervision program.

The crimes which the offender committed to bring them to a state agent are drug related in slightly over one fifth of cases, followed closely behind by DWI and property, with person crimes not too far behind, as provided in **Figure 4.6.**

Figure 4.6. Types of Crimes Because of Which Offenders Were Supervised by Minnesota Department of Corrections Agents in 2013

Number of offenders= 18,456

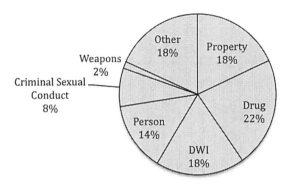

Source: Author created from information obtained from the Minnesota Department of Corrections (2013).

The Department of Corrections also manages three community offender programs.

1. **Sentencing to Service (STS).** This program, developed in 1986, is available only to non-violent offenders who work for free on community improvement projects that could benefit a city, county, township, school district, state, and/or non-profit organization, to include such things as picking up litter, cleaning storm drains, trail development, and river cleanup. It is estimated that the value of the projects STS crews work on is equal to around $5.5 million per year (Minnesota Department of Corrections, 2011). It should also be noted that some counties operate their own STS for both adult and juvenile offenders, which in some cases allows them to work off court fines and fees.

2. **Institution/Community Work Crew (ICWC) Program.** This program developed in 1995 to pay offenders a small wage ($1.50/hour) to be used to pay restitution, family support, and a fund for victims while they work in an organized supervised crew on such things as construction, land restoration, and forestry work (Minnesota Department of Corrections, 2013b).

3. **Work Release.** This program was legislatively created in 1967. It provides close supervision while offenders work full time. Because they are earning a salary they must pay for housing costs, as well as restitution, fines, and other fees (Minnesota Department of Corrections,

2014b). It should also be noted that at the jail level, Minnesota's facilities were listed as the second highest (behind North Dakota) for having a work release or prelease function (Stephan & Walsh, 2011).

When an offender is on probation he/she must obey certain conditions. Violation of any of the conditions could mean a warrant for his/her arrest and subsequent probation revocation. Conditions of probation generally include such things as reporting to a probation officer on a regular basis, not committing any type of crime in any jurisdiction, not possessing a firearm, not using any illegal drugs, and random drug testing. All felony offenders are barred from voting and leaving the state of Minnesota without prior permission. Those on supervised release or on probation are expected to submit to warrantless searches, without probable cause. Discretionary conditions are specific to the offender and can include a range of requirements like completing chemical dependency assessment and treatment, obtaining and maintaining employment, completing domestic violence programing, attending therapy, or attending anger management or parenting classes. They may be required to pay restitution, or child support, stay away from certain individuals or locations, or have no contact with the victims or co-defendants. Probation officers are also allowed to impose intermediate sanctions without going to a court hearing if there are probation violations. For example, a probation officer can require his/her probationer to participate in a Sentence to Serve (STS) Program up to a certain period of time. Whether the violation occurred in a CCA county also dictates the amount of power a probation officer has in regard to imposing various types of intermediate sanctions.

Intensive Supervised Release (ISR)

Minnesota's Intensive Supervision Program was established by the legislature in 1990 (Minnesota Statutes §244.12–244.15). The program requires that certain high-risk offenders be identified while in prison, and that those offenders be placed on intensive supervised release (ISR) upon release from prison. Offenders remain on ISR until they successfully complete the program or until they reach expiration of their sentence. ISR elements include house arrest, electronic monitoring (which may include GPS monitoring, which costs an additional $8–$13 per day, per offender), curfews, random drug/alcohol testing, unannounced residential and work visits by the supervising agent, a mandatory 40 hours per week of work/education, payment of supervision fees, and restitution to victims. Offenders are also required to comply with any special conditions of their release, which may include attending sex offender treatment, Alcoholics Anonymous, and/or anger management classes. ISR consists of six phases, but only level-three predatory offenders are required to complete phases five and six (see Minnesota Department of Corrections, 2012b).

Employment as a Probation Officer

To work as a probation officer (also referred to as corrections agent) for the state of Minnesota, an applicant must meet the following criteria: bachelor's degree in a criminal justice related field and the completion of either (1) a 400-hour internship, (2) two years of experience as a correctional officer/supervisor of Sentence to Serve crew leader, or (3) 6 months of professional level experience as a case manager. It is important to note that in Minnesota, a probation officer is not a licensed peace officer. In other states probation officers are certified by the state's Peace Officer Standards and Training Board. Among other things, this means probation officers in Minnesota are not armed. The salary range is $19 to $27 per hour (Department of Corrections, 2014). The requirements to work in a county as a probation officer are county-specific. The largest county in Minnesota, Hennepin, requires probation agents to have a master's degree in a criminal justice related field with an internship or a bachelor's degree with one year of paid/volunteer approved related experience. The salary range is $18 to $31 per hour for a probation officer, with senior and career probation officers making more (Hennepin County, 2015b).

The job duties of a state probation officer as outlined by the Department of Corrections (2014) include things like providing investigative services to the court, having releasing authority and supervisory and/or referral services to offenders, facilitating law abiding behavior, completing assessments of offenders to determine appropriate levels of supervision, preparing case plans, monitoring offenders in compliance with probation, completing progress reports and detention orders, and testifying in court as needed. If a defendant pleads guilty or is found guilty at trial, for example, a probation officer may be assigned to conduct an investigation before sentencing (known as a pre-sentence investigation or PSI). The probation officer gathers information about the possible sentence for the crime and additional information about the defendant. They may also gather information about the impact of the crime from the victim. The probation officer then gives a report to the judge with recommendations about sentencing.

The job duties of a county probation officer are essentially the same as outlined in **Figure 4.7**.

Figure 4.7. Job Duties of a Probation Officer

The Job Functions of a Probation Officer in Hennepin County, Minnesota

1. Carry an assigned caseload in the investigation and supervision of adult or juvenile offenders under the jurisdiction of the Hennepin County District Court or the jurisdiction of the Minnesota Department of Corrections for adult and juvenile offenders placed on supervised release from state correctional facilities.

2. Evaluate clients to determine initial risk and needs, interpret and assess information to develop treatment or case plans, and make referrals to community/treatment resources when necessary.

3. Conduct on-going motivational interviewing, assess client's readiness for change, and engage client in change process.

4. Provide counseling in relation to personal adjustment and needs for stability, life planning, and compliance with probation and supervised release conditions.

5. Conduct investigations, prepare and write formal court reports, and work with clients to formulate plans for probation. Present recommendations of conditions for probation and/or supervised release to the court.

6. Collaborate with related providers to assess needs, performance, progress, and behavior.

7. Arrange for court appearances for client and families, transporting individuals when necessary.

8. Communicate with other community justice partners regarding clients, including providing information to law enforcement recommending arrest or detention.

9. Maintain accurate documentation of case activity, utilizing department and offender data systems.

10. Recommend revocation, modification, or early dismissal of probation or supervised release as appropriate.

11. Where appropriate, provide on-going monitoring and reporting of client's progress and adjustment as well as service provided by other agencies as a part of the probation or supervised release plan.

12. May be involved in integrated, multidisciplinary or community initiatives and may be housed at community based sites including serving as a liaison between Hennepin County and communities, community organizations, schools, health professionals and service providers and identifying needs and assisting in resolving problems facing individuals and families regarding health and human services issues (including but not limited to housing, employment, financial assistance, and behavioral health).

Source: Hennepin County Job Classification (2015).

Other Issues in Corrections

Cost of Corrections

Like elsewhere, the cost of corrections in Minnesota is not cheap. Minnesota Statutes § 241.018 requires annual reporting of the average department-wide cost per diem of incarcerating inmates in state, county, and regional facilities. In 2013, the general fund budget for the Minnesota Department of Corrections was $481,470,000 (Minnesota Department of Corrections, 2013). In 2010, Minnesota spent an average of $41,364 per inmate. Compared to nationally, this is almost $10,000 more per inmate, with the average cost being $31,286 and more than in the neighboring states of Wisconsin at $37,944, Iowa at $32,925, and North Dakota at $39,271 (Vera Institute, 2012). Minnesota has the 14th highest cost per inmate in the U.S., with Kentucky the lowest at $14,603 and New York the highest at $60,076 (National Institute of Corrections, 2015). These costs not only include the direct cost of the prisons, but also expenditures like administrative costs, employee benefits and taxes, pension contributions, retiree healthcare contributions, capital costs, judgment claims, hospital services, underfunded pensions, and education and training (Vera Institute, 2012).

In reviewing the state's comprehensive financial report from 2010–2014 as a whole, the spending on public safety and corrections is slightly increasing, however, when compared to expenditures in general education, the increase is modest. Minnesota spends significantly more money on general education than on corrections and public safety, however, when looking at higher education in particular, the expenditures are slightly greater for public safety and corrections.

Table 4.7. Expenditures in Minnesota from 2010–2014 (in U.S. dollars)

Year	Public Safety and Corrections (in thousands)	General Education (in thousands)	Higher Education (in thousands)
2010	958,915	8,042,744	981,859
2011	976,261	7,499,159	892,921
2012	952,585	7,890,863	795,389
2013	970,095	8,207,311	849,510
2014	998,054	9,048,212	912,083

Source: Author created from information obtained from Minnesota Management and Budget.

One factor that must be recognized when looking at the costs of prison is healthcare costs. The Pew Chartable Trust (2014) highlights that the three main reasons for growing health expenses are: "(1) aging inmate population, (2) prevalence of infectious and chronic diseases, mental illness, and substance abuse among inmates, many of whom enter prison with these problems, and (3) challenges inherent in delivering health care in prisons, such as distance from hospitals and other providers." Prisoners have a constitutionally guaranteed right to healthcare, therefore, they must be treated. This fact was very publically highlighted when an escaped prisoner, Clarence Moore, who had been on the run for 39 years, turned himself in to the local authorities in April 2015 because he needed healthcare (Johnson, 2015). The ACLU (2012) estimates that releasing elderly prisoners could save an average of $66,294 per inmate. Furthermore, it estimates the cost to incarcerate inmates 50 or more years old, who are relatively low-risk and who total fewer than 250,000 inmates in the U.S., equals $16 billion dollars. Some Minnesota inmates have medical costs that have exceeded $1 million (McEnroe, 2012).

Support Programs in Prisons and Jails

Minnesota prisons have been offering a multitude of programs to try and reduce recidivism, as well as help offenders with education, employment, and substance abuse issues. In 2013, Duwe provided a summary report of evaluations done on various prison programs within Minnesota's Department of Corrections. Results showed programs offered improved public safety, helped with post-release employment, and/or reduced costs to taxpayers. These programs include: (1) EMPLOY, (2) work-release, (3) educational degrees, (4) Minnesota Comprehensive Offender Re-entry Plan, (5) Interchange Freedom Initiative, (6) Minnesota Circles of Support and Accountability, (7) Challenge Incarcerated Program, (8) chemical dependency treatment, (9) sex offender treatment programs, and (10) Affordable Homes Program. After reviewing all of these evaluations, Duwe highlights common threads to include: programs that provided for pro-social support had a positive effect on reducing recidivism; programs that helped with criminal thinking patterns reduced recidivism; programs that targeted chemical abuse reduced recidivism; employment programs yielded higher employment; and that continuum of care from prison to the community was important (Duwe, 2013). The programs highlighted are a sampling of some of the programs available in the DOC, but the list is not exhaustive. Thinking for a Change, which is a cognitive skills building class, Read to Me, which allows inmates to record themselves reading a book that can then be given to their children, and Minnesota Prison

Writing Workshop, which provides all kinds of opportunities for writing in various styles and publishes a literary journal, are other examples.

Support Programs in the Community

There are many non-profit organizations in Minnesota that work directly with offenders while in prison, during their re-entry period, and/or after care to try and help reduce the likelihood of recidivism. Employment is a major factor in helping offenders not recidivate and as such, there are community organizations and groups that work towards this end. For example, the Second Chance Coalition is a partnership of organizations that "advocate for fair and responsible laws, policies, and practices that allow those who have committed crimes to redeem themselves, fully support themselves and their families, and contribute to their communities to their full potential" (Second Chance Coalition, 2015). Some of the recent initiatives they are working on include trying to restore voting privileges, reduce the severity of drug offenses, reduce prison gerrymandering, and rename the crime of "terroristic threats."

Another organization that helps offenders secure employment is Goodwill Easter Seals of Minnesota. Their reentry services start while offenders are incarcerated and continue after release to include such things as advocacy, community resources, employer relationships and education, an employment readiness program, individual case management, mental health/cognitive skills training, mentoring, and a motivational job coach (Easter Seals MN, 2015). Through intensive case management, support with job skills training, support in employment, housing, transportation, and pro-social activities, SOAR's Community Offender Re-entry Program (CORP) helps offenders transition back into the community. In 2012, SOAR worked with 592 offenders in the community on employment and job skills training and provided reentry services to 85 offenders to include services related to sobriety, family relationships, financial responsibility, and pro-social relationships. SOAR participants had a 16% recidivism rate (SOAR Career Solutions, 2012). Amicus is another organization that has a program, Amicus Reconnect, which helps anyone with a criminal record to try and work through the challenges that comes with having a criminal past (Amicus, 2015). They also administer Sisters Helping Sisters to support women prior to and after release to build confidence, have a positive outlook, and live a healthy lifestyle. As with programs inside the prison, the above is sampling of the many organizations and programs that work with offenders in the community.

Professional Organizations

There are several professional organizations that directly assist those individuals who work in a corrections capacity. Some of these organizations and their related function include the following:

- *Minnesota Community Corrections Association*'s purpose is to promote "professionalism and collaboration among individuals and agencies working within community corrections."
- *Minnesota Association of County Probationers*' purpose is to "support the preservation and expansion of professional probation and adjunctive services to the courts of Minnesota ..."
- *Minnesota Restorative Services Coalition*'s purpose is to "promote restorative philosophy and quality restorative services for individuals, communities, and organizations."
- *Minnesota Association of Community Corrections Act Counties* has several main functions including (1) providing a forum to exchange information and resources among the 32 Act Counties, (2) developing policy recommendations, and (3) coordinating and facilitating interaction with the Department of Corrections.
- The *Minnesota Association of Pretrial Services*' purpose is to "create a more safe and just criminal justice system by providing quality training to our members, promoting information to improve pretrial programs and promoting the importance of pretrial services in Minnesota."

Pardons/Commutation/Pardon Extraordinary/ Expungement

In Minnesota, pardons/commutation/pardon extraordinary can be granted under Minnesota Statutes § 638.01 for any criminal offense. A board, consisting of the governor, the chief justice of the Supreme Court, and the attorney general meet two times a year to review applications. A *pardon* is defined as an "act of forgiveness that exempts the convicted person from the punishment imposed by the law." A *commutation* is the "substitution of a lesser or different type of punishment for that imposed in the original sentence." A *pardon extraordinary* is a statutory release. When one is granted, the consequences of criminal convictions are removed. The applicant is "no longer required to report the conviction, except in specific limited circumstances." A convicted offender can apply after it has been ten years since the sentence expired for a violent offense and five years for any other crimes. The board cannot grant these for federal crimes, crimes committed in other states, or crimes committed in foreign countries (Minnesota Department of Corrections, 2015b). As illustrated in **Table 4.8**, pardons or commutations are extremely rare occurrences and pardon/pardon extraordinary are granted on average in less than a third of the cases that applied. An *expungement* is when an offender requests his/her record to be sealed. The records are not destroyed and law enforcement agencies and other public officials can still access them in special cases. Expungements are made possible through Minnesota Statutes § 609A.02 in specified situations such as for drug possession offenses or offenses committed while a juvenile, but tried as an adult. It is should also be noted there is an Innocence Project in Minnesota. They "represent people who were wrongfully convicted for crimes they did not commit, educate attorneys and criminal justice professionals on best practices, and work to reform the procedures that produce such unjust results" (Innocence Project, 2015). At a nationwide level, their efforts have helped over 325 people, serving an average of 13.5 years in prison for a crime they didn't commit, become free (Innocence Project, 2015). See **Chapter One** for an example of a case from Minnesota.

Table 4.8. Minnesota Board of Pardons Activities from 2009–2013

	Applications Requested	Applications Considered/ Pardon Extraordinary or Pardon Extraordinary Waiver of Waiting Period Granted	Applications Considered/ Pardon or Commutation Granted
2013	125	48/11	7/0
2012	117	57/21	16/0
2011	32	45/17	9/0
2010	178	56/18	6/0
2009	175	34/10	7/0

Source: Author created from Annual Reports of the Minnesota Board of Pardons.

Prison Rape Elimination Act (PREA)

In 2003, the Prison Rape Elimination Act took effect in order to eliminate sexual abuse in confinement. As part of this act, a National Standards document was developed to prevent, detect, and respond to prison rape, taking effect in 2012. There are two separate standards: one for adult facilities and another for juvenile facilities (Department of Justice, 2012a; Department of Justice, 2012b). The National PREA Resource Center (2015) provides correctional personnel assistance with the implementation by outlining 12 essential components of these standards that the facilities must address. These include: (1) prevention planning, (2) responsive planning, (3) training and education, (4) screening for risk of sexual victimization and abusiveness, (5) reporting, (6) official response following an inmate/detainee/resident report, (7) investigations, (8) discipline, (9) medical and mental care, (10) data collection and review, (11) audits and state compliance, and (12) other issues including LGBTI and gender-nonconforming inmates and culture change.

The Minnesota Department of Corrections PREA Policy is 202.057 and it states:

> All employees, contractors, and volunteers are expected to have a clear understanding that the Department strictly prohibits any type of sexual relationship with an individual under the Department's supervision, and considers such a relationship a breach of the employee code of conduct. These relationships will not be tolerated. Mandatory staff training and offender education is provided to convey the expectation. (Minnesota Department of Corrections, 2015c)

The Minnesota DOC has a zero tolerance policy on sexual misconduct. It provides inmates with an offender brochure outlining their rights and responsibilities. Each facility has a compliance manager and there is a coordinator that oversees the DOC to make sure it is in compliance with PREA. Jails also must be in compliance with PREA, and like the state facilities, are audited to make sure they meet PREA standards.

Conclusion

While a review of the entire corrections system in Minnesota cannot be accomplished in one chapter, this chapter provided a survey of some of the statistics, structure, programs, employment, history, and legislation that is part of the landscape of corrections. Corrections is multifaceted and an important part of what makes up the criminal justice system. The ultimate goal, of course, is to have less need for corrections, because that would be an indication there is less crime.

Key Terms

Advisory Groups in Corrections
Amicus
Ban the Box
Commissioner of Corrections
Community Corrections Act
Commutation
Correction Officer
Determinate Sentencing
Disproportionate Minority Contact
   Act
Doula Services
Expungement
Innocence Project
Intermediate Sanctions
Jail
Pardon

Parole/Supervised Release
PREA
Prison
Prison Costs
Private Prisons
Programming in Prisons
Programming in the Community
Re-entry Programs
Religion in Prison
Second Chance Coalition
Sentencing to Serve
Transition from Jail to Community
   (TJC) Initiative
Work Crew
Work Release

Discussion Questions

1. What are the benefits of supervised release over incarceration?
2. What do you think the benefits/drawbacks are of private prisons?
3. What services do you think are critical for offenders to have available to them as they re-enter society to help reduce recidivism? Why?
4. Do you think states and the federal government should release older (age 65 and up) offenders into the community? If yes, at what age and for what type of offenses?
5. Are pardons a good thing for the government to offer? Why/why not?
6. Do you think expungement of records is a good practice? In what cases should they be used? Should it be automatic or an application process?
7. Do you think prisoners should earn money while working in prison? What are some arguments for and arguments against? How much should they be allowed to earn?
8. What do you think about infants in prison? Should mothers who give birth while in prison be allowed to keep their newborn in the facility? If yes, for how long?

9. What do you think about allowing religious head coverings and other religious items in prison and jail facilities? Do you think more should be done to help inmates to practice their religious beliefs?
10. Do you support Ban the Box? Why or why not?

Selected Webpages

Amicus
http://www.amicususa.org

American Civil Liberty Union
https://www.aclu.org

Goodwill Easter Seals of Minnesota
http://www.goodwilleasterseals.org/site/PageServer?pagename=serv_other_reentry

Hennepin County Adult Detention Center
http://www.hennepinsheriff.org/jail-gen-info

Innocence Project
http://ipmn.org/

Interstate Commission for Adult Offenders
http://www.interstatecompact.org

Minnesota Association of Community Corrections Act Counties
http://www.maccac.org

Minnesota Association of County Probation Officers
http://www.macpo.net

Minnesota Association of Pretrial Services
http://www.mapsa.us

Minnesota Community Corrections Association
http://www.mnmcca.com

Minnesota Department of Corrections
http://www.doc.state.mn.us/PAGES/

Minnesota Department of Human Rights
http://mn.gov/mdhr/index.html

Minnesota Revisor of Statutes
https://www.revisor.leg.state.mn.us

Minnesota Prison Writing Workshop
http://www.mnprisonwriting.org/who-we-are.html

National Institute of Corrections
http://nicic.gov/statestats/default.aspx?st=mn

National PREA Resource Center
http://www.prearesourcecenter.org/

Second Chance Coalition
http://www.mnsecondchancecoalition.org

Sentencing Project
http://www.sentencingproject.org/template/index.cfm

Transition from Jail to Community Initiative
http://www.urban.org/policy-centers/justice-policy-center/projects/transition-jail-community-tjc-initiative

References

Alexander, M. (2012). *The new Jim Crow: Mass incarceration in the age of colorblindness*. New York: The New Press.

American Civil Liberties Union. (2012). At America's expense: The mass incarceration of the elderly. Retrieved from http://www.aclu.org/files/assets/elderlyprisonreport_20120613_1.pdf

American Civil Liberties Union. (2014). Racial disparities in sentencing. Hearing on reports of racism in the justice system of the United States. Retrieved from https://www.aclu.org/sites/default/files/assets/141027_iachr_racial_disparities_aclu_submission_0.pdf

Amicus. (2015). One-to-One Program. Retrieved from http://www.amicus usa.org/programs/one-to-one/

Beccaria, C. ([1764] 1963). *On crimes and punishments*. Indianapolis, IN: Bobbs-Merrill.

Clear, J., & Pirius, R. (2008). Overview of Minnesota DWI laws. Minnesota House of Representatives. Retrieved from http://www.house.leg.state.mn.us/hrd/pubs/dwiover.pdf

Corrections Corporation of American. (2015). Our history. Retrieved from http://www.cca.com/our-history

Department of Justice, Bureau of Prisons. (2012). Admission and orientation booklet. Retrieved from http://www.bop.gov/locations/institutions/dth/DTH_aohandbook.pdf

Department of Justice. (2012a). Adult facility standards: United States Department of Justice final rule. National standards to prevent, detect, and respond to prison rape under the Prison Rape Elimination Act (PREA). Retrieved from http://www.doc.state.mn.us/pages/files/6313/9879/7157/Adult_Standards.pdf

Department of Justice. (2012b). Juvenile facility standards: United States Department of Justice final rule. National standards to prevent, detect, and respond to prison rape under the Prison Rape Elimination Act (PREA). Retrieved from http://www.doc.state.mn.us/pages/files/2413/9879/7158/Juvenile_PREA_Standards.pdf

Dunn, J. (1960). The Minnesota State Prison during the Stillwater Era, 1853–1914. *Minnesota Historical Society*. Retrieved from http://collections.mnhs.org/MNHistoryMagazine/articles/37/v37i04p137-151.pdf

Durkin, M. (2013, April 5). Duluth prison escapees arrested at Burnsville hotel. *My Fox 9 Twin Cities*. Retrieved from http://www.myfoxtwincities.com/story/21889482/duluth-prison-escapees-arrested-at-burnsville-hotel

Duwe, G. (2013). What works with Minnesota's prisoners: A summary of effects of correctional programming on reducing recidivism, employment, and cost avoidance. *Minnesota Department of Corrections*. Retrieved from http://www.doc.state.mn.us/pages/files/6213/9206/2384/What_Works_with_MN_Prisoners_July_2013.pdf

Duwe, G., & Clark, V. (2103). The effects of private prison confinement on offender recidivism: Evidence from Minnesota. *Criminal Justice Review*, 38(3), 375–394.

Duwe, G., & Johnson, C. (2013). Estimating the benefits of a faith-based correctional program. *International Journal of Criminology and Sociology*, 2, 227–239. Retrieved from http://www.baylorisr.org/wp-content/uploads/benefits_faith-based_correctional_program.pdf

Federal Bureau of Prisons. (2015a). Inmate Race. Retrieved from http://www.bop.gov/about/statistics/statistics_inmate_race.jsp

Federal Bureau of Prisons. (2015b). FMC Rochester. Retrieved from http://www.bop.gov/locations/institutions/rch/

Federal Bureau of Prisons. (2015c). Sentences imposed. Retrieved from http://www.bop.gov/about/statistics/statistics_inmate_sentences.jsp

Gerrity, E. (2013). Prison doulas: An innovative healthcare strategy for incarcerated women. Retrieved from http://www.extension.umn.edu/family/cyfc/our-programs/lessons-from-the-field/traumatic-stress-series/docs/13nov13/gerrity.pdf

Glaze, L., & Kaeble, D. (2014). Correctional populations in the United States, 2013. U.S. Department of Justice, Bureau Statistics. NCJ 248479.

Goodwill Easter Seals Minnesota. (2015). Reentry services. Retrieved from http://www.goodwilleasterseals.org/site/PageServer?pagename=serv_other _reentry

Hennepin County. (2015a). Juvenile detention center. Retrieved from http:// www.hennepin.us/residents/public-safety/juvenile-detention-center

Hennepin County. (2015b). Job classification. Retrieved from http:// www.hennepin.us/jobs/job-classifications

Hennepin County. (2015c). Adult correction facility. Retrieved from http:// www.hennepin.us/residents/public-safety/adult-corrections-facility

Hennepin County Sheriff's Office. (2015). Jail general information. Retrieved from http://www.hennepinsheriff.org/jail-gen-info

Holt v. Hobbs. 574 US _____ (2015).

Innocence Project. (2015). What we do. Retrieved from http://ipmn.org/ what-we-do/

International Center for Prison Studies. (2015). Highest to lowest prison population rate. Retrieved from http://www.prisonstudies.org/highest-to-lowest/ prison_population_rate?field_region_taxonomy_tid=All

Johnson, A. (2015, April 22). Escaped prisoner turns himself in after 39 years for the health care. *NBC News*. Retrieved from http://www.nbcnews.com/ news/us-news/escaped-prisoner-turns-himself-after-39-years-health-care-n345986

Lee v. Weisman, (1992). 505 U.S. 577, 578, 112 S. Ct. 2649, 2655, 120 L. Ed. 2d 467, 480.

Lyden, T. (2015, February 5). Minnesota man who left to join Al-Shabaab is getting out of prison. *KMSP-TV*. Retrieved from http://www.myfoxtwin cities.com/story/28027307/minnesota-man-who-left-to-join-al-shabaab-is-getting-out-of-prison

Maranell, S. (2013, December 12). Volunteers at FCI–Waseca let inmates know that their crime does not define them. Retrieved from http://www.south ernminn.com/waseca_county_news/news/article_b6a02d5f-2e23-5f55-8100-8328b975f7c7.html

McEnroe, P. (2012, April 1). Minnesota's million-dollar inmates. *Star Tribune*. http://www.startribune.com/local/145445035.html

Minnesota Association of Community Corrections Act Counties. (2015). Retrieved from http://www.maccac.org

Minnesota Association of County Probation Officers. (2015). Retrieved from http://www.macpo.net

Minnesota Association of Pretrial Services. (2015). Retrieved from http:// www.mapsa.us

Minnesota Community Corrections Association. (2015). Retrieved from http://www.mnmcca.com

Minnesota Department of Corrections. (1973). Implementation guidelines for the Community Corrections Act of 1973. Retrieved from http://archive.leg.state.mn.us/docs/2010/other/101397.pdf

Minnesota Department of Corrections. (2010). Policy 204.040. Retrieved from http://www.doc.state.mn.us/DocPolicy2/html/DPW_Display_TOC.asp?Opt=204.040.htm

Minnesota Department of Corrections. (2011). Sentencing to Service. Retrieved from: http://doc.state.mn.us/PAGES/files/2614/1279/3637/2-7-14_STS.pdf

Minnesota Department of Corrections. (2012a). *Education overview.* St. Paul, MN. Retrieved from http://www.doc.state.mn.us/pages/files/large-files/Publications/06-12MCECEducationOverview.pdf

Minnesota Department of Corrections. (2012b). *Fact sheet: Intensive supervised release.* St. Paul, MN. Retrieved from: http://www.doc.state.mn.us/pages/files/3113/8694/8314/ISRFactSheet.pdf

Minnesota Department of Corrections. (2013a). Notable statistics, Minnesota Department of Corrections. Retrieved from: http://www.doc.state.mn.us/PAGES/files/6814/1140/1719/notablestatistics.pdf

Minnesota Department of Corrections. (2013b). Institution/Community Work Crew Program. Retrieved from: http://www.doc.state.mn.us/PAGES/files/6113/7971/2216/09-13_ICWC.pdf

Minnesota Department of Corrections. (2014a). Correctional delivery systems. Retrieved from: http://www.doc.state.mn.us/pages/files/5613/9878/6654/DeliverySystemsFactSheet.pdf

Minnesota Department of Corrections. (2014b). Work release fact sheet. Retrieved from: http://doc.state.mn.us/PAGES/files/8514/1279/3663/Work_Release_Fact_Sheet.pdf

Minnesota Department of Corrections. (2014c). Notable statistics. Retrieved from http://www.doc.state.mn.us/PAGES/files/6814/1140/1719/notablestatistics.pdf

Minnesota Department of Corrections. (2014d). Policy 202.045. Retrieved from http://www.doc.state.mn.us/DocPolicy2/html/DPW_Display_TOC.asp?Opt=202.045.htm

Minnesota Department of Corrections. (2015a). Advisory task force on female offenders. Retrieved from: https://forums.doc.state.mn.us/site/fo/default.aspx

Minnesota Department of Corrections. (2015b). Pardon boards. Retrieved from: http://www.doc.state.mn.us/pages/index.php/board-pardons/

Minnesota Department of Corrections. (2015c). PREA information. Retrieved from http://www.doc.state.mn.us/pages/index.php/family-visitor/prea-policy/

Minnesota Department of Corrections. (2015d). Religious programming. Retrieved from: http://www.doc.state.mn.us/DOcpolicy2/html/DPW_Display.asp?Opt=302.300.htm

Minnesota Department of Human Rights. (2013). *Ban the box: Overview for private employers.* Retrieved from http://mn.gov/mdhr/employers/ban box_overview_privemp.html

Minnesota Management and Budget. (2014). Comprehensive annual financial reports from 2010 to 2014. Retrieved from http://www.mn.gov/mmb/accounting/reports/comprehensive-annual.jsp

Minnesota Restorative Services Coalition. (2015). Retrieved from http://www.mnmrsc.org

Minnesota Sentencing Guideline Commission. (2014). 2013 sentencing practices: Annual summary statistics for felony offenders. Retrieved from http://mn.gov/sentencing-guidelines/images/2013%2520Data%2520Report%2520Updated.pdf

National Institute of Corrections. (2015). Correction statistics by state. Retrieved from http://nicic.gov/statestats/default.aspx?st=mn

Office of the Revisor of Statutes. (2014). *2014 Minnesota session laws* (Chapter 234—S.F.No. 2423). Retrieved from: https://www.revisor.mn.gov/laws/?id=234&year=2014&type=0

Pew Charitable Trusts. (2012, June 6). Time served in Minnesota. Retrieved from http://www.pewtrusts.org/en/research-and-analysis/fact-sheets/2012/06/06/time-served-in-minnesota

Pew Charitable Trusts. (2014, May 15). Managing prison health care spending. Retrieved from http://www.pewtrusts.org/en/research-and-analysis/reports/2014/05/15/managing-prison-health-care-spending

PREA Resource Center. (2015). PREA essentials. Retrieved from http://www.prearesourcecenter.org/training-technical-assistance/prea-essentials

Ramsey County. (2015). Detention services. Retrieved from http://www.co.ramsey.mn.us/sheriff/adc/index.htm

Roy, T. (2013). Commissioner letter to House of Representatives on advisory groups. Retrieved from http://www.commissions.leg.state.mn.us/lcpfp/advisory_groups/2013/DOC_AdvisoryGroups.pdf

Sakala, L. (2014). Breaking down mass incarceration in the 2010 Census: State-by-state incarceration rates by race/ethnicity. *Prison Policy Initiative.* Retrieved from http://www.prisonpolicy.org/reports/rates.html

Second Chance Coalition. (2015). 2015 legislative priorities. Retrieved from http://www.mnsecondchancecoalition.org/policy.php

Sentencing Project. (2015). Prison population 1980–2011. Retrieved from http://www.sentencingproject.org/map/map.cfm

Skarbek, D. (2014). *The social order of the underworld: How prison gangs govern the American penal system.* New York: Oxford University Press.

SOAR Career Solutions. (2013). The cost of living. SOAR Career Solutions 2012–2103 Annual Report. Retrieved from http://www.soarcareers.org/documents/2013_soarAnnualReport_Final.pdf

Stafford, M. C. & Warr, M. (1993). A reconceptualization of general and specific deterrence. *Journal of Research in Crime and Delinquency,* 30, 123–135.

Steil, M. (2010, January 8). Tough economy forces shutdown of Appleton prison. *Minnesota Public News.* Retrieved from http://www.mprnews.org/story/2010/01/08/appleton-prison-closing

Stephan, J., & Walsh, G. (2011). Census of jail facilities, 2006. Bureau of Justice Statistics. NCJ 230188.

Stuntz, W. (2011). *The collapse of American criminal justice.* Cambridge, MA: Harvard University Press.

Sykes, G. (1958). *The society of captives: A study of a maximum security prison.* Princeton, NJ: Princeton University Press.

Taub, D. (2010, May 11). Corrections Corp. shows crime pays with private jails. *Bloomberg Business.* Retrieved from http://www.bloomberg.com/news/articles/2010-05-11/corrections-corp-shows-crime-does-pay-as-states-turn-to-private-prisons

Travis, J., Western, B., & Redburn, S. (2014). *The growth of incarceration in the United States: Exploring causes and consequences.* Washington D.C.: National Research Council.

Urban Institute. (2012). Process and systems change evaluation findings from the Transition from Jail to Community Initiative. Retrieved from https://s3.amazonaws.com/static.nicic.gov/Library/026925.pdf

U.S. Census Bureau. (2015). State and county quick facts. Retrieved from http://quickfacts.census.gov/qfd/states/27000.html

U.S. Department of Justice. (2004). Federal Bureau of Prison's program statement on religious beliefs and practices. Retrieved from http://www.bop.gov/policy/progstat/5360_009.pdf

Vera Institute. (2012). The price of prisons. What incarceration costs taxpayers. Retrieved from http://www.vera.org/sites/default/files/resources/downloads/price-of-prisons-updated-version-021914.pdf von Hirsch, A. (1976). *Doing justice: The choice of punishments.* New York: Hill and Wang.

Yuen, L. (2015, February 5). Former al-Shabab recruit turned witness to face deportation. *MPR News.* Retrieved from http://www.mprnews.org/story/2015/02/04/isse-released

Zimring, F. E., & Hawking, G. (1995). *Incapacitation: Penal confinement and the restraint of crime.* Oxford: Oxford University Press.

Chapter Five

Involuntarily Committed: Minnesota's System of Security Hospitals

Learning Objectives

- Explain the legal culpability of offenders afflicted by mental illness in Minnesota
- Describe the M'Naghten Rule and the Model Penal Code Rule for insanity defense
- Summarize the practice of civil commitment in Minnesota and distinguish it from criminal sanctions
- Identify and explain key court cases surrounding the issue of involuntary civil commitment
- Describe the history and factors associated with the civil commitment of sex offenders
- Explain the civil commitment legal process in Minnesota
- Identify conditions of eligibility for involuntary civil commitment
- Summarize the controversy surrounding Minnesota's record of releasing sex offenders from civil commitment
- Explain the concept of stigma
- Identify and describe Minnesota's security hospitals for the involuntarily committed

There has long been a fine line drawn between criminality and destructive or inappropriate acts resulting from mental illness. To the lay person, and even in many cases to the law enforcer, it is difficult to distinguish between someone whose actions are motivated by evil intent and another motivated by insatiable impulses. It is especially difficult when violent crime such as murder or rape is involved. There is such general revulsion in society against acts that viciously and undeservedly harm others that the causes behind the acts are somewhat secondary. What's more, society has a legitimate interest in preventing further acts of harm against the innocent; consequently, pragmatism moves society in a particular direction regardless of what might be going on inside an offender's head. That direction is incapacitation.

However, just what is going on inside an offender's head does in fact matter. It matters on many fronts. If an offender is acting on uncontrollable (or at least difficult to control) impulses, than the rational merit of punishment, rooted in the goal of deterring rationally chosen criminal behavior, fails to deliver for society. Similarly, the notion of punishment as justice for one's evil choices also falls short when an offender is not motivated by evil desires, but rather by mental or physiological pathology.

Indeed, the law in every state recognizes the possibility that some destructive acts—criminal in nature if committed by most people—are sometimes not criminal acts at all. For most crimes, there are two major elements: an unlawful act (*actus reus*) and an accompanying criminal intent (*mens rea*) (see **Chapter One**). The latter element goes to the offender's state of mind. There are many different legal defenses against the existence of criminal intent. Some of these relate to the capacity of one to formulate intent. For example, a five year old who shoots a sibling with a handgun found in the home will not be held criminally liable as a child that age is not accountable for errors in judgment. Even an older juvenile—in Minnesota, anyone under the age of 14— cannot be held *criminally* liable for his or her unlawful actions under any circumstances because the law finds their capacity for legal responsibility to be lacking. Instead, even an intentional, premeditated murder committed by a 13 year old in Minnesota is not a crime at all, but a delinquent act requiring correction. Likewise, most other crimes in Minnesota except for 1st degree murder, when committed by anyone under the age of 18, are deemed delinquent acts which come under the authority of the juvenile justice system because of a juvenile's legal incapacity to make criminal choices. See **Chapter Six**, Table 6.2 for the ages of criminal accountability by state.

Other defenses against a criminal state of mind relate to necessity. For example, if one is coerced or is under duress when committing a criminal act, there is nonetheless no crime as there is no criminal intent. An example might be a motorist who is carjacked by a bank robber and told to flee the police. The motorist will not be charged with fleeing, or aiding and abetting the robber because the motorist had no choice. Or, if one is out in the woods during a blizzard, comes across a vacant cabin, and breaks into the cabin in order to escape the elements, there is no burglary or trespassing here because there is no criminal intent; the break-in was necessary for survival.

Insanity Defense

Still another area of law protecting offenders who lack criminal intent relates to mental illness. In most states, including Minnesota, a criminal defendant deemed legally insane or mentally incapacitated at the time of the offense cannot be held criminal liable. Minnesota Statutes §611.026 reads:

> No person having a mental illness or cognitive impairment so as to be incapable of understanding the proceedings or making a defense shall be tried, sentenced, or punished for any crime; but the person shall not be excused from criminal liability except upon proof that at the time of committing the alleged criminal act the person was laboring under such a defect of reason, from one of these causes, as not to know the nature of the act, or that it was wrong.

To paraphrase the statute, one cannot be tried for a crime or punished for a crime if one has a mental defect which impedes their ability to understand the proceedings. Further, one cannot be held liable for a criminal act if at the time of commission the offender suffered from a mental defect preventing him or her knowing right from wrong.

This is a high bar to meet if you are a defendant or a defense attorney representing such a defendant. The defendant has the burden of proof if an insanity or mental illness defense is going to be offered in court. This is different than most cases in which all burden of proof lies with the prosecutor and the defense need not prove or disprove anything. Further, even if the existence of a mental defect can be established, one still must show that the defect caused the defendant to not know right from wrong. One might be driven by mental, emotional, or physiological impulses which are difficult to control, but if one knows they are to be controlled nonetheless, then one knows right from wrong. If an offender does everything he or she can to evade capture, it will be difficult to argue that he or she did not know the action was wrong in the first place.

One of the most famous insanity defense cases in the United States was that of John Hinckley, who attempted to assassinate President Ronald Reagan in 1981. On March 30, 1981, Hinckley waited outside of the Washington Hilton Hotel where President Reagan had given a speech. Upon President Reagan's emergence from the hotel on his way to his limousine, Hinckley fired several shots with a pistol in the president's direction. He gravely wounded President Reagan, Press Secretary James Brady, Secret Service agent Timothy McCarthy, and Washington DC police officer Thomas Delahanty, before being subdued. All four victims survived, although James Brady suffered permanent brain damage. Evidence at Hinckley's federal trial showed that he had an obsession for actress Jodie Foster. He believed Foster would be pleased at the death of President Reagan and attempted the assassination as a way to win her affection. Hinckley was found not guilty by reason of insanity and was turned over to the custody of a mental hospital for treatment.

Minnesota's law regarding the insanity defense is consistent with the so-called M'Naghten Rule which is subscribed to, in some form, by many states around the country. The emphasis is on the defendant's lack of knowledge of right from wrong at the time of the offense was committed. Some other states have adopted the standard found in the Model Penal Code, developed in the early 1960s. The insanity standard was relaxed. Instead of an inability to know right from wrong, the standard was relaxed to a "substantial incapacity to appreciate right from wrong" (Collins, Hinkebein, & Schorgl, n.d.). A small number of states do not permit an absolution due to insanity at all. Rather, they permit an offender to be found guilty of a crime although legally insane. In these instances, there is still criminal culpability assigned to the offender, along with some combination of punishment and treatment.

Indeed, many criminal offenders have been held criminally liable for their actions despite suffering from some form or another of mental illness. But just how prevalent is mental illness among criminal offenders? In 2005, the U.S. Department of Justice conducted the most recent comprehensive review of mental illness among the incarcerated. The study found that over half of America's prisoners suffered from some form of mental illness. This included nearly 79,000 federal prisoners, 705,600 state prisoners, and 479,900 behind bars in local jails (James & Glaze, 2006). The study relied on self-reported symptoms and matched them against criteria drawn from the *Diagnostic and Statistical Manual of Mental Disorders*, 4th edition (DSM-IV) to indicate the presence of major depression, mania, and psychotic disorders. The *Diagnostic and Statistical Manual of Mental Disorders* is a publication, periodically updated, which serves as the professional standard for classifying mental disorders in the United States.

In the Department of Justice study, major depression included symptoms such as unending sadness, a loss of interest in activities, and insomnia. Symptoms of mania included psychomotor agitation, persistent anger, and constant irritability. Psychotic disorders were identified by signs of delusions or hallucinations. Delusions were defined by the sincere belief of the offenders that other people were controlling their thoughts, could read their minds, or they were being spied on. Hallucinations were indicated by reports of offenders seeing or hearing things that other people around them did not see or hear (James & Glaze, 2006).

Other studies have also been done on smaller scales to gauge the level of mental illness among inmates and those under correctional supervision in the community. Steadman, Osher, Clark Robbins, Case, and Samuels (2009) examined

Table 5.1. Current Basis of Insanity Defense Among the States

Alabama	M'Naghten Rule. The burden of proof is on the defendant.
Alaska	M'Naghten Rule. The burden of proof is on the defendant. A guilty but mentally ill verdict is allowed.
Arizona	M'Naghten Rule. The burden of proof is on the defendant. A guilty but mentally ill verdict is allowed.
Arkansas	Model Penal Code rule. The burden of proof is on the defendant.
California	M'Naghten Rule. The burden of proof is on the defendant.
Colorado	M'Naghten Rule. The burden of proof is on the state.
Connecticut	Model Penal Code rule. The burden of proof is on the defendant.
Delaware	Model Penal Code rule. The burden of proof is on the defendant.
District of Columbia	Model Penal Code rule. The burden of proof is on the defendant.
Florida	M'Naghten Rule. The burden of proof is on the state.
Georgia	M'Naghten Rule. The burden of proof is on the defendant. A guilty but mentally ill verdict is allowed.
Hawaii	Model Penal Code rule. The burden of proof is on the defendant.
Idaho	No insanity defense available. The state allows a guilty but insane verdict.
Illinois	Model Penal Code rule. The burden of proof is on the defendant.
Indiana	Model Penal Code rule. The burden of proof is on the defendant.
Iowa	M'Naghten Rule. The burden of proof is on the defendant.
Kansas	No insanity defense available.
Kentucky	Model Penal Code rule. The burden of proof is on the defendant.
Louisiana	M'Naghten Rule. The burden of proof is on the defendant.
Maine	Model Penal Code rule. The burden of proof is on the defendant.
Maryland	Model Penal Code rule. The burden of proof is on the defendant.
Massachusetts	Model Penal Code rule. The burden of proof is on the state.
Michigan	Model Penal Code rule. The burden of proof is on the state.
Minnesota	M'Naghten Rule. The burden of proof is on the defendant.
Mississippi	M'Naghten Rule. The burden of proof is on the state.
Missouri	M'Naghten Rule. The burden of proof is on the defendant.
Montana	No insanity defense available. Guilty but insane verdict is allowed.
Nebraska	M'Naghten Rule. The burden of proof is on the defendant.
Nevada	M'Naghten Rule. The burden of proof is on the defendant.
New Hampshire	Durham standard, which simply asks whether the accused acted because of a mental disorder. The burden of proof is on the defendant.
New Jersey	M'Naghten Rule. The burden of proof is on the state.
New Mexico	M'Naghten Rule. The burden of proof is on the state.
New York	Model Penal Code rule. The burden of proof is on the defendant.
North Carolina	M'Naghten Rule. The burden of proof is on the defendant.

Table 5.1. Current Basis of Insanity Defense Among the States, *continued*

North Dakota	Model Penal Code rule. The burden of proof is on the state.
Ohio	M'Naghten Rule. The burden of proof is on the defendant.
Oklahoma	M'Naghten Rule. The burden of proof is on the state.
Oregon	Model Penal Code rule. The burden of proof is on the defendant.
Pennsylvania	M'Naghten Rule. The burden of proof is on the defendant.
Rhode Island	Model Penal Code rule. The burden of proof is on the defendant.
South Carolina	M'Naghten Rule. The burden of proof is on the defendant.
South Dakota	M'Naghten Rule. The burden of proof is on the defendant.
Tennessee	Model Penal Code rule. The burden of proof is on the state.
Texas	M'Naghten Rule. The burden of proof is on the defendant.
Utah	No insanity defense available. Guilty but mentally ill verdicts are allowed.
Vermont	Model Penal Code rule. The burden of proof is on the defendant.
Virginia	M'Naghten Rule. The burden of proof is on the defendant.
Washington	M'Naghten Rule. The burden of proof is on the defendant.
West Virginia	Model Penal Code rule. The burden of proof is on the state.
Wisconsin	Model Penal Code rule. The burden of proof is on the defendant.
Wyoming	Model Penal Code rule. The burden of proof is on the defendant.

Source: http://criminal.findlaw.com

the prevalence of serious mental illness among a sample of male and female inmates at the Cook County (Chicago, IL) jail. Their baseline numbers were drawn from the routine assessments which were done at the Cook County jail to determine the mental health status of inmates. Through extrapolation, they estimated that 51% of the U.S. jail population suffered from serious mental illness (Steadman, et al., 2009).

Obviously, the numbers suggest that most offenders who have mental illness are not routinely excused by the law from their criminal liability. In most cases, the mental illnesses that offenders suffer from were not compelling explanations for criminal behavior to be deemed as lacking *mens rea*. However, in some cases the mental illness is a compelling explanation for unlawful, violent behavior. In those cases, particularly when criminal sanctions are not an option, or are no longer an option, the use of involuntary civil commitment has shored up society's desire to incapacitate the dangerous.

Civil Commitment

Civil commitment is defined as "the state-sanctioned involuntary hospitalization of individuals with mental disorders who require treatment, care, or incapacitation because of self-harming or dangerous tendencies" (Melton, Petrila, Poythress, & Slobogin, 2007, p. 325). Every state in the United States, and the federal government, have civil commitment laws which permit the involuntary hospitalization of individuals with one or more mental disorders. Approximately half of the states have laws which further provide for the specific and indeterminate hospitalization of predatory sex offenders deemed to be dangerous (Miller, 2010). Hospitalization in these cases typically involve placement in secure, somewhat prison-like treatment facilities.

History of Civil Commitment

The practice of civil commitment has existed in one fashion or another in the United States throughout its history. The first hospitals established exclusively to mentally ill patients emerged in colonial America in 1773 (Quanbeck, 2014). At various times during the 19th and 20th centuries, laws were passed in a number of states to reform, and then re-reform, the civil commitment process. Reform efforts often resulted in cosmetic rather than substantive changes in civil commitment laws, the improvement of existing facilities, and the building of new ones (Quanbeck, 2014).

Just as state legislatures have evolved on this issue around the country, crafting and implementing various reforms regarding the conditions and circumstances in which commitment and treatment occur, so to have the courts in their analyses of who should be involuntarily committed, what conditions should be in place while in treatment, and under what circumstances should such individuals be released. Today in the United States, for a person to be involuntarily committed into a mental health facility, those seeking the commitment must secure a court order to require it. Courts will give a commitment order to ensure that two goals are accomplished (National Alliance on Mental Illness, 2006):

1. the treatment of individuals with mental illness when they (the patients) are unable or unwilling to seek treatment voluntarily; and
2. to protect the person with mental illness and others from harm due to the illness.

However, the courts have long wrestled with the processes the judiciary uses, as well as those relied upon by government guardians and mental health professionals, to identify just when success has actually been achieved.

In Minnesota, there has been considerable controversy surrounding the state's civil commitment process and practices. The controversy culminated in a 2015 federal class action lawsuit against the Minnesota Department of Human Services and the state's two security hospitals. The lawsuit will be discussed in further detail later in this chapter. But suffice to say, there is a bedrock of major court cases relating to involuntary civil commitment which have preceded the Minnesota experience. Many significant Supreme Court cases have informed the notions of due process and what constitutes treatment success, and therefore the end-game, in the area of involuntary civil commitment. The most significant case law has emerged since the 1970s. In the cases of *Jackson v. Indiana* (1972) and *O'Connor v. Donaldson* (1975), the Supreme Court made it clear that indefinite involuntary commitment is not a blank check by which the government can keep people confined. In *Jackson*, the Court said that mentally ill defendants who are deemed incompetent to stand trial cannot be indefinitely committed on that basis alone. Rather, the nature and duration of civil commitment must bear a reasonable relationship to the purpose of the commitment (Mental Illness Policy Org, 2009).

In *O'Connor v. Donaldson*, the Court considered the appeal of a man who had been confined for nearly 15 years. The purpose of the confinement at a secure mental health facility was for "care, maintenance, and treatment." Over the years, the patient, Kenneth O'Connor, had repeatedly requested to be released from a Florida state hospital, but was denied. State hospital officials had insisted that state law permitted them to keep the "sick" in their custody indefinitely, despite the fact in this case that no treatments were be given to O'Connor and his release was not thought to be potentially harmful. State officials relied on their good-faith understanding of Florida law to shield them from a civil rights lawsuit by O'Connor under 42 USC 1983. A jury had found in favor of O'Connor, believing he was unjustifiably denied his right to liberty, and awarded him damages. A federal appellate court upheld the jury findings.

> The Supreme Court in the case affirmed the finding as well. The Court wrote in the case: [A] State cannot constitutionally confine, without more, a non-dangerous individual who is capable of surviving safely in freedom by himself or with the help of willing and responsible family members or friends, and since the jury found, upon ample evidence, that petitioner did so confine respondent, it properly concluded that petitioner had violated respondent's right to liberty.

Of course, *O'Connor v. Donaldson* involved the commitment of a patient who was not dangerous and evidently in no need of treatment at all. The Court did not foreclose on the indefinite commitment of dangerous persons with genuine mental health issues who pose a real risk to themselves or others. The inevitable question is, what standard should be used? Civil commitment proceedings had always been seen through the lens of civil law. Commitment proceedings were not criminal proceedings. Given this fact, the judicial community and public policy makers alike wrestled with the question of whether a judge or jury should require proof beyond a reasonable doubt that a person was a danger to himself or others and before one should be involuntarily committed. Was the traditional civil law standard of preponderance of the evidence sufficient for such a determination?

The Supreme Court answered that question with an emphatic "neither" in the case of *Addington v. Texas* (1979). The Supreme Court noted:

> The individual's liberty interest in the outcome of a civil commitment proceeding is of such weight and gravity, compared with the state's interests in providing care to its citizens who are unable, because of emotional disorders, to care for themselves and in protecting the community from the dangerous tendencies of some who are mentally ill, that due process requires the state to justify confinement by proof more substantial than a mere preponderance of the evidence.
>
> Due process does not require states to use the "beyond a reasonable doubt" standard of proof applicable in criminal prosecutions and delinquency proceedings ... The reasonable-doubt standard is inappropriate in civil commitment proceedings because, given the uncertainties of psychiatric diagnosis, it may impose a burden the state cannot meet and thereby erect an unreasonable barrier to needed medical treatment. The state should not be required to employ a standard of proof that may completely undercut its efforts to further the legitimate interests of both the state and the patient that are served by civil commitments.

But the Court also said:

> To meet due process demands in commitment proceedings, the standard of proof has to inform the fact-finder that the proof must be greater than the preponderance-of-the-evidence standard applicable to other categories of civil cases.

In the end, the Court landed on a new standard, in part because many states had legislatively adopted it. The Court declared that "clear and convincing evidence" would be the required threshold, under the 14th Amendment's due process protections, to justify the involuntary commitment of a person to a state mental hospital. The Court wrote:

Having concluded that the preponderance standard falls short of meeting the demands of due process and that the reasonable-doubt standard is not required, we turn to a middle level of burden of proof [i.e., clear and convincing evidence] that strikes a fair balance between the rights of the individual and the legitimate concerns of the state.

In subsequent years, the Court continued to define and refine notions of constitutionality regarding the involuntary commitment and treatment of mentally ill persons who may or may not pose a danger to themselves and society.

Civil Commitment of Sexual Predators

A somewhat unique sub-area of civil commitment law, with its own history and idiosyncrasies in application, regards the involuntary treatment and commitment of sex offenders—commonly after the prison terms for the underlying sex offense has already been served. The legislative history regarding the civil commitment of sex offenders in the United States extends back to the early part of the 20th century. As early as 1911, state legislatures were defining sex offenders as "defective" delinquents and criminal "psychopaths" (Miller, 2010). In the 1930s, state legislatures began to pass laws for the civil commitment of sex offenders. This coincided with the emerging medical view of crime and the emphasis on corrections and treatment rather than punishment. Miller (2010) noted that by 1960, 26 states and the District of Columbia had special laws authorizing the civil commitment of those whom the courts had deemed sexual psychopaths. At that time, such civil commitments were an alternative to criminal sentencing, rather than a treatment that would follow the serving of a criminal sentence. Sexual psychopath laws of the kind described above eventually were repealed given that offenders had not shown promise in response to treatments. Increasingly, laws reverted to harsh, determinant criminal sentences for sex offenders (James, Thomas, & Foley, 2008).

In the 1990s, states began to reexamine the utility of a treatment model approach to sexual predators. In 1990, the state of Washington passed the first new-generation civil commitment law for sex offenders. Other states followed suit. By 2010, 20 states had adopted predatory sexual offender involuntary commitment laws (Miller, 2010). Among the states pursuing this approach early-on was Kansas.

In 1994, the state of Kansas passed the Sexually Violent Predator Act. The legislation established procedures for the state to follow by which individuals with a mental or personality disorder which induces predatory sexual violence could be involuntarily committed after serving one's sentence for a sex crime. The first person ever involuntarily committed as a sexual predator under this act was Leroy Hendricks, who had been in prison for a sex offense and had a significant history of molesting children. As a result of a jury trial, Hendricks was committed to a secure state hospital immediately upon his release from prison, having served his sentence there. Hendricks challenged his involuntary and indefinite commitment on the grounds that his 14th amendment due process rights had been violated. He argued that the new trial resulting in his commitment constituted double jeopardy. Additionally, he argued the fact that the Kansas law was passed after he committed the acts which resulted in his commitment was an *ex post facto* law (*Kansas v. Hendricks*, 1997).

In the 1997 case of *Kansas v. Hendricks*, the U.S. Supreme Court rejected Hendricks' claims. The Court noted that there was substantial precedent permitting the states to involuntarily commit individuals suffering from mental illness if they posed a danger to others. The Kansas statute provided for involuntary commitment for persons who had been convicted or charged with a crime of sexual violence, and who suffered from a "mental abnormality or personality disorder which makes the person likely to engage in ... predatory acts of sexual violence." Justice Clarence Thomas, writing the majority opinion of the Court, indicated that the states have always been given considerable latitude in defining mental illness or mental abnormality. The Kansas law was deemed by the Court as adequately defining mental illness and connecting it to the finding of future dangerousness.

The Supreme Court in *Kansas v. Hendricks* also rejected the concerns about double jeopardy and *ex post facto*, both issues of which relate to criminal processes. The Court noted that the Kansas law, while creating procedures for involuntary commitment, did not create criminal proceedings. Rather, the law erected *civil* commitment proceedings. The Court acknowledged that simply labeling a criminal, punishment-oriented process as a "civil" process would not make it so. However, it said this was not the case before them. The Court wrote:

> Although we recognize that a civil label is not always dispositive, we will reject the legislature's manifest intent only where a party challenging the statute provides the clearest proof that "the statutory scheme [is] so punitive either in purpose or effect as to negate [the State's] intention" to deem it "civil." ... In those limited circumstances, we will consider the statute to have established criminal proceedings for constitutional purposes. Hendricks, however, has failed to satisfy this heavy burden.

The Court also rejected due process concerns over the potential of indefinite confinement, which Hendricks saw as a possibly never-ending punishment. Rather, the Court saw indeterminate nature of the confinement as being consistent with the treatment of mental illness. The Court said:

> Hendricks focuses on his confinement's potentially indefinite duration as evidence of the State's punitive intent. That focus, however, is misplaced. Far from any punitive objective, the confinement's duration is instead linked to the stated purposes of the commitment, namely, to hold the person until his mental abnormality no longer causes him to be a threat to others.

Four justices dissented from the majority opinion. Justice Stephen Breyer, writing the dissenting opinion, agreed that the state of Kansas had satisfactorily defined mental illness and properly linked it to future dangerousness, thus legitimizing the civil commitment of sexual predators. However, the state also acknowledged that Hendricks' condition was treatable, and yet no treatments were made available to him in prison, and only inadequate treatment was delivered upon commitment. Therefore, the dissenting justices believed that a primary purpose of the law was indeed to inflict additional punishment on Hendricks and, therefore, violated the Constitution's *Ex Post Facto* Clause.

Some scholars and jurists have argued that involuntary civil commitment should be subject to due process protections and procedures which are comparable to those in the criminal justice system given the loss of personal liberty which comes with it. Quanbeck (2014), for example, lamented that civil commitment proceedings are not subject to Brady requirements. The case of *Brady v. Maryland* (1963) established the long-standing requirement that prosecutors must share with the defense any exculpatory evidence the prosecution has in its possession. For the defense team, in light of *Brady*, there are supposed to be no surprises from the government in criminal cases. However, there is no such requirement in civil commitment proceedings. Government lawyers need not share information or evidence that might mitigate against the appropriateness or the worthwhileness of civilly committing a person with a mental health condition. As evident from cases mentioned previously, courts in this country, and particularly the United States Supreme Court, recognize the need for procedural protections to be accorded to those who are subject to civil commitment, but not on the same level as criminal defendants.

Civil Commitment in Minnesota

Minnesota Statutes Chapter 253B defines and governs the civil commitment process in the state. In Minnesota, a person who is mentally ill is defined in state statute as (Minnesota Statutes § 253B.13):

> any person who has an organic disorder of the brain or a substantial psychiatric disorder of thought, mood, perception, orientation, or memory which grossly impairs judgment, behavior, capacity to recognize reality, or to reason or understand, which is manifested by instances of grossly disturbed behavior or faulty perceptions and poses a substantial likelihood of physical harm to self or others ...

The statute goes on to note that mental illness is demonstrated by a variety of behaviors, including, a failure to obtain food, clothing, shelter, or medical care as a result of the impairment; an inability to obtain necessary food, clothing, shelter, or medical care as a result of the impairment for reasons other than poverty and will likely suffer substantial harm and/or significant psychiatric deterioration or debilitation without treatment; a recent attempt or threat to physically harm oneself or others; or recent and willful conduct involving substantial damage to property.

The civil commitment process is handled through Minnesota's district courts. Under state law, there are six different categories of civil commitment proceedings, as outlined on the webpage of the 4th Judicial District, Hennepin County, Minnesota (2015):

1. Mentally ill persons—Persons that are mentally ill and as a result, pose a danger to themselves or others;
2. Mentally retarded persons—Persons that are developmentally disabled and as a result, pose a danger to themselves or others;
3. Chemically dependent persons—Persons that are chemically dependent, unable to manage personal affairs, and as a result, pose a danger to themselves or others;
4. Persons mentally ill and dangerous to the public—Persons that are mentally ill and as a result, have caused or intended to cause serious physical harm to another and are likely to take such action in the future;
5. Sexual psychopathic personalities—Persons who have an utter lack of power to control their sexual impulses as the result of a mental disorder and therefore pose a danger to the public; and

6. Sexually dangerous persons—Persons who have a mental disorder who have engaged in and are likely to continue to engage in harmful sexual conduct.

Persons who fall under any of the six categories above could be eligible for involuntary civil commitment. Typically, a family member of the patient or a health facility will act as petitioner to have someone committed. A petition to have someone involuntarily committed to a mental health facility is first filed with the county. In many cases, a petition is preceded by an emergency hold placed on someone by a health or mental health care professional (doctoral level), a court, or law enforcement. Involuntary emergency holds can last up to 72 hours, not including weekends and holidays. When a peace officer initiates a hold on someone who the officer believes is a danger to the patient or others, the hold is for 12 hours and is used to admit a person to a hospital emergency room. The hold can be extended to 72 hours by an examining physician or doctoral level psychologist. Persons who are placed under secured care for 72 hours must be informed of their rights. These rights include the freedom to leave after 72 hours absent a court order; the right to a medical examination with 48 hours of being first held; and the right to voluntarily accept treatment (National Alliance on Mental Illness, 2006).

When family members or others desire to file a petition to have someone involuntarily committed, a screening must take place. County health officials will review the petition, conduct a preliminary investigation regarding its merits, and either reject it or endorse it; in the latter case, a report is prepared for the County Attorney's Office articulating the evidence in support of commitment. In compiling their pre-petition report, county health officials must (National Alliance on Mental Illness, 2006):

1. interview the person with the alleged mental illness;
2. identify and investigate the alleged behavior that justifies commitment;
3. identify and consider alternatives to commitment and explain why these alternatives may or may not be appropriate;
4. gather other information about the person with mental illness, such as medications, his or her ability to consent to treatment, the effectiveness of past treatment, and the his or her wishes about treatment;
5. contact the person's insurance company to talk about paying for treatment and determining which doctors and facilities are on the insurance plan; and
6. provide notice about rights, the commitment process, and the legal effects of commitment to the person subject to commitment.

If the County Attorney's Office supports the petition, then it is filed in court and a preliminary hearing on the petition is scheduled before a judge. The court process for involuntary commitments occurs in three phases. The preliminary hearing is the first phase. This hearing often culminates in voluntary agreement between the various parties on a petition. For example, the patient and his or her family who filed the petition may agree on a plan of action for treatment which no longer necessitates court or governmental involvement. If an accord cannot be reached by all parties by the time of the preliminary hearing, the judge will then make a determination if the patient poses a danger to himself or other people. If the patient is deemed dangerous, the judge will order that the patient be held in a secure facility.

It is also during this initial phase that the district court judge who is hearing the case will order an examiner to conduct an examination of the patient. The patient also will select an examiner who will provide an independent review of the patient. The two examiners, who must be licensed mental health professionals, will later submit reports to the court which outline their findings and recommendations in the wake of their examinations.

At this point, a full hearing is scheduled before a district court judge. The County Attorney's office serves as counsel for the petitioner. A court-appointed public defender with specialized training in commitment law will represent the person subject to commitment, unless that person has chosen instead to hire a lawyer of his or her own choosing. During the hearing, the County Attorney may present evidence and call witnesses which support the assertion that the patient requires involuntary confinement and treatment. The patient may also submit evidence and call witnesses demonstrating that he or she does not require confinement, does not pose the kind of danger which might trigger involuntary commitment, and supports less restrictive treatment alternatives (Minnesota 4th Judicial District, 2015).

At the conclusion of the hearing, the judge will make determination as to the petition for involuntary commitment. The judge may embrace the petition's recommendations entirely, or craft a confinement and treatment plan different than that proposed in the petition. If the judge decides that involuntary commitment is proper for the safety of the patient and others, the judge will order the patient to the care of a treatment hospital. As a result of a separate hearing, known as a Jarvis hearing, the judge may order that the patient forcibly receive medication the patient otherwise refuses to receive (Minnesota 4th Judicial District, 2015).

Typically, involuntary civil commitments cannot exceed a period of six months without another full hearing. After that hearing, the commitment order may extend for up to 12 additional months. However, in cases involving persons who are mentally ill and dangerous to the public, sexual psychopaths, or sexually dangerous persons (i.e., justifications #4, #5, and #6 in the list above), the involuntary commitment duration is an indefinite one, subject only to periodic reviews by the court to determine if the confinement in a treatment facility should continue (Minnesota 4th Judicial District, 2015).

Interestingly, prior to 2001, the statute language in Minnesota, with regard to the danger-to-self-or-others requirement, the legislature removed the notions of imminence or immediacy. Those pushing the change wanted to give courts and families wider opportunity to intervene in patients' lives before things became truly harmful (National Alliance on Mental Illness, 2006).

Sex Offender Civil Commitment

For better or worse, Minnesota has been a leader among the states in using civil commitment laws to address sexual offenders. In 1939, Minnesota adopted one of the nation's first sexual psychopath laws, which provided for the civil commitment of persons with "psychopathic personality." This personality disorder was defined in the Psychopathic Personality Act of 1939 as "the existence in any person of such conditions of emotional instability, or impulsiveness in behavior, or lack of customary standards of good judgment, or failure to appreciate the consequences of his acts, or a combination of any such conditions, as to render such person irresponsible for his conduct with respect to sexual matters and thereby dangerous to other persons" (Janus & Walbek, 2000, p. 348). The Minnesota Supreme Court subsequently honed the legislation by determining that the law's effective reach only extended to those persons who lacked the ability to control their sexual urges.

From 1939 to 1969, 474 men were committed to state hospitals in Minnesota under the Psychopathic Personality Act. Many, or even most, of those who were involuntarily committed under the law had been so for offenses which would be considered low-level offenses today, or even legal acts, e.g., homosexual relations (Janus & Walbek, 2000). There were relatively few civil commitments of sex offenders in the 1970s and 1980s in Minnesota. However, in 1989, there were some widely published sex offenses involving parolees that captured the attention of the citizens, victim advocacy groups, and the legislature in Minnesota. A taskforce created by the Attorney General's office examined the prevalence of repeat sex offenders in Minnesota and recommended that civil commitment be used to augment the prison terms of dangerous sexual predators.

In the wake of the task force report, laws were refined and instruments were developed to screen imprisoned sex offenders for consideration of further confinement through civil commitment. Approximately 90% of sex offenders in Minnesota's prisons who are screened are determined to be potential candidates for civil commitment. In recent years, prosecutors have pursued civil commitment for about 61% of the cases referred to them. Ultimately, the rates of those referred who end up being involuntarily committed range from 34% to 67% across the state; 10% of the referred cases are dismissed (Janus, 2013; Janus & Walbek, 2000).

In the early 1990s, the Psychopathic Personalities Act withstood several state constitutional challenges regarding due process, double jeopardy, and ex post facto claims; but the law as practiced was partially invalidated, through inference, by two Minnesota Supreme Court cases in 1994—*In re Linehan* and *In re Rickmyer*. The Minnesota Supreme Court in *Linehan* reinforced the efficacy of the language of the Psychopathic Personalities Act by insisting that the state must present clear and convincing evidence that a person has an utter lack of power to control sexual impulses if one is to be involuntarily committed under that statute. Further, the Minnesota Supreme Court said in *Rickmyer* that the state must reach a high bar to establish the likelihood that an offender would pose harm to others if released, as required under the Psychopathic Personalities Act; this threshold is not necessarily met by single acts of sexual violence, but rather by a pattern of habitual behavior.

As a result of these two cases, the Minnesota legislature enacted a new sex offender law called the "Minnesota Civil Commitment and Treatment Act (MCTA): Sexually Dangerous Persons and Sexual Psychopathic Personalities Act" (Minnesota Statutes § 253D). The law's purpose was to clarify and strengthen the validity of the Psychopathic Personalities Act. The Sexually Dangerous Persons and Sexual Psychopathic Personalities Act permits the involuntary civil commitment of individuals who have engaged in harmful sexual contact or who have a sexual, mental, or personality disorder likely to result in future harmful sexual contact (Janus & Walbek, 2000). The latter law reformed the older law in two ways which made it easier to determine that an offender was either a "sexually dangerous person" or a "sexual psychopathic personality"— either of which become eligible for involuntary civil commitment. First, it removed the "inability to control" language; second, it loosened the "harm" requirement by creating presumptions of harm based on particular criminal acts (Janus & Walbek, 2000).

The Problem of Stigma

Upon securing release from prison or from a secure hospital, sex offenders remain on everyone's radar. Minnesota, like other states, has a "Megan's Law" requiring the registration of labeled sex offenders and notification to certain constituencies when a sex offender moves into a neighborhood. Level I offenders are those who are least likely to re-offend. For those offenders, only law enforcement and victims and witnesses are notified. Level II offenders pose a moderate risk of re-offending. In addition to law enforcement and victims/witnesses, agencies and organizations serving populations at risk are also notified. So, for example, if a sex offender's prior offenses involved children, the area schools and daycare facilities would likely be notified. Level III offenders are those most likely to re-offend. Often, they refused to participate in treatment while in prison or during commitment, or they were unsuccessful in completing the treatment. When Level III sex offenders move into a community anywhere in Minnesota, the entire community is notified. This is done through press releases and town hall meetings.

Table 5.2. Minnesota Sex Offender Classification Scheme

- Level I
  - Least likely to re-offend
  - Who is notified? Law enforcement & victims/witnesses
- Level II
  - Moderate risk of re-offending
  - Who is notified? Law enforcement, victims/witnesses, and agencies serving population at risk (e.g. schools, daycare centers, etc)
- Level III
  - Most likely to re-offend
  - Who is notified? Same as above, AND the community at large

Source: Author created from information obtained from the Minnesota Department of Corrections.

Of course, community members are reminded that the sex offender in question has the right to live in the neighborhood in peace. Residents are warned not to harass the offender, nor to call the police every time the offender is seen. They are reminded that the sex offender has served his or her time behind bars already and owes no further debt to society (except for offenders on probation or parole). Advocacy groups for criminal offenders trying to make a new life for themselves argue that these registration and notification laws, applied against people who have already been punished by the state for their actions, constitutes a second form of punishment—not unlike some arguments made against civil commitment. They claim, with some justification, that the laws make a rehabilitated, normal life impossible to achieve because of the stigma, suspicion, and hostility that is directed toward them by the community.

Stigma is a very powerful force to overcome if one is to lead a normal life. Stigma sets some members of society apart from the rest of society in a way that disadvantages and demeans those to whom stigma is attached. Sociologist Erving Goffman pioneered research and understanding regarding how social stigma impedes the mainstreaming and assimilation of some people in society. Goffman identified three types of social stigma (1963):

1. stigma associated with visible, physical deformities, maladies, and scars
2. stigma associated with ethnicity, nationality, race, and culture;
3. stigma associated with mental illness, criminality, and other anti-social or destructive behavior.

Clearly, those suffering from mental illness, or from irresistible impulses particularly associated with sexual violence and exploitation, fall into the third form of stigma listed above. Sex offenders released from prison into society, or released from involuntary commitment into society, certainly face a range of antipathy from neighbors and the community at large, including suspicion, revulsion, anger, hatred, and other responses which manifest themselves in patently inhospitable living and working conditions. However, legislature in Minnesota as in every state has found that the cost in lost convenience and normalcy in an offender's post-incarceration life is more than offset by the gains in public safety through knowledge and awareness.

Minnesota's Security Hospitals

At the heart of involuntary civil commitment are the facilities where those detained under the Minnesota Sex Offender Program (MSOP) by the Department of Human Services, with the cooperation of the Department of Corrections, must reside. These facilities are Minnesota's security hospitals. The hospitals, while truly serving a therapeutic function, have all the accoutrements of a prison. And an expensive one at that. In 2014, the average cost per custodial client to the Department of Human Services was $341 per day, or $124,000 per year (Minnesota Department of Human Services, 2014).

As already noted, there are two facilities which house involuntary-committed sex offenders in Minnesota: the Minnesota Security Hospital in St. Peter and the Moose Lake State Hospital in Moose Lake. The security hospital in St. Peter houses both sex offenders as well as other dangerous persons who have been civilly committed to custodial care. A wing of the St. Peter hospital is dedicated to housing clients in the Minnesota Sex Offender Program. The Moose Lake facility is entirely dedicated to housing and treating clients in the Minnesota Sex Offender Program. Today, the two hospitals combined serve a total of 715 active clients in the Minnesota Sex Offender Program (Minnesota Department of Human Services, 2015).

Table 5.3. Minnesota Sex Offender Program Statistics (as of April 1, 2015)

Total MSOP clients	715
Location of clients	
Moose Lake	458
St. Peter	257
Age	
18 to 20	0
21 to 25	7
26 to 35	131
36 to 45	176
46 to 55	199
56 to 65	124
Over 65	78
Average age	48
Youngest	21
Oldest	93
Race	
American Indian/Alaskan Native	53
Black/African American	98
White	533
Other or unknown	31
Education	
0 to 8 years	29
9 to 11 years	65
12 years	321
GED	219
High school degree and GED	8
12+ years	44
Unknown	29
Civil commitment by county	
Hennepin	145
Ramsey	71
Other counties	499
Metro counties	298
Non-metro counties	417

Source: Minnesota Department of Human Services (2015)

The Moose Lake facility currently serves 458 clients in the Minnesota Sex Offender Program, but has a capacity of 550. The hospital focuses on the evaluation stage and the transition stage in the treatment of those determined to be sexually psychopathic. Once clients in the program have completed treatment at Moose Lake, the goal is for them to transition to less secure environments in the community while demonstrating their ability to refrain from criminal or dangerous acts (Minnesota Department of Human Services, 2015). In addition to clients who are receiving treatment, the facility also houses individuals who are subject to a petition for civil commitment but have not yet been formally committed by a court, and sex offenders involuntarily committed and who refuse to participate in sex offender treatment. Moose Lake operates a collaborative 50-client program with the Department of Corrections in which individuals serving prison sentences for sex offenses may simultaneously receive sex offender treatment by serving their time at the hospital. These are individuals who are thought likely to be civilly committed and are given an opportunity to begin their treatment early (Minnesota Department of Human Services, 2013).

In 1866, the Minnesota legislature authorized the construction of a hospital for the mentally insane in St. Peter. The City of St. Peter was home to the first of four such facilities, the other three being in Fergus Falls, Rochester, and Anoka. In 1911, the hospital added a secure insane asylum, which years later, in 1957, would become the Minnesota Security Hospital (Minnesota State University, 2015). In the early 1980s, the state legislature authorized the construction of a new campus for the security hospital in St. Peter. This is the campus in use today. The hospital houses approximately 257 sex offenders, but has beds for 300. The St. Peter facility, while the primary location for housing and treating non-sexual but dangerous mentally ill patients, serves as the secondary facility for sex offenders. Clients in the Minnesota Sex Offender program who have shown some promise and have been afforded increased privileges and freedoms to manage their own risks are often transferred from Moose Lake to the sex offender wing at St. Peter.

The hospital in St. Peter has come under considerable criticism in recent years. In January 2014, one patient was beaten and stomped to death by another patient. An independent investigation of what transpired found a general culture of non-intervention and a lack of supervision among the staff. The report indicated that staff members were reluctant to intervene with patients who were disruptive or violent. Ironically, in reports from prior years, the staff had been criticized for being too punitive—using restraints and solitary confinement to punish patients who acted up and became violent. This was precisely the impetus behind hiring David Proffitt in 2011. Proffitt was a staunch opponent of the practice of using restraints and seclusion against patients.

But Proffitt had a rough row to hoe. There had been long-standing morale and leadership troubles at St. Peter's state hospital, and those problems appeared to be exacerbated with Proffitt's hiring. After several staff and physician resignations, a separate investigative report was ordered in January of 2012 by the Department of Human Services concerning complaints about a hostile work environment and a practice of harassment and retaliation that existed at the hospital. In January 2012, the hospital was still led by David Profitt. The report found that Proffitt had not engaged in harassment, retaliation, nor had created a hostile work environment. However, the report did find that Proffitt had contributed to a "poor working atmosphere" and had made inappropriate (although not harassing) comments to staff members.

As already noted, Proffitt was hired as the hospital's chief executive officer in 2011 with the goal of correcting long-standing problems; including correcting the overuse of punishment and restraints by staff against patients. Proffitt's orientation was certainly to minimize the "corrections mindset" that he believed was pervasive among security counselors at the hospital. He once said in a meeting that security counselors had been hired based on their neck size and that they should be afraid to tell him (Proffitt) that they do not like being second-guessed by licensed staff. His lack of sympathy for security personnel was against the backdrop of a 50% increase in staff injuries between 2011 and 2012—most which were caused by assaults committed by patients (McEnroe, 2014). On another occasion, he indicated that he would make sure someone on the staff would go to jail if there was ever a fire and a patient in a personal living suite died. The report found that Proffitt fostered, and perhaps relished, an environment where employees were afraid to make a mistake or show anything other than complete loyalty to Proffitt (Helmers, 2012).

Under pressure from his employer, the Minnesota Department of Human Services, and amid allegations of a confrontational management style which had demoralized staff, Proffitt resigned in March 2012. Carol Olson, the administrator of the Community Behavioral Health Hospitals in Rochester and St. Peter, immediately succeeded Proffitt in the post. Olson has had her hands full. Despite optimism from the Department of Human Services for new leadership, serious misgivings about the hospital have continued, due to missteps and unwelcome publicity. In 2013, a violent offender who was an involuntarily committed patient was accidentally discharged and left at a homeless shelter. In April of 2014, the Minnesota Department of Labor and Industry, Occupational Safety and Health Division, inspected the hospital and ultimately issued a citation for failing to protect employees from workplace violence. And then came the murder of a custodial patient at the hands of another patient in 2015.

There was a baptism by fire for Carol Olson. Even so, it would appear that some things are improving. From 2012 to 2013, under Olson's leadership, staff injuries declined 11% (Minnesota Department of Labor and Industry, 2014). Given they had risen 50% the year before, the 11% decline was still a nearly 40% increase from two years before. But it was moving in the right direction. Additionally, Olson hired 58 new security counselors and increased staff presence in the buildings with the highest rates of incidents and staff injuries (Hegarty, 2015). She also had more security cameras installed to cover blindspots in the facilities. Meanwhile, politicians, bureaucrats in the Department of Human Services in St. Paul, and a wary public continued to wait for another shoe to drop. In December of 2015, the Minnesota Security Hospital in St. Peter was fined $63,000 by the Minnesota Occupational Health and Safety for a total of nine different violations occurring between May and July 2015 in which hospital workers were injured (Ruiter, 2015). While improvements have been made, the Minnesota Legislature will likely insist on additional measures in the future to better secure employee, patient, and visitor safety.

Minnesota Multiphasic Personality Inventory

While the drama involving Minnesota's primary security hospital is somewhat unsettling to the forensic psychiatric professionals, it cannot be denied that Minnesota has a long history of association with successful diagnosis and treatment of mental illness and personality disorders. The fact that the Minnesota Multiphasic Personality Inventory (MMPI) hails from this state is a testament to that.

Prior to the Second World War, there was a need for a broad, standardized assessment of personality and psychopathology (Buchanan, 1994). The MMPI was developed by Dr. Starke Hathaway and Dr. J.C. McKinley at the University of Minnesota in the late 1930s. The MMPI has since become one of the most widely used and frequently studied personality assessments in existence. The original test was re-standardized and updated in the late 1980s as the MMPI-2 (Butcher, Dahlstrom, Graham, Tellegen, & Kaemmer, 1989).

The MMPI-2 is self-administered, though it must be interpreted by a trained psychologist. It uses 568 true/false questions to assess over 120 different aspects of personality and psychopathology. The MMPI-2 includes clinical scales (depression, paranoia, psychopathic traits), content scales (obsessiveness, anger, social discomfort), and validity scales (the lying scale assesses the truthfulness of the respondent). This broad assessment tool is commonly utilized in forensic settings (Archer, Buffington-Vollum, Stredny, & Handel, 2006) for a number of purposes including risk assessment, predicting recidivism, assessing psychopathy, sentencing decisions, predicting prison adjustment, evaluating treatment programs, criminal defense strategies, custody disputes, and assessing malingering (Singh & Fazel, 2010). There have been thousands of published studies examining its reliability and validity across various forensic settings and populations.

One-Way Door

In Minnesota in 2015, there were over 700 persons deemed to be sexually violent predators who are confined involuntarily at either of two state security hospitals—one in St. Peter and the other in Moose Lake. Given that Minnesota is one of only 20 states with special provisions built into statutes for the involuntary commitment of sexual predators, and was one of the forerunners in this area, along with the state of Washington (both having adopted sexual predator laws around 1990), many studies about the civil commitment of sex offenders have focused on Minnesota.

Of particular note, in 2000, Janus and Walbek published a study which examined 116 men who were involuntarily committed as sexually violent predators in Minnesota from 1975 through 1996. The purpose of the study was, in part, to consider the benefits of the Minnesota program relative to its costs. In 1997, the total annual cost of Minnesota sexual offender commitment program was in excess of $15.5 million (Janus & Walbek, 2000). Their study, largely descriptive, nonetheless brought to life many interesting data. For example, it is very difficult to be released from involuntary confinement as a sex offender. They found, as of 1999, that no individual committed after 1983 had ever been granted a direct, unconditional release from custody. For those receiving direct releases prior to 1989, the average time in confinement from commitment to release was approximately 10 years. Based on the trajectory of commitments and releases, the study predicted that 25% of all sexual offenders in confinement by the year 2009 would be so confined due to civil commitment. The study called to question the intended "end game" for civil commitment, if punishment wasn't the goal; over 40% of those offenders examined in the study had never been a participant in sex offender treatment as a patient at their secured hospital (Janus & Walbek, 2000).

The study's predictions were prophetic. In fact, the one-way door (people come in through civil commitment, ostensibly for treatment, but are rarely discharged) identified by Janus and Walbek in 1999 continued without abatement until 2014 when a lawsuit was filed over the very same thing. Dan Gustafson is an attorney for those presently confined under the Minnesota Sex

Offender Program in St. Peter and Moose Lake. He described the program as "hopeless" as "the door only swings one way" (Bierschbach, 2015). The interminability of involuntary commitment of so many of Minnesota's sex offenders led to Gustafson filing a federal class action lawsuit in the federal District of Minnesota.

On February 9, 2015, a trial began in federal court in the St. Paul federal courthouse. Gustafson noted through called testimony the stark contrast with neighboring Wisconsin. That state's modern sex offender program started about the same time as Minnesota's—in the mid-1990s. But Minnesota today has custody of over 700 civilly committed sex offenders to Wisconsin's 362, despite comparable state populations and sex crime rates. What's more, in the past 20 years, Wisconsin has discharged 118 offenders unconditionally and 135 offenders on supervised release. Minnesota has not released anybody in the past 20 years unconditionally and only two offenders have been released with conditions in that time. Minnesota's sex offender program has in custody over 50 men who have no adult criminal records (i.e., their predicate offenses were committed as juveniles); Wisconsin has 2 or 3 of such individuals (Bierschbach, 2015). State officials testified that things are not as bad as the numbers would suggest. They noted that reforms which have been implemented are improving the system. They noted that 57 individuals are in the final stages of treatment, and that only 39 percent of clients are in the initial stages of treatment. It had been 65 percent in 2012; the decline suggests the movement of clients through the treatment phases (Serres, 2015).

The process for an involuntarily committed sex offender to petition the state of Minnesota for release is understandably multi-pronged. The stakes, of course, are high. The petition and hearing process is depicted in **Figure 5.1**. The problem plaintiffs have is less with the process to petition one's release, and more with the fact that the process outcome is, heretofore, universally hollow.

Figure 5.1. Minnesota Civil Commitment Appeal (Petition for Release) Process

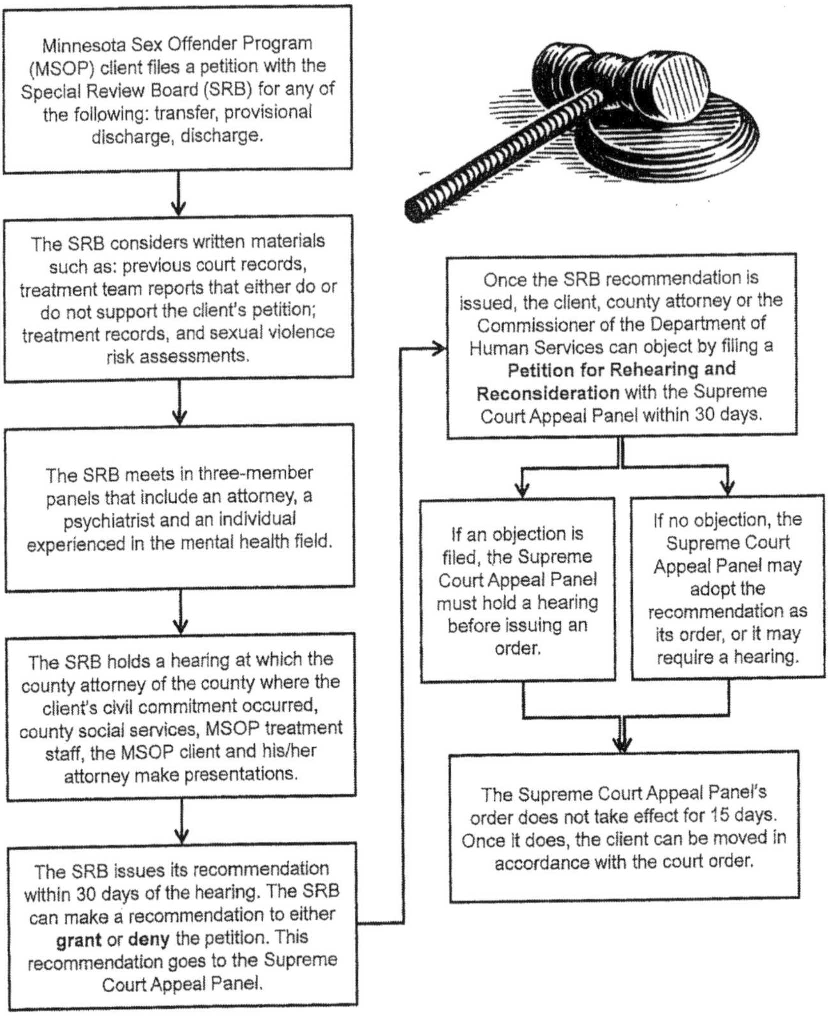

Minnesota Sex Offender Program (MSOP) client files a petition with the Special Review Board (SRB) for any of the following: transfer, provisional discharge, discharge.

The SRB considers written materials such as: previous court records, treatment team reports that either do or do not support the client's petition; treatment records, and sexual violence risk assessments.

The SRB meets in three-member panels that include an attorney, a psychiatrist and an individual experienced in the mental health field.

The SRB holds a hearing at which the county attorney of the county where the client's civil commitment occurred, county social services, MSOP treatment staff, the MSOP client and his/her attorney make presentations.

The SRB issues its recommendation within 30 days of the hearing. The SRB can make a recommendation to either **grant** or **deny** the petition. This recommendation goes to the Supreme Court Appeal Panel.

Once the SRB recommendation is issued, the client, county attorney or the Commissioner of the Department of Human Services can object by filing a **Petition for Rehearing and Reconsideration** with the Supreme Court Appeal Panel within 30 days.

If an objection is filed, the Supreme Court Appeal Panel must hold a hearing before issuing an order.

If no objection, the Supreme Court Appeal Panel may adopt the recommendation as its order, or it may require a hearing.

The Supreme Court Appeal Panel's order does not take effect for 15 days. Once it does, the client can be moved in accordance with the court order.

Source: Minnesota Department of Human Services

During the trial, there were signs that federal judge Donovan Frank, who presided over the case, was finding the plaintiffs' arguments to be at least partially compelling. In earlier rulings on motions, Judge Frank characterized the current system as "clearly broken" and "Draconian" (Bierschbach, 2015). A task force set up by Judge Frank previously to examine the sex offender commitment program in Minnesota said that the system "captures too many people and keeps them too long" (Volpe, 2015). On June 17, 2015, the trial came to a close and Judge Frank issued his 76-page ruling. The Court found that the Minnesota Sex Offender Program, and the underlying statutory scheme, were "unconstitutional on its face and as applied." The Court found that Minnesota law regarding the civil commitment of sex offenders was facially unconstitutional because (*Karsjens, et.al. v. Minnesota Department of Human Services*, et.al., 2015):

- it failed to require periodic risk assessment of offenders;
- it contains no mechanism to allow offenders to access in a timely manner the judicial process to challenge their commitment;
- it renders discharge from the sex offender program more onerous than admission to it;
- it authorizes the burden to petition for a reduction in custody to shift from the state to the offender;
- it contemplates less restrictive alternatives for offenders, but there are no less restrictive alternatives available; and
- it does not require the state to take any affirmative action on behalf of individuals who no longer satisfy the criteria for continued commitment.

The Court also found that Minnesota sex offender commitment laws were unconstitutional as applied. The reasons include:

- the state does not conduct periodic, independent risk assessments and evaluations, absent an offender's petition;
- the risk assessments which have been performed were not done so in a constitutional manner;
- individuals have remained confined in the MSOP even after completing treatment;
- discharge procedures of the MSOP are not working properly;
- there are no less restrictive alternatives to commitment available; and
- the MSOP treatment program structure has been an institutional failure and there is no relationship between treatment and an end to detention.

Judge Frank went on in his ruling to note that Minnesota has severe penalties in its criminal statutes regarding sex offenses. First time offenders committing heinous sex crimes and repeat sex offenders could face as much as mandatory life sentences. But instead, state prosecutors tend to rely on plea agreements for criminal convictions and then the civil commitment process for longevity of confinement. He said of these plea agreements that they were "a disservice to the entire system and have rarely served the interests of justice."

The judge's ruling is a significant blow to the Minnesota Sex Offender Program. The State of Minnesota, in order to comply with Judge Donovan's notions of constitutionality with regard to the civil commitment of sex offenders, would need to completely revamp its civil commitment laws and programs. Judge Donovan's decision made mention of 16 potential substantive changes to the law and program, and suggested there may be more, which might be adopted as court-ordered remedies at a future hearing. Governor Mark Dayton immediately rebuffed the ruling by reiterating his claim that the MSOP is constitutional (Sepic & Cox, 2015). Governor Dayton indicated the ruling will be appealed by the State of Minnesota. However, if the state continues to lose in court as it moves up the appellate chain, then lawmakers, state executives, and public employees involved in the MSOP will certainly have their hands full as they must rebuild the program almost from scratch.

Concluding Remarks

For decades, Minnesota has had codified into law mechanisms for the involuntary commitment of the dangerously mentally ill. Offenders with psychopathic or habitually violent impulses to commit harm may indeed be confined to a secure mental health facility for their own safety and for the safety of others. Violent and repeat sex offenders constitute a subset of the violent mentally ill and are the focus of most civil commitment efforts in Minnesota. Since the 1990s, a fraction of 1% of those individuals who have been involuntarily committed for sexual psychopathy have ever been released to the community, despite having no criminal sanctions hanging over them. Efforts to reform the civil commitment process through lobbying and legal action have been met with varying degrees of success. However, a recent legal victory in federal court by civil liberties advocates for the involuntarily committed may provide impetus in the future for structural change to the civil commitment process in Minnesota and to the sex offender program in particular.

Key Terms

Addington v. Texas
Civil Commitment
In re Linehan
In re Rickmyer
Insanity Defense
Jackson v. Indiana
Kansas v. Hendricks
Level I, II, & III Sex Offenders
M'Naghten Rule
Mental Illness

MMPI
Model Penal Code Rule
O'Connor v. Donaldson
Psychopathic Personality Act
Security Hospital
Sex Offender
Sexually Dangerous Person Act
Sexual Psychopath
Stigma

Selected Internet Sites

American Psychiatric Association
http://www.psychiatry.org/

Minnesota Department of Corrections
http://www.doc.state.mn.us

Minnesota Department of Human Services
www.mn.gov/dhs

Minnesota Revisor of Statutes
www.revisor.leg.state.mn.us

National Alliance on Mental Illness
www.nami.org

U.S. Department of Justice
National Sex Offender Public Website
http://www.nsopw.gov/

Discussion Questions

1. Should criminal liability require an offender to know right from wrong?
2. Is it fair for mentally ill persons who pose a danger to society to be held in custody indefinitely?

3. Under what circumstances should sex offenders be released into the community?
4. What can or should be done to help those stigmatized by mental illness or violent impulses to assimilate into society? Should community notification laws be reformed?
5. Can sex offenders ever be "cured" of their impulses?

References

Addington v. Texas, 441 US 418 (1979).

Archer, R., Buffington-Vollum, J., Stredny, R., & Handel, R. (2006). A survey of psychological test use patterns among forensic psychologists. *Journal of Personality Assessment, 87*, 84–94.

Bierschbach, B. (2015, February 10). Sex offender trial highlights differences between Minnesota, Wisconsin. *MinnPost.*

Brady v. Maryland, 373 US 83 (1963).

Buchanan, R. (1994). The development of the Minnesota mulitphasic personality inventory. *Journal of History of the Behavioral Sciences, 30*, 148–161.

Butcher, J., Dahlstrom, W., Graham, J., Tellegen, A. & Kaemmer, B. (1989). *Manual for the restandardized Minnesota multiphasic personality inventory: MMPI-2.* Minneapolis, MN: University of Minnesota Press.

Collins, K., Hinkebein, G., & Schorgl, S. (n.d.) *The John Hinckley trial and its effect on the insanity defense.* Retrieved from http://law2.umkc.edu/faculty/projects/ftrials/hinckley/hinckleyinsanity.htm#EVOLUTION.

Goffman, E. (1963). *Stigma: Notes on the management of spoiled identity.* New York: Simon and Schuster.

Hegarty, S. (2015, January 20). *DHS requests $10.4 million in emergency funding.* Minnesota House of Representatives Public Information Services. Retrieved from http://www.house.leg.state.mn.us/sessiondaily/SDView.aspx?StoryID=5357.

Helmers, T. (2012). *Minnesota department of human services investigative report.* Minneapolis, MN: Ratwik, Roszak & Mahoney.

In re Linehan, 518 N.W.2d 609 (1994).

In re Rickmyer, 519 N.W.2d 188 (1994).

Jackson v. Indiana, 406 U.S. 715 (1972).

James, D. & Glaze, L. (2006). *Mental health problems of prison and jail inmates.* Bureau of Justice Statistics: Washington, DC.

James, N., Thomas, K., & Foley, C. (2008). *Civil commitment of sexually dangerous persons.* New York: Nova Publishers.

Janus, E. (2013). Preventive detention of sex offenders: The American experience versus international human rights norms. *Behavioral Sciences and the Law*. 31, 328–343.

Janus, E. & Walbek, N. (2000). Sex offender commitments in Minnesota: A descriptive study of second generation commitments. *Behavioral Sciences and the Law*. 18, 343–374.

Kansas v. Hendricks, 521 US 346 (1997).

Karsjens, et.al. v. Minnesota Department of Human Services, et al., Civil No. 11-3659 (2015).

McEnroe, P. (2014, January 1). Minnesota security hospital: Staff in crisis spreads turmoil. *Minneapolis Star Tribune*.

Melton, G., Petrila, J., Poythress, N., & Slobogin, C. (2007). *Psychological evaluations for the courts: A handbook for mental health professionals and lawyers (3rd ed)*. New York: Guilford Press.

Mental Illness Policy Org. (2009). *Supreme court mental health precedent and its implications*. Retrieved from http://mentalillnesspolicy.org/legal/mental-illness-supreme-court.html.

Miller, J. (2010). Sex offender civil commitment: The treatment paradox. *California Law Review*. 98, 2093–2128.

Minnesota 4th Judicial District. (2015). *Mental health civil commitments*. Retrieved from http://www.mncourts.gov/district/4/?page=467.

Minnesota Department of Human Services. (2015). *Minnesota sex offender program statistics*. Retrieved from http://mn.gov/dhs/people-we-serve/adults/services/sex-offender-treatment/statistics.jsp.

Minnesota Department of Human Services. (2014, July 9). Minnesota sex offender program establishes cost of care rate as of July 1, 2014. *Minnesota Department of Human Services Bulletin*.

Minnesota Department of Human Services. (2013). *DHS request for information: Residential and treatment services*. Retrieved from http://www.dhs.state.mn.us/main/groups/business_partners/documents/pub/dhs16_174731~1.pdf.

Minnesota Department of Labor and Industry. (2014). *Notice of contest and service to affected employees*. Filed by the Minnesota Department of Human Services, August 24, 2014.

Minnesota Revisor of Statutes. (2015). *Statutes*. Retrieved from www.revisor.leg.state.mn.us

Minnesota State University. (2015). *St. Peter state hospital collection, 1855–1974*. Retrieved from http://lib.mnsu.edu/archives/fa/smhc/smhc103.html.

National Alliance on Mental Illness. (2006). *Understanding the Minnesota civil commitment process*. St. Paul, MN: NAMI Minnesota.

O'Connor v. Donaldson, 422 US 563 (1975).

Quanbeck, T. (2014). Preventing partisan commitment: Applying Brady protection to the civil commitment of sex offenders. *Case Western Reserve Law Review*, 65(1), 209–249.

Ruiter, D. (2015, December 9). *OSHA fines Minnesota security hospital in St. Peter $63K*. Retrieved from http://www.keyc.com/story/30708519/osha-fines-minn-security-hospital-in-st-peter-63k.

Sepic, M. & Cox, P. (2015, June 17). Federal judge: Minnesota sex offender program unconstitutional. *MPR News*. Retrieved from http://www.mpr news.org/story/2015/06/17/sex-offender-program-unconstitutional.

Serres, C. (2015, March 6). Reforms are taking hold in Minnesota's sex offender program, officials testify. *Minneapolis Star Tribune*.

Singh, J. & Fazel, S. (2010). Forensic risk assessment: A meta-review. *Criminal Justice and Behavior*, 37, 965–988.

Steadman, H., Osher, F., Clark Robbins, P., Case, B., & Samuels, S. (2009). Prevalence of serious mental illness among jail inmates. *Psychiatric Services*, 60, 761–765.

Volpe, T. (2015). *Minnesota sex offenders prepare for civil commitment court battle*. Retrieved from http://www.kare11.com/story/news/investigations/2015/01/29/sex-offenders-treatment-program-moose-lake-civil-committment/22520603/.

Chapter Six

Meet Me at the Mall of America: Minnesota's Juvenile Justice System

Learning Objectives

- Articulate the age-crime curve and criminological theories of juvenile crime
- Describe the history of juvenile justice in Minnesota
- Discover landmark U.S. Supreme Court decisions pertaining to juvenile justice
- Explore arrest and incarceration data for Minnesota youth
- Explain the juvenile justice process in Minnesota
- Examine core legal protections for juveniles
- Identify what constitutes child abuse and neglect
- Describe issues pertaining to bullying and school violence
- Analyze the evolution of youth intervention programming and project evaluation

Since opening its doors in 1992, the Mall of America (MOA) in Bloomington has become a leader in retail, entertainment and attractions. With a gross area of nearly 5 million square feet and unique features such as an aquarium and theme park, MOA is often described as a "city within a city" (Mall of America, 2015a). Thanks to approximately 40 million annual visitors, MOA is also one of the top tourist destinations in the United States. It should come as no surprise, therefore, that children and young people frequent MOA in large numbers.

MOA welcomes "all youth," however on Friday and Saturday evenings, people under the age of 16 must be accompanied by an adult 21 years or older from 4 p.m. until close (Mall of America, 2015b). Why does MOA operate a parental escort policy? Because MOA is concerned about juvenile delinquency.

The Age-Crime Curve

Mall of America's concern about juvenile delinquency is understandable. Research shows crime is most prevalent during mid-to-late adolescence and is in most cases "limited" to adolescence (Moffitt, 1993). In other words, the incidence of crime increases with age until individuals reach about 16 to 20. It then decreases with age in adulthood. Evidence for this "age-crime curve" has been found across samples that vary in terms of demographic and socioeconomic variables (see Farrington, Piquero, & Jennings, 2013). Adolescent crime is almost a prerequisite for adult crime, yet, paradoxically, "most antisocial children do not become antisocial adults" (Robins, 1978, p. 611). This has led some to conclude age has a direct effect on crime and "aging out" is somewhat inevitable, which, if true, renders the entire juvenile justice system irrelevant (Hirschi & Gottfredson, 1983).

A number of criminological theories provide explanations for the age-crime relationship, as follows:

- *Criminal propensity*—youth engage in crime because they have not yet developed internal controls or an ability to see beyond themselves (e.g., impulse control, self-regulation and moral disengagement; Gottfredson & Hirschi, 1990);
- *Rational choice*—youth engage in crime based on a rational calculation of factors such as potential benefits and costs (Cornish & Clarke, 1986; Katz, 1988);
- *Social learning*—exposure to antisocial peers and antisocial peer pressure account for youth crime (Sutherland, 1947; Akers, 2009);
- *Social bond*—youth engage in crime commensurate to their stake in conformity and the extent to which formal or informal social controls, such as parents or teachers, are present (Hirschi, 1969);

- *Strain*—social structures within society pressure youth to commit crime (Merton, 1938). Failure to achieve positively valued goals (e.g., as a result of discrimination), loss of positive stimuli (e.g., death of a loved one), and negative stimuli (e.g., physical or emotional abuse) all constitute sources of "strain" (Agnew 1992); and
- *Procedural justice*—youth engage in crime because previous experiences in the criminal justice system lend them to question the legitimacy of "the law" (Fagan & Tyler, 2005).

There is strong empirical support for social learning theory, owing to the fact most crime is committed in groups and adolescents are particularly susceptible to group processes (Sweeten, Piquero, & Steinberg, 2013). In reality, however, the age-crime relationship cannot be reduced to a single theory or overarching construct. As such, efforts by the juvenile justice system to intervene in the lives of youth involved in crime cannot be discounted (Scott & Steinberg, 2010).

The most basic assumption underlining juvenile justice today is juveniles on the whole do not possess the same *mens rea* or criminal intent as adults because they are not as intellectually, morally, or socially developed as adults (Scott & Steinberg, 2010). The adolescent brain, especially the prefrontal cortex, which controls the brain's most advanced decision-making functions, for example, is still developing, thus risks taken and mistakes made by young offenders may be largely outside of their control (Bonnie & Scott, 2013).

Another basic assumption underlining juvenile justice is *societal reaction* or *criminalization* can potentially transform minor juvenile crime problems into major juvenile crime problems (Becker, 1963; Lemert, 1971). First, juveniles labeled *criminal* or *delinquent* and sanctioned accordingly may interpret their "stigma" as master status, which, in turn, transforms their social identity, and consequently, their behavior (see **Chapter Five**). Second, branded youth also encounter social obstacles that disqualify them from "full social acceptance," such as obtaining meaningful work, earning a high school diploma or post-secondary degree, or building a strong, participatory civic life (Goffman, 1963, p. 9).

A Brief History of Juvenile Justice in Minnesota

In the long history of criminal justice, juvenile justice is a relatively new development (Friedman, 1993). Early in U.S. history, children who broke the law were treated the same as adult criminals. In the early 1800s, alternatives to treating adults and juveniles the same (and housing them together) emerged with the creation of houses of refuge and reformatories. The first juvenile court in the United States was established in Cook County, Illinois, in 1899. This court was the first to have *original jurisdiction* to hear cases that apply to juvenile crime. This means that juveniles under the age of 16 would come before this court first. The court was also granted authority over neglected and dependent children.

Six years later, in 1905, Minnesota established its own juvenile courts for youth under 17 (Feld, 2007). The original law to "regulate the treatment and control of dependent, neglected, and delinquent children" defined a "delinquent child" as anyone under 17 who used "vile, obscene, vulgar, profane or indecent language," was "incorrigible," associated with "thieves, vicious or immoral persons," and knowingly frequented "a house of ill fame" or saloon or pool hall, or wandered "about the streets in the night time" or "about any railroad yards or tracks" (Tiffany, 1910).

Juvenile courts flourished for the first half of the 20th century and the focus on offenders over offenses and rehabilitation over punishment had substantial procedural impact. At this time, the legal concept of *parens patriae* meant that the benevolent state could and should act *in loco parentis*, or in place of the parent, to protect children from adult wrongdoers (Friedman, 1993). As public confidence in indefinite institutionalization (e.g., houses of refuge, reform schools) and the traditional treatment model waned during the 1950s and 1960s, however, formal procedural safeguards for youth were introduced and the juvenile justice system began to take on more characteristics of the adult criminal court. Many of these changes were in response to landmark U.S. Supreme Court decisions pertaining to juvenile justice (see **Table 6.1**).

In Minnesota, a comprehensive revision of the juvenile code in 1959 raised the minimum age of adult prosecution to age 14, where it currently remains (Minnesota Laws 1959 c 685 s 16). In 1973, Minnesota transferred control of juvenile offenders from the Youth Conservation Commission to the Commissioner of Corrections. However, diversion and deinstitutionalization were still the banners of juvenile justice policy (Feld, 2007).

Following a sharp increase in violent juvenile crime in the 1980s and 1990s, the pendulum began to swing toward law and order (Feld, 1984). Spurred by sensationalist media coverage of a "new breed" (DiIulio, 1995, p. 23) of "fatherless, Godless, and jobless" *juvenile superpredators* (Bennett, DiIulio, & Walters, 1996, p. 27) and an impending juvenile "crime wave storm" (Fox, 1996) that never actually materialized (see **Chapter One**), legislatures across the country limited judicial discretion and adopted a more punitive stance toward juvenile offenders. In 1980, for instance, the Minnesota legislature repudiated the "rehabilitative" commitment of the juvenile code to provide "care and guidance ...

Table 6.1. Landmark U.S. Supreme Court Decisions Pertaining to Juvenile Justice

U.S. Supreme Court Decisions	Ruling
Kent v. United States (1966)	Courts must provide the "essentials of due process" in transferring juveniles to the adult system
In re Gault (1967)	Juveniles have basic constitutional rights to notice, counsel, confrontation, and privilege against self-incrimination
In re Winship (1970)	In delinquency matters, the State must prove its case "beyond a reasonable doubt," rather than by the lower, civil "preponderance of the evidence" standard of proof
McKeiver v. Pennsylvania (1971)	Jury trials are not constitutionally required in juvenile court hearings because "due process" required only "accurate fact-finding," which a judge could do as well as a jury
Breed v. Jones (1975)	Waiver of a juvenile to criminal court following adjudication in juvenile court constitutes double jeopardy
Smith v. Daily Mail Publishing Co. (1979)	The press may report juvenile court proceedings under certain circumstances
Eddings v. Oklahoma (1982)	Defendant's youthful age should be considered a mitigating factor in deciding whether to apply the death penalty
Schall v. Martin (1984)	Preventive "pretrial" detention of juveniles is allowable under certain circumstances
New Jersey v. T.L.O. (1985)	Schools can search students if they have reasonable suspicion
Stanford v. Kentucky (1989)	Minimum age for death penalty is set at 16
Veronia School District v. Acton (1995)	Schools can drug test all students who choose to participate in athletics
Board of Education v. Earl (2002)	Schools can drug test all students who choose to participate in extra curricular activities
Roper v. Simmons (2005)	The death penalty for those who had committed their crimes at under 18 years of age was cruel and unusual punishment, thus unconstitutional
Safford Unified School District v. Redding (2009)	Searches in schools using reasonable suspicion cannot be excessively intrusive (i.e. strip searches)
Graham v. Florida (2010)	Juvenile offenders cannot be sentenced to life imprisonment without parole for non-homicide offenses
J.D.B. v. North Carolina (2011)	Age is relevant when determining police custody for Miranda purposes
Miller v. Alabama (2012)	Mandatory sentences of life without the possibility of parole are unconstitutional for juvenile offenders
Montgomery v. Louisiana (2016)	*Miller v. Alabama* applies retroactively

Source: Author created from National Juvenile Defender Center (n.d.).

as will serve the spiritual, emotional, mental and physical welfare of the minor and the best interests of the state" and repurposed the juvenile court "to promote the public safety and reduce juvenile delinquency ... by developing individual responsibility for lawful behavior" (Minnesota Statutes §260.011; Feld, 1981). As a result, the number of offenses for which a juvenile could be tried as an adult increased significantly.

The 1980s and 1990s were busy decades in juvenile justice policy in Minnesota (for a review, see Swayze & Buskovick, 2014a). In 1986, for example, the Minnesota legislature opened to the public delinquency hearings of juveniles 16 years of age or older and charged with a felony level offense (Minnesota Statutes §260.155). In 1991, a "crime committed for the benefit of a gang" was added to the Minnesota statute, thus creating sentencing enhancements for juveniles (see **Chapter Seven**). In 1994, Minnesota authorized a new tier of sentencing called Extended Juvenile Jurisdiction (EJJ), which allowed juveniles to be tried and sentenced in juvenile court, but receive stayed adult sentences. That same year, the legislature expanded juvenile certification, allowing 15-year-olds— now 14-year-olds—to be certified to adult court after showing that retaining the child in juvenile court would not serve public safety (Minnesota Statutes §260B.125). And in 1998, Minnesota created mandatory life imprisonment sentences for "heinous" crimes (Minnesota Statutes §609.106).

In 2012, the U.S. Supreme Court ruled in *Miller v. Alabama* that mandatory life without parole sentences (LWOP) for juveniles convicted of homicide are unconstitutional. However, the Minnesota Supreme Court in 2013, and again in 2014, controversially ruled the *Miller* holding cannot retroactively apply to juveniles given mandatory life without parole sentences. This despite the fact the Minnesota branch of the Department of Justice already conceded *Miller* applies retroactively (Mazurek, 2015). As a result, juveniles within the state of Minnesota face disparate treatment depending on whether the state or federal government prosecutes them (Mazurek, 2015).

Juvenile Crime Data in Minnesota

Over thirty years of juvenile arrest data (**Figure 6.1**) illustrate that juvenile arrests in Minnesota increased 150 percent between 1982 and the peak year of 1998 (see Swayze & Buskovick, 2013). In 1998, there were 134 arrest events for each 1,000 youth aged 10 to 17 in the population. The number and rate of juvenile arrests for *violent crime* peaked in Minnesota and nationally in 1994 (see **Chapter Seven**). Conversely, between 1998 and 2011, juvenile arrests declined in Minnesota by over half (−55%). Ultimately, the number of arrests in 2013 (36,192) was comparable to the number recorded in 1980 (36,008). Minnesota's juvenile arrest pattern, therefore, largely follows the national pattern during the same period, though the rise and fall are more pronounced in Minnesota than nationally (see **Chapter One**).

Consistent with national trends, the number of females in the Minnesota juvenile justice system has also increased over time. Between 1980 and 1990, females accounted for roughly 25 percent of all juvenile arrests. Between 2005 and 2010, females accounted for 33 percent of total juvenile arrests (Swayze & Buskovick, 2013). Of all violent crime, the most juvenile arrests are for aggravated assault followed by robbery. Despite media depictions, the least common juvenile violent crime is murder. Juvenile property crime totals in Minnesota are dominated by the larceny category, which includes all levels of theft ranging from low-level shoplifting to high-value products (Swayze & Buskovick, 2013).

Minnesota court data illustrate a 325 percent rise in juvenile petitions filed between 1984 and 1998, from approximately 15,0000 to more than 63,0000 (Swayze & Buskovick, 2013). Petitions are all cases brought to court in a given year, regardless of when the case comes to conclusion or whether there is a legal finding of guilt. While the number of juvenile petitions filed between 1998 and 2011 declined by 47 percent, the number of youth petitioned in 2011 (33,828) was still over twice the number recorded in 1980. Higher court volume in the 1990s and 2000s is partially attributable to improved data collection and reporting methodologies (namely the introduction of the Minnesota Court Information System [MNCIS] in 2003), but also the larger proportion of arrests petitioned to court than in the 1980s (Swayze & Buskovick, 2013). Many of these petitions are brought by law enforcement.

Youth involved in the juvenile justice system in Minnesota can be placed out of their homes with a Department of Corrections (DOC) or Department of Human Services (DHS) licensed provider after arrest, pending the outcome of court proceedings, or as a dispositional outcome when court-ordered to a residential program. The 50 percent decline in the use of combined secure (e.g., MCF–Red Wing, see **Chapter Four**) and non-secure correctional placements for juveniles in Minnesota between 2001 and 2010 corresponds to the decrease in juvenile arrests and petitions described above, but also the 1999 closing of Minnesota Correctional Facility–Sauk Centre, also known as the *Minnesota Home School* (Justice Policy Institute, 2013). Prior to closing in 1999, all female juvenile offenders under the jurisdiction of the DOC were housed at Sauk Centre. Today, a small number of serious female juvenile offenders are held in DOC contract facilities such as Woodland Hills in Duluth and the Dakota County Juvenile Services Center in Hastings (Swayze & Buskovick, 2013).

On January 1, 2014, there were 22 juveniles (20 males) committed to the Department of Corrections: 30% were for criminal sexual conduct, 15% for felony
theft, 15% for burglary, and the remaining for other crimes (Minnesota House
of Representatives, 2015). Furthermore, there were 7,477 under community supervision, of which 7,471 were on probation. A majority (87%) are supervised
by local agents (Minnesota House of Representatives, 2015).

Figure 6.1. Total Minnesota Juvenile Arrests, 1980–2013

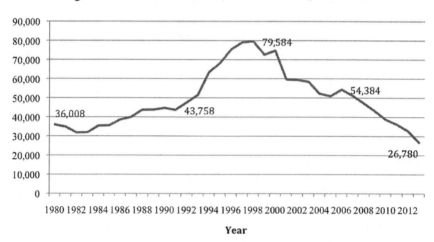

Source: Author created from Swayze and Buskovick (2013)

The Juvenile Justice System in Minnesota

Youth under age 18 presently account for approximately 1.3 million of Minnesota's 5.4 million residents (Swayze & Buskovick, 2014a). Under Minnesota
law, children under the age of 14 years are incapable of committing *crime* (Minnesota Statutes §609.055). Anyone who commits a crime when he or she is between the ages of 10 and 17 is considered a juvenile offender (see **Table 6.2**).
With a few exceptions for especially violent crimes, most juvenile cases remain
in the juvenile court. Younger children are referred to the child welfare system.

Table 6.2. Juvenile Age of Jurisdiction by State

Age	State	N
Upper Age of Jurisdiction		
15	Connecticut, New York, North Carolina	3
16	Georgia, Illinois, Louisiana, Michigan, Missouri, New Hampshire, South Carolina, Texas, Wisconsin	9
17	Alabama, Alaska, Arizona, Arkansas, California, Colorado, Delaware, Florida, Hawaii, Idaho, Indiana, Iowa, Kansas, Kentucky, Maine, Maryland, Massachusetts, **Minnesota**, Mississippi, Montana, Nebraska, Nevada, New Jersey, New Mexico, North Dakota, Oklahoma, Oregon, Pennsylvania, Rhode Island, South Dakota, Tennessee, Utah, Vermont, Virginia, Washington, West Virginia, Wyoming	38
Minimum Age for Delinquency Adjudication		
10	Alabama, Colorado, Kansas, Louisiana, **Minnesota**, Mississippi, Pennsylvania, South Dakota, Texas, Vermont, Wisconsin	11
8	Arizona, Nevada, Washington	3
7	Maryland, Massachusetts, New York	3
6	North Carolina	1
No minimum	Alaska, Arkansas, California, Connecticut, Delaware, Florida, Georgia, Hawaii, Idaho, Illinois, Indiana, Iowa, Kentucky, Louisiana, Maine, Michigan, Missouri, Montana, Nebraska, New Hampshire, New Jersey, New Mexico, North Dakota, Oklahoma, Oregon, Rhode Island, South Carolina, Tennessee, Utah, Virginia, West Virginia, Wyoming	32

N.B. The upper age of jurisdiction is the oldest age at which a juvenile court has original jurisdiction over an individual for law violating behavior.

Source: Author created from Office of Juvenile Justice and Delinquency Prevention (2013)

The juvenile court in Minnesota is authorized to hear cases involving 1) juveniles who commit unlawful acts and 2) Children in Need of Protection or Services (CHIPS) from or by the court, and as such there are two different processes (see **Figure 6.1**). When a juvenile falls under the first category of committing an unlawful act and he or she has not been certified to adult court or committed First Degree Murder, then he/she will be in one of four categories:

1) *Delinquent*—under 18 who commit acts that would be unlawful if committed by an adult except for petty offenses.
2) *Extended Jurisdiction Juveniles*—children 14 or older who commit felony-level delinquent act.

3) *Petty Offenders*—acts that are unlawful because of age (like drinking or smoking) and 1st or 2nd nonviolent misdemeanors (see section below labeled "petty offenses" for more detail).

4) *Juvenile traffic offenders*—age and offense may move the case to adult court.

Each of these categories is discussed below.

As for CHIPS cases, there are many reasons why a child would need protection and services from the court, some of which include: the child is abandoned; he/she needs food, clothing, and shelter; the child is medically neglected; the child is abused physically or sexually; the child is a habitual truant; the child has runway; the parents want to revoke their parental rights; and a child is exposed to criminal activity in the home (Minnesota House of Representatives, 2014).

The juvenile court is also responsible for such matters involving termination of parental rights, appointment and removal of guardians, juvenile marriages, adoption matters, foster care matters, persons who contribute to delinquency or neglect of minor, and reestablishment of legal parent and child relationship (Minnesota House of Representatives, 2014). Parental liability laws in Minnesota are limited, but in some situations parents may be civilly responsible for their children's acts. For example, a parent can be responsible for paying for theft (Minnesota Statutes § 604.14), damages or injuries caused by their child up to a $1,000 (Minnesota Statutes § 540.18), or $5,000 if the crime is bias motivated (Minnesota Statutes § 611A.79). Parents are exempt only if they show they made a reasonable effort to control their child's behavior.

Figure 6.2. Court Process for Delinquency and CHIPS Cases

Delinquency and Other Offenses	• Apprehension • Pretrial Detention • Filing of Petition or Citation • Arraignment Hearing • Certification for Adult Prosecution Hearing or EJJ Hearing (if applicable) • Disposition Hearing • Expungement of Delinquency Records
CHIPS Cases	• Pre-Adjudication Detention • Filing or Petition of Citation • First Appearance • Adjudicatory Hearing • Review of Court-Ordered Placements • Disposition Hearing • Reestablishment of legal parent/child relationship

Source: Author created from Minnesota House of Representatives (2014)

Delinquency

In juvenile court, a defendant is adjudicated *delinquent* rather than found guilty of a *crime*. A delinquent offense is an act committed by a juvenile for which an adult could be prosecuted in criminal court. A delinquent *adjudication* means there has been an admission of guilt by the youth or a legal finding of guilt by a judge; it is the juvenile equivalent of an adult conviction. Adjudications become part of a juvenile's formal criminal record and are often required in order for youth to be placed in certain correctional settings. This can be used to charge or enhance charges. For example, a juvenile is adjudicated on an assault in the first degree. Five years later, the juvenile is now an adult and was arrested for his or her first time as an adult with a firearm. Because of the criminal history showing the adjudication on the assault charge, he or she would be charged at a felony level instead of a possible misdemeanor.

In juvenile court, moreover, there is a *disposition* rather than a *sentence*. The disposition is generally focused on maintaining public safety, but more so rehabilitating the child and returning him or her to law-abiding behavior. Depending on the circumstances of the case, a judge has the ability to order a very broad range of consequences and programming such as:

- Probation supervision
- Restitution
- Community service (also referred to as Sentencing To Service or STS)
- Counseling
- Home detention
- Chemical dependency treatment
- Loss of driver's license
- Placement at a residential juvenile correctional facility such as Boys Totem Town or the state juvenile correctional facility in Red Wing

(Hennepin County Attorney, 2015)

Minnesota has two case outcomes other than adjudication where the court may impose sanctions and supervision without a formal finding of responsibility: *continuance for dismissal* and *stay of adjudication* (Swayze & Buskovick, 2013). In both cases youth may receive court-imposed sanctions and must remain law abiding for a certain period of time to keep charges off their records. This philosophy is different from adult court where there is a greater focus at sentencing on what the punishment should be for a specific criminal act. Still, as with adult court, victims have a right to receive notice of charges, court proceedings, plea negotiations and dispositions (Hennepin County Attorney, 2015).

Other differences in the juvenile justice system compared to the adult system are that juveniles are generally not tried by a jury of one's peers, rather the judge makes the decision. The court proceedings are generally closed to the public to protect privacy. Parents are involved in the juvenile process. The entrance into the juvenile justice system, in addition to official action (arrest, summons, citation), can come from referral by parents, schools, or other interested parties. In addition to the differences in terms used for adults versus juveniles already highlighted, there are many more including such terms as: "Parole" vs. "aftercare," "incarceration" vs. "commitment," "halfway house" vs. "residential care facility," "reduction of charges" vs. "substitution," "jail" vs. "detention facility," etc. And lastly, juveniles also do not have a right to bail; instead they are released to their parents or guardian.

Petty Offenses

The term *status offense* does not exist in Minnesota Statutes or Rules of Procedure, but local practitioners often use the term to describe acts by minors that are illegal by virtue of their age. A status offense is conduct that would not be a crime if committed by an adult. Examples include:

- Truancy—Minnesota Statutes §260A.02 defines continuing truancy as "absent from instruction in a school without valid excuse within a single school year for: (1) three days if the child is in elementary school; or (2) three or more class periods on three days if the child is in middle school, junior high school, or high school."
- Curfew violations—Minnesota Statutes §245A.05 permits a county to adopt a curfew for any unmarried person under the age of 18 and for various times depending on age. For example, in the largest county in Minnesota, Hennepin, the curfew is 9PM for under 12 years old, 10PM for 12–14 years old, and 11PM for 15–17. On the weekends an hour is added to each (Hennepin County Attorney, 2015a).
- Running away
- Underage possession and/or consumption of tobacco products
- Underage alcohol offenses (N.B. The legal drinking age in Minnesota was 19 until 1986. Today, alcohol possession and use by adults aged 18–20 are crimes punishable under state criminal statutes and are not treated as status offenses.)

Females make up a large percentage of juvenile arrests for status offenses in Minnesota, including one-third of arrests for curfew violations and 50 to 60 percent of arrests for runaway (Swayze & Buskovick, 2013).

In Minnesota, the above are all considered *petty offenses* (Minnesota Statutes § 260B.007). While petty offenders are under the delinquency chapter in statute and procedure, the statutes clearly state that petty offenders shall not be adjudicated delinquent. Most traffic offenses, low level theft, disorderly conduct, disturbing the peace, and low level property damage are also offenses which can, and often are, handled as misdemeanor-level petty offenses rather than as misdemeanors, which is their classification if committed by an adult (Hennepin County Attorney, 2015b). Likewise, abused and neglected youth, habitual truants and runaways, youth found in dangerous surroundings, youth engaged in prostitution, and youth committing delinquent acts before the age of 10 are adjudicated as Children in Need of Protection or Services (CHIPS, formerly "dependent and neglected youth") and not adjudicated delinquent (Minnesota Statutes § 260C.007).

Note, non-delinquents can be held in secure juvenile facilities based on "contempt of court" even when their underlying offense would not otherwise meet secure admission criteria. In 1980, the Minnesota Supreme Court ruled in *State ex rel. LEA v. Hammergren* that non-delinquent youth simply had to be notified in advance that failure to follow court conditions could result in secure confinement. The outcome of this decision was the "Hammergren Warning," named after Donald Hammergren, former Hennepin County Juvenile Detention Facility Superintendent, which must be given by a judge in court, on the record, to this effect (Swayze, 2010).

Diversion

As of July 1995, all county attorneys in Minnesota are required to provide at least one juvenile-pretrial diversion program as an alternative to prosecution (Minnesota Statutes § 388.24), although in practice county probation providers are most likely to operate said programs (Swayze & Buskovick, 2012a). Juvenile diversion helps eligible young people who have been cited or arrested for an offense to avoid a charge and a juvenile court record. Young people with little or no juvenile history who have been cited or arrested for a lower-level offense are eligible. So too are lower-level offenses include juvenile petty offenses, most misdemeanor and gross misdemeanor offenses, and with some exceptions, felony property offenses, although there is no uniform standard across Minnesota counties (Swayze & Buskovick, 2012a). Instead of going to court, the offender and his or her parent or guardian attend a diversion intake meeting, complete an assessment, and sign a diversion agreement (Hennepin County Attorney, 2015b).

The diversion agreement typically is a six month contract that requires the offender to accept responsibility for the offense, attend school, adhere to household rules, remain law-abiding by not committing any new offenses, pay restitution to their victim(s), and participate in appropriate programs or services for their needs and circumstances (e.g., mental health and chemical dependency treatment). Although the juvenile is required to accept responsibility for his or her actions, there is no formal guilty plea or record of an admission (Hennepin County Attorney, 2015b). If the youth follows the conditions of that contract, moreover, there is no charge and no juvenile court record. If the youth chooses not to participate or does not follow the conditions of the diversion contract, however, the case is charged and brought to juvenile court.

Adult Certification

When an offense is particularly serious or violent, a juvenile may be certified as an adult and tried in adult criminal court (Minnesota Statutes § 260B.125). Minnesota adopted the term certification as a part of the 1994 Juvenile Court Act. Under the terms of the law, the juvenile must be at least 14 years old, charged with a felony and be a violent or habitual offender to be certified. First-degree murder, however, gives the adult court original jurisdiction (Minnesota Statutes § 260B.007, subd. 6(b)). In other words, a 16- or 17-year-old charged with first-degree murder is automatically tried as an adult. Several other offenses, such as a felony with a firearm, are termed "presumptive" in that it is presumed that the 16- or 17-year-old will be certified as an adult. Under these circumstances, the prosecutor can file motions for adult certification or Extended Juvenile Jurisdiction (EJJ), which allows the court to keep the juvenile in juvenile court until he or she is 21 years old (Hennepin County Attorney, 2015b). Approximately 100 youth each year are certified to stand trial as adults in Minnesota, and in the past decade over 300 inmates who were certified as adults at the time of sentencing have been housed in Minnesota prisons (Swayze & Buskovick, 2013). Minnesota Statutes § 641.14 makes it clear that a minor cannot be detained or confined with adults unless he or she has been indicted for first-degree murder, certified for trial as an adult, or convicted as an adult.

Blended Sentencing

Extended Juvenile Jurisdiction (EJJ) is Minnesota's blended sentencing option intended to retain youth who qualify for adult certification in the juvenile system. Under EJJ, youth can remain under the jurisdiction of the juvenile court until their 21st birthday. An EJJ designation gives a youth both a juvenile disposition and a stayed adult sentence. In the event an EJJ youth commits a new offense or violates their conditions of probation supervision, their EJJ status can be revoked with due process, and the adult sentence imposed (Hennepin County Attorney, 2015b).

Approximately 200 to 250 youth are adjudicated EJJ annually (Swayze & Buskovick, 2013). In order to be eligible for EJJ designation, youth must have committed a felony level offense while between the ages of 14 and 17. A prosecutor then either petitions the case with an EJJ motion, petitions the case with an adult certification motion, or chooses to allow the case to proceed in juvenile court. In cases where the offense is a "presumptive certification" and adult certification is not imposed, EJJ designation is the alternative disposition (Minnesota Statutes § 260B.130).

Juvenile Probation

As introduced in **Chapter Four**, Minnesota has three delivery systems for the supervision of all adult and juvenile offenders on parole, probation, and supervised release (intensive and regular) as established under the Department of Corrections Contract, the County Probation Act (Minnesota Statutes § 244.19) and the Community Corrections Act (Minnesota Statutes § 41) (see **Table 6.3**). Each delivery system dictates how services are paid for and how probation staff are employed (see Minnesota Department of Corrections, 2007). In 27 *Department of Corrections* (DOC) counties, DOC field agents supervise all adult and juvenile offenders of all offense levels. In 28 *County Probation Officer* (CPO) counties, probation officers appointed by the judiciary of the district court supervise all adults and juveniles with the exception of adult felons, who are supervised by DOC agents. And in 32 *Community Corrections Act* (CCA) counties, probation officers hired by the county's Community Corrections Department supervise all adult and juvenile probationers of all offense levels.

Under statute and established rules of procedure, youth do not have to be adjudicated delinquent in Minnesota to be placed on probation. Supervision can be a part of a continuance for dismissal disposition as well as a stay of adjudication disposition. The numbers of Minnesota youth on probation peaked at 18,000 in 1999, but has since fallen over 50% to approximately 8,500 in 2013, comparable to figures in the mid 1980s. Declining court volume is one factor in declining juvenile probation volume in Minnesota (Swayze & Buskovick, 2013).

Table 6.3. Court Services Delivery Systems in Minnesota

System	Counties	N
Department of Corrections Counties	Becker, Beltrami, Benton, Clay, Clearwater, Cottonwood, Douglas, Faribault, Hubbard, Kittson, Lake of the Woods, Le Sueur, Lincoln, Lyon, Mahnomen, Marshall, Martin, McLeod, Murray, Pennington, Pipestone, Redwood, Renville, Roseau, Sibley, Watonwan, Winona	27
County Probation Officer	Benton, Big Stone, Brown, Carver, Cass, Chisago, Freeborn, Goodhue, Grant, Houston, Isanti, Itasca, Jackson, Kanabec, Meeker, Mille Lacs, Mower, Nicollet, Otter Tail, Pine, Pope, Sherburne, Steele, Stevens, Traverse, Wabasha, Waseca, Wilkin, Wright	28
Community Corrections Act	Aitkin, Anoka, Blue Earth, Carlton, Chippewa, Cook, Crow Wing, Dakota, Dodge, Fillmore, Hennepin, Kandiyohi, Koochiching, Lake, Lac qui Parle, Morrison, Nobles, Norman, Olmsted, Polk, Ramsey, Red Lake, Rice, Rock, Scott, St. Louis, Stearns, Swift, Todd, Wadena, Washington, Yellow Medicine	32

Source: Author created from Minnesota Department of Corrections (2007)

Core Protections for Juveniles

The federal Juvenile Justice and Delinquency Prevention Act of 2002 requires that Minnesota monitor its juvenile justice system for four core protections for youth, three of which are related to the appropriate use of secure detention facilities for accused and adjudicated youth (Swayze, 2010). Specifically, the act requires:

1. The deinstitutionalization of non-offenders and status-level offenders from secure facilities;
2. The removal of delinquent youth from adult jails and police lockups;
3. And that juveniles be sight and sound separated from adult inmates whenever they are held in the same facility.

A fourth protection requires that states monitor their juvenile justice system for the over-representation of youth from communities of color, known as Disproportionate Minority Contact (DMC). DMC has shown to exist in most states throughout the U.S. (Kempf-Leonard, 2007). As discussed in **Chapter Four**, youth of color are disparately represented at all stages of justice-system processing in Minnesota. Further, the level of disparity in Minnesota is more severe than both the national average and comparable states (Swayze & Buskovick, 2012c). In 2010, for example, 44 percent of total juvenile arrests were youth of color compared to just 12 percent in 1980. While the population of youth of color has increased from 5 percent to 22 percent of youth ages 10 to 17, youth of color are still substantially overrepresented in Minnesota at the point of arrest (Swayze & Buskovick, 2013).

Child Abuse and Neglect

In September 2015, Minnesota Vikings running back Adrian Peterson, one of the National Football League's top stars, was charged with one count of reckless or negligent injury to a child, a felony, for disciplining his 4-year-old son with a switch. The case was eventually pled down to a single charge of reckless assault, a misdemeanor, but Peterson still missed the entire NFL season and suffered untold damage to his once stellar reputation. More importantly, his actions shone a national spotlight on the fine line between discipline and abuse (Zinser, 2014).

For much of history there were no laws protecting children from physical abuse from their parents, to the extent that the American Society for the Prevention of Cruelty to *Animals* brought the very first case in New York in 1874 (Markel, 2009). Today, Minnesota, acting as a parent, has the authority to intervene in cases involving child abuse and neglect. Child *abuse* is the mistreatment (sexual, physical, or mental) of anyone below 18 years old, whereas *neglect* is when a child is denied basic necessitates or is not provided proper protection or supervision (Minnesota Statutes §626.556). The Minnesota Maltreatment of Minority Act further defines what constitutes each of these behaviors, as outlined in **Table 6.4.** Anyone who knows of cases involving child abuse and neglect should report a case. There are several people who are required by law to report a suspected case of abuse and neglect, including clergy, educators, health care, law enforcement, child care workers, mental health professionals, social services, guardians *ad litem* (see next section), and correctional staff (Minnesota Statutes §626.556, subd. 3). The Child Safety and Permanency Division of the Minnesota Department of Human Services has *A Resource Guide for Mandated Reporters* (2012) to ensure mandated reporters know the process for reporting and associated laws and policies.

The Minnesota Department of Human Services (2015) works with social service agencies in each of the 87 counties and 11 tribal lands in Minnesota who deal with child maltreatment. In 2013, 19,000 reports of child maltreatment were made throughout the state, of which three quarters of the

Table 6.4. Behaviors that Constitute Abuse or Neglect

Sexual (or threatened) Abuse	Physical (or threatened) Abuse	Neglect
Soliciting a child to practice prostitution	Physical injury, mental injury, or threatened injury	Failure to supply necessary food, clothing, shelter, or medical care when reasonably able to do so
Criminal sexual conduct	Inflicted other than by accident physical or mental injury not reasonably explained by the child's history of injuries	Failure to protect a child from serious danger to physical or mental health when reasonably able to do so, including a growth delay, referred to as failure to thrive
Receiving profit derived from prostitution by a child	Aversive or deprivation procedures (e.g., electric shock) not authorized by Department of Human Services rules	Failure to provide necessary supervision or appropriate child care
Hiring or agreeing to hire a child as a prostitute	Regulated interventions (e.g., time out) not authorized by Department of Education rules	Chronic and severe use of alcohol or a controlled substance by a parent or person responsible for the child's care that adversely affects the child's basic needs and safety
Using a minor in a sexual performance or pornographic work		Emotional harm demonstrated by a substantial and observable effect on the child
		Withholding medical treatment, including\medically indicated treatment from a disabled infant with a life-threatening condition
		Prenatal exposure to specified controlled substances
		Failure to ensure that a child is educated in accordance with state law

Source: Author created from Minnesota Statutes §626.556.

reports received a family *assessment* and the remaining a family *investigation*. The later is for when a family will not participate in an assessment or when a child is in immediate or significant danger. After an investigation, if the findings are such, a petition may be filled with the court and brought to a CHIPS Court. In 2000, the Children's Justice Initiative was formed by the Minnesota Supreme Court and the Minnesota Human Services to ensure that any decisions/recommendations made should be from the "eyes of the child" and must achieve at least one of the following: (1) child safety; (2) child stability; (3) permanency for the child; (4) timeliness of process; (5) system accountability; and/or (6) due process protection for the parties (Minnesota Judicial Branch, 2015).

In addition to child abuse and neglect cases, there are several laws in Minnesota that define certain acts committed with or against children as crimes or petty misdemeanors. These acts include such things as providing a tattoo to a minor without parental consent (Minnesota Statutes § 146B.07; § 645.241), allowing a child to tan with ultraviolet light (Minnesota Statutes § 325H.01– 325H.10), giving a lottery ticket to someone under the age of 18 (Minnesota Statutes § 240.13), a pawnbroker making a purchase from someone under the age of 18 (Minnesota Statutes § 325J.08), and marrying someone under the age of 18 without parental consent (Minnesota Statutes § 609.265).

Guardians *ad Litem*

Guardians *ad litem* (GAL) are objective adults, court-appointed to serve as advocates for children involved in a court case. In legal terms, GAL means "guardian of the lawsuit" (State Guardian ad Litem Board, 2013). GAL are spokespersons for the short- and long-term *best interests of the child* appointed in different kinds of cases, including child abuse and neglect cases filed in Juvenile Court (Minnesota Statutes § 260C.163), and divorce or custody cases filed in Family Court (Minnesota Statutes § 518.165).

Guardians *ad litem* in Minnesota include specially trained community volunteers and state employees. They are reimbursed for services at the following rates:

- Abuse, Neglect, and Termination of Parental Rights cases: $1000 total
- All other Juvenile cases: $500 total
- Family cases: $1500 total
- Other cases: $500 total
- Orders For Protection: No charge

(State Guardian ad Litem Board, 2013b)

As outlined by the State Guardian ad Litem Board (2013a), GAL are different from legal guardians because they have no control over the person or property of the child and do not provide a home for the child. GAL also do not function as the child's attorney and provide direct services to the child. Instead, they gather information. GAL interview and observe children and their families. They review social service, medical, school, psychological and criminal records and reports. They attend meetings with the other professionals involved with the children and their families. They outline options and make non-binding written and oral *recommendations* to the court to enable the court to make the best possible decisions. Finally, GAL monitor court ordered plans to ensure children's best interests are being met.

The GAL program emerged in Minnesota following the Federal Child Abuse Prevention and Treatment Act mandate in 1974. With no obvious state agency to administer a statewide GAL program, however, Minnesota delegated responsibility to individual district courts and counties, resulting in a decentralized system. In 1995, in response to concerns raised by citizens to the Legislature about this system, the Office of the Legislative Auditor (1995, p. 47) conducted a statewide review of GAL services and in their report concluded:

> There are 53 local (county-funded) programs. There is little consistency in how counties recruit, select, and supervise guardians. There is no standard training, no system to process complaints and no uniform procedures to remove a GAL. The Supreme Court needs to develop broad guidelines addressing recruitment, selection, supervision, and evaluation for programs to use in administering their program.

Since the Legislative Auditor's Report, there have been a series of reforms to the GAL system, including Rules of GAL Procedure; mandatory statewide training requirements and administrative standards to improve performance and accountability; and an independent GAL Board, thus moving the program outside of the court system (Minnesota Statutes § 480.35).

Bullying and School Violence

For most of the year, children spend more time at school than anywhere else other than their own home. School safety, therefore, is of paramount concern. Violence prevention education has been a mainstay of Minnesota schools since 1992, but only since 2005 have all Minnesota school boards been required to adopt a written policy prohibiting the intimidation or bullying of any student (Swayze & Buskovick, 2014a). After Governor Tim Pawlenty vetoed an anti-bullying measure in 2009, however, Minnesota policy-makers have argued over proper language and measurements that would outline legislation aimed at improving student safety (McGuire, 2015). It took a potential lawsuit against the Anoka-Hennepin school district, Minnesota's largest, for failing to prevent bullying taking place within its schools, to finally force the issue, resulting in the 2014 Safe and Supportive Schools Act (Minnesota Statutes § 121A.031).

The Safe and Supportive Schools Act replaced a 37-word anti-bullying law that was widely considered one of the nation's weakest (McGuire, 2015). The new law requires school districts to track and investigate cases of bullying and train teachers and administrators to prevent it (McGuire, 2014). The new law also includes the following components:

1. A clear definition of bullying and intimidation;
2. Various protective measures for students who are more likely to be bullied or harassed because of their race, color, creed, religion, disability, sex, age etc.; and
3. Specific procedures school staff must follow when an incident of bullying is reported.

(Outfront Minnesota, 2013)

School districts are not required to keep data they gather on bullying or report it, nor require mandatory training for school volunteers. Further, schools are only required to adopt the new legislation if they do not already have an anti-bullying plan in place (McGuire, 2014). Whether or not the new law will reduce bullying within Minnesota schools, therefore, remains to be seen.

Endemic bullying is of course not the only safety concern in Minnesota schools. The 1999 Columbine High School massacre in Columbine, Colorado, and the 2012 Sandy Hook Elementary School shooting in Newtown, Connecticut, are two of the most infamous cases of school violence in America (see Fox & DeLateur, 2014), but Minnesota too has had school shootings (Swayze & Buskovick, 2014b). The first occurred in 1966 in the northern Minnesota town of Grand Rapids. A 15-year-old middle school student shot another student and killed a school administrator in the parking lot at the start of the school day. The first *high profile* school shooting was in 2003 when a freshman opened fire at Rocori High School in the town of Cold Spring, killing two students. But the *most* high profile Minnesota case is the 2005 Red Lake Indian Reservation spree killing (see **Chapter One**), which resulted in the death of two adults in the community and seven people at the high school, including an unarmed security guard at the entrance of the building, a teacher, and five students. Seven other people were injured.

Generally speaking, the safest place for children to be is in school (Robers et al., 2014), but extreme cases such as those aforementioned raise the specter of dangerous schools. Following the Red Lake shooting, for instance, Minnesota established the School Safety Center (MnSSC) within the Department of Homeland Security and Emergency Management and schools began adding *lock-down drills* to their crisis management policies (Swayze & Buskovick, 2014a). Following the 2012 Newtown shootings, which killed 20 children and 6 adult staff members, moreover, National Rifle Association spokesman Wayne LaPierre called for armed guards in every school (Fox & DeLateur, 2014). Civilian teachers from 15 states signed up for armed teacher training. And schools across the country began cracking down on supposedly troublesome behaviors, from making a "gun out of Lego" to playing "cops and robbers" in the playground (Densley, 2013). In reality, however, school crime and violence has been decreasing locally and nationally for two decades (Robers et al., 2014).

Law enforcement has long been present in Minnesota schools (Swayze & Buskovick, 2014b). Minneapolis developed one of the nation's first Police School Liaison Programs (PSLP) in 1967 and through local programs, but also the federal Drug Abuse Resistance Education (D.A.R.E., see Ennett et al., 1994) and Gang Resistance Education and Training (G.R.E.A.T., see Esbensen et al., 2013. See also **Chapter Seven** for a discussion of juvenile gangs) programs in the 1980s and 1990s, respectively, police entered schools in a crime prevention role. It was not until the late 1990s that formal School Resource Officer (SRO) programs to place cops in classrooms emerged. Between 1999 and 2005, for example, 77 Minnesota law enforcement agencies received federal grants to fund the creation of new SRO positions (Swayze & Buskovick, 2014b).

A 2013 survey of SROs in Minnesota schools found that nearly 3-in-10 public schools have them (Swayze & Buskovick, 2014b). In high schools, it is as high as 6-in-10. Minnesota SROs self-reported enjoying working with youth and school staff and believing they are used appropriately in schools. Many reported their SRO work was the most rewarding and useful law enforcement position they ever held. There are challenges, however, such as defining and adhering to the role of SROs in schools; adequate training in youth development and how to interact effectively with children and youth at various developmental stages; and ways to work in partnership with youth, school staff, and the parents of students (Swayze & Buskovick, 2014b).

Survey authors Swayze and Buskovick (2014b) offer six recommendations to improve SRO programs. First, law enforcement agencies should ensure that officers assigned to be SROs are highly motivated to perform this work. Second, schools and law enforcement agencies should develop a memorandum of understanding that states SROs' roles and duties. Third, SROs should be well-trained in preparation for SRO duties. Fourth, SROs and school staff should be cross-trained, so as to facilitate informed cooperation between SROs and school staff. Fifth, SROs should give high priority to preventing crime and disorder in schools rather than focusing on a reactive response after incidents have occurred. Sixth, the impact of SROs on school security and safety should be appropriately evaluated.

There is no clear evidence SROs or other measures such as metal detectors, random searches, drug-sniffing dogs, radio frequency monitors, and surveillance cameras make schools safer (Mukherjee, 2007). Some studies have found a decrease in violence in schools with in-house police officers, while others have found no relationship at all (American Psychological Association, 2006). Part of the problem is that police officers are trained in how to deal with conflict, not how to counsel youth and defuse typical adolescent drama. Student problems, in turn, are redefined as criminal issues requiring a criminal justice response (Na & Gottfredson, 2013; Theriot, 2009). And student problems increase because suspension, expulsion, arrest, etc., fail to address the underlying social and psychological causes of student misbehavior (Densley, 2013). Students cannot speak to appropriate adults if their problems involve criminal activity (e.g., drug use) for fear they will be punished under "zero tolerance" polices that automatically impose severe punishment regardless of circumstances (Skiba & Knesting, 2001).

Indeed, young people throughout the country have been punished for infractions to zero tolerance policies where the intent to commit harm was not readily present. In Anoka, Minnesota, for example, a high school student was suspended for ten days because he left a box cutter in his car that he used for work at a grocery store. Having the box cutter on school grounds was a violation of the school's zero tolerance policy (Kroman, 2008). In 2014, the Obama Administration sent a message to schools to end zero tolerance policies because of their costly disparities and practice. Recommendations were provided to include training in conflict resolution and de-escalation techniques and to more clearly articulate the responsibilities of security personnel to increase understanding about what constitutes a school infraction versus a threat to school safety (Associated Press, 2014).

In his 2010 book, *Homeroom Security: School Discipline in an Age of Fear*, sociologist Aaron Kupchik finds, "the presence of police in schools is unlikely to prevent another school shooting and the potential for oppression of students—especially poor and racial/ethnic minority youth—is a more realistic and common threat than Columbine" (p.82). Indeed, some, including St.

Catherine University professor Katherine Heitzeg (2009), argue too broad educational policies that disproportionately penalize students of color compared to their white peers and lead to school suspension or expulsion constitute a "schoolhouse to jailhouse track" or "school to prison pipeline" (see also, Petteruti, 2011). During the 2012–13 school year, approximately 12% of disciplinary incidents in Minnesota schools, involving 5,476 unique students, involved a referral to law enforcement. It is unknown how many referrals to law enforcement resulted in a formal citation or charges (Swayze & Buskovick, 2014b).

Youth Intervention Programs

A 1974 survey of 231 studies on offender rehabilitation headed by New York sociologist Robert Martinson concluded, "with few and isolated exceptions, the rehabilitation efforts that have been reported so far have had no appreciable effect on recidivism" (p. 25; see also, Lipton, Martinson, & Woks, 1975). In short order, and despite the fact the phrase never appeared in the original report, Martinson's survey came to be known simply as the "nothing works" study (Wilson, 1980). The supposedly incontrovertible truth that *nothing works* in rehabilitating offenders appealed to Left and Right alike (Cullen & Jonson 2009, p. 294). Liberals used the idea to justify an end to indeterminate sentencing tied to vague rehabilitation criteria such as "attitudinal change." Conservatives used the idea to promote retributive *tough on crime* policies such as mandatory prison terms and capital punishment. Two decades of punitive juvenile justice policy practice from "scared straight" programs to correctional boot camps followed (Kleiman, 2009).

The problem was, the null results noted by Martinson and colleagues were tied more to *process* issues of program fidelity (i.e., inappropriate management and implementation) than *outcome* issues of program effectiveness (Cullen & Jonson, 2009). A deeper read of the original study also reveals some rehabilitative programs could be successful contingent upon how success is defined. However, the *nothing works* doctrine took hold, so much so that when Gendreau and Ross (1987) found in fact *many things work*, their findings were discredited and largely dismissed (see Cullen & Jonson, 2009).

As crime continued to rise in the 1990s, and local, state, and federal agencies threw more and more money at the problem, there was increasing recognition that our thinking is really little more than models and interpretations (Barnes, 1990) and funding for crime control programming had to be tied to rigorous and scientifically recognized standards of evidence. One good thing that came out of the "nothing works" ideology was researchers developed more robust means to explain why some interventions were effective and others were not (e.g., Andrews et al., 1990). In 1995, for instance, the National Institute of Justice commissioned an independent review of over 500 program impact evaluations, which concluded, "some prevention programs work, some do not, some are promising, and some have not been tested adequately" (Sherman et al., 1998, p. v). Finally, *something worked*, just not the punitive "scared straight," "shock incarceration," and "boot camp" programs that supplanted rehabilitation during the *nothing works* era. Instead, what worked were programs dedicated to ameliorating underlying *risk factors* at the individual, family, peer, school, and community levels that statistically increase the likelihood of juvenile delinquency (Sherman et al., 1998).

The language of risk factors dominates contemporary discussions of crime prevention (Sherman et al., 2006). In Minnesota, for example, the Risk-Needs-Responsivity (R-N-R) model underlines much juvenile probation policy and practice (Andrews, Bonta, & Hoge, 1990). The risk principle states the level of service should match a juvenile's risk of reoffending. High-risk offenders get more intervention while low-risk offenders receive minimal or no intervention. The need principle states static (e.g., criminal history) and dynamic (e.g., social networks) risk factors should be assessed using actuarial assessment tools such as the Youth Level of Service/Case Management Inventory 2.0 (Hoge & Andrews, 2011) and treatment should be focused on individual *criminogenic needs* such as substance abuse (Andrews & Bonta, 2006). Finally, the responsivity principle essentially entails providing the right treatment at the right level. Agencies provide *cognitive behavioral treatment*, for instance, to maximize a youth's ability to learn from rehabilitative intervention or strength-based services such as *motivational interviewing* to engage families and other key stakeholders in a youth's recovery. However, Minnesota agencies do not always adhere to the R-N-R model. In many counties, for instance, juvenile sex offenders or high profile offenders are supervised at an intense level regardless of risk.

In 2003, Minnesota implemented mental health screenings for most justice system involved youth, contingent upon active parental consent (Minnesota Statutes § 260B.157). Further guided by R-N-R thinking, several Minnesota jurisdictions now limit use of out-of-home placement, providing culturally- and gender-responsive programming in the least restrictive setting necessary to protect public safety (Swayze & Buskovick, 2014a). In 2005, for instance, three of Minnesota's largest counties—Dakota, Hennepin, and Ramsey—adopted the Annie E. Casey Foundation's (2015) Juvenile Detention Alternatives Initiative (JDAI) to divert youth from secure confinement and ensure admissions relied upon objective, validated risk-assessment tools that ascertain risk to public safety (Swayze & Buskovick, 2014a). St. Louis County joined the initiative in 2009.

Specialty courts and diversion programs once deemed "soft" on crime also appear to be gaining a foothold (see **Chapter Three**). Teen courts, for instance, offer a dispositional alternative to the traditional juvenile justice system in which the young offenders' teenage peers hear facts surrounding the incident, deliberate, and determine a disposition, which often includes community service or alcohol or drug treatment (Butts & Buck, 2000). Teen courts are based on assumptions that (a) if antisocial peers can increase antisocial behavior then pro-social peers can encourage pro-social behavior and (b) adolescents are more likely to be influenced by their peers as opposed to adult authority figures in the formal juvenile justice system (Butts & Buck, 2000). In simple terms, teen courts harness the power of positive peer pressure. There are presently no definitive studies about teen court outcomes, and some concerns exist about selection bias in the system, but results are generally positive (see Butts et al., 2012).

In 1976, the Minnesota State Legislature created the Youth Intervention Program (YIP) to provide financial resources to "Youth Intervention Programs." By statute,

> Youth Intervention Program means a nonresidential community-based program providing advocacy, education, counseling, mentoring, and referral services to youth and their families experiencing personal, familial, school, legal, or chemical problems with the goal of resolving the present problems and preventing the occurrence of the problems in the future.
>
> (Minnesota Statutes § 299A.73 Subd. 1)

The 25 organizations that initially received State YIP funding established the Minnesota Youth Intervention Programs Association (YIPA) in 1978 and in 1984 incorporated as a 501(c) (3) nonprofit. YIPA does not directly serve youth, but rather the practitioners and organizations that do. YIPA offers professional development for youth intervention organizations and workers, a forum for collaboration, and advocacy for funding and support for programs throughout Minnesota. In 2012, 51 programs across Minnesota were selected to receive YIP funding (Swayze & Buskovick, 2012b). In addition to the programs identified under YIP, there are many other school, religious, sports, recreation, music, arts, scouting, etc. programs in Minnesota that work with youth to help prevent them from committing crimes in the first place or help them to stop committing further crime.

As mentioned in **Chapter One**, restorative justice has strong roots in Minnesota. This is especially true for responding to juvenile offenders because of diversion. Juveniles engage in restorative justice practices (victim-offender dialogue, conferencing, and circle work) through non-profit agencies to address their individual cases. Incorporating the value of community, offenders engage in the above processes providing conscious healing and culturally relevant responses to harm, which has been identified as a diversionary best practice (Swayze & Buskovick, 2012a). Cass County, in conjunction with the Leech Lake Tribal Court, is a great example of a best practice in providing diversion for first time offending youth. A panel of reservation community members meet with the juvenile and incorporate Ojibwe teachings to respond to the offense. The youth then returns to the community panel with a presentation of their choice illustrating their reflection of the Ojibwe values discussed and their connection realization of the harm as a result of their offense. Another example is in Carver County, where a Youth Empowerment Circle had been created to allow offenders encountering barriers to payment to participate in a circle process to earn monetary credit. These types of programs assist in providing the diversion of further court proceedings and probation revocation for the juveniles while incorporating a community, value-oriented and restoration-focused approach for the psychosocial development of the youth.

Concluding Remarks

Youth involvement in crime in Minnesota is at low levels not see since the 1980s. Is this a lull or a permanent change? Is Minnesota's juvenile justice system working? Perhaps. But we cannot forget those currently in the system. What are their needs? Many juvenile offenders in Minnesota have suffered one or more adverse childhood experiences such as abuse, having a mentally ill parent, domestic violence against a parent, a household member in prison, divorced parents, or a household member with a drug or alcohol problem (Swayze & Buskovick, 2012d). Likewise, many juvenile offenders were themselves victims of crime or exposed to one or more traumatic events that threatened or caused great physical harm in childhood (Swayze & Buskovick, 2012d). The prevalence of trauma in the lives of young people has led to calls for *trauma-informed* juvenile justice that takes steps to reduce the lasting and substantial collateral costs of incarceration on youth—potentially the next evolutionary stage in the system.

Keywords

Abuse
Adjudication
Adult Certification
Age of Jurisdiction
Age-Crime Curve
Blended Sentencing
Bullying
Child Abuse
Children in Need of Protection or
    Services (CHIPS)
Community Corrections Act
Continuance for Dismissal
County Probation Act
Delinquent
Disposition
Disproportionate Minority Contact
Diversion
Extended Juvenile Jurisdiction (EJJ)
Hammergren Warning
Guardians *ad litem*
In loco parentis
Juvenile Detention Alternatives
    Initiative (JDAI)

Juvenile Justice and Delinquency
    Prevention Act of 2002
Mandated Reporter
Mens rea
Neglect
"Nothing Works"
Parental Liability
Parens patriae
Petty Offense
Procedural Justice
Rational Choice Theory
Risk-Needs-Responsivity (R-N-R)
School Resource Officer
School Shootings
School to Prison Pipeline
Social Bond Theory
Social Learning Theory
Stay of Adjudication
Strain Theory
Superpredator
Trauma
Youth Intervention Program
Zero Tolerance

Selected Internet Sites

Annie E. Casey Foundation
http://www.aecf.org/work/juvenile-justice/jdai/

Hennepin County Juvenile Detention Center
http://www.hennepin.us/residents/public-safety/juvenile-detention-center

Juvenile Justice Advisory Committee
https://dps.mn.gov/entity/jjac/Pages/default.aspx

Juvenile Justice Coalition of Minnesota
http://www.jjcmn.com

Minnesota Department of Corrections, Juvenile Services
http://www.doc.state.mn.us/pages/index.php/facilities/juvenile-facilities/

Minnesota Judicial Branch, Juvenile Court
http://www.mncourts.gov/district/4/?page=372

Office of Justice Programs, Youth and Juvenile Justice Reports
https://dps.mn.gov/divisions/ojp/statistical-analysis-center/Pages/youth-juvenile-
justice-reports.aspx

Office of Juvenile Justice and Delinquency Prevention
http://www.ojjdp.gov

Ramsey County Juvenile Services
https://www.co.ramsey.mn.us/cc/juveniles.htm

Discussion Questions

1. What is the relationship between crime and age?
2. Do you think we even need a separate juvenile court system? Why/why not?
3. What are some of the key differences between the adult and juvenile justice process?
4. What do you think is the most important action a parent can do to help their children not become criminal?
5. Under what circumstances, if any, do you think juveniles should be waived to adult court?
6. What do you think should be the punishment for a parent found guilty of neglecting their children and why?
7. What can/should schools do to help stop bullying and prevent violence?
8. Do you think juveniles should have a right to a jury trial?
9. Do you think parents should be held civilly liable for their children's behavior?

References

Agnew, R. (1992). Foundation for a general strain theory of crime and delinquency. *Criminology*, 30, 47–87.

Akers, R. (2009). *Social learning and social structure: A general theory of crime.* New Brunswick, NJ: Transaction.

American Psychological Association. (2006). *Are zero tolerance policies effective in the schools? An evidentiary review and recommendations.* Washington DC: Author.

Andrews, D., & Bonta, J. (2006). *The psychology of criminal conduct* (4th ed.). Newark, NJ: LexisNexis.

Andrews, D., Bonta, J., & Hoge, R. (1990). Classification for effective rehabilitation: Rediscovering psychology. *Criminal Justice and Behavior, 17,* 19–52.

Andrews, D., Zinger, I., Hoge, R., Bonta, J., Gendreau, P., & Cullen, F. (1990). Does correctional treatment work? A psychologically informed meta-analysis. *Criminology, 28,* 369–404.

Annie E. Casey Foundation (2015) *Juvenile Detention Alternatives Initiative.* Retrieved from http://www.aecf.org/work/juvenile-justice/jdai/

Associated Press. (2014, January 8). Obama Administration recommends eliminating "zero tolerance" policies in the schools. PBS News Hour. http://www.pbs.org/newshour/rundown/obama-administration-recommends-ending-zero-tolerance-policies-in-schools/

Barnes, J. (1990). *Models and interpretations.* New York: Cambridge University Press.

Becker, H. (1963). *Outsiders: studies in the sociology of deviance.* New York: Free Press.

Bennett, W., Dilulio J., & Walters, J. (1996). *Body count: moral poverty, and how to win America's war against crime and drugs.* New York: Simon & Schuster.

Bonnie, R. & Scott, E. (2013). The teenage brain: Adolescent brain research and the law. *Current Directions in Psychological Science, 22,* 158–161.

Butts, J., & Buck, J. (2000). *Teen courts: A focus on research.* OJJDP Juvenile Justice Bulletin. Washington, DC: Office of Juvenile Justice and Delinquency Prevention, Office of Justice Programs, U.S. Department of Justice.

Butts, J., Roman, J., & Lynn-Whaley, J. (2012). Varieties of juvenile court: Non-specialized courts, teen courts, drug courts, and mental health courts. In B. Feld and D. Bishop (Eds.), *Oxford Handbook of Juvenile Crime and Juvenile Justice* (pp. 606–635). New York: Oxford University Press.

Cornish, D. & Clarke, R. (1986). *The reasoning criminal: rational choice perspectives on offending.* Berlin: Springer-Verlag.

Croman, J. (2008, September 17). Tool from teen's job, gets him suspended from school. Kare 11. Retrieved from http://archive.kare11.com/news/article/524796/0/Tool-from-teens-job-gets-him-suspended-from-high-school

Cullen, F. & Jonson, C. (2011). Rehabilitation and treatment programs. In J. Wilson & J. Petersilia (Eds.), *Crime and public policy* (pp. 293–344). New York: Oxford University Press.

Densley, J. (2013, February 28). After Sandy Hook, 'zero-tolerance' policies are making schools less safe. *MinnPost.* Retrieved from: http://www.minn

post.com/community-voices/2013/02/after-sandy-hook-zero-tolerance-policies-are-making-schools-less-safe

Dilulio, J. (1995). The coming of the super-predators. *The National Review*, November 27, 23–28.

Ennett, S., Tobler, N., Ringwalt, C., & Flewelling, R. (1994). Resistance education? A meta-analysis of Project D.A.R.E. outcome evaluations. *American Journal of Public Health*, 84, 1394–1401.

Esbensen, F-A, Osgood, D., Peterson, D., Taylor, T., & Carson, D. (2013). Short- and long-term outcome results from a multisite evaluation of the G.R.E.A.T. program. *Criminology & Public Policy*, 12, 375–411.

Fagan, J., & Tyler, T. (2005). Legal socialization of children and adolescents. *Social Justice Research*, 18, 217–241.

Farrington, D., Piquero, A, & Jennings, W. (2013). *Offending from childhood to late middle age: Recent results from the Cambridge Study in Delinquent Development*. New York: Springer.

Feld, B. (1981). Juvenile court legislative reform and the serious young offender: Dismantling the 'rehabilitative ideal.' *Minnesota Law Review*, 65, 167.

Feld, B. (1984). Criminalizing juvenile justice: Rules of procedure for the juvenile court. *Minnesota Law Review*, 69, 141.

Feld, B. (2007). Juvenile justice in Minnesota: framework for the future. In Council on Crime and Justice (ed.), *Justice, where art thou: A framework for the future* (pp. 49–57). Minneapolis, MN: Author. Retrieved from http://www.crimeandjustice.org/researchReports/FINAL%20REPORT%2010.4.07.pdf

Fox, J. (1995). The calm before the crime wave storm. *Los Angeles Times*, October 30. Retrieved from http://articles.latimes.com/1995-10-30/local/me-62753_1_crime-wave

Fox, J. & DeLateur, M. (2014). Mass shootings in America: Moving beyond Newtown. *Homicide Studies*, 18, 125–145.

Friedman, L. (1993). *Crime and punishment in American history*. New York: Basic Books.

Gendreau, P. & Ross, R. (1987). Revivification of rehabilitation: Evidence from the 1980s, *Justice Quarterly*, 4, 349–407.

Goffman, E. (1963). *Stigma: Notes on the management of spoiled identity*. New York: Simon and Schuster.

Gottfredson, M., & Hirschi, T. (1990). *A general theory of crime*. Stanford, CA: Stanford University Press.

Heitzeg, N. (2009). Education or incarceration: Zero tolerance policies and the school to prison pipeline. *Forum on Public Policy*. Retrieved from http://forumonpublicpolicy.com/summer09/issuesineducation.html

Hennepin County Attorney. (2015a). Curfews. Retrieved from http://www.hennepinattorney.org/prevention/students-youth/curfew

Hennepin County Attorney. (2015b). *Juvenile prosecution.* Retrieved from http://www.hennepinattorney.org/cases/Juvenile/juvenile-prosecution

Hirschi, T. (1969). *Causes of delinquency.* Berkeley: University of California Press.

Hirschi, T, &. Gottfredson, M. (1983). Age and the explanation of crime. *American Journal of Sociology, 89,* 552–584.

Hoge, R. & Andrews, D. (2011). *Youth level of service/case management inventory 2.0.* Toronto, ON: Multi-Health Systems Inc.

Justice Policy Institute. (2013). *On common ground: Lessons learned from five states that reduced juvenile confinement by more than half.* Retrieved from http://www.justicepolicy.org/uploads/justicepolicy/documents/common-ground_online.pdf

Katz, J. (1988). *Seductions of crime: Moral and sensual attractions in doing evil.* New York: Basic Books.

Kempf-Leonard, K. (2007). Minority youths and juvenile justice: Disproportionate minority contact after nearly 20 years of reform efforts. Youth Violence and Juvenile Justice, 5(1), 71–87.

Kleiman, M. (2009). *When brute force fails: How to have less crime and less punishment.* Princeton, NJ: Princeton University Press.

Kupchik, A. (2010). *Homeroom security: School discipline in an age of fear.* New York: NYU Press.

Lemert, E. (1971). *Instead of court: diversion in juvenile justice.* Rockville, MD: National Institute of Mental Health.

Lipton, D., Martinson, R., & Wilks, J. (1975). *The effectiveness of correctional treatment: A survey of treatment valuation studies.* New York: Praeger Press.

Mall of America. (2015a). *About MOA.* Retrieved from http://www.mallof america.com/about/moa/overview

Mall of America. (2015b). *Parental escort policy.* Retrieved from http://www.mallofamerica.com/guests/escorts

Markel, H. (2009, December 14). Case shined first light on abuse of children. *New York Times.* Retrieved from http://www.nytimes.com/2009/12/15/health/15abus.html

Martinson, R. (1974). What works? Questions and answers about prison reform. *The Public Interest, 35,* 22–54.

Mazurek, A. (2015). Criminal law: No looking back: Narrowing the scope of the retroactivity doctrine for juveniles sentenced to life without release—Roman Nose v. State. *William Mitchell Law Review, 41,* 330–365.

McGuire, K. (2012, April 10). Dayton signed anti-bullying bill. *Star Tribune*. Retrieved from http://www.startribune.com/dayton-signs-anti-bullying-bill/254659091/

Merton, R. (1938). Social structure and anomie. *American Sociological Review*, 3, 672–682.

Miller v. Alabama, 567 U.S. ___ (2012).

Minnesota Department of Corrections. (2007). *The delivery systems change process*. Retrieved from http://www.doc.state.mn.us/publications/documents/Deliverysystemschangeprocess.pdf

Minnesota Department of Human Services. (2012). Resource guide for mandated reporters. Retrieved from https://edocs.dhs.state.mn.us/lfserver/Public/DHS-2917-ENG

Minnesota Department of Human Services. (2015). Child protection. Retrieved from http://www.dhs.state.mn.us/main/idcplg?IdcService=GET_DYNAMIC_CONVERSION&RevisionSelectionMethod=LatestReleased&dDocName=id_000152

Minnesota House of Representatives. (2014). Youth and the law: A guide to legislatures. Retrieved from http://www.house.leg.state.mn.us/hrd/pubs/youthlaw.pdf

Minnesota House of Representatives. (2015). Juvenile offenders. Retrieved from http://www.house.leg.state.mn.us/hrd/databook/juvcorr.aspx.

Minnesota Judicial Branch. (2015). CHIPS Court. Retrieved from http://www.mncourts.gov/district/8/?page=1117

Moffitt, T. (1993). Adolescence-limited and life-course persistent anti-social behavior: A developmental taxonomy. *Psychological Review*, 104, 674–701.

Mukherjee E. (2007). *Criminalizing the classroom: The over-policing of New York City schools*. New York: New York Civil Liberties Union.

National Juvenile Defender Center. (n.d.). United States Supreme Court juvenile justice jurisprudence. Retrieved from http://njdc.info/practice-policy-resources/united-states-supreme-court-juvenile-justice-jurisprudence/

Na, C. & Gottfredson, D. (2013). Police in schools: Effects on school crime and the processing of offending behaviors. *Justice Quarterly*, 30, 619–650.

Office of Juvenile Justice and Delinquency Prevention. (2013). *Upper and lower age of juvenile court delinquency and status offense jurisdiction, 2013*. Retrieved from http://www.ojjdp.gov/ojstatbb/structure_process/qa04102.asp?qaDate=2013

Office of the Legislative Auditor. (1995). *Guardians ad litem*. St. Paul, MN: Program Evaluation Division, State of Minnesota.

Outfront Minnesota. (2014). *Safe & supportive Minnesota schools law*. Retrieved from https://www.outfront.org/safeschools/bill

Petteruti A. (2011). *Education under arrest: The case against police and schools.* Washington, DC: Justice Policy Institute.

Robers, S., Kemp, J., Rathbun, A., & Morgan, R. (2014). *Indicators of school crime and safety: 2013 (NCES 2014-042/NCJ 243299).* Washington, DC: National Center for Education Statistics, U.S. Department of Education, and Bureau of Justice Statistics, Office of Justice Programs, U.S. Department of Justice.

Robins, L. (1978). Sturdy childhood predictors of adult antisocial behavior: Replications from longitudinal studies. *Psychological Medicine,* 8, 611–622.

Sutherland, E. (1947). *Principles of criminology (4th edition).* Philadelphia, PA: Lippencott.

Tiffany, F. (1910). *Revised laws of Minnesota, supplement 1909.* St. Paul, MN: West Publishing. Retrieved from https://www.revisor.mn.gov/statutes/?id=73A&year=1909

Scott, E. & Steinberg, L. (2010). *Rethinking juvenile justice.* Cambridge, MA: Harvard University Press.

Sherman, L., Farrington, D., Walsh, B., & MacKenzie, D. (Eds). (2006). *Evidence-based crime prevention* (Revised Edition). London: Routledge.

Sherman, L., Gottfredson, D., MacKenzie, D., Eck, J. Reuter, P., & Bushway, S. (1998). *Preventing crime: what works, what doesn't, what's promising, a report to the United States congress.* Washington DC: National Institute of Justice.

Skiba, R. & Knesting, K. (2001). Zero tolerance, zero evidence: An analysis of school disciplinary practice. *New Directions for Youth Development,* 92, 17–43.

State Ex Rel. LEA v. Hammergren, 294 N.W.2d 705 (1980).

State Guardian ad Litem Board. (2013a). *What is a GAL?* Retrieved from http://mn.gov/guardian-ad-litem/Program_Info/What_is_a_GAL.jsp

State Guardian ad Litem Board. (2013b). *GAL fees.* Retrieved from http://mn.gov/guardian-ad-litem/Program_Info/GAL_fees.jsp

Swayze, D. (2010). *The federal juvenile justice and delinquency prevention act vs. Minnesota statutes and rules of juvenile procedure.* St. Paul, MN: Minnesota Department of Public Safety, Office of Justice Programs.

Swayze, D. & Buskovick, D. (2012a). *Minnesota juvenile diversion: A summary of statewide practices and programming.* St. Paul, MN: Minnesota Department of Public Safety, Office of Justice Programs.

Swayze, D., & Buskovick, D. (2012b). *Minnesota youth intervention programs: A statistical analysis of participant pre- and post-program surveys.* St. Paul, MN: Minnesota Department of Public Safety, Office of Justice Programs.

Swayze, D., & Buskovick, D. (2012c). *On the level: Disproportionate minority contact in Minnesota's juvenile justice system.* St. Paul, MN: Minnesota Department of Public Safety, Office of Justice Programs.

Swayze, D., & Buskovick, D. (2012d) *Youth in Minnesota correctional facilities and the effects of trauma: Responses to the 2010 Minnesota student survey.* St. Paul, MN: Minnesota Department of Public Safety, Office of Justice Programs.

Swayze, D., & Buskovick, D. (2013). *Back to the future: Thirty years of juvenile justice data in Minnesota, 1980–2010.* St. Paul, MN: Minnesota Department of Public Safety, Office of Justice Programs.

Swayze, D., & Buskovick, D. (2014a). *Back to the future: Thirty years of Minnesota juvenile justice policy and practice, 1980–2010.* St. Paul, MN: Minnesota Department of Public Safety Office of Justice Programs.

Swayze, D. & Buskovick, D. (2014b). *Law enforcement in Minnesota schools: A statewide survey of school resource officers.* St. Paul, MN: Minnesota Statistical Analysis Center.

Sweeten, G., Piquero, A., & Steinberg, L. (2013). Age and the explanation of crime, revisited. *Journal of Youth and Adolescents, 42,* 921–938.

Theriot, M. (2009). School resource officers and the criminalization of student behavior. *Journal of Criminal Justice, 37,* 280–287.

Wilson, J. Q. (1980). What works revisited: New findings on criminal rehabilitation. *The Public Interest, 61,* 3–17.

Zinser, L. (2014, November 4). Adrian Peterson agrees to plea deal in child-abuse case. *The New York Times.* Retrieved from http://www.nytimes.com/2014/11/05/sports/football/vikings-adrian-peterson-reaches-plea-deal-in-child-abuse-case.html?_r=0

Chapter Seven

The Shame of the Cities: Minnesota's Gangs and Gangsters

Learning Objectives

- Identify some of the infamous gangsters of Minnesota's past
- Describe the causes and consequences of Prohibition
- Analyze the O'Connor System of policing in St. Paul
- Describe the origins of state and federal gun laws
- Discuss problems with defining gangs and using gang member databases
- Identify some of the major gang branches in Minnesota
- Critique the Metro Gang Strike Force
- Explore gang intervention efforts in Minnesota
- Define hate crimes
- Explore the role of drug cartels in the Minnesota drug trade

A walk through Minnesota's history reveals storied tales of violence, vice, corruption, and extortion that blemish the "Minnesota-nice" reputation. After all, it was here that "Public Enemy Number One" John Dillinger vacationed and the notorious James-Younger Gang met their demise (Maccabee, 1995). It didn't help Minnesota's "Nice" image that nepotistic politicians and police were in lockstep with the criminals, securing safe havens and accepting bribes, among other crooked practices. The pages that follow, therefore, illuminate the causes and consequences of Minnesota's very special relationship with gangs and gangsters. One consistent theme throughout the chapter is the connection between Minnesota and Chicago, Illinois, from the business ties between criminals in both places to the migration of gang members from one place to another.

History of Gangs in Minnesota

We begin with a historical approach to examine gangs and organized crime, for as philosopher George Santayana once argued, "Those who cannot remember the past are condemned to repeat it." As **Figure 7.1** highlights, as of today we have not fully remembered the past, since gangs have been part of the Minnesota landscape for more than 125 years.

Figure 7.1. Timeline of Minnesota Gang History

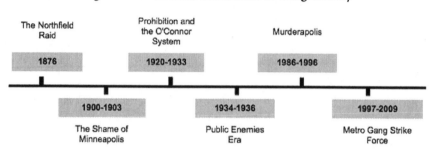

The Northfield Raid and the James-Younger Gang

On September 7, 1876, eight notorious outlaws—Jesse James and his brother Frank; the Younger brothers, Cole, James, and Robert; Charlie Pitts; Clel Miller; and William Stiles—attempted to rob the First National Bank in Northfield (Northfield Historical Society, n.d.). Northfield was (and still is) a college town approximately one hour south of the Twin Cities—home to Carleton and St. Olaf colleges. The James-Younger Gang, educated in violence during the American Civil War, robbed banks and trains and killed uncooperative employees, cultivating a Robin Hood image of stealing from the rich to give to the poor (Riedel & Welsh, 2011). The local bank was thought to be an easy target. The James-Younger gang thought wrong.

In a textbook James-Younger robbery, three gang members entered the bank, drew their weapons, and announced the holdup. Cashier Joseph Lee Heywood was told to open the safe. Heywood refused, citing a time-delay lock that could not be opened, and subsequently was shot dead (Minnesota History Center, n.d.). Meanwhile, the citizens of Northfield engaged the remaining members of the James-Younger Gang in a gun battle on the street. In the melee that followed, Clel Miller and William Stiles were killed. Cole and Bob Younger were wounded. The others were forced to flee. It was the beginning of the end for the band of outlaws that had elicited a response between fear and fascination for more than a decade following the Civil War.

The Youngers were eventually captured in Madelia after another gun battle in which gang member Charlie Pitts was killed. The three Younger brothers were tried in Faribault, found guilty of murder, and sentenced to life in the state prison at Stillwater. Bob Younger died in prison in 1889; Jim was pardoned in 1901 and committed suicide in 1902; Cole, also pardoned in 1901, helped found the prison's first newspaper, *The Prison Mirror*, and eventually died in 1916 (Minnesota History Center, n.d.).

The Shame of Minneapolis

Minneapolis has produced countless upstanding citizens who have contributed greatly to society. There are, however, a few individuals the city would rather forget, chief among them Albert Alonzo "Doc" Ames (January 18, 1842–November 16, 1911). Ames held four non-consecutive terms as mayor of Minneapolis between 1876 and 1902. Ames was known for his assistance of the poor, sometimes giving medical treatment to those who could not afford it. But following the 1903 publication of "The Shame of Minneapolis," an article by New York-based muckraking journalist Lincoln Steffens for the influential *McClure's Magazine* (see Steffens, 1957), Ames became better known for creating one of the most corrupt municipal governments in American history.

Upon election to his final term as mayor in 1900, Ames "set out upon a career of corruption for which deliberateness, invention, and avarice has never been equaled" (Steffens, 1957, p. 42). First, he employed his brother Fred as Minneapolis' chief of police. Next, he picked an easily corruptible former gambler, already acquainted with the underworld, for chief of detectives. Then, using the *spoils system* (a practice in which politicians, after winning election, give government jobs to their patrons as a reward for working toward victory, and an incentive to keep working on their behalf), Ames fired officers appointed under previous administrations and sold their badges to the professional criminals he consulted for advice (Nathanson, 2010).

The deck was stacked. Ames and colleagues organized a citywide system to extract bribes from gambling parlors, opium joints, and houses of prostitution forbidden under city law (Steffens, 1931). This arrangement, and the systematic release of known criminals from local jails, attracted more criminals to the city, many of whom arranged with the police to be left alone. Illegal businesses multiplied. At one point, there were more saloons than churches in the city of Minneapolis (Nathanson, 2010). There was even some evidence of women setting up candy stores for children as fronts for brothels (Steffens, 1957).

Ames extorted huge sums of protection money from illegal businesses, but his organization quickly swirled out of control when the police and politicians began cheating each other (Steffens, 1957). A city grand jury, under the leadership of foreman Hovey C. Clarke, finally brought Ames down. Members of the grand jury paid out of their own pockets several private detectives to investigate Ames and his coconspirators (Kaplan, 1974). The investigators submitted numerous indictments. The mayor fled the state and lived in exile until he was eventually arrested in New Hampshire in February 1903.

Ames was extradited to Minnesota and tried for receiving a $600 bribe from a prostitute (Nathanson, 2010). He was found guilty and sentenced to six years in the Minnesota State Prison at Stillwater, but served no time in jail. His sentence was overturned on appeal and following two mistrials, all legal action against him ceased. Ames' brother Fred, however, served several years in state prison, and many others also wound up behind bars.

After Ames, alderman D. Percy Jones, the City Council president, took control as acting mayor. He tossed out the bad apples on the police force and named a church deacon and personal friend as chief (Steffens, 1957). Ames' crimes are explained in part by his supposed alcoholism (Zink, 1930). Alcohol also features prominently in life of the next elected official, although in a very different way.

Prohibition

Minnesotan Andrew John Volstead (October 31, 1860–January 20, 1947) was a Republican member of the United States House of Representatives from 1903–1923. A lawyer by training, Volstead served as chairman of the House Judiciary Committee from 1919 to 1923. Most famously, however, Volstead collaborated with Wayne Wheeler of the Anti-Saloon League to draft, sponsor, and champion the National Prohibition Act of 1919. The so-called Volstead Act was enacted to carry out the intent of the Eighteenth Amendment to the U.S. Constitution, which from 1920 until its repeal in 1933, prohibited the sale, manufacture, distribution, and importing of intoxicating liquors in the United States.

Prohibition was an effort to reverse the perceived negative influence of alcohol on public health, safety, and morality. The Woman's Christian Temperance Union, for example, advocated for the law as a means of preventing abuse from drunken husbands (Bordin, 1981). Prohibition succeeded in reducing liquor consumption in America, the police arrested fewer people for drunkenness, and the cost of alcohol and liquor became too high for many to afford (National Archives, 2015). It also took a lot of resources on behalf of the government, who could not enforce every violation. The unintended consequences were many, including illicit drinking, consumption of unregulated and often toxic forms of alcohol, disrespect for the law, government corruption, and increased organized crime (see Riedel & Welsh, 2011). And so it was that a law named after a Minnesotan became the catalyst for a new episode of gangsterism throughout the state and nation.

Perhaps the most notorious gangster in Minneapolis' history is Romanian-Jewish immigrant Isadore "Kid Cann" Blumenfeld (September 8, 1900–June 21, 1981). Cann's rise from Northside nickel-and-dime pimp and bookmaker to Midwest godfather is almost cinematic. With the onset of Prohibition, Cann and his brothers Jacob and Harry, began *legally* importing industrial grade alcohol from Canada, ostensibly for the processing of fur (their father was a furrier), and diverting it to *illegal* distilleries in the forests near Fort Snelling (Karlen, 2014). The Cann family also purchased large quantities of premium corn liquor moonshine (the only "branded" moonshine produced in the U.S. during Prohibition) from local farmers in Stearns County to sell on to the Chicago Outfit, bossed by the legendary Al Capone (Davis, 2007)—the first of many Chicago connections outlined in this chapter. The power and influence of Cann's "Minneapolis Combination," as it came to be known, has been compared to that of Capone's Chicago Outfit, but so too has the mythology surrounding it. For example, Cann's organized crime group supposedly enjoyed ties to the Genovese crime family, one of the "Five Families" of New York and among the most powerful mafias in the United States (Karlen, 2014). See **Figure 7.2** for definitions of organized crime and mafias.

A number of deaths are attributed to Cann and his gang, including journalists who were assassinated for exposing the inner workings of his organization and its ties to corrupt politicians. Cann also was implicated in the 1924 murder of cab driver Charles Goldberg, the attempted murder of police officer James H. Trepanier at the Cotton Club in Minneapolis, and the 1935 murder of Walter Liggett. Liggett, the founder and editor of *The Midwest American* newspaper, reported a link between Cann and his childhood friend, Minnesota Governor Floyd B. Olson. As a result, Liggett was arrested on trumped-up morals charges and machine-gunned to death in the alley behind his home at 1825 2nd Ave. S, right across from Stevens Square Park (Sparber, 2011). Cann was indicted, but suspiciously acquitted of the crime despite eyewitness testimony from Liggett's wife and daughter, among others, identifying him as the shooter.

Cann held considerable power over the Jewish neighborhoods in North Minneapolis and oversaw illegal activities such as bootlegging, prostitution, and labor racketeering. He later graduated to trucking distribution routes, illegal gambling, and real estate deals throughout the American Sun Belt. He is perhaps the most famous of local crime figures in Minnesota, but often ignored when compared to the national gangsters who frequented St. Paul (Karlen, 2014).

Figure 7.2. Definition of a Gang, Organized Crime Group, and Mafia

> **Gang:** any durable, street-oriented youth group whose involvement in illegal activity is part of its group identity. Group names, colors, symbols, tattoos, and other elements ascribed to gangs and their members are *descriptors* not *definers*.
>
> **Organized crime group:** attempts to regulate and control the production and distribution of a given commodity or service unlawfully. For example, a drug syndicate or cartel may aspire to be the sole supplier of drugs in a given domain.
>
> **Mafia:** a type of organized crime group that attempts to control the supply of protection. The scope of a Mafia group is much wider than that of an organized crime group, since it aspires to protect *any* transaction, not just those related to, say, drugs, in a given domain.

Source: Author created from Klein and Maxson (2006, p. 4) and Varese (2010, pp.14–17).

The O'Connor System and Big Tom Brown

In the 1920s and 1930s, St. Paul was either home to or a stopping place for the most notorious gangsters of modern folklore. John Dillinger, Pretty Boy Floyd, Babyface Nelson, Machine Gun Kelly, Ma Barker and her boys, and others all frequented the capital city at one point or another during their criminal careers (Maccabee, 1995). In 1936, in an article illustrated by Ludwig Bemelmans, author of the Madeline children's books, *Fortune Magazine* named St. Paul the best place in America to hire a hit man (MinnPost, 2008). Part of the reason was Israel "Icepick Willie" Alderman, an assassin who punctured victims' brains via their eardrums with his namesake tool to avoid signs of homicide during an autopsy, was in town (Karlen, 2014). St. Paul was also cited as a destination for money laundering and fencing stolen property.

What explains this history? St. Paul's police chief at the time, John J. O'Connor (October 29, 1855–July 4, 1924), had established a *Layover Agreement* that offered criminals a safe haven within the city limits of St. Paul provided they followed three very simple rules: (1) check in with police upon arrival; (2) commit no serious criminal activity within the borders of the city; and (3) pay all necessary bribes (Maccabee, 1995). O'Connor served two terms as police chief between 1900 and 1920, but his agreement, known as *The O'Connor System*, was policy and practice in the City of St. Paul until the mid-1930s.

With unilateral authority, O'Connor reorganized the St. Paul Police Department and created a quid-pro-quo system he believed eliminated major crime, but in reality only displaced or encouraged it. The O'Connor System at-tracted gangsters on the run from around the country. Nightspots like The Green Lantern, at 10th and Wabasha, and the "Hollyhocks," on Mississippi River Boulevard, catered to them. The notorious Alvin "Creepy" Karpis, FBI Director J. Edgar Hoover's last "Public Enemy Number One," once said of this time in history, "If you were looking for a guy you hadn't seen for a few months, you usually thought of two places: prison or St. Paul. If he wasn't locked up in one, he was probably hanging out in the other" (as cited in Gorn, 2009, p.88). Case in point: after John Dillinger escaped from an "escape proof" In-diana jail and eluded a nationwide manhunt in March 1934, he wound up in St. Paul (Federal Bureau of Investigation, n.d.). The Uptown Theater at Ox-ford and Grand was one of Dillinger's favorite haunts—apparently he liked aisle seats for quick getaways (Maccabee, 1995).

On March 31 of that year, the *St. Paul Daily News* reported two major sto-ries under the headline "Machine Guns Blaze as Jury Whitewashes Police" (as cited in Thayer, 2009). First, Dillinger had evaded FBI agents by shooting his way out of an apartment building on Lexington Parkway (N.B., before 1934, federal agents did not have the right to carry weapons or arrest criminals, re-lying instead on local police). Second, a St. Paul grand jury concluded a lengthy investigation by declaring that the city, contrary to rumors, did not have a gangster problem (MinnPost, 2008). The irony was thick. City Mayor William Mahoney, running for reelection at the time, responded, saying, "If there are any gangsters here, it is because they have been invited by the newspapers," a slight at critic Howard Kahn (1934), *St. Paul Daily News* editor, who was ac-tively using his First Amendment free-press rights to expose corruption.

During the *Public Enemies* era (June 1934 to May 1936) in which the FBI la-beled Dillinger, Floyd, Nelson, and Karpis, in that order, "Public Enemy Num-ber One," police posts were politically charged mayoral appointments. In 1930, for example, "Big" (he was 6 foot 5 inches tall) Tom Brown became chief after a stint in the so-called "Purity Squad," a special St. Paul police unit designed to identify and shut down speakeasies (places that sold alcohol illegally) but notorious for its repeated failure to find any illegal activity (Mahoney, 2013). Brown is credited with enabling Ma Barker and her boys to kidnap William Hamm Jr., the Hamm Beer Company heir, and Edward Bremer, founder of Bremer Bank, for ransom (Mahoney, 2013). Brown also was involved in the 1934 killing of former ally and Dillinger associate, Homer Van Meter. Police ambushed Van Meter and egregiously machine-gunned him to death at the corner of Marion Street and University Avenue, allegedly to get at his money, which was pocketed by the perpetrators (Mahoney, 2013). Police even acquired

Van Meter's automobile and pressed it into service as a squad car (Saint Paul Police Historical Society, 1984).

Eventually, the law caught up with Brown, but he never saw the inside of a prison cell. The "Houdini of gangster-cops" simply retired to collect his pension and run a tavern up north (Mahoney, 2013, p. 4). To prevent future O'Connor Systems, however, St. Paul changed the law to select police chiefs on merit, not political connections.

The O'Connor System enabled criminals to organize and build coast-to-coast crime syndicates (Maccabee, 1995, p. 50–7), but the true underlying mechanism was Prohibition. Prohibition failed because it was unenforceable. It confused Americans about what was right and wrong—people became criminals overnight for enjoying alcohol, and had to interact with criminals to obtain it. Prohibition's coincidence with the "speed graphic era" of photojournalism also fast-tracked the ambivalence toward violence and culture of public investigation seen in contemporary media (Millett, 2004, 2008). The sensationalized run of such criminals as John Dillinger, whose robberies of banks and railroads made him popular among poor people, only increased admiration for the "outlaw as social bandit" (Riedel & Welsh, 2011, p.49). National Prohibition was eventually repealed in 1933, leaving the issue up to individual states. Minnesota legalized liquor, and like the gangsters before them, taxed it. But the end of easy money through booze simply triggered a new era of kidnappings and bank robberies among the criminal elite.

Guns and Gun Laws in Minnesota

The gangs and gangsters that arose after passage of the Volstead Act used guns to devastating effect. Since Al Capone's Chicago Outfit orchestrated the 1929 St. Valentine's Day Massacre of six North Side mob associates and a mechanic in Chicago, for example, the Thompson submachine gun forever lives in infamy. One year after the Twenty-First Amendment brought an end to Prohibition, therefore, Congress also levied sharp regulations and high taxes on gun sales, with emphasis on weapons generally associated with gangster violence: "A shotgun or rifle having a barrel of less than eighteen inches in length, or any other weapon, except a pistol or revolver, from which a shot is discharged by an explosive if such weapon is capable of being concealed on the person, or a machine gun." The *1934 National Firearms Act* became the first federal regulation on guns in U.S. history.

Today, the United States has by far the highest rate of gun ownership in the world. The Small Arms Survey (2007) estimates there are 270 million civilian-owned firearms in the U.S., which translates to 89 guns for every 100 people. More guns, however, does not necessarily translate into more gun owners—three-quarters of people with guns own two or more and the prevalence of gun ownership has declined steadily in the past few decades (Small Arms Survey, 2007). In a state like Minnesota, it is not surprising that the general public would own guns, and multiple ones at that, as this state is known for hunting. Hunting is big business in Minnesota (see **Chapter Two**). The first weekend in November operates much like a state holiday with the opening of deer hunting season.

In Minnesota, a permit to purchase is required to transfer/purchase "military-style assault weapons" and handguns through Federal Firearms License (FFL) dealers (Minnesota Statutes § 624.7131). A permit to carry also acts as a permit to purchase for Minnesota residents. Traditional rifles and shotguns (primarily used in hunting) may be purchased without a permit, but Minnesota is a "shall issue" state, meaning a permit to carry a pistol is required to carry handguns. Minnesota Statutes § 624.714 observes "a person, other than a peace officer ... who carries, holds, or possesses a pistol in a motor vehicle, snowmobile, or boat, or on or about the person's clothes or the person, or otherwise in possession or control in a public place without first having obtained a permit to carry the pistol is guilty of a gross misdemeanor." Concealment is permitted but not required, and only handguns may be carried concealed. To obtain a permit to carry, people must first complete authorized firearms training.

It is important to note, persons listed in Minnesota's criminal gang investigation system (see below) and persons less than 21 years of age are prohibited from possessing a firearm. Yet, juvenile gang members still commit the vast majority of gun murders (Decker & Pyrooz, 2011). In reality, gang members get their guns from corrupt firearm dealers, theft, and friends and other criminals in their social networks (Cook et al., 2007).

Figure 7.3. A Brief History of Guns in America

The Second Amendment of the United States Constitution reads, "A well-regulated militia being necessary to the security of a free State, the right of the people to keep and bear arms shall not be infringed." Here "arms" refer to military weapons and those used by a "well-regulated militia" when the Second Amendment was signed in 1787, which were mostly long arms that could discharge only once before they had to be reloaded; very different from the arms used by Al Capone and his contemporaries.

During the American Revolutionary War (1775–1783), militiamen were largely dependent on publicly supplied muskets with bayonets. The Second Amendment was ratified in case the federal government should neglect to sufficiently arm and discipline the militia (Sweeny & Saul, 2013). The danger was not a tyrannical federal government bent on disarming the people, but rather the people disarmed because of federal inaction! In 1792, federal law mandated every eligible man to purchase a military-style gun and ammunition for

Figure 7.3. A Brief History of Guns in America, *continued*

his service in the citizen militia, and militiamen of course defeated the British Army to win independence for the original 13 colonies.

After the Revolutionary War, the standing Continental Army was disbanded (as per Article 1, Section 8 of the U.S. Constitution) and subsequent wars (e.g., the War of 1812, the Mexican War, the U.S. Civil War, and the Spanish-American War) were all fought primarily with state militias called to temporary federal service. By the middle of the nineteenth century, the United States had a standing army, but only mobilization of National Guard units coupled with a massive conscription effort created a force large enough to fight World War I and World War II overseas. Only after WWII did a large (and well funded) standing army become a permanent fixture of the American landscape.

When the Civil War ended in 1865, demobilized Union and Confederate troops were permitted to take home their arms. Such establishes a base for the modern culture of personal weapons (Riedel & Welsh, 2011). The National Rifle Association (NRA) was founded in 1871, in part to promote firearms safety education and marksmanship training for this new generation of gun owners.

For most of its history, the NRA was primarily a sporting and hunting association (Lepore, 2012). The NRA endorsed both the 1934 National Firearms Act and the 1938 Federal Firearms Act, which together created a licensing system for dealers and imposed tax and registration requirements on the "gangster guns" used by the Public Enemies of the world. But the 1968 Gun Control Act, enacted after assassinations of Robert F. Kennedy and Martin Luther King Jr., banning mail-order gun sales (N.B., President John F. Kennedy was killed in 1963 by a gun purchased through a mail-order advertisement in the NRA's *American Rifleman* magazine), sales to "dangerous" categories of persons (e.g., juveniles, convicted felons, drug users, former mental patients), and restricting importation of military-surplus firearms, divided the NRA (Winkler, 2011).

At this time, establishing a constitutional right to carry a gun for the purpose of self-defense became central to the mission of the Black Panther Party. Inspired by Malcolm X's call for self-defense "by whatever means necessary," Huey Newton, Bobby Seale, and other young African Americans very publicly tested a California law that allowed people to carry guns in public providing they were visible and not pointed at anyone in a threatening way (Winkler, 2011). In doing so, the Black Panther Party took the instrument that once enforced Jim Crow and white supremacy and turned it into a symbol of black empowerment. Subsequent law-and-order legislation that disarmed black radicals under the auspices of fighting crime and controlling civil unrest roused the sleeping NRA (Winkler, 2011). Following a coup d'état at the group's annual membership meeting in 1977, the NRA began advancing the argument that the Second Amendment guarantees an individual's right to carry a gun as a means of *self-defense*, rather than the people's right to form armed militias to provide for the *common defense*.

The idea that owning and carrying a gun is both a fundamental American freedom and an act of citizenship only gained wide acceptance in the decades since. The NRA's interpretation of the Second Amendment achieved new legal authority in 1986 with the passage of the Firearms Owners Protection Act, which repealed parts of the 1968 Gun Control Act by invoking "the rights of citizens ... to keep and bear arms under the Second Amendment." States, in turn, widely adopted "concealed carry" and "stand your ground" legislation, the latter pertaining to an extension of the so-called castle doctrine, exonerating from prosecution citizens who use deadly force when confronted by an assailant, even if they could have retreated safely. Then, in 2008, in *District of Columbia v. Heller*, the Supreme Court ruled un-

Figure 7.3. A Brief History of Guns in America, *continued*

constitutional Washington, D.C.'s 1975 Firearms Control Regulations Act, specifically the ban on handguns and prohibition of long guns for self-defense. But nothing in the opinion, Justice Antonin Scalia wrote, should "be taken to cast doubt on longstanding prohibitions on the possession of firearms by felons and the mentally ill, or laws forbidding the carrying of firearms in sensitive places such as schools and government buildings, or laws imposing conditions and qualifications on the commercial sale of arms" (as cited in Winkler, 2011).

New Gang City: Murderapolis

On June 30, 1996, in an article headlined "Nice City's Nasty Distinction: Murder Soars in Minneapolis," the *New York Times* gave Minneapolis a controversial new name: "Murderapolis" (Johnson, 1996). The name reflected a record 97 murders in the city in 1995, or 27 per 100,000 people, many of them attributed to gangs. This was not news to local residents, who had endured years of gang violence, such as the 1994 arson killing of the Coppage family—five children ages 2 to 11—wherein the 6-0 Tre Crips firebombed the home of a former gang member, who escaped, in revenge for a suspected breach of the gang's "code of silence" (Lee, 2003). Two half-brothers were eventually convicted. Fast-forward two decades and Minneapolis now is a much safer city: there were 39 murders in 2012 or 10 per 100,000. But the reality of gangs still looms large in the Twin Cities.

Migration or Mimicking?

The 1980s and 1990s were decades of gang *proliferation*, wherein communities across the United States increasingly reported the existence of gangs and gang problems (Maxson, 1998). Street gangs are now found in about 3,300 jurisdictions across the U.S., including Minnesota (Egley & Howell, 2013). *Gang migration*—the movement of gang members from one city to another—was one popular explanation for this trend, encompassing both temporary relocations (e.g., visits to relatives, short trips in search of new criminal markets or to develop new criminal enterprises, and longer stays while escaping crackdowns on gangs or gang activity) and more permanent changes, such as residential moves and court placements (Maxson, 1998). During this time, gang members from Chicago and other large Midwest cities certainly converged on Minneapolis, supposedly drawn to the city's more generous housing and social welfare policies (Worthington, 1993). At the same time, however, Minnesota young people began looking at gang culture popularized in the media and adapting styles to local conditions, taking on affiliations with "supergangs" from Chicago and Los Angeles (see Table 7.1) that were more imagined than real (Howell, 2007). As such, the precise mechanisms underlying gang proliferation in Minnesota are unclear.

Table 7.1. Typology of "Supergang" Branches in Minnesota

Gang	Vice Lords	Gangster Disciples	Bloods	Crips	Latin Kings
Alliance	People Nation	Folk Nation	People Nation	Folk Nation	People Nation
Ethnicity	African-American	African-American	African-American	African-American	Hispanic
Founded	1957	Late 1960s	1972	1969	1940s/1986
Founders	Edward Perry, Alfonso Alfred, Bobby Gore	Larry Hoover, David Barksdale	Sylvester Scott, Benson Owens	Raymond Washington, Stanley Williams	Luis "King Blood" Felipe
Home	North Lawndale, Chicago, IL	South Side, Chicago, IL	Piru Street, Compton, CA	South Los Angeles, CA	Chicago, IL, and New York State Collins Correctional Facility
Colors	Red and Black	Blue and Black	Red and Black	Blue and Black	Black and Gold
Sports Apparel	Chicago Bulls, University of Nevada–Las Vegas	Detroit Lions, Georgetown Hoyas, Duke Blue Devils, San Francisco Giants	Chicago Bulls, Kansas City Chiefs, Philadelphia Phillies	British Knights, Dallas Cowboys, Orlando Magic	Los Angeles Kings, Pittsburgh Pirates
Represent	Left	Right	Left	Right	Left
Greeting	"All is well"	"All is one"	"What it B like, Blood"	"What it C like, Cuz"	N/A
Symbols	Five point star, pitchforks down	Six-point Star of David (Barksdale), pitchforks up, 74 (seventh and fourth letters of the alphabet)	MOB (Member of Bloods), CK (Crip Killer) 031 / 021	Six-point star, Bs crossed out	Five or three-point "sacred crown," "Kingism" ideology

Source: Author created from the Midwest Gang Investigators Association, Minnesota chapter.

Generally speaking, motivations for joining gangs can be understood in terms of pushes and pulls (Decker & Van Winkle, 1996). Push factors speak to the economic, social, and political forces that propel youth toward gang involvement; such as concentrated disadvantage in the urban ghetto following economic restructuring and the flight of black working- and middle-class families (Wilson, 1987). Pull factors pertain to the attractiveness of gangs and the perceived advantages of gang membership. Gangs facilitate certain imperatives for young people, for example, the search for protection, the search for money, the search for pleasure and moral transcendence, and the search for respect and recognition (see Densley, 2015). The irony of course is youth join gangs for protection, yet gang membership increases their risk of victimization (Melde, Taylor, & Esbensen, 2009). Youth join gangs for excitement, yet gang life is generally "a boring life" (Klein, 1995, p.11). Youth join gangs for kinship, yet there is no honor among thieves (Densley, 2013). And youth join gangs for "quick money," yet gang members are poorly compensated for their efforts (Levitt & Venkatesh, 2000). Further, selection into gangs is a two-way process (i.e., people choose gangs, but also gangs choose people), which means there are inherent costs and risks to gang membership that gangs themselves fail to disclose (Densely, 2012). You might say gangs are not held to the same *truth in advertising* standards as legitimate organizations.

United for Peace and the Murder of Patrolman Jerry Haaf

In the early 1980s Sharif Willis, a Chicago Vice Lord "minister of justice," migrated to Minneapolis. The Vice Lords are one of the largest and oldest gang branches in Chicago, and founding members of the People Nation alliance (Howell & Griffiths, 2015; see Table 7.1). During the 1980s and 1990s, the Vice Lords fought with their Folk Nation rivals, the Gangster Disciples, for control of transportation and distribution of crack cocaine and retail distribution of powdered cocaine and heroin in Minneapolis. Willis rose to prominence when he killed a man over $5 in a crap game dispute and served six years of a 10-year prison sentence for the crime. The city embraced him after his release, and although still tied to the Vice Lords, Willis vowed to end escalating gang violence in Minneapolis.

With city funding, Willis set up United for Peace, a coalition of gang leaders and inner-city civic leaders that organized *gang summits*, modeled on peace talks between warring nations, and used donated portable cellular phones to dispatch gang members to police calls in an effort to mediate disputes (Police

Officers Federation of Minneapolis, 2015). United for Peace was housed under The City Inc., a nonprofit organization that provided alternative high schools, day cares, parenting classes, and job programs for inner-city youth. In this regard, parallels can be drawn between Minneapolis in the 1990s and Chicago in the early 1970s, when the Black P Stone Nation and Jeff Fort secured public and private support for their Youth Organizations United (Worthington, 1993). The Chicago project ended when a U.S. Senate investigation found evidence of fraud. Fort was later convicted for narcotics trafficking.

The unusual Minneapolis police-gang cooperative agreement, United for Peace, ended in far more shocking circumstances. On September 25, 1992, 30-year police veteran Jerry Haaf was shot in the back and killed in the Pizza Shack restaurant, a popular cop hangout, during his morning coffee break. Haaf was only a few months from retirement. Hours earlier, a police-community meeting in north Minneapolis turned tense when protestors accused the Minneapolis Police Department and Metro Transit Police Department of manhandling a blind, disabled black man over unpaid bus fare (Hughes, 2002). Police, in turn, accused United for Peace of trying to incite a disturbance and then complain about police brutality. Four alleged members of the Vice Lords were eventually tried and convicted of Haaf's murder, which investigators found was planned at Sharif Willis' house—although whether or not Willis was present is unclear (Hughes, 2002). In 1995, Sharif Willis was sentenced to almost 27 years in federal prison for separate drug and gun-related crimes.

Not all gangs in Minnesota are connected to Chicago "supergangs" such as the Vice Lords. But just like the first gangs in 1920s Chicago (Thrasher, 1927), ethnicity and migration feature prominently in the etiology of Minnesota's criminal landscape, including Hmong and Native American gangs.

Asian Gangs

The Hmong people, originally from the mountainous regions of China, Thailand, Laos, and Vietnam, were U.S. allies during the Second Indochina War (also called the Vietnam War, 1955–1975). After the United States pulled out of Vietnam, the Hmong—considered traitors—were left behind to face retaliation from hostile political regimes. Displaced by the war, hundreds of thousands of Hmong refugees fled to resettlement camps in Thailand. Thousands eventually resettled in the United States and during the 1980s, many Hmong arrived in the Twin Cities area because of a multi-million dollar program started by the University of Minnesota Agricultural Extension Service providing education, equipment, and land to Hmong farmers and their families. Today, some 66,000 ethnic Hmong call Minneapolis-St. Paul home and the Twin Cities has become the "cultural and socio-political center of Hmong life in the U.S." (Grigoleit, 2006, p. 2).

Like generations of immigrants before them, the Hmong (and more recently Cambodian, Karen, and Vietnamese peoples) experienced difficulty integrating into American society. And like generations of immigrants before them (Thrasher, 1927), second-generation Hmong youth formed gangs as a subcultural adjustment to their anomic situation and in accordance with illegitimate opportunity structures in their community (Tsunokai & Kposowa, 2002). The first Hmong gang in Minnesota was the Cobra gang (Straka, 2003). The gang originally comprised teenage friends who lived together in housing projects, played together on a soccer team, and banded together to protect themselves and other Hmong youths from racist bullying (Straka, 2003). From benign origins, however, the group — like many gangs (Densley, 2014) — evolved into a criminal entity. What started out as fights, thefts, and other minor delinquency transformed into more serious crimes like aggravated assault and auto theft (Straka, 2003).

Around 1988, a new Hmong gang was formed outside of the Cobra gang (Straka, 2003). Hmong youths who were barred from joining the Cobra gang on the grounds they were too young, banded together to form The White Tigers. The White Tigers are credited with ushering Hmong gangs into a new, more violent, era. In 1992, for example, gang members crashed through the front door of a Federal Firearms Licensee in a stolen vehicle and took 100 guns (Straka, 2003). Hmong gangs today are primarily involved in automobile theft for parts, home invasions, burglaries (whereby gangs exploit the Hmong cash-economy and an absence of guardianship during lengthy cultural and spiritual events), and illegal gambling. Some gangs also use immigrant community networks to traffic marijuana grown for personal consumption in California over to Minnesota.

In the City of St. Paul, Hmong gangs have taken up a loose stylistic affiliation with the Bloods and Crips of Los Angeles. Examples include the Asian Crips 357, comprised primarily of second- and third-generation Hmong-Americans, the True Bloods 22, comprised of newer Thai and Hmong immigrants, Purple Brothers 162, and Menace of Destruction 301, which identifies as Blood in Minnesota, but Crip in California. Such gangs, concentrated in the University Avenue, Frogtown, Northend, and Eastside areas of St. Paul will come into conflict at big cultural events like the annual July 4, Hmong soccer tournament and the Hmong New Year celebration (McIntee, 2010). Many of them have branched out into prostitution and sexual violence, exploiting the stigma attached to extramarital sex in Hmong communities to secure immunity from prosecution (Straka, 2003). Indeed, owing to the "bride price" (Nqi poj niam) tradition in Hmong marriages, whereby the groom pays money or goods to the bride's family for her hand in marriage (essentially to compensate the family for their "loss" of domestic help), victims of sexual violence are assumed promiscuous and are literally worth less.

Native American Gangs

According to 2010 census data, more than 25,000 Native American people live in the Twin Cities metro area. Between 1992 and 2002, Native Americans experienced violent crimes at double the rate of the rest of the nation (Perry, 2004). Alcoholism mortality rates are 514 percent higher than in the general population and Native American teens experience the highest suicide rate in the country (Center for Native American Youth at the Aspen Institute, 2011). Native American children in Minnesota are six times as likely to make contact with child protective services as white children, eight times as likely to experience neglect and 12 times as likely to spend time in out-of-home care (Minnesota Department of Human Services, 2010). These problems, and more, have deep roots. In 1862, for example, President Abraham Lincoln ordered the hanging of 38 Santee Sioux men in the largest mass execution in American history. The hanging in Mankato came in the aftermath of the Sioux Uprising, in which Dakota tribal members attempted to drive white settlers from their territory after being robbed, cheated, and starved by local, state, and federal officials (Minnesota History Center, 2012). After the hangings, many Natives were removed to Nebraska, and over the next 100 years, the area's remaining tribes and bands underwent brutal changes— moving to reservations, sending culture and tradition underground, and migrating from their homelands to cities like Minneapolis (see **Chapter Nine**). This explains in part why distrust of police is still part of daily life for the city's Native American community. The American Indian Movement was born in Minneapolis in the 1960s because of police brutality in the Indian community (Birong-Smith, 2009). In the 1990s, moreover, Minneapolis police arrested two intoxicated American Indian men and decided to transport them to a hospital in the trunk of their car (Human Rights Watch, 1998).

Native American gangs trace their roots back to the 1980s and 1990s, when city gangs first introduced themselves to Indian Country (Ahtone, 2015). Until the early 1990s, gangs in Minneapolis' Native American neighborhoods primarily existed for protection. As discussed, gangs from Chicago, Detroit, and other major Midwest cities had begun migrating into the area, and Native young people often banded together to resist the growing number of threats. Groups like the Clubsters, the Naturals, and the Death Warriors were small, all-Native groups, vying for legitimacy with primarily black gangs. Minnesota's two most prominent Native American gangs, the Native Mob and the Native

Disciples, however, evolved out of the high-profile murder of Randy Pacheco. Pacheco, a Native member of the Vice Lords, was shot in 1994 following an altercation with Shinob-Mob members Joe and Terry Bercier. Terry was convicted for the murder, while his brother Joe was acquitted (Ahtone, 2015).

With Joe out on the street, Vice Lords' members sought permission to avenge Pacheco's death. The Vice Lords' predominately black leadership refused. Pacheco's Native American compatriots struck anyway and were excommunicated. In turn, they formed their own gang, Native Mob, affiliation with which was signified by wearing red and black clothing. Predictably, Joe Bercier's murder prompted further retaliation, this time from the Gangster Disciples—another Chicago-based gang that had emerged in Minneapolis—who had ties to the Bercier family (Ahtone, 2015). Reciprocal violence escalated, and Native members of the Gangster Disciples in the East Phillips neighborhood soon found themselves at war with Native Mob and the Vice Lords. Lacking support from the Gangster Disciples' black leadership, Native members split to form their own Native Disciples (Ahtone, 2015).

Native Mob grew to more than 200 members across cities and reservations in Minnesota, Wisconsin, and North and South Dakota. The group was implicated in crimes such as drug trafficking, weapons sales, assault, witness intimidation, murder, human trafficking, sexual assault, and racketeering (United States Attorney's Office Minnesota, 2014). But this all ended in 2013, when local, state, and federal officials launched a takedown of Native Mob, resulting in dozens of arrests and convictions under the RICO or Racketeer Influenced Corrupt Organizations Act (United States Attorney's Office Minnesota, 2014). In maintaining strict codes of conduct and hierarchical structures, Native Mob was the exception, not the rule, among street gangs (Howell & Griffiths, 2015). Still, Ahtone (2015) observes, "With arrests and indictments having resulted in the temporary absence of Native Mob, a power vacuum exists in Minnesota's Indian gang world. And while both new and old gangs are eager to fill it, the Native Disciples may be the only group with the organization and manpower to do so."

Defining Gang Membership in Minnesota

Defining gangs is not as easy as it sounds. Minnesota gangs are increasingly splintered into smaller "cliques" and crews running a few blocks, some of which are small subsets of more established gangs (Williams, 2015). This, in turn, has made defining gangs even more difficult. As the father of gang research, Frederick Thrasher (1927) observed, no two gangs are exactly alike in form and function. Criminologists, in turn, struggle with or challenge the term "gang" because, after 100 years of trying, still no uniform definition exists and, as we shall see, the arbitrary and capricious labeling of benign peer groups as gangs has catastrophic consequences (Katz & Jackson-Jacobs, 2004; McCorkle & Miethe, 2002). Gang definitions, for instance, often fail to separate the actions of gang members as individuals from the actions of gangs as organizations (see Densely, 2013). In this sense, *gang member* activity is simply any independent action taken by people who happen to be gang members. *Gang-related* activity speaks to individual action taken in furtherance or support of the gang, whereby individuals in gangs act as agents of the organization (Sánchez-Jankowski, 2003).

Minnesota Statutes § 609.229 defines a "criminal gang" as any ongoing organization, association, or group of three or more persons, whether formal or informal, that:

1) has, as one of its primary activities, the commission of one or more of the offenses listed in section 609.11, subdivision 9, including murder in the first, second, or third degree; assault in the first, second, or third degree; burglary; kidnapping; false imprisonment; manslaughter in the first or second degree; aggravated robbery; simple robbery; first-degree or aggravated first-degree witness tampering; criminal sexual conduct; escape from custody; arson in the first, second, or third degree; drive-by shooting; possession or other unlawful use of a firearm;
2) has a common name or common identifying sign or symbol; and
3) includes members who individually or collectively engage in or have engaged in a pattern of criminal activity.

This legal definition is obviously more prescriptive than Klein and Maxson's (2006, p. 4) "consensus Eurogang definition" of gangs as durable and street-oriented youth groups whose involvement in illegal activity is part of their group identity (see **Figure 7.2**), in part because since the late 1980s crimes committed to benefit a gang in Minnesota carry longer prison sentences (National Gang Center, n.d.). The Eurogang definition, however, is sufficiently general to capture the essence of the gangs described in this chapter.

GangNET and the Metro Gang Strike Force

Minnesota once had a coordinated approach to corroborating gang information and challenging gang activity. The state's use of a collaborative task force, comprehensive gang criteria, and computerized gang databases, was celebrated as a potential model for other states to follow (Barrows & Huff, 2009).

Recent scandals have halted progress, however, and today Minnesota lacks both a centralized repository for counting gangs and gang members and a clear mandate for policing them (Huff & Barrows, 2015).

In 1997, the Minnesota Legislature (by Minnesota Statutes §299C.091) established the "Criminal Gang Investigative Data System" or "Pointer File," administered and maintained by the Minnesota Bureau of Criminal Apprehension (BCA) to tally and track gang members (see Barrows & Huff, 2009). The legislature also established 10-point criteria for entry into the system, as follows:

1. Admits to being a gang member;
2. is observed to associate on a regular basis with known gang members;
3. has tattoos indicating gang membership;
4. wears gang symbols to identify with a specific gang;
5. is in a photograph with known gang members and/or using gang-related hand signs;
6. name is on gang document, hit list, or gang-related graffiti;
7. is identified as a gang member by a reliable source;
8. arrested in the company of identified gang members or associates;
9. corresponds with known gang members or writes and/or receives correspondence about gang activity; and
10. writes about gang (graffiti) on walls, books and paper.

(Aba-Onu et al., 2010, p. 225)

Individuals had to meet three of the ten criteria, be at least 14 years old, and commit a gross misdemeanor or felony to be entered into the file, and the BCA was tasked with "cleaning" it every three years. If within the three-year period an individual in the Pointer File had not been arrested or convicted of a crime, they were to be removed (Barrows & Huff, 2009). By 2009, 2,000 potential gang members were named in the Pointer File.

In 1998, however, the Ramsey County Sheriff's Department received state funding to create their own database of potential gang members, called GangNET (Gottfried, 2009). Criteria for entry into GangNET—private, proprietary software developed by Orion Scientific Systems—was not as strict as criteria for entry into the state's rival Pointer File (Aba-Onu et al., 2010). GangNET, for example, included people who met any *one* of the 10-point criteria, had no age limit, and did not require that an individual commit a crime to be entered. Further, the data were cleaned only every ten years. As a result, GangNET reportedly had eight times more gang members than the Pointer File database, totaling approximately 16,000 (Aba-Onu et al., 2010).

The community eventually began to question the validity of the GangNET system, not least because, contrary to popular belief, gang membership is generally of short duration, typically less than two years (Pyrooz & Sweeten, 2015), and police and rival gang members may perceive *former* gang members listed in the database as *current* gang members and arrest or attack them as such (Decker, Pyrooz, & Moule, 2014). Tensions increased in 2007 when the BCA audited 219 of the 2052 files in the Pointer File database (Gottfried, 2009). Despite an 85% success rate, the BCA found discrepancies in who gets entered into the database and for what reasons.

Further evaluation of the supposedly confidential Pointer File and GangNET databases in 2010 raised additional concerns about the methods used to track gangs and criminal activity (see Aba-Onu et al., 2010). Specifically, (1) individuals (or their parents) were never notified when they were entered into either system; (2) not all individuals entered were *bona fide* gang members; (3) blacks were overrepresented; (4) who had access to the data was not defined within the legislation; (5) and there was no appeals process for people misidentified or no longer in a gang.

Ramsey County Sheriff Matt Bostrom officially closed GangNET in August 2011, although in reality the system's use by law enforcement agencies had dwindled since the Metro Gang Strike Force was shut down two years earlier in 2009 (Xiong, 2011). Although the Pointer File is not formally closed, no new information is being added, since GangNET was feeding the Pointer File (Huff & Barrows, 2015).

The Minnesota Gang Strike Force, created in 1997 by Minnesota Statutes §299A.64 alongside the Criminal Gang Oversight Council, was a statewide task force of gang officers, "to eliminate the harm caused to the public by criminal gangs and their illegal activities within the state of Minnesota." Due to funding issues, the Minnesota Gang Strike Force was disbanded in 2005, restructured to have only one office stationed in New Brighton, and renamed the Metro Gang Strike Force (MGSF). In 2009, a legislative audit report into the MGSF found at least $18,126 in cash seized from suspects was unaccounted for and 13 out of 80 confiscated vehicles were missing (Furst, 2011). A former strike force commander, quoted as saying "the Strike Force is the best task force that the state of Minnesota has ever funded," also illegally sold a seized television to a student employee in his office (Furst, 2011). A later report found the MGSF guilty of widespread impropriety, excessive force, and illegal searches and seizures; concluding that much of the task force's police work was ineffective (Luger & Egelholf, 2009). In the end, the MGSF was unable to account for 202 of its 545 cash seizures, totaling $165,650 (Hurst, 2011).

The MGSF was disbanded in 2009 and eventually ordered to pay $3 million to victims of misconduct (Nelson, 2010). This included $6,000 for a two-year-old toddler who was kicked in the head by one Task Force officer during an illegal search for drugs, and $35,500 for two immigrants who were afraid to report their experience of excessive force out of fear of deportation. The two immigrants were also awarded special visas to stay in the United States (Furst, 2012). In total, the money addresses "wrongdoing and improper seizure" and funds "statewide training to keep similar misconduct from happening again" (Nelson, 2010, p. 2).

The MGSF scandal led to significant changes in police policy and practice, including establishment of the new nine-point gang criteria (see **Figure 7.4**) and a curtailing of agency-specific gang units in Minnesota (see Huff & Barrows, 2015). The FBI Safe Streets Task Force in Minneapolis largely replaced the MGSF, although some agencies, including the St. Paul Police Department, maintained their own gang units. In April 2015, Minneapolis Police Chief Janeé Harteau announced her department would form a new unit comprised of five officers and a supervisor to address gangs and stem retaliatory shootings during the summer months (Roper, 2015). The unit would also monitor social media and YouTube rap videos for online insults and chatter about retaliatory violence. The announcement came shortly after social media and gang *pointers* again got police in trouble, during an episode known as "Pointergate."

Figure 7.4. The Nine-Point Criteria for Gang Membership in Minnesota

A "gang member" in Minnesota is an individual who is 14 years of age or older and meets at least three of the nine criteria listed below:

1. Admits gang membership
2. Arrested with a gang member
3. Displays a gang tattoo or brand
4. Wears clothing or symbols intended to identify with a gang
5. Appears in a photograph or image with a gang member engaging in gang-related activity or displaying gang signs or symbols
6. Name appears on a gang roster
7. Identified as a member of a gang by a reliable source
8. Is regularly observed or communicates with a gang member in furtherance or support of gang-related activity
9. Produces gang-specific writing or graffiti in furtherance or support of gang-related activity.

A "confirmed gang member" is a gang member per the above who has been adjudicated or convicted of a violent crime.

Source: Minnesota Violent Crime Coordinating Council (2012).

In response to a 2014 photograph of Minneapolis Mayor Betsy Hodges posing with "convicted felon" Navell Gordon, "law enforcement sources," for KSTP-TV, including police union chief John Delmonico, conflated Hodges' extended pointer finger with a "known gang sign" and argued the photo "could jeopardize public safety and put their officers at risk" (Kolls, 2014). The Twitter hashtag "Pointergate" went viral and the story even featured on the *Daily Show with Jon Stewart* (Wemple, 2014). The public condemned police for politicking (Hodges had been outspoken in her criticism of the Minneapolis Police for resisting her body-camera initiative, see **Chapter Ten**) and racial stereotyping (Gordon was a young black male, not a gang member) and found KSTP-TV guilty of the lesser offenses of sensationalism and poor taste.

Gang Intervention in Minnesota

So far, police have not come off well in this chapter. The good news is Minnesota is also the site of some innovative best practices in policing gangs and gang violence. Minneapolis, for example, was the first city after Boston, Massachusetts, to pilot Group Violence Intervention (GVI), a well-documented gang violence reduction strategy that began life as "Operation Ceasefire" in the 1990s (see Kennedy & Braga, 1998) and now is codified by the National Network for Safe Communities (2013). GVI is a focused-deterrence strategy comprised of various tactics. GVI begins with a problem analysis, such as a systematic review of all violent incidents and an audit or mapping of all violent groups in any given jurisdiction (see **Chapter Ten**). Once the key players are identified, coordinated law enforcement action against the most violent group follows in an effort to demonstrate to other groups that violence will not be tolerated. Next, community moral voices and social service providers partner with law enforcement to engage directly with violent group members (and through them, their associates) in a "call-in," or face-to-face meeting, at a venue of civic importance (Kennedy, 2011).

There is "strong empirical evidence" for GVI's effectiveness (Braga & Weisburd, 2012, p. 25). Some of that evidence comes courtesy of the St. Paul Police Department (see Densley & Jones, 2016). After the Metro Gang Strike Force fiasco, the St. Paul Police Department became one of the only law enforcement agencies in the state to maintain its own stand-alone gang unit. In early 2011, the unit identified an escalation in retaliatory violence between local factions of two rival Latino gangs— 18th Street and Sureños 13. Intelligence from social media and a confidential informant also indicated the 18th Street gang was poised to initiate a large number of girls into their ranks through a process that included sexual assault. Immediate intervention was needed.

Utilizing gang intelligence and criminal records, the St. Paul Police Department Gang Unit served an unconventional search warrant on active members of the gang; one that included a search, but in lieu of automatic arrest, an invite to dinner at a local community center for conversation about the need to stop the violence now before it was too late. Initially, this unorthodox plan to search but not arrest gang members was condemned as being "soft on crime" (Gervais, 2011). However, the Gang Unit persisted and mobilized community leaders and service providers to help the gang members desist from gang life. To gain parental input, the Gang Unit recruited the Mexican Consulate to mitigate fears of deportation and unlock some of the failed narratives that had alienated police from the Latino community in the past. They eventually conducted a "call-in" with the 18th Street gang and all interested parties.

A key partner in this effort was the Neighborhood House's Gang Reduction and Intervention Program (GRIP), a social service initiative that steers young people away from gangs and crime toward a brighter future. The Neighborhood House is a landmark social service agency in St. Paul where people can meet over Latin American cuisine to learn about Latino culture and celebrate friendship and personal responsibility. GRIP includes weekly meetings with speakers and field trips, free gang-tattoo removal (plastic surgeons and nurses donate their time to perform the laser treatments), tutoring, boxing lessons, social support systems, and volunteer work in the community (Gervais, 2011). The program's director, Enrique "Cha-Cho" Estrada, continues to put his own moral voice behind the SPPD and offer services to gang members.

Paul Iovino, who was commander of the Gang Unit at the time, recalls internecine violence between 18th Street and Sureños gang members declined immediately after the call-in (Gervais, 2011). Today, "clique" gangs such as Hit Squad, Ham Crazy, Gutter Block Goons, and Selby Side, are the most active of the approximately 30 gangs resident in the City of St. Paul (Williams, 2015). For further discussion of juvenile crime and violence intervention, see **Chapter Six**.

Hate Groups, Outlaw Motorcycle Clubs, and Drug Cartels: Gangs by Any Other Name

There are eight active "hate groups" in Minnesota, according to the Southern Poverty Law Center (SPLC, 2015). Nationwide, there were 784 active hate groups in 2014 that "have beliefs or practices that attack or malign an entire class of people, typically for their immutable characteristics" (SPLC, 2015). Hate itself is not a crime because it is protected under the First Amendment right to freedom of speech and expression. But crime motivated by hate is not protected, hence Congress defines a "hate crime" as any "criminal offense motivated, in whole or in part, by the offender's bias against a race, religion, disability, sexual orientation, ethnicity, gender, or gender identity" (Federal Bureau of Investigation, n.d.). From 2003–2013, Minnesota was responsible for approximately 1–3% of all the hate crimes committed nationally. The motivations for these crimes are displayed in **Table 7.2**. As shown, victims are most likely to be targeted because of their race, both in Minnesota and nationally.

Hate groups in Minnesota include: the Aryan Strikeforce, a racist skinhead group; the Israelite Church of God in Jesus Christ, a Black Separatist group; a National Socialist Movement franchise of Neo-Nazis; the Parents Action League, an anti-lesbian, -gay, -bisexual, and -transgender (LGBT) group; The Remnant Press, a radical traditional Catholicism group; the Vinlanders Minnesota, another racist skinhead group; Weisman Publications, a Christian identity group; and You Can Run But You Cannot Hide, another anti-LGBT group. From 2004 through 2012, SPLC lists 59 incidents of hate-related crimes in Minnesota, many of which were related to vandalism, threats, and harassment.

Outlaw motorcycle clubs also have a presence in Minnesota. Since the 1980s, the Hells Angels Motorcycle Club has established itself as the dominant motorcycle gang in the state and via creation of the Minnesota Motorcycle Clubs Coalition (MMCC), controls most of the smaller motorcycle clubs in Minnesota, including Hells Outcasts, the oldest motorcycle gang in the state, formed in 1947, and Los Valientes, another Saint Paul club, formed in 1976. The Hells Angels maintain a truce with The Sons of Silence, which has active chapters in Faribault, Hutchinson, Mankato, Rochester, and St. Cloud. The Outlaws are the Hells Angels' main rivals, with a large presence in the neighboring state of Wisconsin. While outlaw motorcycle gang activity is largely hidden from public view, these so-called "one-percenter" clubs (a reference to a comment made by the American Motorcyclist Association that 99 percent of motorcyclists were law-abiding citizens, implying that the last one percent were outlaws) are used by their members as conduits for criminal enterprise, specifically trafficking and cross-border smuggling of guns and drugs (Barker, 2007).

Outlaw motorcycle clubs control some of Minnesota's narcotics market, but Mexican drug cartels are the primary producers, transporters, and distributors of illicit and prescription drugs in the state (Tarm, 2013). The I-35 corridor that runs from just north of the U.S.-Mexico border in Laredo, Texas, up through Minnesota is partly responsible, but more so is Minnesota's proximity to Chicago, which in 2010 was the only U.S. city to rank in the top five for shipments of all four major drug categories—heroin, marijuana, cocaine, and methamphetamine (U.S. Department of Justice, 2010). The powerful Sinaloa Cartel enjoys a virtual monopoly on the Chicago drug trade, to the extent that Cartel leader Joaquín "El Chapo" Guzmán Loera once referred to the city as his "home port" (McGahan, 2013). In 2013, El Chapo was declared Chicago's Public Enemy Number One, a distinction last held by Al Capone. And his ties

Table 7.2. Motivation for Hate Crimes in Minnesota and Nationally

Year	Total Number in MN/US	Race % in MN/% in US	Religion % in MN/% in US	Sexual Orient. % in MN/% in US	Ethnicity % in MN/% in US	Disability % in MN/% in US	Gender % in MN/% in US	Gender Identity % in MN/% in US	Multiple-Bias % in MN/% in US
2003	215/7489	71/51	10/18	17/17	2/14	0/.4	NA	NA	NA/.05
2004	239/7,649	66/53	13/18	14/16	7/13	.4/.8	NA	NA	NA/.09
2005	206/7,163	52/55	12/17	13/14	23/13	1.5/.7	NA	NA	NA/.04%
2006	137/7,722	72/52	9.5/19	15/15	4/13	0/1	NA	NA	NA/.03
2007	157/7,624	50/51	12/18	17/17	20/13	1/1	NA	NA	NA/.04
2008	164/7,783	59/51	8/20	18/17	15/11	.6/1	NA	NA	NA/.04
2009	153/ 6,604	56/48	10/20	18/19	14/12	1/1.5	NA	NA	NA/.09
2010	127/6,628	54/47	7/20	17/19	22/13	0/.6	NA	NA	NA/.06
2011	148/ 6,222	49/47	16/20	23/21	12/12	.7/.9	NA	NA	NA/.09
2012	72/5,796	56/48	15/19	17/20	13/12	0/1.6	NA	NA	NA/.10
2013	144/5,928	58/48	13/17	21/21	8/11	.7/1.4	0/.3	0/.5	NA/.1

Source: Author created from information provided by Federal Bureau of Investigation.

to Minnesota were exposed in 2014, when the Sinaloa Cartel reportedly hired MS-13 gang members to fly from Los Angeles, California, to St. Paul to find the people they suspected of stealing 30 pounds of meth and $200,000 from a stash house (Gottfried, 2014).

Concluding Remarks

In the 90 years since Frederic Thrasher (1927) first documented 1,313 gangs in Chicago, street gangs remain an enduring and challenging social problem facing adolescents and young adults, particularly in urban America. Over 30,000 homicides in the U.S. are attributed to street gangs since the 1990s (Howell & Griffiths, 2015). Such homicides are often very public and characterized by cyclical and retaliatory exchanges (Papachristos, Hureau, & Braga, 2013). As a result, gang members have homicide victimization rates that are at least 100 times greater than the general public (Decker & Pyrooz, 2010). This is a national problem with local implications. This chapter has explored Minnesota's unflattering history of gangs and gangsters. We hope as students of criminal justice, you advance this knowledge in the continuing fight against corruption and serious youth violence.

Key Terms

1934 National Firearms Act	Murderapolis
Doc Ames	National Rifle Association
Gang	Neighborhood House (GRIP)
Gang Migration	O'Connor System (Layover agreement)
Gang Summit	Organized Crime Group
GangNET	Outlaw Motorcycle Clubs
Group Violence Intervention	Pointer File
Hate Crimes	Prohibition
Jerry Haff	Public Enemies Era
John Dillinger	Speakeasy
Layover Agreement	Spoils System
Mafia	Supergangs
Metro Gang Strike Force	Volstead Act

Selected Internet Sites

First National Bank of Northfield
https://firstnationalnorthfield.com/about/history/

Midwest Gang Investigators Association
http://www.mgia.org

Minnesota Historical Society, Inventory of Criminal History Files
http://www2.mnhs.org/library/findaids/pubsaf08.xml#a9

National Gang Center
https://www.nationalgangcenter.gov

Northfield Historical Society
http://www.northfieldhistory.org/bank-site/

St. Paul Gangster Tours
www.wabashastreetcaves.com

Violent Crime Coordinating Council
https://dps.mn.gov/divisions/ojp/Pages/violent-crimes-coordinating-council.aspx

Discussion Questions

1. What is a gang? What are the differences between gangs in the 1920s and gangs today?
2. What is the Volstead Act and what effect did it have on gun laws in the United States and Minnesota?
3. Compare and contrast GangNET and the Pointer File.
4. What were some of the concerns raised about the GangNET and Pointer File databases?
5. What are some push and pull factors for juveniles to join gangs in Minnesota?
6. Research organizations in Minnesota that are helping to *prevent* gang membership and/or *intervene* in gang violence. What are their methods?
7. Besides gang task forces and other strategies discussed in this chapter, what more do you think police departments can or should do to help respond to gang problems in the community?
8. Do you think a lot of hate crimes go unreported? Why would someone not want to report being a victim of a hate crime?

References

Aba-Onu, U., Levy-Pounds, N., Salmen, J., & Tyner, A. (2010). Evaluation of gang databases in Minnesota and recommendations for change. *Information & Communications Technology Law*, 19, 223–254.

Alhtone, A. (2015, January 23). Boys in the woods: A Saturday night in White Earth with the Native Disciples. *Al Jazeera America*. Retrieved from http://projects.aljazeera.com/2015/01/native-gangs/native-disciples.html

Baran, M. (2015, February 21). Mall of America increases security after being named in apparent al-Shabab video. *MPR News*. Retrieved from http://www.mprnews.org/story/2015/02/21/cbs-news-alshabaab-video-calls-for-attack-on-mall-of-america

Barker, T. (2007) *Biker gangs and organized crime*. Newark, NJ: Anderson.

Barrows, J., & Huff, R. (2009). Gangs and public policy: Constructing and deconstructing gang databases. *Criminology and Public Policy*, 8, 675–703.

Birong-Smith, C. (2009). *The influence of police brutality on the American Indian movement's establishment in Minneapolis, 1968–1969*. Retrieved from http://www.ais.arizona.edu/thesis/influence-police-brutality-american-indian-movements-establishment-minneapolis-1968-1969.

Bordin, R. (1981). *Women and temperance: The quest for power and liberty, 1873–1900*. Philadelphia: Temple University Press.

Braga, A., & Weisburd, D. (2012). The effects of focused deterrence strategies on crime: A systematic review and meta-analysis of the empirical evidence. *Journal of Research in Crime and Delinquency*, 49, 323–358.

Brennan Center for Justice. (2015). *Countering Violent Extremism (CVE): A resource page*. Retrieved from https://www.brennancenter.org/analysis/cve-programs-resource-page.

Center for Native American Youth at the Aspen Institute. (2011). *Fast facts on Native American youth and Indian Country*. Retrieved from http://www.aspeninstitute.org/sites/default/files/content/images/Fast%20Facts.pdf

Chanen, D. (2003, April 21). Asian gangs: A rise in influence, the fall of a young man; killing highlights young members' taste for revenge. *Star Tribune*. Retrieved from http://search.proquest.com.ezproxy.metrostate.edu/docview/427548602/3154B0C628834B41PQ/11?accountid=12415

Cook, P., Ludwig, J., Venkatesh, S., & Braga, A. (2007). Underground gun markets. *Economic Journal*, 117, F558–88.

Davis, E. (2007). *Minnesota 13: Stearns County's 'wet' wild prohibition days*. Helena, MT: Sweet Grass Publishing.

Decker, S., & Pyrooz, D. (2010). Gang violence worldwide: Context, culture, and country. In *Small Arms Survey 2010: Gangs, Groups, and Guns* (pp. 128–55). Cambridge: Cambridge University Press.

Decker, S., Pyrooz, D., & Moule, R., Jr. (2014). Disengagement from gangs as role transitions. *Journal of Research on Adolescence*, 24, 268–283.

Decker, S., & Van Winkle, B. (1996). *Life in the gang: Family, friends, and violence*. Cambridge, UK: Cambridge University Press.

Densley, J. (2012). Street gang recruitment: Signaling, screening, and selection. *Social Problems*, 59, 301–321.

Densley, J. (2013). *How gangs work: An ethnography of youth violence*. New York: Palgrave Macmillan.

Densley, J. (2014). It's gang life, but not as we know it: The evolution of gang business. *Crime & Delinquency*, 60, 517–546.

Densley, J. (2015). Joining the gang. In S. Decker & D. Pyrooz (eds.), *The handbook of gangs*. New York: Wiley.

Densley, J., & Jones, D. (2016). Pulling levers on gang violence in London and St. Paul. In C. Maxson & F.-A. Esbensen (eds.), *Gang transitions and transformations in an international context*. New York: Springer.

Egley Jr., A., & Howell, J. (2013). *Highlights of the 2011 National Youth Gang Survey*. Washington, DC: U.S. Department of Justice, Office of Juvenile Justice and Delinquency Prevention.

Federal Bureau of Investigation. (n.d.). *Famous cases and criminals: John Dillinger*. Retrieved from http://www.fbi.gov/about-us/history/famous-cases/john-dillinger

Federal Bureau of Investigation. (n.d.). *Hate crime: Overview*. Retrieved from http://www.fbi.gov/about-us/investigate/civilrights/hate_crimes/overview

Fortune Magazine. (1936, April). Revolt in the Northwest, 13, 112–19.

Furst, R. (2011, March 23). Gang Strike Force shut down after audit finds $18,000, 13 cars missing. *Star Tribune*. Retrieved from: www.startribune.com/local/minneapolis/45485362.html

Furst, R. (2012, August 5). Payouts reveal brutal, rogue Metro Gang Strike Force. *Star Tribune*. Retrieved from: http://www.startribune.com/local/165028086.html

Gervais, B. (2011, December 3). St Paul employs 'smarter, not softer' approach to gangs. *Pioneer Press*. Retrieved from http://www.twincities.com/minnesota/ci_19459543

Gorn, E. (2009). *Dillinger's wild ride: The year that made America's public enemy number one*. New York: Oxford University Press.

Gottfried, M. (2009, September 20). Gang database: Just how accurate, how fair? *Pioneer Press*. Retrieved from: http://www.twincities.com/ci_13370332

Gottfried, M. (2014, May 6). Suspected Mexican drug cartel enforcers indicted in St. Paul torture-kidnap case. *Pioneer Press*. Retrieved from http://www.twincities.com/crime/ci_25706693/accused-drug-enforcers-indicted-st-paul-torture-kidnap

Grigoleit, G. (2006). Coming home? The integration of Hmong refugees from Wat Tham Krabok, Thailand, into American society. *Hmong Studies Journal*, 7, 1–22.

Howell, J. (2007) Menacing or mimicking? Realities of youth gangs. *Juvenile and Family Court Journal*, 58, 39–50.

Howell, J., & Griffiths, E. (2015). *Gangs in America's Communities* (2nd ed). Thousand Oaks, CA: Sage.

Huff, C., & Barrows, J. (2015). Documenting gang activity: Intelligence databases. In S.H. Decker & D. Pyrooz (eds.), *Handbook on Gangs and Gang Responses*. New York: Wiley.

Human Rights Watch. (1998). *Incidents: Minneapolis*. Retrieved from http://www.hrw.org/legacy/reports98/police/uspo86.htm

Johnson, D. (1996, June 30). Nice city's nasty distinction: Murder soars in Minneapolis. *New York Times*. Retrieved from http://www.nytimes.com/1996/06/30/us/nice-city-s-nasty-distinction-murders-soar-in-minneapolis.html

Kahn, H. (1934, 6 April). Mayor Mahoney expresses satisfaction with St. Paul police conditions. *St. Paul Daily News*, 1.

Kaplan, J. (1974). *Lincoln Steffens: A biography*. New York: Simon and Schuster.

Karlen, N. (2014). *Augie's Secrets: The Minneapolis mob and the king of the Hennepin strip*. St. Paul, MN: Minnesota Historical Society Press.

Katz, J., & Jackson-Jacobs, C. (2004). The criminologists' gang. In C. Sumner (ed.), *The Blackwell companion to criminology* (pp. 91–124). Malden, MA: Blackwell.

Kennedy, D. (2011). *Don't shoot: One man, a street fellowship, and the end of violence in inner-city America*. New York: Bloomsbury.

Kennedy, D., & Braga, A. (1998). Homicide in Minneapolis: Research for problem solving. *Homicide Studies*, 2, 263–290.

Klein, M. (1995). *The American street gang*. New York: Oxford University Press.

Klein, M., & Maxson, C. (2006). *Street gang patterns and policies*. Oxford: Oxford University Press.

Kolls, J. (2014, November 7). Mpls. mayor flashes gang sign with convicted felon; law enforcement outraged. *KSTP*. Retrieved from http://kstp.com/news/stories/S3612199.shtml?cat=1

Lapore, J. (2012, 23 April). Battleground America: One nation under the gun. *The New Yorker*. Retrieved from: http://www.newyorker.com/reporting/2012/04/23/120423fa_fact_lepore

Lee, A. (2003). *Code of silence: The Andre Coppage story.* Bloomington, IN: 1st Book Library.

Levitt S., & Venkatesh, S. (2000). An economic analysis of a drug-selling gang's finances. *The Quarterly Journal of Economics*, 115, 755–789.

Luger, A., & Egelholf, J. (2009). *Report of the Metro Gang Strike Force review panel.* Retrieved from https://dps.mn.gov/divisions/co/about/Documents/final_report_mgsf_review_panel.pdf

Maccabee, P. (1995). *John Dillinger slept here: A crooks' tour of crime and corruption in St. Paul, 1920–1936.* St. Paul, MN: Minnesota Historical Society Press.

Mahoney, T. (2013). *Secret partners: Big Tom Brown and the Barker gang.* St. Paul, MN: Minnesota Historical Society Press.

Maxson, C. (1998). *Gang members on the move.* Washington, DC: U.S. Department of Justice, Office of Juvenile Justice and Delinquency Prevention.

McCorkle, R., & Miethe, T. (2002). *Panic: The social construction of the street gang problem.* Upper Saddle River, NJ: Prentice Hall.

McGahan, J. (2013, September 17). Why Mexico's Sinaloa Cartel loves selling drugs in Chicago. *Chicago Magazine.* Retrieved from http://www.chicagomag.com/Chicago-Magazine/October-2013/Sinaloa-Cartel/

McInte, M. (2010, November 27). Violence mars Hmong New Year celebration in St. Paul. *The Uptake.* Retrieved from http://theuptake.org/2010/11/27/violence-mars-hmong-new-year-celebration-in-st-paul/

Melde, C., Taylor, T., & Esbensen, F.-A. (2009). 'I got your back': An examination of the protective function of gang membership in adolescence. *Criminology*, 47, 565–594.

Millett, L. (2004a). *Murder has a public face: Crime and punishment in the speed graphic era.* St. Paul, MN: Borealis Books.

Millett, L. (2004b). *Strange days, dangerous nights: Photos from the speed graphic era.* St. Paul, MN: Borealis Books.

Minnesota Department of Human Services. (2010). *Minnesota child welfare disparities report.* Retrieved from http://www.mncourts.gov/Documents/0/Public/Childrens_Justice_Initiative/Disparities_-_Minnesota_Child_Welfare_Disparities_Report_(DHS)_(February_2010).pdf

Minnesota History Center. (2012). The U.S.-Dakota War of 1862. Retrieved from http://www.usdakotawar.org

Minnesota History Center. (n.d.). *Northfield raid & the James-Younger gang.* Retrieved from http://libguides.mnhs.org/northfieldraid

Minnesota Violent Crime Coordinating Council. (2012). *Gang criteria recommendation to the commissioner of public safety.* Retrieved from: https://dps.mn.gov/divisions/ojp/forms-documents/Documents/Gang%20Criteria/Gang%20Criteria%20Report%20to%20Commissioner-FINAL.pdf

MinnPost. (2008, July 2). 150 Minnesota moments we'd just as soon forget. *MinnPost*. Retrieved from http://www.minnpost.com/politics-policy/2008/07/150-minnesota-moments-wed-just-soon-forget

Nathanson, I. (2010). *Minneapolis in the twentieth century*. St. Paul, MN: Minnesota Historical Society.

National Archives. (2015). *Teaching documents: The Volstead Act and related Prohibition documents*. Retrieved from http://www.archives.gov/education/lessons/volstead-act/

National Center for Education Statistics. (2008). *Status and trends in the education of American Indians and Alaska Natives: 2008*. Retrieved from http://nces.ed.gov/pubs2008/nativetrends/highlights.asp

National Gang Center. (n.d.). *Gang-related legislation by state: Minnesota*. Retrieved from https://www.nationalgangcenter.gov/Legislation/Minnesota

National Network for Safe Communities. (2013). *Group violence intervention: An implementation guide*. Washington, DC: U.S. Department of Justice, Office of Community Oriented Policing Services. Retrieved from http://nnscommunities.org/our-work/guides/group-violence-intervention/group-violence-intervention-an-implementation-guide

National Network for Safe Communities. (2014). *National initiative for building community trust and justice announced*. Retrieved from http://nnscommunities.org/our-work/commentary/national-initiative-for-building-community-trust-and-justice-announced

Nelson, T. (2010, August 25). Gang Strike Force victims reach $3M settlement. *MPR News*. Retrieved from: http://www.mprnews.org/story/2010/08/25/strike-force-settlement

Northfield Historical Society. (n.d.). *The First National Bank of Northfield*. Retrieved from http://www.northfieldhistory.org/bank-site/

Papachristos, A., Hureau, D., & Braga, A. (2013). The corner and the crew: The influence of geography and social networks on gang violence. *American Sociological Review, 78*, 417–47.

PBS Newshour. (2013, September 23). Kenyan foreign minister says 'two or three' Americans involved in mall attack. Retrieved from http://www.pbs.org/newshour/bb/africa-july-dec13-kenyaminister_09-23/

Perry, S. (2004). *American Indians and crime: A BJS statistical profile, 1992–2002*. Washington DC: U.S. Department of Justice. Retrieved from http://www.justice.gov/sites/default/files/otj/docs/american_indians_and_crime.pdf

Police Officers Federation of Minneapolis. (2015). *Jerome (Jerry) Haaf*. Retrieved from http://www.mpdfederation.com/jerome-jerry-haaf/

Pyrooz, D., & Sweeten, G. (2015). Gang membership between ages 5 and 17 years in the United States. *Journal of Adolescent Health, 56*, 414–19.

Riedel, M., & Welsh, W. (2011). *Criminal violence: Patterns, causes, and prevention.* (3rd ed.). New York: Oxford University Press.

Roper, E. (2015). Mpls. police will launch new gang unit. *StarTribune*, April 22. Retrieved from http://www.startribune.com/local/blogs/300965 331.html

Saint Paul Police Historical Society. (1984). *The long blue line.* Retrieved from http://www.spphs.com/history/blue_line.php

Sánchez-Jankowski, M. (2003). Gangs and social change. *Theoretical Criminology*, 7, 192–216.

Small Arms Survey. (2007). *Guns and the City.* Cambridge: Cambridge University Press.

Southern Poverty Law Center. (2015). *Hate map.* Retrieved from http://www.splcenter.org/hate-map

Sparber, M. (2011, February 11). Come along for my tour of Minneapolis crime history. *MinnPost.* Retrieved from: https://www.minnpost.com/max-about-town/2011/02/come-along-my-tour-minneapolis-crime-history

Stanek, R. (2012). *Testimony of Richard W. Stanek to the subcommittee on crime, terrorism, and homeland security.* Retrieved from http://judiciary.house.gov/_files/hearings/Hearings%202012/Stanek%2007252012.pdf

Steffens, L. (1931). *The autobiography of Lincoln Steffens.* New York: Harcourt, Brace, and Company. 376–377.

Steffens, L. (1957). *The shame of the cities.* New York: Sagamore Press.

Straka, R. (2003). The violence of Hmong gangs and the crime of rape. *FBI Law Enforcement Bulletin*, 72, 12–16.

Sweeny, K., & Saul, C. (2013). All guns are not created equal. *Chronicle of Higher Education*, February 1, B4–5.

Tarm, M. (2013, April 1). AP IMPACT: Cartels dispatch agents deep inside US. *Associated Press.* Retrieved from http://bigstory.ap.org/article/ap-impact-cartels-dispatch-agents-deep-inside-us

Thayer, S. (2009). *Saint mudd.* St. Cloud, MN: North Star Press.

Thrasher, F. (1927). *The gang: A study of 1,313 gangs in Chicago.* Chicago, IL: University Of Chicago Press.

Tsunokai, G. T., & Kposowa, A. J. (2002). Asian gangs in the United States: The current state of the research literature. *Crime, Law & Social Change*, 37, 37–50.

United States Attorney's Office Minnesota. (2014). *Native Mob gang leader sentenced to 43 years in prison.* Retrieved from http://www.justice.gov/usao/mn/nativemobsentencing.html

United States Department of Justice. (2010). *Drug movement into and within the United States.* Retrieved from: http://www.justice.gov/archive/ndic/pubs38/38661/movement.htm

Varese, F. (2010). What is organized crime? In F. Varese (ed.), *Organized Crime*, (pp. 1–33). London: Routledge.

Wemple, E. (2014, November 13). Jon Stewart tilts at #Pointergate. *Washington Post*. Retrieved from http://www.washingtonpost.com/blogs/erik-wemple/wp/2014/11/13/jon-stewart-tilts-at-pointergate/

Williams, B. (2015, April 22). "Clique" gangs vex prosecutors, youth workers. *MPR News*. Retrieve from http://www.mprnews.org/story/2015/04/22/gangs

Wilson, W.J. (1987). *The truly disadvantaged: The inner city, the underclass, and public policy*. Chicago: University Of Chicago Press.

Winkler, A. (2011, September). The secret history of guns. *The Atlantic*. Retrieved from: http://www.theatlantic.com/magazine/archive/2011/09/the-secret-history-of-guns/308608/

Worthington, R. (1993, August 28). Plan to rehab Vice Lords remake of 1970s Chicago. *Chicago Tribune*. Retrieved from http://articles.chicagotribune.com/1993-08-28/news/9308280100_1_gang-leaders-gang-members-national-gang

Xiong, C. (2011, August 14). Ramsey County's GangNet database goes dark Monday. *Star Tribune*. Retrieved from: http://www.startribune.com/local/east/127697703.html

Zink, H. (1930). *City bosses in the United States*. Durham, NC: Duke University Press.

Chapter Eight

The State and District of Minnesota: The Federal Criminal Justice System at Work

Learning Objectives

- Describe those powers enumerated in the U.S. Constitution as belonging to the federal government and contrast those with the powers belonging to the states
- Explain key elements of the Judiciary Act of 1789
- Identify the early manifestations of federal law enforcement in the United States
- Contrast the responsibilities of federal law enforcement with those of state and local law enforcement
- Explain the presence of the federal courts in Minnesota
- Distinguish district court judges from magistrate judges
- Summarize the role of the United States Attorney in the federal criminal justice system

- Describe the jurisdiction of the Federal Bureau of Investigation and other key federal agencies
- Identify and describe federal correctional facilities in Minnesota

Most of this book is focused on elements of the criminal justice and legal systems in Minnesota which are delivered by the state and local governments. However, a significant portion of the business of criminal justice within the state, as in every state, is a product of the United States federal government. Indeed, within Minnesota, the United States government is visibly present through many federal law enforcement agencies, federal corrections facilities, and the federal courts.

History of Federal Criminal Justice in the United States

Before examining the details of the federal criminal justice apparatus in Minnesota today, it is helpful to understand the history and nature of the federal criminal justice system. Having an understanding of this system enables one to better contrast the role of federal criminal justice organizations in Minnesota with those belonging to Minnesota's state and local governments.

The United States Constitution, at least in its explicit language, envisions a limited criminal justice role for the national government. There is no general police power bestowed on the federal government. Instead, general powers including police powers are reserved to the states. James Madison, the chief author of the Constitution, wrote in *Federalist 45* that the powers of the national government, under the Constitution, were "few and defined" and related principally to external objects such as war, peace, foreign commerce, and taxation relating to foreign commerce. By contrast, the powers of the states, Madison wrote, were "numerous and indefinite" and related to the lives, liberties, and properties of the people, the internal order, improvement and prosperity of the state (Madison, 1788).

This principle was solidified in the 10th Amendment of the Constitution, which reads:

> The powers not delegated to the United States by the Constitution, nor prohibited to the States, are reserved to the States respectively, or to the people.

The states were considered sovereigns; sovereign governments can police their own people and territory as they see fit.

However if the states were given the general powers to police their citizens, what powers did the federal government have under the Constitution, particularly as related to criminal justice matters? The federal government was indeed assigned by the Constitution specific areas to regulate. Article I, Section 8, known as the Necessary and Proper Clause, states that Congress has the authority to "make all laws which shall be necessary and proper for carrying into the execution the foregoing powers, and all other powers vested by this Constitution in the government of the United States ..."

The foregoing powers mentioned in the Necessary and Proper clause relate to:

- taxation
- interstate and international commerce
- immigration and naturalization
- bankruptcy
- counterfeiting securities and coin
- piracy
- insurrection

These various domains for Congress, and by extension the federal government, to operate within are among Congress' enumerated powers. These are the regulatory areas specified in the Constitution as belonging to the federal government rather than to the states. Most federal criminal laws are connected in some way (sometimes very tenuously) to the enumerated powers above.

Perhaps the single most important piece of legislation with regard to America's federal criminal justice system was the Judiciary Act of 1789. While many elements of this law have been amended and modified over time, the basic framework for the criminal justice and legal systems at the national level, handed down via the Judiciary Act of 1789, remains in place today. Through this law, Congress exercised its Constitutional prerogative to create a federal court system. While the United States Constitution established a Supreme Court to serve as a co-equal branch of government with the Congress and the Presidency, the set-up of district and appellate courts was left to the Congress. Article III, Section 1 of the Constitution reads:

> The judicial Power of the United States shall be vested in one supreme Court, and in such inferior Courts as the Congress may from time to time ordain and establish. The Judges, both of the supreme and inferior Courts, shall hold their Offices during good Behavior, and shall, at stated Times, receive for their Services a Compensation, which shall not be diminished during their Continuance in Office.

The Judiciary Act created the basic 3-tiered structure of the federal court system in place today, which include district courts, circuit courts of appeal, and the Supreme Court. The federal judiciary in the whole was to adjudicate all civil and criminal matters under the authority of the United States, bankruptcy matters, treaty disputes, and disputes between states.

United States Attorney

The Judiciary Act also created the office of United States Attorney for each federal judicial district. In 1789, each of the 13 original states constituted the boundaries of a federal judicial district. Many states today contain more than one judicial district; however (then and now), no state contains fewer than one complete judicial district. The responsibility of the United States Attorney in each district was to "prosecute and conduct all suits in such Courts in which the United States shall be concerned and to give his advice and opinion upon questions of law when required by the President of the United States and when requested by the Heads of any of the Departments, touching any matters that may concern their departments" (Bumgarner, 2006, p. 30).

United States Marshal

Still another important creation of the Judiciary Act of 1789 was the office of United States Marshal for each federal judicial district. United States Marshals and the deputy U.S. marshals they appointed to work for them arguably constitute America's first federal law enforcement officers as these officials were the first created by statute to possess exclusively law enforcement-related duties. The responsibilities of U.S. marshals early in America's history resembled those of local sheriffs—with the significant caveat that their authority was derived from the national government. The duties of U.S. marshals and deputy U.S. marshals in the late 18th century (and continuing to this day) included the serving of federal court orders, capturing and delivering to court federal fugitives, and compelling citizens to serve on federal juries within their districts (Calhoun, 1989).

The U.S. marshals in each district also served as the primary federal investigative agency throughout the 19th century. U.S. marshals were responsible for enforcing the Alien Act of 1798 (which required the deportation of foreigners deemed dangerous), the Sedition Act of 1798 (which criminalized criticism of the United State government), anti-slave trade laws and, ironically, at the same time, the Fugitive Slave Act. In other words, U.S. marshals were simultaneously responsible for enforcing federal laws to restrict and even suffocate the slave trade while also protecting the property interest of slave owners in individual slaves who escaped their captivity and fled to northern states where slavery was illegal (Bumgarner, Crawford, & Burns, 2013). Over time, the investigative responsibilities of U.S. marshals with regard to federal crimes diminished as new federal law enforcement agencies were created, most notably the Justice Department's Bureau of Investigation in 1908 (later to become the Federal Bureau of Investigation).

Other Early Federal Law Enforcement Agencies

While the U.S. marshals certainly were among the earliest to carry out law enforcement responsibilities at the federal level, they were not entirely alone. Indeed, early post-colonial America saw federal law enforcement manifest itself in at least four ways, with law enforcement service to the federal judiciary being only one of them. The early manifestations were (Bumgarner, et al, 2013):

1. Serving the Judiciary
2. Enforcing tariffs and taxes on imports
3. Protecting the postal system
4. Protecting federal real property

The enforcement of taxes and tariffs was a major manifestation of federal law enforcement in America's early history. Several federal law enforcement agencies today trace their origin to this early governmental mission, including the U.S. Coast Guard, the Bureau of Immigration and Customs Enforcement, and the Internal Revenue Service. In 1789, Congress passed two very important pieces of legislation relating to the collection of tariffs. The Tariff Act of 1789 authorized the federal government to collect duties on imported goods. In tandem with this law, the Fifth Act of Congress was passed to create the first federal agency: U.S. Customs. The Customs Bureau was placed under the control of the U.S. Department of the Treasury. The Customs Bureau employed "collectors" in each of the 59 customs districts. U.S. Customs also employed "surveyors" and naval officers to assist the collectors in securing owed tariffs (Saba, 2003).

In 1790, Congress appropriated to U.S. Customs 10 naval warships to be used by surveyors and naval personnel to enforce tariff and trade laws. These ships became the fleet of the Revenue Cutter Service. The Revenue Cutter Service, which was part of the Treasury Department's Customs Bureau, also enforced smuggling, piracy, and anti-slave trade laws, including one law from 1794 which barred the use of American-flagged vessels in the slave trade and another in 1808 which prohibited the introduction of new slaves from Africa into the United States (U.S. Coast Guard, 2002).

Another manifestation of federal law enforcement early in America's history related to the United States Post Office (later to become the U.S. Postal Service). The United States Constitution gives the federal government exclusive authority to establish and maintain a postal system. America's post-colonial postal system was based on the colonial postal system set up by Benjamin Franklin, who became the colonial postmaster general in 1753. He held that position for many years. In 1772, he created the position of "surveyor." Surveyors for the postal system were responsible for enforcing postal regulations and carrying out audit functions. In 1792, the Postal Service was established as a permanent federal agency. In 1801, the working title for surveyors was changed to "special agent," which is perhaps the earliest example of the use of this term for federal criminal investigators (U.S. Postal Service, 2012).

By 1830, the Postal Service created within itself the Office of Instructions and Mail Depredations. The term "depredation" means "raid, an attack, or damage and/or loss." The term was fitting for the title of the office, given its duties. Postal service special agents were organized into this bureau and formally served as the investigative and inspection branch of the United States Post Office. Special agents were responsible for investigating and preventing embezzlement, robberies of mail riders, stage coaches, steamboats, and later, trains. Postal special agents possessed statutory authority to carry firearms and make arrests (Bumgarner, 2006).

Still another early manifestation of federal law enforcement related to the securing and policing of federal property. In 1790, Congress began to meet temporarily in Philadelphia for a 10-year period while public buildings were constructed in the newly established District of Columbia, which was designated to be the nation's capital. It was thought that the capital of the United States should be located on federal territory not belonging to any particular state. A congressional commission was formed to manage federal real property in the District of Columbia during and after construction was completed (Senate Historian, nd). The Commission initially hired six night watchmen to protect federal buildings in Washington DC. In 1802, a superintendent of federal buildings was appointed who oversaw the activities of the watchmen. A few years later, in 1816, the Office of the Commissioner of Public Buildings was established as the management of federal property became too complex for a lone superintendent. Likewise, the policing of federal property became more complex as the number of public buildings grew and the federal footprint on the ground was enlarged (Bumgarner, 2006). In 1828, Congress formally authorized a Capitol Police Force. The responsibilities of this police force included patrolling the Capitol grounds and other public buildings. Much later, in 1849 when the Department of Interior was established, the organization of the Capitol Police were moved under the umbrella of the Interior Department. Today, several uniformed federal police organizations look to the appointment of those six night watchmen in 1790 as a part of their heritage. These agencies include today's Capitol Police, the Supreme Court Police, the Federal Protective Service, the U.S. Park Police, and many other federal police and security agencies (Bumgarner, et al., 2013).

Interestingly, the four early manifestations of federal law enforcement (i.e, serving the judiciary, taxes and tariff enforcement, protecting the postal system, and securing federal property) still exist through various federal agencies today. What's more, agencies which are engaged in these functions, and in many others, are all present in Minnesota.

The Federal Courts

Minnesota is a state which possesses only one federal judicial district. The District of Minnesota is a part of the Eighth Circuit Court of Appeals. The Eighth Circuit includes the districts of Minnesota, North Dakota, South Dakota, Nebraska, Northern Iowa, Southern Iowa, Western Missouri, Eastern Missouri, Western Arkansas, and Eastern Arkansas.

Figure 8.1. Federal District and Appellate Court Map

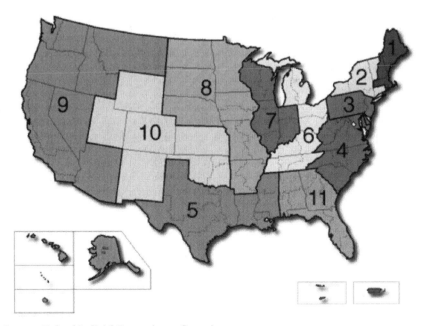

Source: Federal Judicial Center (www.fjc.gov)

Although a single judicial district, federal justice is dispensed through four federal courthouses in Minnesota. The two main federal court buildings are located in St. Paul and Minneapolis. However, there are also federal courthouses in Duluth and Fergus Falls. The St. Paul federal courthouse is home to five federal district court judges and four federal magistrates. The Minneapolis federal courthouse is home to six federal district court judges and two magistrate judges. Additionally, the courthouses in Duluth and Fergus Falls each house a magistrate judge (unless there is a vacancy). Further, a magistrate judge currently sits in Bemidji as well (given the significant federal case traffic from the nearby Red Lake Indian Reservation); however, there is no federal courthouse facility in Bemidji. There are five federal bankruptcy judges in Minnesota as well; two are seated in St. Paul and three are seated in Minneapolis.

District court judges are on the frontline of the federal criminal and civil justice systems. Federal district court serves as the court of general and original jurisdiction for most federal matters. A court of general jurisdiction is one that may handle all legal matters, including civil and criminal cases. A court of original jurisdiction is one in which cases are first heard and considered. Federal district judges are known as "Article III judges" as they are afforded protections under Article III of the Constitution—namely, appointment for a life term, salary protections, and forced removal from office only through impeachment. District judges preside over federal civil and criminal trials and supervise federal grand juries. The workload of federal district judges can vary considerably from one judicial district to another. Normally, as a district's caseload increases, Congress will respond by appropriating funding for additional judicial positions. However, politics can sometimes get in the way as a Congress dominated by one party may not wish to give a president from the other party an opportunity to expand the federal judicial bench with appointees who presumably share the president's legal philosophy.

Another mechanism for addressing workload concerns of federal district judges is the magistrate judge. A federal magistrate judge has the power to conduct misdemeanor-level criminal trials, as well as various routine preliminary hearings, including initial appearances and the issuance of subpoenas and warrants. While district judges are appointed by the President, confirmed by the Senate, and can serve for life, magistrate judges are appointed by district court judges. Full-time magistrates can serve for up to two consecutive 8-year terms. Part-time magistrates may serve up to 4-years per term. The position of magistrate judge was created in 1968 as a way to lighten the workload of federal district judges. In the United States, there are over 500 full-time and 45 part-time magistrate judges (Mays, 2012).

Table 8.1. Types of Cases Heard in Federal and State Courts

The Federal Court System	The State Court System
Cases that deal with the constitutionality of a law;	Most criminal cases, probate (involving wills and estates)
Cases involving the laws and treaties of the U.S.;	Most contract cases, tort cases (personal injuries), family law (marriages, divorces, adoptions), etc.
Cases involving ambassadors and public ministers;	State courts are the final arbiters of state laws and constitutions. Their interpretation of federal law or the U.S. Constitution may be appealed to the U.S. Supreme Court. The Supreme Court may choose to hear or not to hear such cases.
Disputes between two or more states;	
Admiralty law;	
Bankruptcy; and	
Habeas corpus issues.	

Source: "Comparing Federal and State Courts" retrieved from http://www.uscourts.gov/about-federal-courts/court-role-and-structure/comparing-federal-state-courts

Federal Grand Juries

A grand jury is a panel of citizens called to grand jury duty who consider the facts and evidence of a criminal case and determine whether criminal charges should be filed. They are different from a trial jury in that they do not determine whether or not someone is guilty. Rather, they simply determine whether or not sufficient evidence exists, based on probable cause, for someone to be charged and tried with a crime. If a grand jury determines that there is enough probable cause for someone to be charged, they issue a charging document called an indictment, also called a "true bill." If they determine that there is not sufficient evidence for someone to be charged with a crime, they issue a "no bill." In the Minnesota criminal justice system, grand juries are used for only for certain types of cases. In particular, Minnesota grand juries are utilized in cases involving police officer use of deadly force and for crimes in which the maximum sentence is life in prison (Brown, 2014).

At the federal level, grand juries are used much more routinely than is the case under Minnesota state law. Indeed, federal grand juries are relied upon to secure charges in almost all felony-level offenses. Federal misdemeanor charges come in form of an information. Likewise, informations are used as charging documents in some federal felony cases in which a suspect would like to resolve the case quickly and plead guilty. However, in the majority of federal felony cases, indictments must be issued. This is consistent with the constitutional requirement under the 5th amendment, which reads in part *"no person shall be held to answer for a capital, or otherwise infamous crime, unless on a present-ment or indictment of a grand jury ...".*

Federal grand juries consist of 23 citizens drawn for jury duty from the ju-dicial district in which the grand jury is impaneled. A quorum is required for the grand jury to conduct business. A quorum is defined by 16 of the 23 ju-rors being present (U.S. Courts, n.d.). For an indictment to be issued, a min-imum of 12 grand jurors must vote in favor of a true bill. As with state grand juries, the work of a federal grand jury, and its deliberations, are secret. In-deed, it is a criminal offense to leak grand jury information — that is, evi-dence or testimony considered or presented before the grand jury and any information about the deliberations of grand jurors regarding a particular case (U.S. Courts, n.d.).

U.S. Probation and Pretrial Services

An important component of the United States Courts is the office of U.S. Probation and Pretrial Services. The work of U.S. Probation and Pretrial Serv-ices officers includes investigating and reporting on the background of the ac-cused appearing in federal court so that judges can make appropriate bail determinations; investigating and reporting on compliance with court-ordered conditions of release for those awaiting trial or for those convicted of crimes and serving sentences of probation; and assisting defendants and convicts in finding opportunities within the community for work and treatment to im-prove their lives and facilitate productive assimilation back into society (U.S. Probation and Pretrial Services, 2002).

Federal probation officers have been working in Minnesota since 1930. The number of federal probation officers grew in Minnesota from one in 1930 to six officers in 1970. The number of officers grew further as the state popula-tion and federal caseload grew. There were 14 federal probation officers in the mid-1980s and 28 by the early 1990s. By 2010, there Probation and Pretrial Services for the District of Minnesota had over 50 officers and nearly 30 sup-port staff (U.S. Probation and Pretrial Service, n.d.).

The work of probation officers at the state and federal levels can be danger-ous. Because of this, many states permit their probation officers to carry firearms in the course of official duties. As outlined in Chapter Four, the state of Min-nesota does not permit probation officers to carry firearms as they are not li-censed peace officers. Although state probation officers in Minnesota are unarmed, federal officers employed by U.S. Probation and Pretrial Services are permitted to carry firearms. Title 18, Sections 3603 and 3154, of the United States Code permits U.S. probation and pretrial services officers to carry firearms if approved by the federal judicial district in which they work, and the District of Minnesota does so approve.

U.S. Attorney for the District of Minnesota

The Office of United States Attorney in every federal judicial district in the United States shares the same responsibilities: the prosecution of criminal cases brought by the federal government; the litigation and defense of civil cases in which the United States is a party; the handling of criminal and civil appellate cases before the United States Courts of Appeals; and the collection of debts owed the federal government that are administratively uncollectable (Bumgarner, et al., 2013). The United States Attorney for the District of Minnesota and in the other 93 judicial districts come under the organizational umbrella of the U.S. Department of Justice and the U.S. Attorney General as the head of the department. Consequently, individual offices of United States Attorneys must align their own missions with the priorities of the U.S. Justice Department. The Justice Department explains the purpose for its existence in the form of several broad mission goals (Bumgarner, et al., 2013):

- enforce the law and defend interests of the US according to the law;
- ensure public safety against threats, foreign and domestic;
- provide federal leadership in preventing and controlling crime;
- seek just punishment for those guilty of unlawful behavior; and
- ensure fair and impartial administration of justice for all Americans.

Ultimately, the work of the U.S. Attorney's Office in Minnesota, and that of all Justice Department agencies, must comport with these above goals.

The U.S. Attorney's Office in Minnesota has existed since 1849 when Congress established Minnesota as a territory and federal judicial district (Office of United States Attorney, 2015). The U.S. Attorney for any of the 94 judicial districts, including Minnesota, is appointed by the President and confirmed by the Senate. Given the appointment process, most U.S. Attorneys have some political connections to the party of the President in power. However, they also typically have risen through the ranks as career federal or local prosecutors. Prosecutorial experience is an important consideration for appointment.

While U.S. Attorneys are appointed and serve at the pleasure of the President, most of the work is done by career staff attorneys known as assistant U.S. attorneys. Assistant U.S. attorneys (AUSAs) are the line-level prosecutors in the U.S. Attorney's Office. Nationwide, there are nearly 6,000 AUSAs. However, Minnesota employs only a little over 50 AUSAs.

The pace of work for AUSAs is robust—especially given the complex nature of many federal cases. In fiscal year 2010, U.S. Attorney offices around the country filed nearly 61,529 criminal cases involving nearly 84,000 defendants. Approximately 39% of the cases were immigration-related, 21% were narcotics-related, and 20% involved violent crime charges. The conviction rate in federal cases is consistently above 90%, with over 80% of those convicted receiving federal prison time (DOJ, 2014). In the District of Minnesota, during fiscal year 2013, 226 new criminal cases were filed involving 305 criminal defendants. Additionally, there were 396 cases pending against 621 defendants at the beginning of fiscal year 2013 (DOJ, 2014).

The conviction rate was higher than the national average in fiscal year 2013. A total of 389 defendants in Minnesota either pled guilty or were found guilty at trial; only 2 defendants were found not guilty. Cases against a total of 31 defendants were dismissed (DOJ, 2014).

The U.S. Attorney's Office in Minnesota consists of four divisions:

- Criminal Division
- Civil Division
- Appellate Division
- Administrative Division

The Criminal Division is the largest division of the U.S. Attorney's Office. It consists of 40 assistant United States attorneys. The Criminal Division itself is broken into four distinct sections (Office of United States Attorney, 2015). The sections are:

- Fraud and Public Corruption—includes cases relating to mail fraud, wire fraud, bank fraud, mortgage fraud, environmental crime, and bribery.
- Major Crimes and Priority Prosecutions—includes cases related to terrorism, cybercrime, human trafficking, child exploitation, immigration violations, bank robbery, federal program fraud, and crimes in Indian Country.
- OCDETF and Violent Crimes—includes cases which emerge from the Organized Crime and Drug Enforcement Task Force (OCDETF), repeat federal offender crimes involving guns, gangs, and drugs, and other criminal organization cases.
- Special Prosecutions—focuses on cases which span the other three areas, but are especially long-term and resource-intensive in nature.

The Civil Division focuses on civil cases relating to federal program fraud, fair housing and employment, environmental regulations, civil rights, and asset forfeiture. The 11 assistant U.S. attorneys in the Civil Division in Minnesota are also responsible for defending the United States government in cases involving the Federal Tort Claims Act, employment laws, immigrations laws, and Constitutional claims. The Appellate Division monitors cases going to, and coming out of, the Eight Circuit Court of Appeals and evaluates those decisions for precedent and other implications. Finally, the Administrative Division is responsible for providing support services to the Office of United States Attorney, including human resources, information technology, budget and procurement, facilities management, and other areas (Office of United States Attorney, 2015).

Minnesota's Federal Law Enforcement Community

The federal executive branch of government is organized into regions across the United States. Minnesota is a part of Region 5, which also includes Wisconsin, Illinois, Indiana, Michigan, and Ohio. For large federal agencies, one will typically find a full-fledged field office in Minneapolis or St. Paul. For smaller federal agencies, the nearest field office is likely located in Chicago and the presence in Minnesota comes in the form of smaller, resident offices which answer to the regional office in Chicago.

Nationwide, there were 120,000 federal law enforcement officers in 2008. This is the most recent year that a census of federal law enforcement officers was tabulated by the Bureau of Justice Statistics. Of the 120,000 federal officers, approximately 37% were in jobs which primarily involved criminal investigative responsibilities, 21% were in positions primarily consisting of police patrol responsibilities, and 15% were engaged in immigration and border inspection job functions (Reaves, 2012).

Within the state of Minnesota, there were 1,160 federal law enforcement officers in 2008. Of these, 376 officers were engaged primarily in criminal investigative responsibilities. Another 127 officers were primarily engaged in police patrol responsibilities. Inspection-related duties was the job focus of 212 officers. The remaining federal law enforcement officers in Minnesota were engaged in other duties, including court operations, physical security, corrections, and other functions (Reaves, 2012). Minnesota had a federal law enforcement officer to citizen population ratio of 22 per 100,000 residents. This is in contrast to a high of 130 officers per 100,000 citizens for the state of New Mexico and a low of 9 officers per 100,000 citizens for the states of Iowa and Wisconsin (Reaves, 2012).

The number of federal law enforcement officers in Minnesota has grown gradually over the years. From 2002 to 2008, the number of federal officers and agents in Minnesota expanded by 19%. At the same time, the population of the state also grew, so the ratio of federal officers to Minnesotans climbed only modestly. In 2002, Minnesota was home to 976 federal law enforcement officers (Reaves and Bauer, 2003). By 2004, the number of federal officers and agents working in Minnesota increased to 1,067 (Reaves, 2006). The ratio of federal law enforcement officers to Minnesota citizens, per 100,000, in 2002 and 2004 were 19 and 21, respectively. This represents a 16% increase in the density of federal officers within Minnesota from 2002 to 2008.

Table 8.2. Number and Job Function of Federal Law Enforcement
Officers in Minnesota by Year

Primary Job Function	2002	2004	2008
Criminal Inv & Patrol	414	406	503
Other (incl inspection)	563	661	657
Total	976	1,067	1,160

Source: U.S. Department of Justice, Bureau of Justice Statistics

Federal Bureau of Investigation

The agency with the largest federal law enforcement presence in Minnesota is the Federal Bureau of Investigation, or FBI. The FBI's main field office in Minnesota is in Brooklyn Park, a suburb of Minneapolis, and is one of 56 FBI field offices around the country. However, the FBI also maintains resident offices with small numbers of special agents in the cities of St. Paul, Bemidji, Duluth, Mankato, St. Cloud, and Rochester. The Special Agent in Charge of the Minneapolis field office also supervises the resident offices in South Dakota (Rapid City, Aberdeen, Pierre, and Sioux Falls) and North Dakota (Bismarck, Minot, Grand Forks, and Fargo). Further, in response to escalating crime in the Bakken oil field region, the Minneapolis Division of the Federal Bureau of Investigation (FBI) announced plans in 2014 to open a permanent field office in Williston, North Dakota, which it went on to do. The oil boom created an influx of highly paid temporary workers living in sprawling "man camps" with limited spending opportunities and law enforcement oversight (Horwitz, 2014). Such conditions spawned a market for illicit drugs, prostitution, and sex trafficking, which, in turn, attracted organized criminals and increased levels of violence, especially against women (Horwitz, 2014).

As federal law enforcement agencies go, the FBI is a relative new-comer, having not been created until the 20th century. The U.S. Department of Justice was created in 1870. However, the department did not have a detective bureau of its own. Instead, when it wanted to have a criminal investigation conducted, it had to borrow investigators from other agencies, such as the Secret Service, or hire private investigators such as the Pinkertons. By the turn of the 20th century, Congress became increasingly wary of expanding the investigative powers of existing federal agencies for fear of creating a national secret police organization. Consequently, laws were passed restricting the use of private detectives and the loaning out of special agents from the Secret Service to other government bureaus (Jeffreys-Jones, 2007). Congressman James Tawney from southern Minnesota was instrumental in passing these laws (Fox, 2003).

Having recognized a need for an investigative unit within the Department of Justice—particularly after the availability of investigators from other sources dried up due to the legislation mentioned above, Attorney General Charles Bonaparte elected to administratively create a detective unit within the Department of Justice in 1908. He did so by transferring in 9 ex-Secret Service agents and hiring an additional 25 people new to government service to become agents (DOJ, 2008).

In 1909, George Wickersham became Attorney General under newly elected President William Taft. Wickersham embraced the importance of a detective unit with the Department of Justice and secured permanent funding for the outfit. He named the unit the Bureau of Investigation. It wasn't until 1935, however, that the FBI director J. Edgar Hoover renamed the organization the Federal Bureau of Investigation, having finally secured statutory arrest and firearms authority in 1934 (Bumgarner, et al., 2013).

Today, the FBI continues to be a key agency within the U.S. Department of Justice. The agency employed 35,664 people in 2012, including 13,778 special agents 21,886 support staff.

The support staff includes professional positions such as crime and intelligence analysts, language specialists, forensic scientists, computer specialists, attorneys, and others (Bumgarner, Crawford, & Burns, 2013). The exact numbers of FBI agents in Minnesota is not publicly released, but the Minneapolis field office, along with its resident offices, is considered a "medium-sized" field office within the agency.

Prior to the 9/11 terror attacks in 2001, the FBI focused most of its resources and attention on violent crime, white collar crime, and government fraud. Indeed, the FBI has the broadest investigative jurisdiction of any federal agency, possessing authority to investigate over 200 federal crimes. However, after September 11, 2001, the FBI deliberately changed its investigative footing to focus much more attention on homeland security and counterterrorism. The FBI's stated investigative priorities are listed below. It is no accident that the first three priorities relate to protection of the United States from terroristic threats (FBI, 2015).

1. Protect the United States from terrorist attack.
2. Protect the United States against foreign intelligence operations and espionage.
3. Protect the United States against cyber-based attacks and high-tech crimes.
4. Combat public corruption at all levels.
5. Protect civil rights.
6. Combat transnational and national criminal organizations and enterprises.
7. Combat major white-collar crime.
8. Combat significant violent crime.
9. Support federal, state, county, municipal, and international partners.
10. Upgrade technology to successfully perform the FBI's mission.

The shift by the FBI toward homeland security and counterterrorism investigations is certainly as observable in Minnesota as it is anywhere else in the country. The FBI office in Minneapolis sponsors a very active Joint Terrorism Task Force (JTTF) consisting of FBI agents and law enforcement officers from a myriad of other federal, state, and local agencies. Counterterrorism investigations in Minnesota have gained national attention as many young men from the large Somali refugee population in Minnesota have sought to travel to Syria and Iraq to fight with the Islamic State in Iraq and Syria (ISIS), which is in violation of federal law (see **Chapter Ten**).

Other Federal Law Enforcement Agencies

In addition to the FBI, the state and District of Minnesota is home to several other federal law enforcement agencies. Many Americans are unaware of just how many federal law enforcement agencies exist. Due to television, cinematic, and news media portrayals, they might be aware of the FBI, Secret Service, the Drug Enforcement Administration (DEA), the Bureau of Alcohol, Tobacco, Firearms, and Explosives (ATF), and the Naval Criminal Investigative Service (NCIS). Few have ever heard of the Department of Agriculture's Office of Inspector General or the Environmental Protection Agency Criminal Investigation Division. In fact, there are dozens of federal agencies which possess law enforcement authority (defined as the authority by employees to carry firearms and make arrests for violations of federal law).

Figure 8.2. Federal Law Enforcement Agencies and Officers

U.S. Department of Agriculture
  U.S. Forest Service (rangers and special agents)

U.S. Capitol
  U.S. Capitol Police (police officers)

U.S. Department of Commerce
  Office of Export Enforcement (special agents)
  NOAA Fisheries Office of Law Enforcement (patrol officers and special agents)

U.S. Department of Defense
  Air Force Office of Special Investigations (special agents)
  Army Criminal Investigation Division (special agents)
  Naval Criminal Investigative Service (special agents)
  Department of Defense Police (police officers)

U.S. Environmental Protection Agency
  Criminal Investigation Division (special agents)

U.S. Health and Human Services
  Food and Drug Administration, Office of Criminal Investigation (special agents)

U.S. Department of the Interior
  Bureau of Indian Affairs (police officers and special agents)
  Bureau of Land Management (rangers and special agents)
  Bureau of Reclamation (police officers)
  National Park Service (rangers and special agents)
  U.S. Park Police (police officers)
  Fish and Wildlife Service (rangers and special agents)

U.S. Department of Justice
  Federal Bureau of Investigation (special agents)
  U.S. Marshals Service (marshals and deputy marshals)
  Bureau of Alcohol, Tobacco, Firearms and Explosives (special agents)
  Drug Enforcement Administration (special agents)

U.S. Department of Homeland Security
  Immigration and Customs Enforcement (special agents)
  Federal Protective Service (police officers, inspectors, and special agents)
  Customs and Border Protection (inspectors)
  U.S. Secret Service (police officers and special agents)
  U.S. Coast Guard (security officers and special agents)
  U.S. Border Patrol (border patrol agents)
  Federal Air Marshal Service (air marshals)

U.S. Department of the Treasury
  Internal Revenue Service (special agents)

Figure 8.2. Federal Law Enforcement Agencies and Officers, *continued*

U.S. Department of the Treasury, continued
  Bureau of Engraving and Printing Police (police officers)
  U.S. Mint Police (police officers)

U.S. Department of State
  Bureau of Diplomatic Security (special agents)

U.S. Department of Veterans Affairs
  VA Police (police officers)

U.S. Postal Service
  Postal Inspection Service (postal inspectors)
  Postal Service Police (police officers)

U.S. Supreme Court
  U.S. Supreme Court Police (police officers)

National Railroad Passenger Corporation
  Amtrak Police (police officers)

Smithsonian Institution
  Smithsonian Police (police officers)

Tennessee Valley Authority
  TVA Police (police officers)

Offices of Inspector General
(all agencies listed below employ special agents/criminal investigators)
  Agency for International Development
  Central Intelligence Agency
  Corporation for National and Community Service (AmeriCorps)
  Department of Agriculture
  Department of Commerce
  Department of Defense (Defense Criminal Investigative Service)
  Department of Education
  Department of Energy
  Department of Health and Human Services
  Department of Homeland Security
  Department of Housing and Urban Development
  Department of the Interior
  Department of Justice
  Department of Labor
  Department of State
  Department of Transportation
  Department of the Treasury
  Department of Veteran Affairs
  Environmental Protection Agency
  Federal Deposit Insurance Corporation
  Federal Reserve Board
  Federal Trade Commission
  General Services Administration
  Government Printing Office

Figure 8.2. Federal Law Enforcement Agencies and Officers, *continued*

Offices of Inspector General, continued
  Legal Services Corporation
  National Aeronautics and Space Administration
  National Archives and Records Administration
  National Endowment for the Arts
  National Endowment for the Humanities
  Nuclear Regulatory Commission
  Office of Personnel Management
  Peace Corps
  Railroad Retirement Board
  Security and Exchange Commission
  Small Business Administration
  Smithsonian Institution
  Social Security Administration
  Tennessee Valley Authority
  Treasury Inspector General for Tax Administration
  U.S. International Trade Commission
  United States Postal Service

Source: Bumgarner, J. (2006).

In addition to the FBI, the U.S. Department of Justice houses several key federal law enforcement agencies. These include the U.S. Marshals Service, the Drug Enforcement Administration (DEA), and the Bureau of Alcohol, Tobacco, Firearms, and Explosives (ATF). As noted earlier, the U.S. Marshals Service functions as the federal government's sheriff's department. It is responsible for court security, custody and transportation of federal prisoners prior to serving prison sentences, serving court processes, and apprehending federal fugitives. The DEA is the agency responsible for investigating violations of our nation's drug laws, which are codified in Title 21 of the United States Code.

The ATF was transferred to the Justice Department from the Treasury Department in 2003 as a result of the Homeland Security Act of 2002. The ATF has primary jurisdiction in federal bombing cases, unless the event is considered terrorism-related, in which case the FBI has primary jurisdiction. The ATF also investigates federal firearms violations, which are articulated in the Gun Control Act of 1968 and its amendments.

Before the terror attacks on September 11, 2001, the two cabinet-level departments primarily known for their federal law enforcement assets were the Department of Justice and the Department of Treasury. Historically, treasury agents were as remarkable in the eyes of the public as FBI agents, the former of which included federal sleuths such as Eliot Ness. The Treasury Department had included agencies such as the Secret Service, U.S. Customs, ATF, and the

Internal Revenue Service (IRS). However, with the Homeland Security Act of 2002, most Treasury law enforcement agencies other than the IRS were relocated to other departments. As already noted, the ATF was moved to the Justice Department. The Secret Service and U.S. Customs both were moved to the newly created Department of Homeland Security. Through the reorganization, the investigative components of the U.S. Customs Service and the Immigration and Naturalization Service (INS) were combined to form the investigative branch of the Bureau of Immigration and Customs Enforcement (ICE)—which is today known as Homeland Security Investigations (HSI). The uniformed branches of Customs and INS, including the U.S. Border Patrol, were combined to become the Bureau of Customs and Border Protection (CBP). All of these agencies have offices in Minnesota. In fact, ICE-HSI is commonly the lead agency on human trafficking investigations—many of which have resulted in high-profile criminal prosecutions within Minnesota (see **Chapter Ten**).

Another Department of Homeland Security agency maintaining a presence in Minnesota is the U.S. Secret Service. The Secret Service was created as a Treasury Department agency in 1865 to confront the widespread problem at the time of counterfeit currency and fraud committed against the U.S. Government. Today, the Secret Service is also known for dignitary protection—particularly the U.S. President, U.S. Vice-President, and their families. The Secret Service is also responsible for investigating computer/electronic transfer crimes and credit card fraud. Finally, given its physical and personal security expertise, the Secret Service has been made the lead agency in protecting national special security events. These large-scale, high-profile events include the Super Bowl and national political party conventions (see **Chapter Ten**).

As mentioned previously, the IRS was one agency which did not transfer out of the Department of the Treasury. The history of the IRS goes to the year 1919 when an intelligence unit was created within the Treasury Department. This unit was responsible for investigating tax evasion. The intelligence unit, over time, would see its name change but not its mission. Today, it is known as the Criminal Investigation Division (CID) of the Internal Revenue Service and it has exclusive jurisdiction to investigate violations of Title 26 (which articulates federal tax and financial crimes).

Some of the truly under-heralded, but very important, members of the federal law enforcement community are the Offices of Inspector General (OIGs). OIGs can be found in every federal cabinet-level department, every major independent agency, and in many other federal independent agencies. The mission of the Offices of Inspector General is to prevent and detect fraud, waste, and abuse in federal programs under the auspices of their parent federal agency or department (Bumgarner, 2014). Historically, OIG special agents had varying degrees of law enforcement authority, depending on specific OIG. However, the Homeland Security Act of 2002 granted uniform firearms and arrest authority across the majority of OIGs. Nationwide, there are a little over 2,000 OIG special agents. Dozens of OIG special agents from several agencies are located within the state of Minnesota. Crimes commonly investigated by OIGs include program fraud, contract fraud, collusion, bribery, threats, assaults, thefts, embezzlement, and conspiracy.

Perceptions of Federal Law Enforcement

All of the agencies above, and many others on the list in Figure 8.2 maintain offices of varying sizes in Minnesota—primarily in the Twin Cities of St. Paul and Minneapolis—but also in other regional centers of the state. The federal law enforcement community works with state and local law enforcement throughout Minnesota to accomplish the common goal of abating criminality within the state. To that end, cooperation between federal agents and state and local police officials is certainly a must. And yet, in Minnesota and elsewhere, there has historically been tension between federal law enforcement —especially the FBI—and everybody else in the law enforcement community.

In an effort to begin to gauge the relationship between local and federal law enforcement officials in Minnesota, a small pilot study was conducted in 2011 to assess among local law enforcement officers their knowledge and opinions about federal law enforcement. A total of 63 police officers and sheriff deputies at five Minnesota agencies participated in a survey (Bumgarner, 2011). Seventy-nine percent of these officers had at least some experience working with federal law enforcement officers.

The survey instrument was designed to illicit attitudinal/opinion measures along various constructs, including the appropriate mission of federal law enforcement, the capabilities of federal law enforcement officers, and general impressions and favorability toward federal law enforcement. The survey results suggested that, in the aggregate, officers possessed some misgivings about the reach and scope of federal law enforcement. But just as true, they expressed relatively high levels of confidence in the abilities of federal agents to perform their jobs.

With regard to questions relating to the mission and scope of federal law enforcement, a plurality of respondents tended to view the federal government as too large and too over-reaching. For example, in response to the statement "The federal government is too big," approximately 40% agreed or strongly agreed, while only 17% disagreed or strongly disagreed. There was also a consistent chorus in support of the idea that states and localities should play the lead in most criminal and public policy matters. A full 60% of the surveyed officers agreed or strongly agreed with the statement "Most public policy issues should be handled by state and local government agencies," while about 5% disagreed or strongly disagreed.

Regarding the capabilities of federal agents, there was some good news for federal law enforcement. The idea of a federal agents being stuffy, inflexible, and lacking common sense or good judgment is well-represented in the popular culture. The movie *Die Hard* was just one of countless cinematic productions over the years that have shown federal agents acting in ill-advised, immature, rigidly by-the-book, or otherwise unsophisticated and unintuitive manner— which always serves to simply make the job of the real cops that much harder. However, less than 10% of the officers surveyed here agreed with the notion that federal agents have no street smarts, and only one officer taking the survey was willing to agree with the explicit declaration that federal agents lack common sense. Finally, federal law enforcement tended to fare well with respondents' general perceptions. A full 52% of respondents recorded a favorable or extremely favorable view of federal law enforcement. About 5% of the respondents reflected a generally unfavorable or extremely unfavorable view.

This Minnesota-specific study lacked experimental controls and surveyed only a small number of officers. Therefore, there are limits to the conclusions one can draw from the study. But in so far as the officers surveyed in the study were concerned, there was some good news to be had for the federal law enforcement community in Minnesota. The notion that federal law enforcement has to overcome stereotypes about poor judgment and incompetence was largely not supported by the survey results. By and large, local police officers and deputies in the study expressed confidence in the law enforcement abilities of federal agents. What's more, local officers who had experience working with federal agents in Minnesota tended to reflect favorable views of the agents who helped constitute those experiences. Minnesota officers who participated in the study tended to like and respect the federal agents they have had occasion to work with, but remain somewhat unsatisfied with a lack of cooperation and mission encroachment at the organizational level of federal agencies. An implication for the federal government seeking stronger ties with local law enforcement in wide array of criminal investigation and homeland security arenas is that federal agencies might try to "get out of the way" (institutionally) as much as possible and let the individual, collaborative, and competent federal agents working for them be the face of the federal government to their local law enforcement partners.

Effective law enforcement—particularly as it relates to homeland security—requires cooperation and coordination across all levels of government. Law enforcement agencies must have confidence in their partner organizations and, to the extent possible, avoid the distractions of interagency and intergovernmental squabbling. Among officers and agents, respect for one another as professionals and respect for the organization and mission to which the professionals belong likely go a long way toward reducing counterproductive infighting.

Federal Corrections in Minnesota

The U.S. Federal Bureau of Prisons (BOP) is an agency within the U.S. Department of Justice and is responsible for designing, operating, and maintaining the federal correctional system. The BOP employs over 39,000 people and supervises the prison sentences of 208,000 federal inmates. The BOP operate 148 facilities nationwide, with security conditions ranging from minimum security to high security (Federal Bureau of Prisons, 2015).

Minnesota is the home to four facilities operation by the Federal Bureau of Prisons (also see **Chapter Four**). The facilities are:

- Duluth Federal Prison Camp (minimum security)
- Sandstone Federal Correctional Institute (low security)
- Waseca Federal Correctional Institute (low security)
- Rochester Federal Medical Center (administrative security)

The Duluth Federal Prison Camp houses 759 male inmates. As a minimum security facility, the Duluth Federal Prison Camp utilizes dormitory housing for inmates. There is no perimeter fencing to secure inmates at the facility. And, with minimum security camps, the staff to inmate ratio is relatively low. The focus with minimum security federal facilities is on providing inmates with opportunities for work and programs to improve life-skills and occupational readiness (Federal Bureau of Prisons, 2015). The Duluth Federal prison camp is one of seven minimum security federal facilities in the United States.

The Sandstone and Waseca federal correctional institutes, as low security facilities, do have some accoutrements of prison. For example, low security facilities managed by the Bureau of Prisons include double-fenced perimeters. They also have a larger staff to prisoner ratio than minimum security facilities. The life of an inmate is more structured and participation in work and programming is expected. The Sandstone Federal Correctional Institute houses 1,310 male inmates. The Waseca Federal Correctional Institute houses 974 female inmates. Interestingly, there are 35 low security federal correctional institutes in the United States and two of them are in Minnesota (Federal Bureau of Prisons, 2015).

Finally, Minnesota is home to the Rochester Federal Medical Center. This facility is one of six medical referral centers managed by the U.S. Bureau of Prisons. The Rochester Federal Medical Center houses 800 male inmates. The facility is located on the grounds of a former state hospital. The center delivers to inmates specialized medical and mental health services. Notable inmates in the past include former televangelist Jim Bakker, political activist Lyndon LaRouche, and Sheikh Omar Abdel Rahman, the latter of whom was sentenced to life in prison for the 1993 bombing of the World Trade Center in New York (Walsh, 2010).

Concluding Remarks

The federal government of the United States, as sovereign government sharing power with the states, maintains a criminal justice apparatus of its own. The federal government's criminal justice presence is visible in every state of the union, including Minnesota. Within the federal judicial district of Minnesota, the federal government operates out of four courthouses, four correctional facilities, and several law enforcement agencies. Cooperation, informed by respect, between federal, state, and local criminal justice authorities is essential for delivering on the promise of a secure homeland, justice for crime victims, and safety for the general public.

Key Terms

Article III Judges

Bureau of Alcohol, Tobacco, Firearms, and Explosives (ATF)

Bureau of Immigration and Customs Enforcement (ICE)

Circuit Court of Appeals

Charles Bonaparte

Drug Enforcement Administration (DEA)

Enumerated Powers

Federal Bureau of Investigation (FBI)

Federal Bureau of Prisons

Federal Correctional Institute (Low Security)

Federal Prison Camp (Minimum Security)

Fifth Act of Congress

General Jurisdiction

Grand Jury

Homeland Security Investigations (HSI)

Information

Indictment

Internal Revenue Service (IRS)

Joint Terrorism Task Force (JTTF)

Judiciary Act of 1789

Necessary and Proper Clause

Office of Inspector General (OIG)

Organized Crime and Drug Enforcement Task Force (OCDETF)

Original Jurisdiction

Tariff Act of 1789

United States Attorney

United States District Court

United States Marshal

United States Secret Service

Selected Internet Sites

Bureau of Alcohol, Tobacco, Firearms, and Explosives
https://www.atf.gov/

Council of the Inspectors General on Integrity and Efficiency
https://www.ignet.gov/

Drug Enforcement Administration
http://www.dea.gov/index.shtml

Eighth Circuit Court of Appeals
http://www.ca8.uscourts.gov/

Federal Bureau of Investigation
https://www.fbi.gov/

Federal Bureau of Prisons
http://www.bop.gov

Federal Judicial Center
http://www.fjc.gov

Immigration and Customs Enforcement
http://www.ice.gov/

Offices of the United States Attorneys
http://www.justice.gov/usao

U.S. Bureau of Justice Statistics
http://www.bjs.gov/index.cfm

U.S. District Court of Minnesota
http://www.mnd.uscourts.gov/

United States Marshals Service
http://www.usmarshals.gov/

Discussion Questions

1. What role, if any, should the federal government have in policing general crimes commonly addressed by local law enforcement? Does the expansion of federal criminal laws give rise to concerns about a national police force?
2. Given the FBI's many criminal investigative responsibilities, should the United States create a new federal agency which focuses exclusively on counterterrorism?

3. Many scholars and activists have raised concerns about federal prison sentences and their tendency to be longer than sentences imposed at the state level. Is it appropriate that federal prosecutions are sometimes pursued instead of state prosecutions in order to secure tougher punishments for offenders?
4. There are dozens of federal law enforcement agencies with firearms and arrest authority. Are there too many federal law enforcement agencies in existence today? Should many of these agencies be consolidated? Should some of these agencies be eliminated altogether? Explain.
5. It is currently a federal felony to possess any amount of marijuana. And yet, many states have decriminalized marijuana in their own state statutes. Should federal law be amended to permit the legal use of marijuana? If not, should federal prosecutions continue even in states that have chosen to legalize marijuana?

References

Brown, H. (2014, August 20). Good question: What is a grand jury? WCCO CBS Minnesota. Retrieved from http://minnesota.cbslocal.com/2014/08/20/good-question-what-is-a-grand-jury/

Bumgarner, J. (2014). Federal law enforcement In J. Albanese (Ed.) *Encyclopedia of Criminology and Criminal Justice*. Malden, MA: Wiley-Blackwell.

Bumgarner, J., Crawford, C., & Burns, R. (2013). *Federal law enforcement: A primer*. Durham, NC: Carolina Academic Press.

Bumgarner, J. (2011). "Exploring the Intersection of Policing and Federalism: Peace Officer Perceptions of American Federal Law Enforcement," presented at the Academy of Criminal Justice Sciences, Toronto, ON, Canada.

Bumgarner, J. (2006). *Federal agents: The growth of federal law enforcement in America*. Westport, CT: Praeger.

Calhoun, F. (1989). *The lawmen: United States marshals and their deputies*. Washington, DC: Government Printing Office.

Federal Bureau of Investigation. (2015). *Today's FBI Facts & Figures 2013–2014*. Washington DC: FBI Office of Public Affairs.

Federal Bureau of Prisons. (2015). *About our facilities*. Retrieved from http://www.bop.gov/about/facilities/federal_prisons.jsp

Fox, J. (2003). *The birth of the Federal Bureau of Investigation*. Washington, DC: Office of Public/Congressional Affairs.

Horowitz, S. (2014). Dark side of the boom. *Washington Post*, September 28. Retrieved from http://www.washingtonpost.com/sf/national/2014/09/28/dark-side-of-the-boom/

Jeffreys-Jones, R. (2007). *The FBI: A history.* New Haven, CT: Yale University Press.

Madison, J. (1788). Alleged dangers from the powers of the Union to the state governments considered [Federalist 45]. *Independent Journal.* January 26.

Mays, C.L. (2012). *The American courts and the judicial process.* New York: Oxford University Press.

Office of United States Attorney. *About us.* Retrieved from http://www.justice.gov/usao-mn/about-us

Reaves, B. (2012). *Federal law enforcement officers, 2008.* Washington, DC: Bureau of Justice Statistics.

Reaves, B. (2006). *Federal law enforcement officers, 2004.* Washington, DC: Bureau of Justice Statistics.

Reaves, B. and Bauer, L. (2003). *Federal law enforcement officers, 2002.* Washington, DC: Bureau of Justice Statistics.

Saba, A. (2003). U.S. customs service: Always there ... ready to serve. *U.S. Customs Today.* February.

U.S. Coast Guard. (2002). *U.S. coast guard: An historical overview.* Washington, DC: USCG Historian's Office.

U.S. Courts. (n.d.) *Handbook for federal grand juries.* Washington, DC: Administrative Office of the United States Courts.

U.S. Department of Justice. (2014). *United States Attorneys' annual statistical report.* Washington, DC: U.S. DOJ.

U.S. Department of Justice. (2008). *The FBI: A centennial history, 1908–2008.* Washington, DC: Government Printing Office.

U.S. District Court. (2015). *District of Minnesota.* Retrieved from http://www.mnd.uscourts.gov/

U.S. Postal Service. (2012). *History of the United States postal service 1775–2006.* Retrieved from https://about.usps.com/publications/pub100.pdf

U.S. Probation and Pretrial Services. (2002). *Charter for excellence.* Retrieved from http://www.mnp.uscourts.gov/pdf/charter.pdf

U.S. Probation and Pretrial Services. (n.d.). *District of Minnesota.* Retrieved from http://www.mnp.uscourts.gov/index.html

U.S. Senate Historian. (n.d.). *The capitol police.* Retrieved from http://www.senate.gov/artandhistory/history/common/briefing/Capitol_Police.htm

Walsh, J. (2010, May 19). Land of four federal prisons. *Star Tribune.* Retrieved from http://www.startribune.com/land-of-four-federal-prisons/94314029/

Chapter Nine

The Death of the Death Penalty: The History of Capital Punishment in Minnesota

Learning Objectives

- Explain the consequentialist and retributivist perspectives on punishment
- Articulate arguments for and against capital punishment
- Describe public sentiment in the United States regarding the death penalty
- Summarize key court cases relating to the imposition of the death penalty
- Explain the history of capital punishment in Minnesota, including the first and last executions
- Explain the circumstances surrounding the federal government's mass execution of 38 Sioux Indians in Mankato, Minnesota, in 1862
- Identify elements of 1st degree murder under Minnesota statutes
- Identify the objectives of criminal sentencing according to the federal Sentencing Reform Act of 1984
- Describe the use of sentencing guidelines in Minnesota

Criminal justice as an academic and applied field of inquiry and practice is replete with controversial topics. Issues regarding race, fairness, equity, vengeance, and others regularly surface in criminal justice. One particular criminal justice issue, embodying all the above, has served more than most to represent all that is controversial and contested in criminal justice and criminology over the past several years. That issue is capital punishment.

About the Death Penalty

Capital punishment refers to the imposition of a sentence of death by execution for the proscribed crimes deemed to be so heinous as to warrant no less a penalty. In 2012, a total of 58 countries around the world still utilized capital punishment for certain offenses; 140 countries had abolished the death penalty (Amnesty International, 2013). Interestingly, the United States is the only western country to still have capital punishment.

Of course, in the United States, the individual states are sovereign. Some states have capital punishment as their maximum penalty, while others do not. As of 2015, 19 states had abolished the death penalty, leaving 31 states with capital punishment in place. The State of Minnesota is one of the 19 states without the death penalty, having abolished it in 1911. Among the 31 states with the death penalty, several have placed moratoriums on the imposition and carrying out of the death penalty while matters regarding errors in convictions, inequalities in sentencing, and problems with lethal injection methods are examined and sorted out. The primary mechanism of execution is lethal injection, although some states have alternative methods available. In 2015, a law was passed in Utah reinstating the use of firing squads as a method of execution if lethal injection drugs cease to be available (McCombs, 2015).

The fact that two-thirds of the states still permit the use of capital punishment for their most serious and vicious offenders is reflective of the views of the American people on the whole. Approximately 63% of Americans favor the death penalty as an appropriate state response to some offenses. This margin of support has held steady for several years throughout the 2000s, but represents a decline from a peak of 80% support in the early 1990s (Saad, 2013).

Despite the popularity of the death penalty, and despite its availability as an option for punishing murderers, it is a punishment that is rarely imposed. In 2014, there were only 35 executions in the United States. In 2013, there were 39 (Death Penalty Information Center, 2015a). However, there are over 3,000 people on death row and there are many thousands of homicides committed in the United States each year. Americans like the idea of offenders paying the ultimate price for brutally killing others, but have not really mustered the political pressure to force legislators and government officials to actually impose this penalty with any urgency or consistency. In fact, the death penalty is only sought in 1% of capital murder cases (Armour & Umbreit, 2012).

Figure 9.1. States Without the Death Penalty

     Indicates states which have abolished capital punishment

Source: Author created from deathpenaltyinfo.org

Arguments For and Against the Death Penalty

There are several arguments for and against the death penalty which are compelling. Generally, the arguments for the death penalty tend to be either consequentialist or retributivist. The consequentialist arguments focus on the utility of the death penalty. For example, if the death penalty has a deterrent effect and therefore results in fewer homicides, this is a positive consequence of that punishment. Additionally, if the death penalty at a minimum has an incapacitation effect (those put to death have been incapacitated from doing further harm), this too would be a positive outcome. Consequentialist, or utilitarian, arguments of punishment are associated with philosophers such as Jeremy Bentham from 18th to 19th century England. Bentham emphasized that punishment should be parsimonious, i.e., the idea that no more punishment than necessary to gain compliance by offenders with the rules should be employed. In other words, the least severe punishment should be imposed which still meets social purposes. Bentham also said that society should take into account the offender's sensibilities when meting out punishment; in other words, punishment should be tailored to the offender. This approach has served as the primary rationale for indeterminate sentencing in the 20th century (Tonry, 2011).

Interestingly, opponents of the death penalty also tend to rely on consequentialist arguments. They note that the death penalty does not have a deterrent effect (and therefore has no societal gain in that regard). However, the death penalty does have costs (expensive to navigate due to multiple appeals, the potential for unfair application, no opportunity for rehabilitation, maintaining death row units, etc.) which arguably result in a societal net loss. They also point to the principle of parsimony and argue that legitimate goals of punishment can be accomplished with non-lethal penalties. Hence, opponents of the capital punishment say we need to look in other directions for society's response to heinous crimes.

The retributivist argument for capital punishment has little concern for consequences—positive or negative—of the death penalty. Retributivist philosophies espoused by the likes of Immanuel Kant and George Hegel suggest that punishment is appropriate for punishment's sake. Punishment, including the maximum punishment of death for some offenses, is proper because it is the just and proportionate thing to do. Retributivists note that utilitarian opponents of capital punishment show an amoral approach to punishment and fail to view the convicted offender as a rational human being, thereby denying him human dignity.

In fact, C.S. Lewis once penned an essay against the "humanitarian theory of punishment." Humanitarian justifications for punishment focus on society's gain through an offender's involuntary rehabilitation. Lewis stated that this approach to addressing crime, including as applied to the abolition of the death penalty, does several things (Lewis, 1949):

1) it removes the concepts of moral culpability and proportionality from punishment;
2) it treats offenders like children, imbeciles, or animals, rather than morally autonomous adults;
3) it risks injustices predicated on well-meaning and tyrannical motives; and
4) it necessarily authorizes the punishment of the innocent (for their own good).

As Hegel noted, the humanity of an offender, and the rational choices he or she makes which result in "wrongs", require "cancellation." In some cases, the maximum penalty is the only sufficient penalty to cancel a wrong brought about by an offender. Respect for the moral autonomy of the criminal and his or her capacity for making moral choices require punishment apportioned to the crime (Tonry, 2011).

The Risk of Error

One concern many opponents offer regarding capital punishment is that there is often a risk of the penalty being applied mistakenly against someone who does not deserve it. The concern relates to all forms of criminal sanction, but time lost due to error is compensable; life lost is irreversible. Concern over errors in the application of the death penalty have given birth to advocacy and public interest groups such as the Innocence Project (see **Chapter Four**). The Innocence Project traces its beginnings back to the early 1990s when a couple of law professors from New York City set out to address the substantiated notion that many wrongful criminal convictions occur because of eyewitness testimony rooted in error or malice. The ramifications of faulty eyewitness testimony are most severe in murder and stranger-rape cases given the long prison terms, and in some cases death sentences, that attach to those convictions. The Innocence Project evaluates thousands of cases every year for faulty evidence, prosecutorial misconduct, and inadequate defense. To date in the United States, there have been 329 convicted individuals who have been exonerated on reexamined DNA evidence alone; intervention by the Innocence Project was directly responsible for over half of these exonerations (Innocence Project, 2015).

Some proponents of the death penalty would counter the concern over mistakes by reserving capital punishment for only the most certain of cases. Effectively, after such a reform were put in place, the death penalty would only be levied in "smoking gun cases." A bank robber shoots and kills a teller and then is wounded and captured in an ensuring police shootout at the bank entrance. A registered pedophile's semen is found in a little girl's dead body on his property. A prison inmate is captured on video camera stabbing and killing a cafeteria worker before being wrestled to the ground by prison guards. In these cases, the reasonable doubt threshold has not only been met, but arguably so has proof beyond *all* doubt. Some reformers would reserve a swift and certain death penalty for these types of offenders under these types of circumstances. However, significant changes in the laws, and perhaps even the Constitution, would need to occur before such a system could be implemented.

Cruel and Unusual Punishment

One argument against capital punishment today is less about philosophy and more about legality. In particular, opponents point to the Eighth Amendment of the U.S. Constitution and its prohibition against cruel and unusual punishment. They argue that the bar for objectionable punishment has been lowered over time as society has matured and as the community of democratic nations around the world has rejected capital punishment and other harsh forms of retribution.

Through several court decisions over the years, the U.S. Supreme Court has essentially identified two manifestations of cruel and unusual punishment: barbaric punishments of the kind incompatible with a civilized society and punishments which are disproportionate to the crime (De Leon & Fowler, 2013). Opponents of the death penalty have used both criteria to argue in the courts against it. They have claimed that capital punishment in the modern age is barbarism. They have also claimed that capital punishment, in particular cases, was a disproportionate response to the crime given the circumstances known about the offender and other factors.

With regard to the argument that the death penalty, in and of itself, is barbaric, the Supreme Court has consistently rejected that notion. The Supreme Court first articulated with specificity what it understood cruel and unusual punishment to be in the case of *Wilkerson v. Utah* (1878). In the Court's decision, it noted that some forms of punishment which no longer existed in the United States or the civilized world, such as drawing and quartering, public dissecting, burning offenders alive, and disemboweling, were indeed cruel and unusual under the Constitution. However, Utah's use of the firing squad was not. The Supreme Court has acknowledged, however, that the death penalty has a potential for barbarism. In a case concerning the use of the electric chair (*In re Kemmler*, 1890), the Court said a legitimate method of execution must not involve anything other than what merely causes death. Further, death should be relatively instantaneous and not involve extended and unnecessary pain.

With regard to the principle that punishment must be proportionate to the crime, lest it be deemed cruel and unusual, the Supreme Court first insisted upon this in the case of *Weems v. U.S.* (1910). The principle of proportionality handed down in *Weems* was later incorporated into the Fourteenth Amendment and therefore applied to the states as a result of *Robinson v. California* (1962). Since then, the U.S. Supreme Court has found a number of crimes and circumstances for which the death penalty had been statutorily proscribed to be disproportionate, including:

- *Coker v. Georgia* (1977)—rape of an adult
- *Thompson v. Oklahoma* (1988)—15-year-old murderer
- *Atkins v. Virginia* (2002)—murderer who is intellectually impaired
- *Roper v. Simmons* (2005)—murderer under 18
- *Kennedy v. Louisiana* (2008)—rape of a child

Interestingly, in the case of *Roper v. Simmons* in which the Supreme Court barred under the Constitution the execution of anyone whose capital crimes were committed when the offender was under the age of 18, the Court cited "evolving standards of decency that mark the progress of a maturing society." Many opponents of the death penalty recognize this as an opening of the door for the Court to someday abolish the death penalty altogether under the justification of evolving societal standards. Supporters of the death penalty respond that no institution of government better represents the true pulse of society than democratically elected state legislators who are responsible for passing laws relating to the use or abolition of capital punishment. They note that if societal standards of decency on this subject do evolve in the direction of abolition, the legislative process will reflect it. Until then, they say, the Court should butt out.

Death Penalty as a Deterrent?

The utilitarian arguments against the death penalty that it is not a deterrent and that it is discriminatory against minorities is still an open debate. In 2000, University of Maryland criminologist Raymond Paternoster conducted a study of the potential for racially discriminatory death sentence practices. He found a significant difference in the sentencing patterns of convicted white murderers from that of convicted black murderers. In particular, he found that black defendants who murdered white victims were more likely to be charged with capital murder and sentenced to death than with any other racial combination of offenders and victims (Paternoster & Brame, 2003).

However, in 2005, statistician and sociologist Richard Beck of the University of California, Los Angeles, and colleagues, re-examined the data from the Paternoster and Brame study. Beck found that race played either no role or a small and unidentifiable role in death sentences. If race did play a role, it was in the other direction than identified by Paternoster and Brame, as Beck found that cases with a black defendant and a white victim were less likely to result in a death sentence (Berk, Li, & Hickman, 2005).

David Muhlhausen (2007) identified several longitudinal studies which have shown that capital punishment does have a deterrent against future murders. One study of capital punishment in Georgia by Emory University economists found that each execution resulted in 18 fewer homicides (Muhlhausen, 2007). Another study, by Emory University law professor Joanna Shepherd (2004) found that:

1) each execution was associated with three fewer murders;
2) each execution was associated with fewer murders of blacks, followed by whites, over other racial groups; and (importantly) ...

3) shorter periods of time on death row before execution was associated with an increased deterrent effect—for each 2.75 year reduction in time on death row, one murder was deterred.

Certainly, many social scientists would take issue with the findings in these and other studies which support the notion that an efficacious death penalty deters homicidal violence. It is safe to say at the very least that the consequences of the death penalty are not settled science.

History of the Death Penalty in Minnesota

For the first half-century following Minnesota's statehood, premeditated murder was punishable by death in the state. Minnesota was created as a territory in 1849, and officially became a state in 1858. According to the Death Penalty Information Center, Minnesota executed 27 people from 1860 until 1906; the method of execution in Minnesota was death by hanging.

Ann Bilansky

The first hanging in the state of Minnesota was that of St. Paul resident Ann Bilansky in 1860. Bilansky was also the only woman every executed in Minnesota. Bilansky was involved in a love triangle between herself, her husband Stanislaus Bilansky, and her lover John Walker. On March 11, 1859, Stanislaus Bilansky died after a 9-day illness. The next day, March 12, Stanislaus was placed in a coffin for visitation and a funeral to follow. Several friends and family members gathered at the Bilansky house in St. Paul to pay their last respects, along with John Walker who did carpenter work for Bilansky's. However, before the funeral procession to the cemetery could commence, the Ramsey County coroner, John Wren, showed up at the Bilansky home with three doctors, a coroner's jury, and witnesses in tow (Trenerry, 1985). The doctors examined the body and the coroner held an inquest right there, calling witnesses to testify. It was determined that Bilansky had died of natural causes from the illness he came down with on March 2, but that Ann's care for him during the illness was wanting—especially since she never called for a doctor. The funeral then was allowed to proceed.

Immediately following the funeral, Ann, John Walker, and Bilansky's house servant, Rosa Scharf, returned to the Bilansky home. Scharf observed that Walker apparently had no intention of leaving; indeed, later that evening, Scharf observed Ann undress in front of Walker. It was widely rumored among Bilansky friends that Ann and Walker had some sort of relationship. Walker had actually facilitated Ann meeting Stanislaus in 1858, culminating in the Bilansky marriage in May of that year. Walker had referred to Ann as his aunt, but it was clear there was amorous affection between them. It was also well known that Stanislaus was an unpleasant and abusive person. It was unclear why Ann, who was charming, attractive, and already a widow from a previous marriage would agree to marry Stanislaus. By the time Stanislaus Bilansky had taken ill, he had complained many times to his saloon friends about Walker's apparent relationship with Ann. And Ann had done little to conceal how she felt about Stanislaus, telling others that she hated him and would not sleep with him (Trenerry, 1985).

By March 13, Ann Bilansky and John Walker were under suspicion of murder. On March 14th, an autopsy was ordered for Stanislaus. The exam revealed that his stomach and intestinal track was inflamed, and that his tongue was brownish and cracked. The doctor performing the autopsy later testified that this was consistent with arsenic poisoning. Additional testimony from one of Ann's friends indicated that she and Ann had gone shopping in late February, and that Ann had purchased arsenic for poisoning rats. The drug store clerk tried to sell Ann something that purportedly worked even better on rats, but Ann insisted that it must be arsenic.

Ultimately, Ann Bilansky was charged and tried for the murder of her husband based on a significant pile of circumstantial evidence. On June 3, 1859, the jury reached and delivered a verdict of "guilty." At that time in Minnesota, the automatic penalty for premeditated murder was death. Later, in 1868, the Minnesota legislature changed the law to require an affirmative choice by juries to sentence a convicted murderer to death. That modification to the law remained in place for 15 years before reverting back to the mandatory death penalty for 1st degree murder (Armour & Umbreit, 2012).

Immediately after the death sentence was handed down, political pressure began to mount for the governor to commute her sentence. Many around the state, including those who believed she was guilty, did not abide with the idea of imposing the maximum penalty on a woman. In fact, the very day that the Minnesota Supreme Court upheld her conviction upon appeal, Justice Charles Flandrau wrote Governor Henry Sibley asking that he commute the sentence of Bilansky. He wrote (Trenerry, 1985, p. 38):

> It is my firm conviction that a strict adherence to the penal code will have a salutary influence in checking crime in the State, but it rather shocks my private sense of humanity to commence by inflicting the extreme penalty on a woman. I believe she was guilty, but nevertheless hope that if you can consistently with your view of justice and

duty, you will commute the sentence which will be pronounced, to imprisonment.

Governor Sibley took no action as his term in office was about to expire.

On January 1, 1860, Alexander Ramsey became Governor of Minnesota. While considerable debate and hand-wringing took place among the governor's advisors and in the legislature regarding the propriety of the death penalty for women, and also for men, Governor Ramsey eventually issued the death warrant to the Ramsey County Sheriff, instructing him to carry out the sentence. On March 23, 1860, Ann Bilansky was hung just after 10 a.m. The anti-death penalty movement in Minnesota was born (Armour & Umbreit, 2012).

Mass Hanging of 38 Sioux Indians

Despite Minnesota's modern association with antipathy for the death penalty, the state ironically was the stage for the largest mass execution in U.S. history. This too happened in close proximity to the state's founding. The largest mass execution ever to take place in the United States was the hanging of 38 Sioux Indian combatants in Mankato, on December 26, 1862. However, in fairness, the State of Minnesota, per se, was not responsible for the mass execution; the federal government was.

On August 17, 1862, four Sioux Indians raided two farmhouses in Acton Township, located in the south-central part of the state, killing five white settlers there. The raid on the farm houses culminated in part from desperation Sioux Indians had felt due to the failure to honor commitments by the federal government and particularly local government officials. Reportedly a couple days previous, on August 15, negotiations between hungry Indians, governmental officials, and traders broke down when trader Andrew Myrick said of the Indians, "So far as I am concerned, if they are hungry let them eat grass or their own dung."

Word of the attack against the settlers made its way to the Lower Sioux Reservation near present day Morton, along the Minnesota River Valley. A decision was made among tribal members to preemptively go to war with the white settlers as reprisals would certainly follow after the Acton killings. The following day, on August 18, 1862, the U.S.-Dakota War began as bands of Sioux Indians attacked white settlers at their farmsteads and in small towns along the Minnesota River Valley. White men, women, and children were massacred in droves. In some documented accounts, Sioux warriors became drunk and made sport out of the killing of the settler children. Many women and teenage girls were reported to have been raped. On the other hand, many women and children were taken into captivity rather than murdered. It signaled the varied approaches of the many Sioux bands and tribes to the conflict. The town of New Ulm, where hundreds of area settlers fled to, was placed under siege by the Indians and much of the town burned before the Indians were pushed back.

Governor Ramsey pled with the Abraham Lincoln administration, somewhat busy with the U.S. Civil War at the time, to make available thousands of troops and munitions. He noted that panic in the region had depopulated entire counties, and that a battle front had been drawn by the Indians extending 200 miles (Nichols, 2012). Initially, President Lincoln dispatched General John Pope to Minnesota to lead a newly created "War Department of the Northwest" which consisted of several army regiments. But initially the regiments were slow to muster. Pope made urgent requests to the War Department for more troops.

Pope wrote in his request for more soldiers (as cited in Nichols, 2012, p. 88):

> You have no idea of the wide, universal and uncontrollable panic everywhere in this country. Over 500 people have been murdered in Minnesota alone and 300 women and children now in captivity. The most horrible massacres have been committed; children nailed alive to trees and houses, women violated and then disemboweled—everything that horrible ingenuity could devise. It will require a large force and much time to prevent everybody leaving the country, such is the condition of things.

Eventually, Pope received the troops he needed. The Sioux uprising lasted for six weeks before federal troops and state militia finally defeated the Indians.

After the surrender of the Indians, thousands of Sioux men, women, and children were rounded up, and 303 Sioux braves were charged and tried by military tribunals for what would be termed war crimes today and were sentenced to death. Both General Pope and Governor Ramsey were eager to impose this sentence as the cry for vengeance among whites in Minnesota was deafening. There was real concern that the rule of law could break down if the government did not adequately assuage the anger of Minnesotans. There was also concern that soldiers themselves holding hundreds of Indian men, women, and children might act out in vengeance against their non-combatant prisoners if the condemned 303 were not put to death. President Lincoln was very reluctant to execute so many people and to orphan so many children. It was not that atrocities were not committed by the Indians against settlers; they most certainly were. But in every case, was it these 303 Indians who committed them?

Lincoln decided to take a closer look at the trial records of the condemned Indians. He found that many appeared to be convicted on very flimsy testimony and in some cases, only because they were present or in the vicinity when other braves committed the criminal acts. In the end, Lincoln found middle ground. He wrote, in response to a Senate resolution sponsored by the Minnesota delegation urging that the death sentences be carried out (as cited in Nichols, 2012, p. 112):

> Anxious to not act with so much clemency as to encourage another out-
> break on the one hand, nor with so much severity as to be real cru-
> elty on the other, I ordered a careful examination of the records of
> the trials to be made, in view of first ordering the execution of such
> as had been proved guilty of violating females.

As a result of that review, Lincoln ordered that 39 particular Indians be executed on December 19. Later, the date was extended to December 26. Just prior to the execution date, one of the 39 was pardoned in light of additional evidence. The remaining 38 Sioux Indians were executed by hanging on December 26th at 10 a.m. A large crowd gathered and observed the executions, but did not resort to lynch-mob violence against other Indians being held. It later came to light that one of the Indians executed was not a person against whom a death sentence had been ordered, but was included in the group by mistake (Nichols, 2012).

The execution of the 38 Sioux Indians has become a cause célèbre for Na-
tive Americans in Minnesota and the Upper Midwest. There have been parks created, commemorative bike runs, annual pow wows, and other events to fos-
ter "reconciliation" between Indians and whites which have emerged—especially in Mankato and other parts of southern Minnesota—to honor the 38 who were hung. These 38 have come to represent all the injustice that many Sioux Indians have experienced in Minnesota since the United States government established it as a territory. Often lost in the discussion is that, at the very least, most of these Indians certainly were guilty of war atrocities against unarmed women and children. Many Minnesotans today with ancestral ties to the settlers who endured or succumbed to the Sioux uprising wonder if these 38 who were hung most appropriately epitomize government injustice against Native Americans. They note that reconciliation goes both ways, or at least it should.

William Williams

The execution to end all executions in Minnesota was that of William Williams in 1906. On April 15, 1905, at approximately 1:00 a.m., gun shots were heard by Emma Kline while she lay in bed in her St. Paul apartment. Moments later, William "Bill" Williams knocked on Kline's apartment door. When she answered, she recognized the man to be Williams, who was an occasional visitor to the Kellers in the apartment upstairs. He told her that the Mrs. Keller and her son had been shot and that she should go upstairs to tend to them. When Kline arrived upstairs, she found Mary Keller was shot and sitting in a chair. Mary told Kline that "Bill shot my boy and nearly killed me too" (Trenerry, 1985). She then asked Kline to check and see if her boy was dead. Kline found Johnny Keller in his bed with two gunshots to the head. He was still breathing, but later succumbed to his wounds, as did his mother Mary.

After Williams had instructed Emma Kline to check on the Kellers, he had gone directly to the St. Paul central police station and told officers there that he had shot the Kellers after an argument with Mary. He said he had left the revolver there in the Keller apartment. Williams was placed under arrest while police officers checked on the Kellers. At the apartment, they found the two victims, mortally wounded, and the revolver.

During Williams' trial, doctors testified about the nature of the wounds to Johnny Keller. They noted that he had been shot from close range to the back of the head while he was in bed. Johnny had been coldly executed. The jury also heard the testimony of Emma Kline and the police account of Williams' confession. Also introduced into evidence were several letters written by Williams to Johnny Keller which helped paint the motive. It turned out that Williams had a homosexual relationship with Johnny. He wanted Johnny to leave with him that night, but Johnny did not want to. Further, Johnny's parents forbad the relationship and wanted Williams to have no more contact with him. William was a lover scorned—scorned by the parents of his lover and the lover himself.

On May 19, 1905, the jury convicted Williams of 1st degree murder. The jury had had the option of convicting Williams instead of 2nd degree murder. In fact, during deliberations, the jury asked the judge if it would still be 1st degree murder if John Keller and Mary Keller had been shot after an argument and scuffle, but not with prior intent or planning to kill. The judge simply reread the charge regarding 1st degree and 2nd degree murder (Trenerry, 1985). Williams was immediately sentenced to death by hanging.

The execution took place on February 13, 1906, at 12:31 a.m. at the Ramsey County Jail in St. Paul. The execution took place after midnight because of the John Day Smith Law of 1889. This law required that executions take place at night and that journalists not be present. The rationale behind the law was that many previous executions had become rowdy public spectacles. Although executions in the state would always take place at night after the passage of the law, the ban against coverage by journalists was never enforced (Tanick, 2011).

When Williams was dropped from the gallows, he hit the ground. It turned out that the rope being used was several inches too long. Sheriff's deputies rushed in and hoisted Williams up by the neck by pulling on the rope. It was approximately 15 minutes before Williams was declared dead. The reporters there to cover the execution were uniformly horrified at what had happened. The next day, front page stories appeared in the paper about the botched hanging. Minnesotans had been growing queasy about capital punishment. There had been a vibrant anti-death penalty movement in Minnesota for decades. The news accounts of this hanging gone awry were the tipping point. Death penalty opponents convinced the legislature to abolish capital punishment five years later. In 1911, life imprisonment (with the possibility of parole) became the penalty for premeditated murder.

Resurgence of Interest in Capital Punishment in Minnesota

In the century since the abolition of the death penalty in Minnesota, there have been many attempts to bring it back. Most recently, in 2004, Governor Tim Pawlenty unsuccessfully lobbied for a referendum to consider the reinstatement of the death penalty in Minnesota. Critics of Pawlenty's proposal argued that the death penalty was too expensive, too unfair against the poor and minorities, and too often errant (in that innocent people are sentenced to death). Pawlenty said his proposal would mitigate against those concerns in very specific ways. His proposal included (Death Penalty Information Center, 2015b):

- a requirement that DNA evidence link a suspect to the crime;
- it would apply only to 1st degree murder of 2 or more persons, or a public safety official, or involving a sexual assault or other heinous or cruel actions;
- require unanimous jury decision;
- county attorney's decision to pursue death penalty would have to be confirmed by peer review of fellow prosecutors;
- Minnesota Supreme Court would automatically review all death sentences;
- clemency board would be established which could urge the governor to grant a reprieve;
- death penalty would not be imposed on defendants under 18 or those found to be mentally disabled;
- would not apply when eyewitness testimony is by a jail informant;
- lethal injection would be the sole execution method.

Pawlenty's proposal was in 2004. Since then, the U.S. Supreme Court has already mandated some of the provisions Pawlenty offered to include, such as no death penalty for crimes committed by juveniles or the mentally impaired, and no death sentences by other than a unanimous jury. Since Pawlenty's effort, there has been no serious proposal in Minnesota to bring back capital punishment.

Punishment in Minnesota Today

While Minnesota does not have the death penalty, it does provide for severe sanctions for premeditated 1st degree murder. In 1911, the state made a life sentence the mandatory sentence for such offenders. However, there had always been the possibility of parole. Minnesotans, content with foregoing Governor Pawlenty's proposal and remaining a capital-punishment-free state in the mid-2000s, were not content with the prospect of violence and vicious 1st degree murderers ever roaming the streets of Minnesota. So, in 2005, the state legislature changed the law, assigning a mandatory penalty of life without the possibility of parole for 1st degree murderers. Murder in the 1st degree in Minnesota is defined as (Minnesota Statutes § 609.185):

(1) causing the death of a human being with premeditation and with intent to effect the death of the person or of another;

(2) causing the death of a human being while committing or attempting to commit criminal sexual conduct in the first or second degree with force or violence, either upon or affecting the person or another;

(3) causing the death of a human being with intent to effect the death of the person or another, while committing or attempting to commit burglary, aggravated robbery, kidnapping, arson in the first or second degree, a drive-by shooting, tampering with a witness in the first degree, escape from custody, or any felony violation of chapter 152 involving the unlawful sale of a controlled substance;

(4) causing the death of a peace officer, prosecuting attorney, judge, or a guard employed at a Minnesota state or local correctional facility, with intent to effect the death of that person or another, while the person is engaged in the performance of official duties;

(5) causing the death of a minor while committing child abuse, when the perpetrator has engaged in a past pattern of child abuse upon a child and the death occurs under circumstances manifesting an extreme indifference to human life;

(6) causing the death of a human being while committing domestic abuse, when the perpetrator has engaged in a past pattern of do-

mestic abuse upon the victim or upon another family or household member and the death occurs under circumstances manifesting an extreme indifference to human life; or

(7) causing the death of a human being while committing, conspiring to commit, or attempting to commit a felony crime to further terrorism and the death occurs under circumstances manifesting an extreme indifference to human life.

A charge of 1st degree murder requires an indictment by a grand jury.

Life without the possibility of parole has also been extended as a penalty to certain 1st degree criminal sexual conduct (involving sexual penetration) and 2nd degree criminal sexual conduct (involving sexual contact but not penetration) offenders if two or more heinous elements are present in the offense, or if one heinous element is present and the assailant is a repeat offender. Heinous elements include conduct such as torture, mutilation, and other forms of extreme violence and depravity. As of 2012, there were 569 prisoners serving life-terms in Minnesota (Armour & Umbreit, 2012).

The federal Sentencing Reform Act of 1984 articulates a number of sentencing objectives that have guided sentencing judges around the country in their leniency or harshness toward convicted defendants. Some of the more important objectives of sentencing are (Champion, 2008):

- to promote respect for the law;
- to reflect the seriousness of the offense;
- to provide just punishment for the offense;
- to deter the defendant from future crime;
- to protect the public from the convicted offender; and
- to provide the convicted offender with educational/vocational training or other rehabilitative assistance.

These goals of sentencing have not only guided judges but state legislatures in their effort to craft effective and appropriate sentencing schemes. What is interesting about the objectives is that all but the last one implies or implores the use of harsher sentences against criminal offenders. Certainly, by the mid-1980s when the Sentencing Reform Act had passed, the need for stronger penalties was broadly subscribed to in American society and in Minnesota.

In fact, even before the federal Sentencing Reform Act of 1984, Minnesota had already begun to move toward a tougher stand against criminal offenders by limiting the use of indeterminate sentencing (which allows correctional officials and judges to release offenders from prison when they were deemed to be rehabilitated rather than after having served a set minimum sentence). In

1980, Minnesota adopted the use of a sentencing guideline grid. Minnesota was the first state in the Union to adopt sentencing guidelines (Minnesota Sentencing Guidelines Commission, 2015). Since then, the laws in Minnesota have been further honed to result in longer prison sentences for various types of criminal offenders.

Minnesota's guidelines-based grid sentencing is a form of presumptive sentencing. With this form of sentencing, a specific sentence for an offender appears in a grid and is expressed as a range of months for each and every offense or offense class. The sentences prescribed in the sentencing grid are expected to be imposed in all but exceptional cases where there are aggravating or mitigating circumstances. Usually sentencing grids, such as the one used by Minnesota, have the current offense under consideration listed on the vertical axis and the prior criminal record of the offender on the horizontal axis. The point where these two intersect is the sentencing range. The number of months listed below the range is the presumptive sentence. However, a judge can sentence someone to any amount within the range without justification. A judge may depart from the range in a higher or lower direction depending on aggravating or mitigating circumstances, respectively. These are called upward and downward departures and they require the judge's written explanation justifying the departure.

In 2014, Minnesota joined 28 other states and passed legislation to compensate individuals wrongfully convicted of a crime and who served time in prison. Minnesota Statutes §590.11 describes the elements necessary for an individual to file a claim. The statute requires a prosecutor to join the petition for compensation in the interest of justice. It further requires of exonerees (Minnesota Statutes §590.11):

- they were convicted of a felony and served any part of the imposed sentence in prison;
- in cases where they were convicted of multiple charges arising out of the same behavioral incident, they were exonerated for all of those charges;
- they did not commit or induce another person to commit perjury or fabricate evidence to cause or bring about the conviction; and
- they were not serving a prison term for another crime at the same time.

Those receiving compensation under this law may receive between $50,000 and $100,000 for each year of wrongful incarceration, and $25,000 to $50,000 for each year wrongfully placed on supervised release.

Figure 9.2. Minnesota Sentencing Guidelines Grid

Presumptive sentence lengths are in months. Italicized numbers within the grid denote the discretionary range within which a court may sentence without the sentence being deemed a departure. Offenders with stayed felony sentences may be subject to local confinement.

SEVERITY LEVEL OF CONVICTION OFFENSE (Example offenses listed in italics)		CRIMINAL HISTORY SCORE						
		0	1	2	3	4	5	6 or more
Murder, 2nd Degree (intentional murder; drive-by-shootings)	11	306 *261-367*	326 *278-391*	346 *295-415*	366 *312-439*	386 *329-463*	406 *346-480[2]*	426 *363-480[2]*
Murder, 3rd Degree Murder, 2nd Degree (unintentional murder)	10	150 *128-180*	165 *141-198*	180 *153-216*	195 *166-234*	210 *179-252*	225 *192-270*	240 *204-288*
Assault, 1st Degree Controlled Substance Crime, 1st Degree	9	86 *74-103*	98 *84-117*	110 *94-132*	122 *104-146*	134 *114-160*	146 *125-175*	158 *135-189*
Aggravated Robbery, 1st Degree Controlled Substance Crime, 2nd Degree	8	48 *41-57*	58 *50-69*	68 *58-81*	78 *67-93*	88 *75-105*	98 *84-117*	108 *92-129*
Felony DWI; Financial Exploitation of a Vulnerable Adult	7	36	42	48	54 *46-64*	60 *51-72*	66 *57-79*	72 *62-84[2, 3]*
Controlled Substance Crime, 3rd Degree	6	21	27	33	39 *34-46*	45 *39-54*	51 *44-61*	57 *49-68*
Residential Burglary Simple Robbery	5	18	23	28	33 *29-39*	38 *33-45*	43 *37-51*	48 *41-57*
Nonresidential Burglary	4	12[1]	15	18	21	24 *21-28*	27 *23-32*	30 *26-36*
Theft Crimes (Over $5,000)	3	12[1]	13	15	17	19 *17-22*	21 *18-25*	23 *20-27*
Theft Crimes ($5,000 or less) Check Forgery ($251-$2,500)	2	12[1]	12[1]	13	15	17	19	21 *18-25*
Sale of Simulated Controlled Substance	1	12[1]	12[1]	12[1]	13	15	17	19 *17-22*

[1] 12[1]=One year and one day

☐ Presumptive commitment to state imprisonment. First-degree murder has a mandatory life sentence and is excluded from the Guidelines under Minn. Stat. § 609.185. See section 2.E, for policies regarding those sentences controlled by law.

▦ Presumptive stayed sentence; at the discretion of the court, up to one year of confinement and other non-jail sanctions can be imposed as conditions of probation. However, certain offenses in the shaded area of the Grid always carry a presumptive commitment to state prison. See sections 2.C and 2.E.

[2] Minn. Stat. § 244.09 requires that the Guidelines provide a range for sentences that are presumptive commitment to state imprisonment of 15% lower and 20% higher than the fixed duration displayed, provided that the minimum sentence is not less than one year and one day and the maximum sentence is not more than the statutory maximum. See section 2.C.1-2.

[3] The stat. max. for Financial Exploitation of Vulnerable Adult is 240 months; the standard range of 20% higher than the fixed duration applies at CHS 6 or more. (The range is 62-86.)

Source: Minnesota Sentencing Guidelines Commission (2015).

Federal Death Penalty

Although Minnesota does not have capital punishment, there is always the possibility that a criminal offense committed in Minnesota will result in a death sentence. This is because federal criminal law applies in the State of Minnesota as it does throughout the country, and there are several federal offenses for which the death penalty could be imposed.

The case of the murder of Dru Sjodin exemplifies this point. On November 22, 2003, in the late afternoon, University of North Dakota college student Dru Sjodin was kidnapped from a Grand Forks, North Dakota mall parking lot; she had just ended her work shift at a store inside the mall. A week later, police arrested Alfonso Rodriguez, Jr. in connection with Sjodin's disappearance. Rodriguez was a 50-year-old, registered Level III sex offender. Those labeled "Level III" are sex offenders deemed most likely to reoffend. The police had been able to connect Rodriguez to the mall and items of Sjodin's to Rodriguez' car. In April of 2004, once the snow drifts began to melt, Sjodin's body, with her hands tied behind her back, was found just west of Crookston, Minnesota. Crookston is located 25 miles to the east of Grand Forks, North Dakota, and was where Rodriguez was living with his mother. An autopsy showed that Sjodin had been raped, beaten, and stabbed and cut several times. Additional forensic evidence on the body linked Rodriguez to the crime.

The outrage over the crime by residents of both North Dakota and Minnesota was widespread and intense. Neither North Dakota nor Minnesota have the death penalty. However, because Sjodin was kidnapped in one state and brought across states lines to another, the federal government had concurrent jurisdiction. Rodriguez was charged under the federal kidnapping statute and was convicted in federal court in the District of North Dakota on September 22, 2006. Because the kidnapping resulted in death, Rodriguez was eligible for the death penalty. The federal jury, consisting of North Dakota citizens, recommended a death sentence—despite North Dakota not having a death penalty of its own. On February 8, 2007, Rodriguez was formally sentenced to death and sent to federal death row at the federal prison in Terre Haute, Indiana.

The same dynamic is played out with the Boston Marathon bombing trial of Dzhokhar Tsarnaev, who was the surviving member of a pair of brothers accused of detonating two pressure cooker bombs near the finish line of the Boston Marathon in 2013. Tsarnaev was tried in federal court in Boston and convicted on 30 counts relating to his terroristic acts. All along, prosecutors indicated their intention to pursue the death penalty despite the state of Massachusetts having no such penalty of its own. Jurors were selected in part because of their willingness to consider the death penalty. The support for seeking the death penalty for Tsarnaev was generally popular in the Boston area and throughout New England. On May 15, 2015, the federal jury of seven women and five men unanimously determined that Tsarnaev should die for his crimes. The sentence is another example of citizens sensing that the only appropriate and just penalty for certain heinous criminal acts is the penalty of death, despite those same citizens permitting their own state to forego such penalties as too costly and uncivilized. It is perhaps an unintended consequence, unforeseen by the framers, that one of the chief blessings of America's model of government—federalism—permits incongruity in criminal sentencing, even on matters as fundamental as life and death.

Concluding Remarks

Over 100 years ago, Minnesota chose to abandon the death penalty as a punishment for the most heinous of offenders. Since then, the state has wrestled with questions concerning what punishments are most proper for violent offenders and other criminals. In an effort to minimize subjectivity and unfair or unjust variability in criminal sentencing, Minnesota was among the first states to adopt sentencing guidelines, presumptive sentencing, and mandatory sentences for certain types of offenses. However, some Minnesotans remain convinced that the death penalty is the only appropriate penalty for the most callous and scheming of homicidal offenders. The federal criminal justice system does provide a method for imposing the death penalty on certain offenders who may commit crimes in Minnesota which are simultaneous capital federal offenses. However, to date, no federal offenders have ever been handed a death sentence for crimes committed and prosecuted in Minnesota.

Key Terms

Ann Bilansky
Atkins v. Virginia
Capital Punishment
Coker v. Georgia
Consequentialist Theory
Death Penalty
Determinate Sentencing
Deterrence
Dru Sjodin
Exoneree Compensation
Federal Death Penalty
Kennedy v. Louisiana

Presumptive Sentence
Retributivist Theory
Robinson v. California
Roper v. Simmons
Sentencing Grid
Sentencing Guidelines
Sentencing Reform Act of 1984
U.S.-Dakota War
Weems v. U.S.
Wilkerson v. Utah
William Williams

Selected Internet Sites

Amnesty International
http://www.amnestyusa.org/

Death Penalty Information Center
http://www.deathpenaltyinfo.org/

Innocence Project
http://www.innocenceproject.org/

Minnesota Revisor of Statutes
www.revisor.leg.state.mn.us

Minnesota Sentencing Guidelines Commission
http://mn.gov/sentencing-guidelines/

Robina Institute of Criminal Law and Criminal Justice
http://www.robinainstitute.org/

U.S. Bureau of Justice Statistics
http://www.bjs.gov/index.cfm

Discussion Questions

1. What are the strongest arguments for the death penalty? Against the death penalty?
2. What is cruel and unusual punishment?
3. In what ways do sentencing guidelines contribute to fairness and equality?
4. Should politicians in Minnesota examine the reinstatement of the death penalty if the majority of Minnesotans want it?
5. What should the state do for individuals who have been wrongfully convicted of a crime and later exonerated after serving a portion or all of a prison sentence?
6. Should the federal government pursue the death penalty in capital cases which happen to take place in states that do not have the death penalty?

References

Amnesty International (2013). *Death sentences and executions 2012*. London, UK: Amnesty International Publications.

Armour, M. & Umbreit, M. (2012). Assessing the impact of the ultimate penal sanction on homicide survivors: A two state comparison. *Marquette Law Review, 96*, 1–131.

Atkins v. Virginia, 536 U.S. 304 (2002).

Berk, R., Li, A., & Hickman, L. (2005). Statistical difficulties in determining the role of race in capital cases: A re-analysis of data from the state of Maryland. *Journal of Quantitative Criminology, 21*(4), 365–390.

Champion, D. (2008). *Probation, parole, and community corrections.* Upper Saddle River, NJ: Prentice Hall.

Coker v. Georgia, 433 U.S. 584 (1977)

Death Penalty Information Center (2015a). *Executions by year.* Retrieved from http://www.deathpenaltyinfo.org/executions-year

Death Penalty Information Center (2015b). *Minnesota.* Retrieved from http://www.deathpenaltyinfo.org/Minnesota-0

Death Penalty Information Center (2015c). *Legislative activity—Minnesota.* Retrieved from http://www.deathpenaltyinfo.org/legislative-activity-minnesota

De Leon, J. & Fowler, J. (2013). Cruel and unusual punishment. In J. Albanese (ed.) *Encyclopedia of Criminology and Criminal Justice.* Malden, MA: Wiley-Blackwell.

Innocence Project (2015). *About us.* Retrieved from http://www.innocenceproject.org/about-innocence-project

In re Kemmler, 136 U.S. 436 (1890)

Kennedy v. Louisiana, 554 U.S. 407 (2008)

Lewis, C.S. (1949). The humanitarian theory of punishment. *The Twentieth Century: An Australian Quarterly Review, 3*(3), 5–12.

Macombs, B. (2015, March 24). Utah will return to the firing squad: How will that work? *Christian Science Monitor.* Retrieved from http://www.csmonitor.com/USA/2015/0324/Utah-will-return-to-the-firing-squad-How-will-that-work-video

Minnesota Revisor of Statutes. (2015). *Statutes.* Retrieved from www.revisor.leg.state.mn.us

Minnesota Sentencing Guidelines Commission (2015). *35th anniversary of the guidelines.* Retrieved from http://mn.gov/sentencing-guidelines/

Muhlhausen, D. (2007). *The death penalty deters crime and saves lives.* Testimony before the Subcommittee on the Constitution, Civil Rights, and Property Rights of the Committee on the Judiciary, United States Senate. June 28, 2007.

Nichols, D. (2012). *Lincoln and the Indians: Civil war policy and politics.* St. Paul, MN: Minnesota Historical Society Press.

Paternoster, R. & Brame, R. (2003). *An empirical analysis of Maryland's death sentence system with respect to the influence of race and legal jurisdiction.* Department of Criminology, University of Maryland.

Robinson v. California, 370 U.S. 660 (1962)

Roper v. Simmons, 543 U.S. 551 (2005)

Saad, L. (2013). U.S. death penalty support stable at 63%: Decade long decline in support after 2001 seen mostly among Democrats. *Gallup.* Retrieved from http://gallup.com/poll/159770/death-penalty-support-stable.aspx

Shepherd, J. (2004). Murders of passion, execution delays, and the deterrence of capital punishment. *Journal of Legal Studies, 58* (3), 791–846.

Tanick, M. (2011). Looking back: A century without executions. *Bench & Bar.* March 14.

Thompson v. Oklahoma, 487 U.S. 815 (1988)

Tonry, M. (2011). *Why punish? How much?* Oxford, UK: Oxford University Press.

Trenerry, W. (1985). *Murder in Minnesota.* St. Paul, MN: Minnesota Historical Society Press.

Weems v. U.S., 217 U.S. 349 (1910)

Wilkerson v. Utah, 99 U.S. 130 (1878)

Chapter Ten

The Times They Are A-Changin': The Future of Crime and Criminal Justice in Minnesota

Learning Objectives

- List the positive and negative effects of marijuana
- Describe the key elements of human trafficking
- Define the Safe Harbor Law
- Explain homelessness and its link to trafficking
- Discuss the current response to clergy sexual abuse
- Define violent extremism
- Identify strategies for improving policing in the twenty-first century
- Examine the "Black Lives Matter" movement
- Articulate reasons why racial and ethnic minorities are under-represented in law enforcement
- Identify the arguments for and against drone use
- Discuss pros and cons of police body cameras
- Describe how maps are used to fight crime

There are a number of "new" and emerging crime trends and issues pertaining to criminal justice in Minnesota that warrant special attention and focus. We place "new" in quotation marks because some of these issues technically are not new, but because of increased awareness, technology, changes in legislation, or some other reason, they are the subject of much conversation and debate in the news, in criminal justice agencies, in classrooms, and around the dinner table. The issues highlighted in this chapter, from medical marijuana to human trafficking, and clergy sex abuse to violent extremism, are not uniquely Minnesotan, but focus is largely on what these issues look like in this state.

Medical Marijuana

Marijuana refers to the dried leaves, flowers, stems, and seeds from the hemp plant, *Cannabis sativa* (National Institute on Drug Abuse, 2014). The plant contains the psychoactive chemicals cannabidiol (CBD) and tetrahydro-cannabinol (THC), among other related compounds. Marijuana is the most commonly used illicit drug in the United States (National Institute on Drug Abuse, 2014) and bipartisan legislation passed in 2014 created a new process allowing seriously ill Minnesotans to use a *medicinal* version of the drug to treat certain conditions (Minnesota Department of Health, 2015).

Minnesota is the twenty-second medical marijuana state, although its law is more restrictive than some. Only patients who are legal Minnesota residents and have been diagnosed with one of the following qualifying conditions are eligible to receive medical cannabis in Minnesota:

- Cancer associated with severe/chronic pain, nausea or severe vomiting, or cachexia or severe wasting;
- Glaucoma;
- HIV/AIDS;
- Tourette Syndrome;
- Amyotrophic Lateral Sclerosis (ALS);
- Seizures, including those characteristic of epilepsy;
- Severe and persistent muscle spasms, including those characteristic of Multiple Sclerosis;
- Crohn's Disease;
- Terminal illness, with a life expectancy of less than one year, if the illness or treatment produces severe/chronic pain, nausea or severe vomiting, cachexia or severe wasting.

(Minnesota Statutes § 311 — S.F. No. 2470)

It should also be noted that beginning in August 2016, patients certified as suffering from intractable pain will also qualify. Minnesota Statutes § 152.125 defines intractable pain to be "a pain state in which the cause of the pain cannot be removed or otherwise treated with the consent of the patient and which, in the generally accepted course of medical practice, no relief or cure of the cause of the pain is possible, or none has been found after reasonable efforts."

Medical cannabis is not available via a pharmacy through a prescription from a doctor, but rather a patient registry maintained by the state. There is an annual $200 registration fee, in addition to the actual cost of the drug, although low-income patients can get a reduced $50 fee (Minnesota Department of Health, 2015). The cost of medical marijuana is generally out of pocket for a patient. By November 2015, approximately 750 patients had enrolled, along with 450 health care practitioners. With the addition of intractable pain as a qualifying condition, the number of patients enrolled is expected to grow in 2016.

Patients enrolled on this registry can obtain medical cannabis to be consumed only in pill, oil, or vapor form (i.e., non-smoking methods that do not require the use of dried leaves or plant form) directly from one of eight authorized, regulated, and inspected dispensaries located in Eagan, Eden Prairie, Hibbing, Minneapolis, Moorhead, Rochester, St. Cloud, and St. Paul (Minnesota Department of Health, 2015). Medical cannabis is manufactured in Minnesota by one of two manufactures: Minnesota Medical Solutions and Leafline Labs.

Minnesota's law enforcement community largely opposed the 2014 medical marijuana bill, citing concerns over regulation and public safety (Flaherty et al., 2014). This was largely expected given state and federal drug policy has for 40 years erred on side of criminalization, and law enforcement has a vested financial interest (tied to federal grants) in the continued prohibition of drugs (Lynch, 2012). Admittedly, public health professionals in Minnesota also had reservations, owing to the fact clinical studies are ongoing and for many conditions, marijuana's effectiveness remains uncertain (see Table 10.1). Marijuana still is a Schedule I Controlled Substance and although minor possession is only a petty misdemeanor in Minnesota, the drug accounts for the largest portion of drug-related arrests in the state (Gettman, 2009). Table 10.2 below highlights Minnesota's marijuana possession and sales laws and penalties. As it deals with medical cannabis specifically, Minnesota Statutes § 152.33 makes it a felony for anyone who intentionally diverts medical marijuana to anyone other than the patient. It is important to highlight that there is a 23-member Medical Cannabis Task Force that was created by legislation that is tasked with conducting hearings and analyzing medical cannabis in this state.

Table 10.1. The Positive and Negative Effects of Marijuana

Positive	Negative
Alzheimer's: Potentially slows the progression of the disease	Immediate effects include rapid heartbeat and impairment to balance, posture, coordination, and reaction time. Some users suffer panic attacks, or anxiety
Cancer: Increases appetite and reduces chemotherapy-related nausea in the short term	Temporary sterility in men
HIV/AIDS: Potentially boosts weight gain	Blockage of memory formation
Glaucoma: Lowers pressure inside the eye, relieving discomfort	Prenatal or adolescent exposure can lead to altered brain development
Epilepsy: Animal studies suggest THC may work as an antiepileptic agent	Youthful exposure can lead to earlier onset and more severe psychoses, including schizophrenia
Multiple sclerosis: Can be an effective treatment of neuropathic pain, disturbed sleep, and spasticity	Increased risk of depression for young people who have a genetic vulnerability
Other: Helps reduce chronic pain and inflammation	One in ten people who experiment with marijuana become dependent

Source: Author created from Barcott (2015).

The long "war on drugs" that began in earnest in 1971 when President Richard Nixon declared drug abuse "public enemy number one," stems in part from the complex connection between drugs and crime (Dufton, 2012). Goldstein (1985) famously explained the drug-crime relationship as resulting from (1) the pharmacological effects of drug use (i.e., intoxicated people commit crime), (2) the economic-compulsive nature of drug-addiction (i.e., people commit crime to feed their habit), and (3) the systemic violence associated with the illicit drug trade.

On the latter point, *prohibition* against drugs, not drugs per se, causes the vast majority of drug-related violent crime (Roth, 1994). The illegality of drugs creates a situation where at any point in the drug supply chain, disputes between buyers and sellers over price, quality, and quantity, and disputes between sellers over customer base and product availability cannot be resolved by a legal third party (i.e., you cannot call the police when someone steals your drugs, although throughout the U.S. there are cases, albeit rare, of drug dealers who have called the police because their money and/or drugs were stolen), but rather through force and the threat of force (Kleiman, 2009). This set up in-

Table 10.2. Marijuana Penalties in Minnesota

Offense	Penalty	Prison	Max. Fine
Possession			
Less than 42.5 g	misdemeanor	N/A	$200
42.5 g–10 kg	felony	5 years	$5,000
10–50 kg	felony	20 years	$250,000
50–100 kg	felony	25 years	$500,000
More than 100 kg	felony	30 years	$1,000,000
More than 1.4 g inside one's vehicle (except the trunk)	misdemeanor	90 days	$1,000
Sale			
Less than 42.5 g without remuneration	misdemeanor	N/A	$200
42.5 g–5 kg	felony	5 years	$10,000
5–25 kg	felony	20 years	$250,000
25–50 kg	felony	25 years	$500,000
More than 50 kg	felony	30 years	$1,000,000
Importing 50 kg or more	felony	35 years	$1,250,000
To a minor	felony	20 years	$250,000
Within a school zone or other specified areas	felony	15 years	$100,000
More than 25 kg in a school zone	felony	30 years	$1,000,000

Source: Author created from Minnesota Statutes § 152.

centivizes dealers to "create and sustain a reputation for being at least as tough and at least as well-armed as their competitors" (Boyum, Caulkins, & Kleiman, 2011, p. 371). As outlined in **Chapter Seven**, when alcohol was prohibited "alcohol dealers settled their differences with firearms; just as cocaine dealers do today" (Kleiman, 2009, p. 150).

The fact that drug dealers are armed and dangerous forces law enforcement to develop new and aggressive tactics for policing the drug market. Drug dealing typically is a crime with a cooperating witness or victim (because both buyer and seller mutually seek one another out), thus drug enforcement is forced to rely on "unusually intrusive investigative techniques" predicated on low "reasonable suspicion" standards of evidence (Klieman, 2009, p. 155). Aggressive *profiling* and *stop and frisk* tactics, in turn, create an environment of distrust between high-crime neighborhoods and law enforcement.

The strain between the police and public can also be criminogenic "since police work relies heavily on cooperation with the public" (Boyum, Caulkins, & Klieman, 2011, p. 373). As discussed below, community perceptions of police illegitimacy play into the obligation community members feel to obey (or not obey) law enforcement (Gau & Brunson, 2015). Evidence of this strain between police and community is especially true within communities of color (Alexander, 2012). The war on drugs has "disproportionately impacted Black America through mass incarceration, societal disenfranchisement, and community and family disruption and destruction" (Eversman, 2014, p. 31).

Medicinal marijuana laws can be a precursor to the decriminalization or even legalization and regulation of marijuana per se. But marijuana is not the only issue. Minnesota has among the cheapest and purest heroin in the country, and heroin-related deaths have surged in recent years (Case & Godar, 2014). This has led to adoption of "harm reduction" drug treatment methods such as needle exchange programs, opiate maintenance therapy (e.g., methadone and buprenophrine), and opioid antagonist use (e.g., Naloxone to counter the effects of a heroin overdose, see **Chapter One** for more details) throughout the state. Opponents of harm reduction policies argue drugs are illegal for a reason—they are addictive and contribute to social decay and crime. They further criticize harm reduction for helping maintain a negative addiction to drugs (Boyum, Caulkins, & Kleiman, 2011, p. 369). Yet, the goal of harm reduction is "supporting and prioritizing efforts to reduce the consequences of drug use" (Eversman, 2014, p. 30). Owing to the fact the criminal justice system represents one of the largest contact points through which those struggling with drug addiction can access the services and treatment they need, harm reduction may be the first step in connecting those with drug problems to appropriate resources (Boyum, et al., 2011). One such way that is showing promise is through the use of drug courts (see **Chapter Three**).

Drug crimes are often held up as the quintessential *mala prohibita* or legally proscribed offenses (see **Chapter One**). Gambling, speeding, vagrancy, public intoxication (not illegal in Minnesota), and prostitution are other examples. On the subject of prostitution, however, there is increasingly recognition that sex work is, at best, a constrained choice, and sex trafficking, our next topic, is perhaps better conceived as a *mala in se* or morally proscribed offense.

Human Trafficking

Under the Trafficking Victims Protection Act of 2000 (Gov Track, 2013), which makes human trafficking a federal crime and provides a framework for prevention and intervention, human trafficking is defined as the recruitment, harboring, transportation, provision, or obtaining of a person for one of three purposes:

- Labor or services, through the use of force, fraud, or coercion for the purposes of subjection to involuntary servitude, peonage, debt bondage, or slavery.
- A commercial sex act through the use of force, fraud, or coercion.
- Any commercial sex act, if the person is under 18 years of age, regardless of whether any form of coercion is involved.

According to the U.S. Department of Homeland Security (2014), human trafficking is "a modern-day form of slavery involving the illegal trade of people for exploitation or commercial gain." People who traffic use a variety of methods to lure their victims, including force, fraud, or coercion. As shown in **Figure 10.1**, there are three key elements to trafficking: (1) the act; (2) the means; and (3) the purpose (United Nations Office of Drugs and Crime, 2015).

Figure 10.1. Key Elements of Human Trafficking

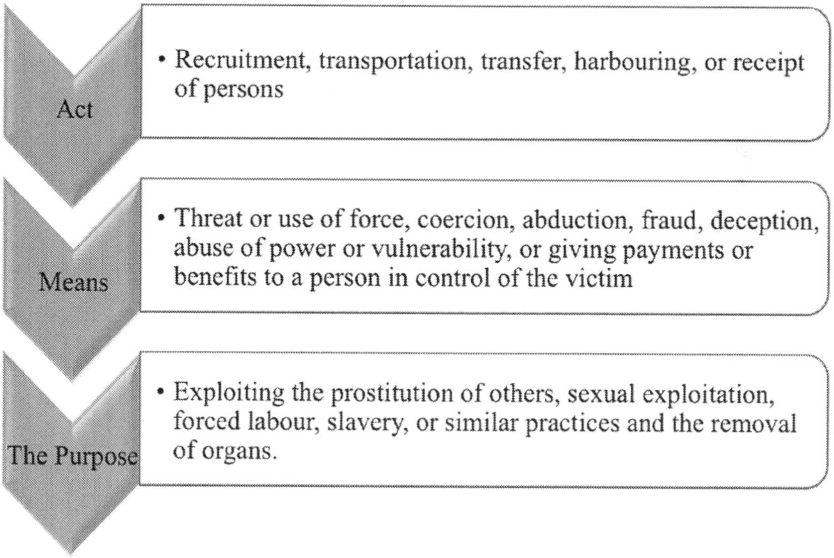

Act
- Recruitment, transportation, transfer, harbouring, or receipt of persons

Means
- Threat or use of force, coercion, abduction, fraud, deception, abuse of power or vulnerability, or giving payments or benefits to a person in control of the victim

The Purpose
- Exploiting the prostitution of others, sexual exploitation, forced labour, slavery, or similar practices and the removal of organs.

Source: Author created from United Nations Office of Drugs and Crime (2015).

Human trafficking is a global issue, with an estimated 21 million or more victims worldwide (more women and adults than children and men), of which 14.2 million are forced into labor exploitation, 4.5 million are forced into sexual exploitation, and 2.2 million are state-imposed forced labor (International Labor Organization, 2012). Domestically, the true nature and extent of human trafficking is unknown, in part because offenders and victims are quintessential hidden populations (Minnesota Office of Justice Programs, 2012). Most offenders are never arrested, therefore, never charged or convicted. And most victims avoid contact with police or service providers (like those that deal with domestic violence, sexual assault, homelessness, other victim services, etc.).

There are, however, some official crime counts as it relates to human trafficking. According to U.S. Department of Justice data, federally funded human trafficking task forces opened 2,515 cases for investigation between January 2008 and July 2010, 82% of which were for sex trafficking (Banks & Kyckelhahn, 2011). Analyses of these cases (see Banks & Kyckelhahn, 2011) reveal confirmed sex trafficking victims were overwhelmingly female, whereas labor trafficking victims were both male and female. Sex trafficking victims were more likely to be white or black, compared to labor trafficking victims, who were more likely to be Hispanic or Asian. Sex trafficking victims were also younger on average than labor trafficking victims. Most confirmed human trafficking *suspects*, by contrast, were male U.S. citizens between the ages of 18 and 34. Sex trafficking suspects were more likely to be black, whereas labor trafficking suspects were more likely to be identified as Hispanic.

Human trafficking affects Minnesotans, hence the state passed legislation in 2005 mandating biannual reporting on the crime (Minnesota Statutes §299A.785). Further, Minnesota Statutes §609.282 deals with labor trafficking whereby anyone found guilty of knowingly engaging in the labor trafficking of another can be sentenced to 15 years in prison and/or a fine of $30,000. If the person is under 18, the prison sentence increases to 20 years and/or a fine up to $40,000.

Minnesota Statutes §609.322 deals with the solicitation, inducement, and promotion of prostitution by articulating the following:

(a) Whoever, while acting other than as a prostitute or patron, intentionally does any of the following may be sentenced to imprisonment for not more than 20 years or to payment of a fine of not more than $50,000, or both:

   (1) solicits or induces an individual under the age of 18 years to practice prostitution;

   (2) promotes the prostitution of an individual under the age of 18 years;

(3) receives profit, knowing or having reason to know that it is derived from the prostitution, or the promotion of the prostitution, of an individual under the age of 18 years; or

(4) engages in the sex trafficking of an individual under the age of 18 years.

In 2011, Minnesota passed the landmark Safe Harbor for Sexually Exploited Youth, which redefined prostituted children as *victims* not *delinquents*. As of 2014, thirty-one states had adopted similar legislation (National Corporation of State Legislators, 2015). U.S. Senator Amy Klobuchar (D-MN) subsequently helped adapt Minnesota's Safe Harbor Law for the federal level. In April 2015, the Justice for Victims of Trafficking Act, S. 178, introduced by Senator John Cornyn (R-TX) was passed (Polaris Project, 2015). The federal law mandates that juveniles be viewed as victims and survivors, *not* criminals. The Minnesota law does five key things to help juveniles who have been sexually trafficked (as outlined by the Minnesota Department of Health, 2015):

1. Added the definition of sexually exploited youth in Minnesota's child protection codes.
2. Increased the penalties against commercial sex abusers or purchasers.
3. Directed the Commissioner of Public Safety to work with stakeholders to create a victim-centered, statewide response for sexually exploited youth.
4. Excluded sexually exploited youth under 18 from the definition of delinquent child.
5. Implemented state service model called No Wrong Door—making available resources and services for sexually exploited youth.

The 2014 Minnesota Human Trafficking Report (Minnesota Office of Justice Programs, 2014), which consists of results of a survey sent out to service providers and law enforcement agencies who are most likely to come in contact with human trafficking victims, showed that 70% of service providers throughout the state had helped a victim of either sex or human trafficking and 8% of law enforcement had a labor trafficking arrest or investigation. Labor trafficking victims were U.S. citizens or permanent residents from other countries, exploited in domestic situations (e.g., as housekeepers and nannies), restaurants, hotels, agriculture, landscaping, construction, massage parlors, and door-to-door sales. Sex trafficking victims were involved in forced prostitution, forced pornography, and forced stripping. The Minnesota Office of Justice Programs (2014) cautions, however, not all service providers and law enforcement were represented due to underreporting. Without a standardized data collection method for tracking this crime, this is but one way to uncover some of the reality of this crime in Minnesota.

Minnesota's No Wrong Door Model, as a result of the 2011 Safe Harbor Legislation, published a 2013 report outlining a comprehensive, multi-disciplinary plan to respond to sexually exploited youth in Minnesota. The plan included 11 recommendations, to include things like "provide comprehensive training on juvenile exploitation, provide appropriate and accessible supported services to exploited youth, and support efforts to prevent the sexual exploitation of youth" (Department of Public Safety, Office of Justice Programs, 2013). The plan is premised on the idea that anyone who comes in contact with a juvenile who may be exploited may recognize it and know where to direct the youth for effective services. There are several validated assessment tools that have been developed to screen for trafficking victims (like the Trafficking Victim Identification Tool (TVIT) and Human Trafficking Interview and Assessment Measure/HTIAM-14) as well as other assessments that have not yet been validated (like the Rapid Screening Tool for Child Trafficking, Comprehensive Human Trafficking Assessment and U.S. Department of Health and Human Services (HHS) Human Trafficking Screening Tool) (West Coast Children's Clinic, 2015). In the 2014 state report of human trafficking in Minnesota, it was estimated $13.5 million per annum was needed to sustain the No Wrong Door model. For FY16/17, the base budget is only $5 million.

Task forces have been set up both at national and state levels to respond to human trafficking. This is in part as a result of the Trafficking Victims Protection Act of 2000, but also because task forces bring together varied talents and expertise to share and coordinate efforts, and increase capacity which can produce more effective results. Two examples of task forces in Minnesota are the Minnesota Human Trafficking Task Force, led by the Minnesota Department of Health, and the Gerald D. Vick Human Trafficking Task Force, led by the St. Paul Police Department and named in honor of a St. Paul police officer killed in the line of duty in 2005 while working an undercover prostitution case.

Furthermore, the Intelligence Reform and Terrorism Prevention Act of 2004: Title VII—Implementation of 9/11 Commission Recommendations, requires a Human Smuggling and Trafficking Center at the federal level. Among its tasks are to:

> serve as a clearinghouse with respect to all relevant information related to facilitation of migrant smuggling and trafficking of persons; ensure cooperation to improve effectiveness and to convert all information of migrant smuggling and trafficking of persons into tactical, operational, and strategic intelligence that can be used to combat such

illegal activities; and assess vulnerabilities in the United States and foreign travel system that may be exploited by international terrorists, human smugglers and traffickers, and their facilitators.
(United States Department of State, 2004).

It should be noted that human smuggling is not synonymous with human trafficking (see **Table 10.3**).

**Table 10.3. U.S. Department of State Distinction between
Human Trafficking and Human Smuggling**

Human Trafficking	Human Smuggling
Must Contain an Element of Force, Fraud, or Coercion (actual, perceived or implied), unless under 18 years of age involved in commercial sex acts.	The person being smuggled is generally cooperating.
Forced Labor and/or Exploitation.	There is no actual or implied coercion.
Persons trafficked are victims.	Persons smuggled are complicit in the smuggling crime; they are not necessarily victims of the crime of smuggling (though they may become victims depending on the circumstances in which they were smuggled).
Enslaved, subjected to limited movement or isolation, or had documents confiscated.	Persons are free to leave, change jobs, etc.
Need not involve the actual movement of the victim.	Facilitates the illegal entry of person(s) from one country into another.
No requirement to cross an international border.	Smuggling always crosses an international border.
Person must be involved in labor/services or commercial sex acts, i.e., must be "working."	Person must only be in country or attempting entry illegally.

Source: U.S. Department of State (2006).

There are several organizations that deal directly with victims of human trafficking in Minnesota. One such organization is Breaking Free, whose mission is to "educate and provide services to women and girls who have been victims of abuse and commercial sexual exploitation (prostitution/sex trafficking) and need assistance escaping the violence in their lives." They do this by providing such things as housing, pre-court diversion, and outreach (Breaking Free, 2015). Breaking Free is unique from other organizations in Minnesota by offering a "johns" school for convicted offenders. A judge may order the offender to complete the schooling as a condition of probation or as part of their sentence (Breaking Free, 2015). Other service providers in Minnesota include such organizations as Catholic Charities, Heartland Girls Ranch, Minnesota Indian Women Resource Center, PRIDE Program, the Link, American Indian Community Housing Organization, Mission 21, Life House, Program for Aid to Victims of Sexual Assault, and Safe Haven Shelter (Minnesota Human Trafficking Task Force, 2015).

Minnesota Girls Are Not for Sale is a public awareness campaign to help stop sex trafficking in this state. It is a five-year, $5 million project, started in 2012 by the Women's Foundation of Minnesota. Its main goals include to "decrease demand for child prostitution through effective law enforcement and policies and educate and mobilize public support and activism to end the prostitution of Minnesota girls" (Women's Foundation of Minnesota, 2015). The focus is the pimps who sell the girls and the adults who use them. One of the places where this exchange happens is online. One website in particular, Backpage.com, has come under heavy scrutiny for allowing traffickers to sell underage girls for sex online (see **Figure 10.2**). This webpage, owned by Village Voice Media, is an online advertisement site similar to Craigslist. It is big business, as in 2012, it was said that Backpage was bringing in $22 million annually from prostitution advertising (Kristof, 2012).

Homelessness

A discussion of human trafficking in Minnesota would be remiss not to look at the issue of homelessness in this state, especially as it relates to homeless youth. In order to provide some idea of the scope of homelessness in Minnesota, the Wilder Foundation conducts a statewide survey every three years. Like other survey reports, it is believed the numbers are underreported since not all homeless are in shelters, utilize outreach services, and/or are known about on the day the study was administered. The most recent survey data from October 25, 2012, showed there were 10,214 homeless people throughout the state; 9% were veterans and 46% were under the age of 21. On any given night, it estimated there are 14,000 who are homeless in Minnesota. The reasons for why people become homeless are varied, but the most common is because they could not afford rent or a mortgage. Other more frequently cited reasons are personal conflict or a drinking or drug problem.

Figure 10.2. Human Trafficking Cases in Minnesota That Used
Backpage.com to Sell Victims for Sex

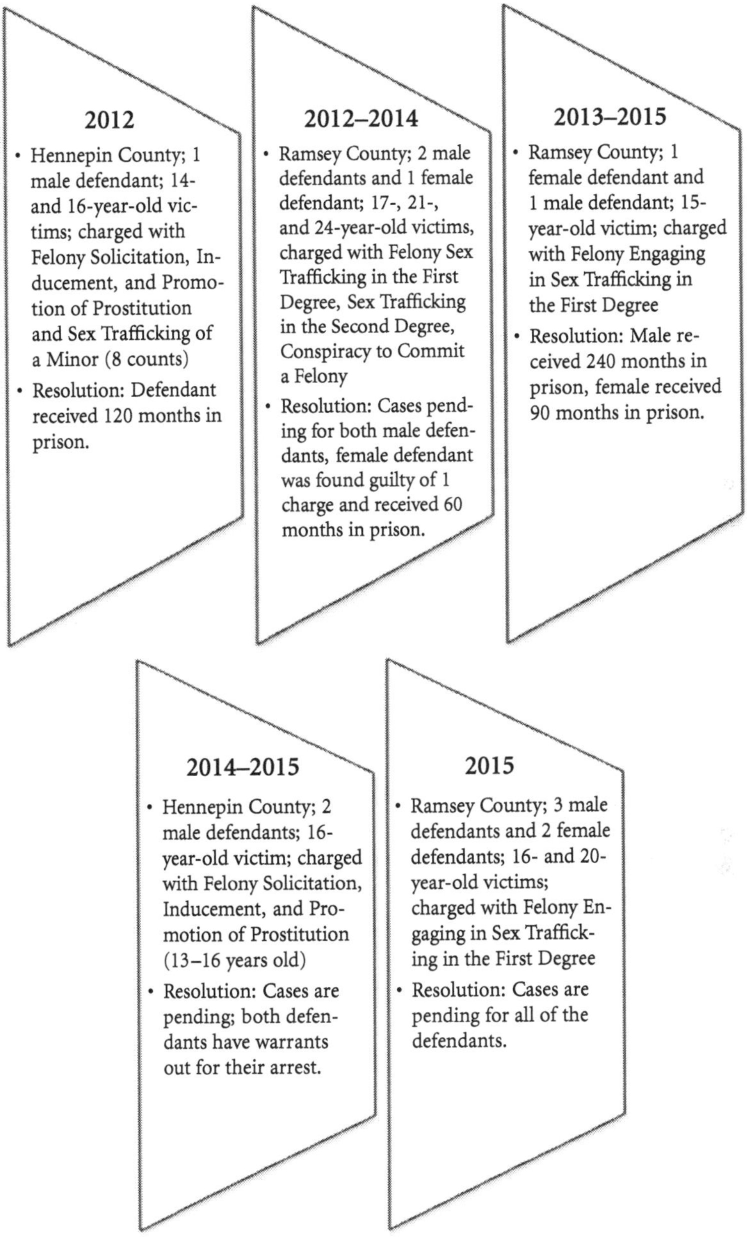

2012

- Hennepin County; 1 male defendant; 14- and 16-year-old victims; charged with Felony Solicitation, Inducement, and Promotion of Prostitution and Sex Trafficking of a Minor (8 counts)
- Resolution: Defendant received 120 months in prison.

2012–2014

- Ramsey County; 2 male defendants and 1 female defendant; 17-, 21-, and 24-year-old victims, charged with Felony Sex Trafficking in the First Degree, Sex Trafficking in the Second Degree, Conspiracy to Commit a Felony
- Resolution: Cases pending for both male defendants, female defendant was found guilty of 1 charge and received 60 months in prison.

2013–2015

- Ramsey County; 1 female defendant and 1 male defendant; 15-year-old victim; charged with Felony Engaging in Sex Trafficking in the First Degree
- Resolution: Male received 240 months in prison, female received 90 months in prison.

2014–2015

- Hennepin County; 2 male defendants; 16-year-old victim; charged with Felony Solicitation, Inducement, and Promotion of Prostitution (13–16 years old)
- Resolution: Cases are pending; both defendants have warrants out for their arrest.

2015

- Ramsey County; 3 male defendants and 2 female defendants; 16- and 20-year-old victims; charged with Felony Engaging in Sex Trafficking in the First Degree
- Resolution: Cases are pending for all of the defendants.

Source: Author created from information by Eccher (2014), Mohr (2015), and Xiong (2015).

Homelessness is associated with violence. The Wilder study showed that approximately 20% of the homeless adults and homeless youth indicated histories of being a victim of sexual or violent assault while being homeless. In looking at homeless youth, more than half of them experienced some type of abuse or neglect, with girls more likely to report sexual victimization (Wilder Foundation, 2013). Fifteen percent of girls and 18% of homeless male youth indicated they have been sexual with someone for the purposes of gaining shelter, clothing, or food. It is important to distinguish that some argue the term *survival sex* should be used for adults who trade sexual acts for basic needs. However, when this involves someone under the age of 18, they should be referred to as victims of sex trafficking (Bigelsen & Vuotto, 2013). In a random sample of homeless youth from the Covenant House in New York, it was found that 48% of those involved in the commercial sex industry entered because they didn't have a safe place to sleep. These youth regretted this decision and felt it was degrading and traumatizing (Bigelsen & Vuotto, 2013). When looking at ways to reduce human and sex trafficking, therefore, addressing homelessness is an important step.

Clergy Sexual Abuse

Sexual abuse cases involving clergy are a major topic of concern among the public, faith-based communities, law enforcement agencies, academics, and others who have been directly or indirectly impacted. The Catholic Church has been under heavy scrutiny for cases involving priest pedophilia/hebephilia/pedohebephilia worldwide. While Pope Francis has called for a "zero tolerance" policy and has said that bishops and those involved in the cover-ups will be held accountable, organizations like the Survivors Network of those Abused by Priests (SNAP) do not feel enough is being done to stop further abuse and want the Pope to "expose and remove clerics who commit and conceal heinous crimes against the most vulnerable" (Blain, 2014). As more information becomes available (i.e., files are being made public) more is being uncovered about what these crimes look like and how administrators (i.e., bishops, cardinals, and others in positions of authority) responded behind closed doors.

Uncovering the actual numbers of clergy involved in sexual abuse is difficult. In May 2014, the Vatican reported to the United Nations that since 2004, 848 priests or deacons had been defrocked and 2,572 more had been otherwise punished for sexual abuse of a minor (Associated Press, 2014). This equates to over 3,400 "credibly accused" of rape or molestation in 10 years. The term "credibly accused" is somewhat ambiguous, however, not least because there does not appear to be a precise definition for what actions justify "credibly accused."

Bishopaccountability.org is a non-scientific, publically available database created to "document the abuse crisis in the Roman Catholic Church." It publishes information about priests, nuns, brothers, deacons, and seminarians publically accused of sexual abuse in the United States. For Minnesota, the database lists 175 individuals, in neighboring Wisconsin there are 122 and in Iowa 82. Between July 1, 2013, and June 30, 2014, the United States Conference of Catholic Priests reported 620 survivors of child sexual abuse had come forward (most likely self-reported, followed by reports by attorneys), with 657 allegations of victimization stemming from as early as 1920 to present time. The status of the allegation on June 30, 2014, showed that 130 of the cases were substantiated, 62 were unsubstantiated, 243 the investigations were still ongoing, 210 cases were unable to be proven, and 12 cases resulted in some other outcome (United States Conference of Catholic Priests, 2015). In 37 cases, the victims involved were still minors, thus they were reported to the local authorities. Six of these cases were substantiated, 11 were unsubstantiated, 12 were unable to be proven, and the investigation is ongoing for the eight remaining.

In 2002, the United States Conference of Catholic Bishops created the *Charter for the Protection of Children and Young People* (approved in 2005 and then revised and approved in 2011), which is a standard operating procedure for bishops to address allegations of sexual abuse of minors. It is not a law, but viewed by the bishops as a moral contract. The *Charter* includes 17 articles that center around four main themes:

1) to promote healing and reconciliation with victims/survivors of sexual abuse of minors;
2) to guarantee an effective response to allegations of sexual abuse of minors;
3) to ensure the accountability of procedures; and
4) to protect the faithful in the future.

A 2014 annual report regarding implementation of the *Charter* highlights that the United States Conference of Catholic Bishops conducted background checks of over 2 million staff, volunteers, clerics, and candidates for ordination, trained 98% of their two million staff and volunteers in creating a safe environment and preventing child sexual abuse, and prepared 4.4 million children in recognizing and protecting themselves from abuse.

In 2013 Minnesota passed legislation that "changes the statue of limitation applied to civil legal claims for survivors of childhood sexual abuse" (Minnesota Coalition Against Sexual Violence, 2014). The Minnesota Child Victim

Act (Minnesota Statutes § 541.073) provides individuals who were older than 24 years of age at the time the law took effect (May 25, 2013) three years (until May 24, 2016) to bring a civil claim forward (i.e., suing an individual for assault and/or an organization for negligence).

In October 2013, St. Paul police opened an investigation into the handling of allegations of child sexual abuse by former priest Curtis Wehmeyer, who was arrested in 2012 and pled guilty to sexually abusing two sons of a parish employee and possession of child pornography (Baran, 2014). Wehmeyer was sentenced to five years in prison. A Minnesota Public Radio investigation subsequently uncovered evidence that several church officials did not immediately report allegations of abuse to police (Baran, 2014). A local law firm, *Jeff Anderson & Associates PA*, began pursuing civil litigation against the Church and is now recognized as one of the main voices in the fight against clergy sexual abuse.

Since 2013, the law firm has published on their webpage the names and details of approximately 200 priests in Minnesota who have been credibly accused (see http://www.andersonadvocates.com/Disclosures/Priests). As they retrieve the personal files of the priests, they add them to their webpage. Some of the files contain hundreds of pages of information. The law firm is currently working with an interdisciplinary research team to try and find a way to categorize and make the information in the files more accessible and usable. As more files are released and more people come forward, more information about these crimes will be known which will allow for further assessment, analysis, awareness, and application to hopefully prevent future cases of child sexual abuse by the clergy and others in positions of authority.

In January 2015, the Roman Catholic Archdiocese of St. Paul became the twelfth U.S. diocese to seek bankruptcy protection in connection with claims of sex abuse by priests (Nienstedt, 2015). In June 2015, the Archdiocese of St. Paul was criminally charged with allegedly turning a "blind eye" to sexual abuse against minor boys (Collins & Baran, 2015), after which it was announced by the Vatican, the Archbishop and Auxiliary Bishop of Twin Cities had resigned (Margolin, 2015). This was also the same week the Vatican announced Pope Francis accepted a proposal from the Counsel of the Cardinals to create a church tribunal (part of the Congregation for the Doctrine of the Faith) to judge "abuse of office" cases whereby bishops did not protect children from sexual abuse (Vatican, 2015).

Violent Extremism

Violent extremists are defined as "individuals who support or commit ideologically motivated violence to further political goals" (U.S. Department of Homeland Security, 2015). The Department of Homeland Security, in an attempt to counter violent extremism, works to achieve three main objectives: (1) understand violent extremism, (2) support local communities, and (3) support local law enforcement (U.S. Department of Homeland Security, 2015). In February 2015, Minneapolis-St. Paul became one of three pilot sites, alongside Boston and Los Angeles, for a strategy to integrate law enforcement agencies and social service providers to counter violent extremism (U.S. Department of Justice, 2015). From an enforcement perspective, this sounds promising, but from a community perspective there is concern. Local Somalis are worried about the exploitation of community outreach for intelligence purposes and an overreliance on the debunked theory of "radicalization" (see Brennan Center for Justice, 2015).

With the collapse of the Somali government in 1991 and the ensuing civil war, refugees from East Africa fled to Minnesota and made much of Minneapolis' south side—specifically, the Cedar Riverside neighborhood—their home. Minnesota is a "designated U.S. Refugee Resettlement Area," with a Somali population ranging from 80,000 to 125,000—the largest in America (Stanek, 2012). Still, serious racial tensions among rival clan and family structures, and with indigenous populations, escalated into violence. Somali youth, suffering from trauma and "multiple marginality," turned to gangs such as the Somali Hot Boyz, the Somali Mafia, and Madhibaan, as a form of "street socialization" (Vigil, 2002). In July 2008, the Somali Outlawz burglarized a gun store in Minnetonka, Minnesota, taking 57 handguns, some of which were sold and used in homicides, aggravated assaults, shootings, and robberies (Stanek, 2012).

In recent years, there has been increased focus on the disappearance of young Somali men from Minnesota, who are believed to have been recruited into Islamist terror groups al-Shabaab and the Islamic State (Yuen, Ibrahim, & Aslanian, 2015). Following the Westgate Shopping Mall attack in Kenya in 2013, for example, in which al-Shabaab terrorists murdered 67 people and wounded 175, Kenyan authorities revealed that one of the attackers was an American who had lived in Minnesota (PBS Newshour, 2013). Al-Shabaab released a video in 2015 calling for similar attacks on shopping malls in the United States, specifically Minnesota's Mall of America (Baran, 2015). Two months later, the FBI's Joint Terrorism Task Force arrested six people in Minneapolis and San Diego for providing support to the self-proclaimed Islamic

State and planning to travel to Syria to fight for the terror group (Yuen & Ibrahim, 2015).

Moving forward, we must be careful not to make "disaffected Muslim youth" a constructed class. Radicalization, like joining a gang, is a negotiated process, not a definitive destination state (Densley, 2014). Individual immersion within extremist groups, or "embeddedness" (Pyrooz, Sweeten, & Piquero, 2013), is a latent continuous construct based on contact with the group, position in the group, importance of the group, the balance of non-group to group peers, and participation in group activities. For many Muslims, religion is the defining factor of identity. Militancy rests upon convincing believers that a " 'neglected duty' exists in the fundamental, mainstream part of the religion" (O'Connor, 2008, p. 30), which is easier in times of political uncertainty, where anger at U.S. foreign policies and wars in the Middle East is left to fester.

With a tendency to *externalize* blame and consider themselves as victims of mistreatment, jihadists typically think problems reside in others, not themselves (Sageman, 2008). Revenge against "others," therefore, is a popular motive for action. The incentive structures of fundamentalist Islam, in turn, make violence an appealing choice. Young men who spend hundreds of hours per year in prayer groups and become leaders in their local mosque communities may come to view extremism as the only sure path to Heaven or paradise (Wikorowicz & Kaltenthaler, 2006). People may initially join extremist groups because they are confused, isolated, or have no other choices, but before long they sincerely believe radical Islam is the right path. Extremist groups provide to participants an insular sense of meaning that previously did not exist in the larger world (Sageman, 2008).

The broader Somali community, like other communities of color, thus seeks a degree of *procedural justice*, whereby they are given opportunities to participate in the fight against violent extremism and police treat them with fairness and respect (Jackson, 2015a). Somalis also seek to remedy police *implicit bias* (an automatic and unconscious process, in contrast to *explicit bias*, which operates at a conscious level) and *micro-aggressions* cultivated by public perceptions of *all* Somalis as potential jihadists (see Banjai & Greenwald, 2013). Many law-abiding Muslims feel unduly persecuted because since the September 11, 2001, terror attacks, "extremists affiliated with a variety of far-right wing ideologies, including white supremacists, anti-abortion extremists and anti-government militants, have killed more people in the United States than have extremists motivated by al Qaeda's ideology" (Bergen & Sterman, 2014). Prior to 9/11, moreover, the deadliest terrorist attack on American soil was the 1995 Oklahoma City bombing, masterminded by far-right extremist Timothy McVeigh. Yet it is jihadist violence that continues to dominate the news and the attention of policy makers.

In the end, there is no progress without *reconciliation*, or recognition from both police and the community that they are individually responsible for mistakes made in the past, but collectively willing and able to reject the past to build a safe future together (National Network for Safe Communities, 2014). The good news is experimental evaluations are presently underway to ensure training of officers in procedural justice and implicit bias actually translates into quantifiable improvements in field outcomes (Police Foundation, 2014).

Twenty-First Century Policing

The above brings us to a related issue of police reform. In December 2014, President Barack Obama launched a *Task Force on 21st Century Policing* in response to several high-profile cases of black suspects dying in police custody (President's Task Force on 21st Century Policing, 2015). The successive deaths of Eric Garner in Staten Island, New York, Michael Brown in Ferguson, Missouri, Tamir Rice in Cleveland, Ohio, Walter Scott in North Charleston, South Carolina, and Freddie Gray in Baltimore, Maryland, sparked an ongoing series of protests and civil disorder from which Minnesota was not immune. The November 2015 fatal police shooting of 24-year-old Jamar Clarke in North Minneapolis, for example, prompted days of tense protest outside the 4th police precinct, organized under the "black lives matter" banner (Black Lives Matter Minneapolis, 2015). Black Lives Matter had earlier protested police brutality at the 2015 Minnesota State Fair, where a chant aimed at law enforcement, "Pigs in a blanket, fry 'em like bacon," caused some controversy, and at the Mall of America in Bloomington, where, in December 2014, 25 people were arrested for trespassing on private property.

The "black lives matter" phrase and Twitter hashtag was born in 2013 after the acquittal of George Zimmerman in the killing of Trayvon Martin, and has since grown into a national movement. Black Lives Matter resonates in Minnesota for a reason. In February 2015, the *Washington Post* published an article titled, "If Minneapolis is so great, why is it so bad for African Americans?" outlining racial disparities related household income, homeownership, and educational attainment (Guo, 2015). And racial disparities in the criminal justice system have long been held "an embarrassment to all Minnesotans" (Johnson & Heilman, 2001).

Minneapolis police in particular draw a lot of negative publicity at the local and national level. In December 2013, for example, two white Minneapolis cops were fired for using racial slurs while off-duty in Green Bay, Wisconsin (Furst, Chanen, & McKinney, 2013). In May 2015, a Minneapolis police officer hit a 10-year-old with a chemical irritant while spraying protestors at another Black Lives Matter protest (Feshir & Cox, 2015). Two weeks later, the American Civil Liberties Union of Minnesota (2015) reported black people were 8.7 times more likely than white people to be arrested by Minneapolis police officers for low-level offenses (e.g., minor driving offenses, curfew violations, public consumption or trespassing). The study of 96,000 low-level arrests made from January 2012 through September 2014 found black people accounted for 19 percent of the population and 59 percent of the suspects.

St. Paul police too have had their fair share of controversy. In 2012, for instance, their crime lab was shut down because of a host of problems, including errors in drug testing, training, and documentation (Nelson, 2013). In recent years, moreover, St. Paul police have used *deadly force* more than any other law enforcement agency in Minnesota. From 2004 to 2014, for example, St. Paul officers shot and killed 13 men, ten of whom were people of color. By comparison, Minneapolis police were involved in eight fatal shootings (Norfleet & Walsh, 2015).

Some read these deadly force encounters as symptomatic of an increasingly distrustful and aggressive relationship between communities of color and police—problems that could lead to more fatal encounters. Others, including St. Paul Chief Smith, attribute them to more guns on the street and more police interactions with intoxicated or mentally ill people (Norfleet & Walsh, 2015).

Either way, the elephant in the room is that for every young black male killed by a white police officer there are hundreds more killed by other young black males. Public silence on this issue has lead some to argue, "Some Black Lives Don't Matter" (Lowry, 2015). Violent crime is largely intra-racial for all groups, but Centers for Disease Control and Prevention (2015) data reveal blacks were 55% of shooting homicide victims in 2010, despite constituting only 13% of the total U.S. population. A young black man is about five times more likely to be killed by a gun than a young white man. These numbers, dramatic as they are, understate the problem because most gun deaths are ruled accidental or the result of suicide, but in 82 percent of cases where a black person is killed by a gun, it is judged a homicide (Centers for Disease Control and Prevention, 2015).

Gun violence is the number one cause of death among black men aged 20 to 24 in America and it is concentrated in the same small geographic areas where police officers are most likely to be involved in problematic citizen encounters. Police *legitimacy* (see Tyler, 2004) and public *trust* in Minnesota, therefore, are paramount. In general, if an agency is viewed as *legitimate*, there is a match between the actions the agency engages in and the acceptable norms of behaviors in the community (Jackson, 2015a). When an agency is viewed as *trusted* they are looked upon as acting with the right intentions and are "fair, honest, reliable, competent, [and] responsive" (Jackson, 2015b, p. 3). To police by consent, legitimacy and trust are required.

To enhance police legitimacy, the President's Task Force on 21st Century Policing (2015) recommends practices that promote respectful and dignified interactions between police and communities, new technologies to enhance public trust and public safety, and policies that prioritize de-escalation and avoid provocative tactics. Some police departments in Minnesota are doing this well and have received national recognition for their efforts in community policing. For example, in 2012 the Columbia Heights Police Department received the prestigious 2012 International Association of Chiefs of Police Community Policing Award for agencies serving populations less than 20,000 people. They were selected because of their many department initiatives, some of which include: hot spot policing, Neighborhood Watch, youth mentoring, open gym, landlord training, All-Hands Day, and fundraising for local non-profits (Nadeau, 2012).

In 2014, the Attorney General announced the creation of a nationwide program, the National Initiative for Building Community Trust and Justice, to

1. Enhance procedural justice;
2. Reduce implicit bias; and
3. Support racial reconciliation.

In March 2015, Minneapolis was selected as one of the six pilot sites for this initiative because of its willingness and capacity to participate as well as its

> history of social tensions, level of violence, economic conditions, police department size, and historical strategies for addressing procedural fairness, implicit bias, and reconciliation at the local level. Through this process, the team gained insight into the potential for measurable gains within sites and which sites include the special subpopulations on which the National Initiative will focus (LGBTQI, youth, victims of domestic violence and sexual assault, Latino, and one neighborhood per site that will implement targeted youth violence and/or gang reduction strategies). (National Institute for Building Community Trust and Justice, 2015)

To improve accountability and transparency, in June 2015, a bill was introduced by U.S. Senators Booker and Boxer to require the systematic tracking (to be submitted to the Attorney General) of police shootings and use of force incidents across the nation. This senate bill, the Police Reporting Information, Data, and Evidence (PRIDE) Act of 2015, would require the following information:

- The gender, race, ethnicity, and age of each individual who was shot, injured, or killed;
- The date, time, and location of the incident;
- The number of officers and number of civilians involved in the incident;

- Whether the civilian was armed with a weapon; and
- The type of force used against the officer, the civilian, or both, including the types of weapons used.

(Booker, 2015)

The President's task force further recommends police better reflect the communities they serve. Minneapolis police, for example, have about half the black and Hispanic officers they need to accurately reflect the city's population (McKinney, 2014). After years of diversity plans and legal action, however, the lack of racial and ethnic diversity in Minnesota law enforcement is not for want of trying.

Hartman (2015) outlines some of the reasons agencies struggle to recruit minorities, including the stigma attached to being a police officer; some minority communities do not look favorably on law enforcement, therefore, it is not a desirable profession to pursue. There is also a lack of minority role models, which is critical in the recruitment process. Another issue cited is that applicants cannot get past the credit and criminal history check. Minneapolis Police Chief Janee Harteau posits that the high financial and opportunity costs associated with Professional Peace Officer Education (PPOE) compared to traditional police academies (see **Chapter Two**), potentially dissuade diverse or "second career candidates" from entering the profession (Ramsay & Harteau, 2014). Of course, the image of law enforcement today also affects recruitment. In spring 2015, an unprecedented seven students dropped out of the law enforcement program at Hennepin Technical College in Brooklyn Park, for example, no longer wanting to be officers out of fear (Xiong, 2015). At the time, police officers nationwide were on high alert after colleagues in New York City were shot and killed, ostensibly in retaliation for black deaths in police custody (Mueller & Baker, 2014).

In an effort to counter the national narrative of rampant problem police officers, the Minnesota Police and Peace Officer Association (MPPOA) announced in 2015 that it would launch a public relations campaign to highlight the good work that the state's peace officers are doing in their communities (Scheck, 2015). A statewide poll taken in June of 2015 found that 85% of the 450 Minnesotans polled trusted law enforcement officers to make sound deadly force decisions; 79% indicated their perceptions of Minnesota police officers had not been changed by the bad publicity police had received nationally in recent months (Scheck, 2015). The MPPOA hopes to keep favorable perceptions high, and even improve upon them, through the announced ad campaign.

In sum, Minnesota, like many other states, faces two related challenges for the future: improving police-community relations and reducing inner-city gun violence. If the public is not satisfied that police are working towards this end, they will let the police and others know through protests and other means. As has been seen in the past, the law enforcement response to expressions of public dissatisfaction matters, especially in an era where everything is recorded and disseminated through social media and 24-hour news cycles. In 2012, Hilal and Densley wrote an article for the *Minnesota Police Chief Magazine* asking if law enforcement was prepared for a new era of protests and called on law enforcement agencies to look critically at their policies in how best to respond to civil disobedience in their communities, especially since agencies were viewed as increasingly militaristic, including in regard to the actual weapons in use. In May 2015, President Obama announced that the federal government would stop providing local police agencies with military equipment, like tanks and grenade launchers, and require more strict restrictions and conditions for the use of other types of equipment (Johnson, 2015).

Twenty-First Century Technology

As discussed above, the President's Task Force on 21st Century Policing (2015) calls for law enforcement to embrace twenty-first century technology in its day-to-day operations and interactions with the public. After all, "A typical smart phone has more computing power than Apollo 11 when it landed a man on the moon" (Gibbs, 2012). There are many areas where technological advances are being utilized in law enforcement that can have both intended and unintended consequences. Law enforcement agencies, for example, use social media tools to build public relations, report human-interest stories, humanize police, connect with the community, disseminate crime alerts, even enlist the help of the public in solving crimes or locating missing persons (Lieberman et al., 2013). Similarly, police use technology tools, such as portable speed signs, to gain *cooperative compliance*. Police officers need to partner with citizens to gain compliance through education and building consensus that laws need to be followed. Technology can assist this goal because it can enhance order in a community without requiring a law enforcement officer to be there to enforce infractions.

Technological advances can be divided into *soft* and *hard* technologies (Byrne & Marx, 2011, p.19). Soft technologies include "new software programs, classification systems, crime analysis techniques, risk assessment instruments, and data sharing/system integration techniques." Examples include AMBER Alert, facial recognition, crime mapping, criminal history databases, sex offender registries, etc. Hard technologies are "new materials, devices, and equipment that can be used to either commit crime or prevent and control crime." Examples include closed circuit televisions, body armor, weapons, ignition interlock systems, biometrics, metal detectors, etc. (Byrne & Marx, 2011, p.20). While a discussion of all technological inventions, uses, advancements, and concerns is beyond the scope of this chapter, below we provide highlights a few of the areas that dominate news headlines in Minnesota and elsewhere.

Police Body Cameras

The issue of the use of police body cameras has been in the works for years, but because of some very high-profile cases involving shootings of unarmed black men in 2014 and 2015, there is a sense of urgency for agencies and states to implement policies and procedures for the utilization and access to the footage captured on camera. There is a need to build consensus on what standards should be used when using body cameras or other technologies to monitor and respond to police actions and behaviors (Jackson, 2015a). In May 2015, the U.S. Department of Justice announced it would provide $20 million ($75 million over 3 years) for police departments to (1) purchase 50,000 body cameras, (2) study the effectiveness of the cameras, and (3) provide training and assistance (Jackson, 2015b). This stems from President Obama's December 1, 2014, announcement where he pledged funds for cameras to help improve police community relations, especially within minority communities.

While body cameras "change the equation of transparency and accountability" (Jackson, 2015a, p.2.), issues of privacy (especially recording in the home), public access, data retention, and data control remain unresolved. There is also the high price tag in terms of costs for the technology, data storage, and the resources to respond to requests for copies of the videos. This also leads to the question of where should the videos be housed—in a locked evidence room or in an encrypted cloud service (Kaste, 2015)? Minnesota law would currently classify all body camera data as "public" (with a couple of exceptions) unless it is part of an active, ongoing criminal investigation. The International Association of Chiefs of Police, who creates model policies on many different law enforcement-related topics, issued a press release in June 2014 stating that they "lead the way on body-worn camera policies" and released three reports: Body-Worn Camera Model Policy, Body-Worn Camera Concepts and Issues Paper, and the Technology Policy Framework at no cost to its 23,000 membership list. In March 2015, the ACLU issued a Version 2.0 of their policy white paper on police body cameras. The first was published in 2013, but they have since updated it in light of the events in Ferguson, Missouri, and nationwide protests. While they are against widespread government surveillance, they believe body cameras could promote police accountability. They state:

> we think they can be a win-win—but only if they are deployed within
> a framework of strong policies to ensure they protect the public with-

out becoming yet another system for routine surveillance of the public, and maintain public confidence in the integrity of those privacy protections. Without such a framework, their accountability benefits would not exceed their privacy risks. (Stanley, 2015, p.2)

Some agencies in Minnesota utilize body cameras. Burnsville Police Department was one of the first to adopt them in 2010. According to Burnsville Police Chief Eric Gieseke, "It's the wave of the future in one way, shape, or form. If we aren't recording ourselves, someone else is" (as cited in Bierschbach, 2014). In December 2014, Minneapolis Police Department, the largest agency in the state, launched a body camera pilot program to determine the best policy and equipment for their agency. They created a standard operation procedure for the cameras that is subject to change after the pilot study is completed (Minneapolis Police Department, 2014). At a state level, the legislature is working through the process to provide some regulation on the use of body cameras. In May 2015, for example, the Minnesota Senate passed a bill that was attached to another bill on law enforcement technology dealing with license plate readers that would make the video captured largely private information (Simons, 2015).

While the message from the Obama Administration is clear that they want to see the use of police body cameras nationwide, it is important to recognize that like other technologies, there are some limitations. Table 10.4 provides a list of 10 such limitations as outlined by the Force Science Institute. This research institute examines the "true physical and psychological dynamics of force encounters by conducting groundbreaking research into officer and suspect behaviors during rapidly unfolding, high-stress confrontations."

Table 10.4. Ten Limitations of Body Cameras as Outlined by the Force Science Institute

1. A camera doesn't follow your eyes or see as they see.
2. Some important danger cues can't be recorded.
3. Camera speed differs from the speed of life.
4. A camera may see better than you do in low light.
5. Your body may block the view.
6. A camera only records in 2-D.
7. The absence of sophisticated time-stamping may prove critical.
8. One camera may not be enough.
9. A camera encourages second-guessing.
10. A camera can never replace a thorough investigation.

Reprinted with permission from Force Science News, published by the Force Science Institute (2014). www.forcescience.org.

Drones

The use of Unmanned Aerial Vehicles (UAVs) or drones by law enforcement presents many opportunities, but also challenges (Sengupta, 2013). A drone is an aircraft without a human pilot aboard that is controlled either via remote control or via autonomous onboard computers. The control system, such as the ground control station, the control link or specialized data connection, and other related support equipment, constitute the other elements of an unmanned aircraft system (UAS). Police use them for search-and-rescue missions, but more often for surveillance. As such, drone technology has to be weighed in light of the Fourth Amendment to the United States Constitution, which states:

> [t]he right of the people to be secure in their persons, houses, papers, and effects, against unreasonable searches and seizures, shall not be violated, and no Warrants shall issue, but upon probable cause, supported by Oath or affirmation, and particularly describing the place to be searched, and the persons or things to be seized.

In the past, the U.S. Supreme Court has ruled use of certain surveillance technologies without a warrant violates of the Fourth Amendment. In the 2001 case of *Kyllo v. United States*, for example, the Court ruled that use of thermal imaging to detect heat in a home should be defined as a search, thus requiring a warrant. Likewise, in the 2012 case of *United States v. Jones*, the Court decided placement of a Global Positioning System (GPS) tracking device on a vehicle constitutes a search under the Fourth Amendment.

While the U.S. Supreme Court has not ruled on the use of drones specifically, states have wrestled with the issue. In 2013, some states put a moratorium on the drone use, except in cases of emergency, until their legal ramifications could be more clearly articulated (Bohm, 2013; Virginia Legislative Information System, 2013). In 2014, California Governor Jerry Brown vetoed a bill that would require a warrant to use drones (Scott, 2014). And in 2015, in Minnesota, Senator Scott Dibble introduced SF 1299 and Representative John Lesch introduced HF 1491 in an attempt to regulate the use of drones by law enforcement. Neither bill was passed into law, in part because they contained significant limitations and reporting requirements on the law enforcement usage of this technology.

As was the case with policy body cameras, the ACLU (2015) weighed in on drone use, saying, "deployed without proper regulation, drones equipped with facial recognition software, infrared technology, and speakers capable of monitoring personal conversations would cause unprecedented invasions of our privacy rights." Invasion of privacy is one common cited reason against drone use, but there are others (see **Figure 10.3**). At time of this writing, the U.S. Department of Justice is funding a project through the Office of Community Oriented Policing Services to create a guidebook to "address and defuse potential tensions between the community and law enforcement. The guidebook will include detailed UAV/UAS usage guidelines that police can adopt voluntarily and informational materials, such as talking points, that law enforcement executives can use to inform the public" (Police Foundation, 2015).

**Figure 10.3. Arguments For and Against the
Law Enforcement Use of Drones**

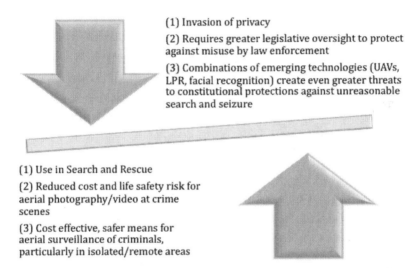

(1) Invasion of privacy

(2) Requires greater legislative oversight to protect against misuse by law enforcement

(3) Combinations of emerging technologies (UAVs, LPR, facial recognition) create even greater threats to constitutional protections against unreasonable search and seizure

(1) Use in Search and Rescue

(2) Reduced cost and life safety risk for aerial photography/video at crime scenes

(3) Cost effective, safer means for aerial surveillance of criminals, particularly in isolated/remote areas

Source: Author created.

Geographic Information Systems (GIS) and Crime Analysis

Crime mapping and spatial analysis are natural tools for law enforcement, with origins as far back as the early to mid-1800s and the "moral statistics" of French sociologists André-Michel Guerry and Adolphe Quetelet (Beirne, 1987). In the United States, principles of crime mapping hail primarily from the work of "Chicago School" sociologists Robert Park, Ernest Burgess, Clifford Shaw, and Henry McKay. Shaw and McKay (1943), for instance, linked crime rates to neighborhood ecological characteristics, specifically the degree of *social distance* between community residents (a symptom of racial/ethnic heterogeneity and residential instability) and their *social isolation* from both "parochial" (e.g., schools and businesses) and "public" (e.g., government and economy) means of social control (Bursik & Grasmick, 1993). Later theories of environmental criminology, moreover, state that crime is "routine" and predictably located in place and in time (Brantingham & Brantingham, 1991; Cohen & Felson, 1979).

Crime mapping in the twenty-first century is a lot more advanced than in the days of Shaw and McKay, to the extent that "algorithmic" or "computational" criminology (a mixture of criminology, computer science, and applied mathematics) is fast becoming its own sub-discipline. Brantingham (2011) concludes:

> The field of computational criminology involves using computational power to identify: (1) patterns and emerging patterns; (2) crime generators and crime attractors; (3) terrorist, organized crime and gang social and spatial networks as well as co-offending networks; and, (4) cybercrime.

The "big data" revolution and coming of the digital age of perfect remembering (Mayer-Schönberger & Cukier, 2014) has allowed police departments to do such things as deploy its resources in a more effective manner, track offenders, identify gang hazards, and understand crime more fully.

The push to use crime mapping gained momentum in 1996 when the National Institute of Justice created a Mapping Research Center from funds obtained through the Omnibus Appropriations Act of 1996 (National Institute of Justice, 2009). The National Institute of Justice MAPS (Mapping and Analysis for Public Safety) program helps fund research projects throughout the country that will: "(1) lead to more effective deployment of resources, (2) better use of public safety resources, (3) stronger crime policies, and (4) greater understanding of crime" (National Institute of Justice, 2009). Furthermore, throughout the country there are certificate programs designed specifically for criminal justice personnel interested in learning how to data map and collect and analyze geographic data.

One technique that addresses the issue of effective deployment of resources is the use of "hot spot" patrols. A hot spot is a cluster of crime in a small geographic area. When a hot spot is determined, more or specialized police resources are deployed to this area. In a classic randomized control experiment that took place in Minneapolis to test the general deterrent effect of hot spot patrols, it was determined the presence of police had a moderate deterrent effect on crime. Furthermore, the crime difference is proportional to the presence of police (Sherman & Weisburd, 1995). Since then many studies have been conducted to examine this crime prevention strategy. In a meta-analysis of these studies, the evidence continues to show hot spot patrolling is effective at reducing crime (Braga, Papachristos, & Hureau, 2012). As such, in spring 2015, with the help of a $125,000 federal grant and in partnership with the Domestic Abuse Project, the Minneapolis Police Department began piloting a program to deal with hot spot domestic violence calls whereby a hot spot domestic violence location will have officers, along with an anti-abuse advocate who is trained in crisis intervention, respond to work with the victim (McDonough, 2015). The hope is this program will help reduce domestic abuse and recidivism.

As outlined, the idea of deploying police resources to areas most likely to have crime is necessary because of limited resources. It is prudent that police administrators use their resources in the most effective manner. Closely related to this is the idea of *purposeful policing*. When officers are not responding to a call for service, they should have a pre-determined plan for how best to utilize their time to prevent crime and work with the community. In order to identify a plan, they can turn to an analyst. Crime analysis refers to "the qualitative and quantitative study of crime and law enforcement information in combination with socio-demographic and spatial factors to apprehend criminals, prevent crime, reduce disorder, and evaluate organizational procedures" (Boba, 2001, p. 9). There are several different types including (1) administrative, (2) tactical, (3) strategic, and (4) investigative and criminal investigation (Boba, 2001). Crime analysts are becoming more widely used in city, county, state, and federal law enforcement agencies.

Cyber Crime

While drones, body cameras, and GIS are all tools to help law enforcement, technology has also created an opportunity for a different, but very costly type of crime, cyber crime. The internet offers a low-risk opportunity for piracy, fraud and the sale of stolen or counterfeit goods, as well as for blackmail and harassment. Corporations and individuals in Minnesota and across the United States are affected. For instance, Minnesota-based Target Corporation announced in 2013 that data from around 40 million credit and debit cards were stolen (Target Brands Inc., 2015). This data breach cost Target an estimated $162 million (Lunden, 2015).

Minnesota Statutes § 609.527 states that "A person who transfers, possesses, or uses an identity that is not the person's own, with the intent to commit, aid, or abet any unlawful activity is guilty of identity theft." The scope of this crime is not fully known since people often report being a victim to private companies (e.g., credit card providers) not public law enforcement agencies. The Minnesota Attorney General requests victims report identity theft and other cyber crimes to their local police or sheriff. In some instances, federal jurisdiction applies, which would then mean the FBI and Secret Service are involved. There is also the opportunity to report victimization to the Internet Crimes Complaint Center, which is a federal clearinghouse established by the FBI and the National White Collar Crime Center,

> to receive, develop, and refer criminal complaints regarding the rapidly expanding arena of cyber crime. The IC3 gives the victims of cyber crime a convenient and easy-to-use reporting mechanism that alerts authorities of suspected criminal or civil violations. For law enforcement and regulatory agencies at the federal, state, local, and international level, the IC3 provides a central referral. (Internet Crimes Complaint Center, 2015)

Either way, one future challenge for law enforcement is reconciliation of jurisdictional issues and education and training in technical competencies.

Concluding Remarks

This book has provided an overview of what the system of justice looks like in Minnesota. While there are some notable differences, the police, courts, and corrections across the United States all work in tandem to respond to crime and serve the public. There is no state that has figured out how to do it perfectly because no state has the absence of crime. In fact, some argue, including one of the founders of sociology, Emile Durkheim, that crime is normal and serves a function for society; we need it to help define the norms of a society.

While crime is unlikely to disappear, as discussed in **Chapter One**, crime is in decline and it has been for several decades. Why there is a crime drop is up for debate, but there is no denying that crime continues to fall. Nevertheless, this fact is not comforting to the people who are still victims of crime, some of which is violent, nor the taxpayers who still see a large percentage of their tax dollars going to fund the criminal justice apparatus. While practitioners, researchers, educators, politicians, advisory boards, task forces, and many others are working to prevent crime and deliver justice, it cannot be done without the support and buy in from the general public. Being educated in the realities of how the justice systems operates is an important step; so is building trust. This book provides the education, which helps lay the foundation for trust. Lest we forget, in the words of Dr. Martin Luther King Jr., "Justice denied anywhere diminishes justice everywhere."

Key Terms

Backpage

Black Lives Matter

Body Cameras

Charter for the Protection of Children and Young People

Clergy abuse

Cooperative Compliance

Crime Analyst

Drones

Fourth Amendment

GIS

Hot Spots

Human Smuggling

Human Trafficking

Identity Theft

Implicit bias

Legitimacy

Medical Marijuana

Minnesota Child Victim Act

Minnesota Girls Are Not for Sale

National Institute for Building Community Trust and Justice

No Wrong Door Model

Procedural Justice

Purposeful Policing

Safe Harbor

Sex Trafficking

Survival Sex

Technology (Hard and Soft)

Trafficking Victims Protection Act

Violent Extremism

War on Drugs

Selected Internet Sites

Jeff Anderson & Associates PA
http://www.andersonadvocates.com/Documents/Index

Bishopaccountability.org
http://bishop-accountability.org

American Civil Liberties Union of Minnesota
http://www.aclu-mn.org

Black Lives Matter
http://blacklivesmatter.com

Breaking Free
http://www.breakingfree.net

Brennan Center for Justice
http://www.brennancenter.org

Internet Crimes Complaint Center
http://www.ic3.gov/default.aspx

Minnesota Department of Health
http://www.health.state.mn.us

Minnesota Human Trafficking Taskforce
http://mnhttf.org/our-role-purpose/about/

Minnesota Office of Revisor of Statutes
https://www.revisor.leg.state.mn.us

National Council of State Legislators
http://www.ncsl.org/research/civil-and-criminal-justice/human-trafficking-
  overview.aspx

National Human Trafficking Resource Center
http://traffickingresourcecenter.org

National Institute for Building Community Trust and Justice
http://trustandjustice.org

Survivor Network of those Abused by Priests
http://www.snapnetwork.org

United Nations Office of Drugs and Crime
http://www.unodc.org/unodc/en/human-trafficking/what-is-human-traffick
  ing.html

United States Department of Homeland Security
http://www.dhs.gov

Wilder Foundation
https://www.wilder.org/Pages/default.aspx

Women's Foundation of Minnesota
http://www.wfmn.org/mn-girls-are-not-for-sale/educate/resources/

Discussion Questions

1. Do you think marijuana should be decriminalized? Why/why not?
2. What do you think can/should be done in schools and communities to help protect children from sex trafficking?
3. Do you think the Catholic Church is doing enough to respond to and protect its members from clergy abuse? If no, what more would you like to see being done?
4. What can the average citizen do to protect themselves or others from violent extremism?

5. What role does "purposeful policing" or patrolling with a pre-determined strategy play in the patrol tactics of a street-level officer? Do you agree with the adage of "random patrol nets random results"? How would you obtain relevant data to determine proactive patrol strategies?
6. What do you think can be done to improve legitimacy and trust in law enforcement?
7. If you were on the Supreme Court and a case involving drones and whether under the Fourth Amendment a warrant is needed came before the court, how do you think you would rule and why?
8. Do you think there can be too much transparency? Should the public be allowed to see what an officer does throughout his/her shift? Would you want to be recorded the entire time you are working?
9. Are there new hard or soft technologies that you don't think police should use? Why or why not?

References

Alexander, M. (2012). *The new Jim Crow: Mass incarceration in the age of colorblindness*. New York: The New Press.

American Civil Liberties Union. (2015). *Domestic drones*. Retrieved from https://www.aclu.org/issues/privacy-technology/surveillance-technologies/domestic-drones

American Civil Liberties Union of Minnesota. (2015). *Picking up the pieces: Policing in America, a Minneapolis case study*. Retrieved from https://www.aclu.org/feature/picking-pieces

Associated Press. (2014, May 7). Vatican reveals how many priests defrocked for sex abuse. *CBS News*. Retrieved from http://www.cbsnews.com/news/vatican-reveals-how-many-priests-defrocked-for-sex-abuse-since-2004/

Banaji, M., & Greenwald, A. (2013). *Blindspot: Hidden biases of good people*. New York: Delacorte Press.

Banks, D., & Kyckelhahn, T. (2011). *Characteristics of suspected human trafficking incidents, 2008–2010*. Washington, DC: U.S. Department of Justice, Office of Justice Programs Bureau of Justice Statistics. Retrieved from http://www.bjs.gov/content/pub/pdf/cshti0810.pdf

Baran, M. (2014, February 19). Number of alleged sex abusers greater than archdiocese has revealed. *MPR News*. Retrieved from http://minnesota.publicradio.org/collections/catholic-church/2014/02/19/investigation-more-priests-accused-of-sexual-abuse-in-twin-cities-catholic-church/

Baran, M. (2015, February 21). Mall of America increases security after being named in apparent al-Shabab video. *MPR News*. Retrieved from http://www.mprnews.org/story/2015/02/21/cbs-news-alshabaab-video-calls-for-attack-on-mall-of-america

Barcott, B. (2015). *Weed the people: The future of legal marijuana in America*. New York: Time Books.

Beirne, P. (1987). Adolphe Quetelet and the origins of positivist criminology. *American Journal of Sociology*, 92, 1140–116.

Bergen, P., & Sterman, D. (2014, April 15). U.S. right wing extremists more deadly than jihadists. *CNN*. Retrieved from http://www.cnn.com/2014/04/14/opinion/bergen-sterman-kansas-shooting

Bierschbach, B. (2014, January 2). Police departments in Minnesota focus on police body camera. *MinnPost*. Retrieved from https://www.minnpost.com/politics-policy/2014/01/police-departments-minnesota-focus-body-cameras

Bigelsen, J., & Vuotto, S. (2013). *Homelessness, survival sex, and human trafficking as experienced by the youth of Covenant House New York*. Retrieved from http://traffickingresourcecenter.org/sites/default/files/Homelessness%2C%20Survival%20Sex%2C%20and%20Human%20Trafficking%20-%20%20Covenant%20House%20NY.pdf

Black Lives Matter Minneapolis. (2015). Facebook profile. Retrieved from https://www.facebook.com/BlackLivesMatterMinneapolis/

Blain, B. (2014, July 7). Victims meet the Pope, SNAP Responds. Press Release. http://www.snapnetwork.org/rome_victims_meet_the_pope_snap_responds

Boba, R. (2001). Introductory guide to crime analyst and mapping. U.S. Department of Justice: Community Oriented Police Services. Retrieved from http://www.cops.usdoj.gov/html/cd_rom/tech_docs/pubs/Introductory GuidetoCrimeAnalysisMapping.pdf

Bohm, A. (2013). The first state laws on drones. Retrieved from https://www.aclu.org/blog/first-state-laws-drones

Booker, C. (2015, June 2). Booker, Boxer introduce Bill to bring transparency and accountability to police departments nationwide. Corey Booker, United States Senator for New Jersey. Retrieved from http://www.booker.senate.gov/?p=press_release&id=247

Boyum, D., Caulkins, J., & Kleiman, M. (2011). Drugs, crime, and public policy. In J. Wilson & J. Petersilia (Eds.), *Crime and public policy* (p. 411–436). New York: Oxford University Press.

Braga, A., Papachristos, A., & Hureau, D. (2012). Hot spot policing effects on crime. *Campbell Systematic Review*. Retrieved from www.campbellcollaboration.org

Brantingham, P. (2011). Computational criminology. *Proceedings of the 2011 European Intelligence and Security Informatics Conference.* Washington, DC: IEEE Computer Society.

Brantingham, P., & Brantingham, P. (1991). *Environmental criminology.* Prospect Heights, IL: Waveland Press.

Breaking Free. (2015). Retrieved from http://www.breakingfree.net

Brennan Center for Justice. (2015). *Countering Violent Extremism (CVE): A resource page.* Retrieved from https://www.brennancenter.org/analysis/cve-programs-resource-page

Bursik, R., Jr., & Grasmick, H. (1993). *Neighborhoods and crime: The dimensions of effective community control.* New York: Lexington.

Byrne, J., & Marx, G. (2011). Technological innovations in crime prevention and policing. A review of research implementation and impact. *Cahiers Politiestudies Jaargang, 3,* 17–40.

Case, C., & Godar, B. (2014, January 20). Twin Cities, Minnesota trying to cope with flood of cheap, pure heroin. *MinnPost.* Retrieved from http://www.minnpost.com/politics-policy/2014/01/twin-cities-minnesota-trying-cope-flood-cheap-pure-heroin

Centers for Disease Control and Prevention. (2015). *National Violent Death Reporting System.* Retrieved from http://wisqars.cdc.gov:8080/nvdrs/nvdrsDisplay.jsp

Cohen, L., & Felson, M. (1979). Social change and crime rate trends: A routine activity approach. *American Sociological Review, 44,* 588–605.

Collins, J., & Baran, M. (2015, June 5). Twin Cities archdiocese criminally charged in priest child abuse case. *MPR News.* Retrieved from http://www.mprnews.org/story/2015/06/05/archdiocese-investigation

Densley, J. (2014, October 7). ISIS: The street gang on steroids. *CNN.* Retrieved from: http://www.cnn.com/2014/10/07/opinion/densley-isis-gangs/

Department of Public Safety, Office of Justice Programs. (2013). A comprehensive approach to Safe Harbor for Minnesota's sexually exploited youth. Retrieved from https://dps.mn.gov/divisions/ojp/forms-documents/Documents/!2012%20Safe%20Harbor%20Report%20(FINAL).pdf

Dufton, E. (2012, March 26). The war on drugs: How President Nixon tied addiction to crime. *The Atlantic.* Retrieved from http://www.theatlantic.com/health/archive/2012/03/the-war-on-drugs-how-president-nixon-tied-addiction-to-crime/254319/

Eccher, M. (2014, November 20). St. Paul prostitution ring busted by runaway, 17, police say. *Pioneer Press.* Retrieved from: http://www.twincities.com/localnews/ci_26970301/st-paul-prostitution-ring-busted-by-runaway-17

Eversman, M. (2014) 'Trying to find the middle ground': Drug policy and harm reduction in black communities. *Race and Justice*, 4, 29–44.

Feshir, R., & Cox, P. (2015, May 15). Protesters march in support of boy, 10, hit by pepper spray. *MPR News*. Retrieved from http://www.mprnews.org/story/2015/05/15/mpls-protest

Flaherty, D., Kingrey, J., Franklin, J., & Skoogman, A. (2014, April 29). Medical marijuana: Law enforcement is open to careful first steps. *Star Tribune*. Retrieved from http://www.startribune.com/medical-marijuana-law-enforcement-is-open-to-careful-first-steps/257252761/

Force Science Institute. (2014). Ten limitations of body cameras. Retrieved from http://www.forcescience.org/whoweare.html

Furst, R., Chanen, D., & McKinney, M. (2013, December 31). Two white MPLS cops fired over racial slurs incident in Green Bay. *Star Tribune*. Retrieved from http://www.startribune.com/two-white-mpls-cops-fired-over-racial-slurs-incident-in-green-bay/234280301/

Gau, J., & Brunson, R. (2015). Procedural injustice, lost legitimacy, and self-help: Young males' adaptations to perceived unfairness in urban policing tactics. *Journal of Contemporary Criminal Justice*, 31, 132–150.

Gettman, J. (2009). Marijuana in Minnesota: Arrests, usage, and related data. *The Bulletin of Cannabis Reform*. Retrieved from http://www.drugscience.org/States/MN/MN.pdf

Gibbs, N. (2012, August 16). Your life is fully mobile. *Time Magazine*. Retrieved from http://techland.time.com/2012/08/16/your-life-is-fully-mobile/

Goldstein, P. (1985). The drugs/violence nexus: A tripartite conceptual framework. *Journal of Drug Issues*, 15, 493–506.

Gov Track. (2013). *H.R. 898 (113th): Trafficking Victims Protection Reauthorization Act of 2013*. Retrieved from https://www.govtrack.us/congress/bills/113/hr898

Guo, J. (2015, February 17). If Minneapolis is so great, why is it so bad for African Americans? *Washington Post*. Retrieved from http://www.washingtonpost.com/blogs/govbeat/wp/2015/02/17/if-minneapolis-is-so-great-why-is-it-so-bad-for-black-people/

Hartman, M. (2015, May 29). Why it is difficult for minorities to become cops. *Marketplace*. Retrieved from http://www.marketplace.org/topics/world/behind-blue-line/why-its-difficult-minorities-become-cops

International Association of Chiefs of Police. (2014, June 9). IACP leads the way on body-worn camera policies. Press Release. Retrieved from http://www.theiacp.org/ViewResult?SearchID=2413

International Labor Organization. (2012). 21 million people are now victims of forced labour, ILO says. Retrieved from http://www.ilo.org/global/about-the-ilo/newsroom/news/WCMS_181961/lang--en/index.htm

Internet Crime Complaint Center. (2015). Retrieved from http://www.ic3.gov/about/default.aspx

Jackson, B. (2015a). Respect and legitimacy—a two-way street: Strengthening trust between the police and the public in an era of increased transparency. Rand Corporation. Retrieved from http://www.rand.org/content/dam/rand/pubs/perspectives/PE100/PE154/RAND_PE154.pdf

Jackson, D. (2015b, May 1). Obama team will fund police body camera project. *USA Today*. http://www.usatoday.com/story/news/nation/2015/05/01/obama-police-body-cameras-josh-earnest-baltimore/26696517/

Jeff Anderson & Associates PA. (2015). *Document and priest files*. Retrieved from http://www.andersonadvocates.com/Documents/Index

Johnson, A. (2015, May 18). Obama: US cracking down on militarization of police. *NBC News*. Retrieved from http://www.nbcnews.com/news/us-news/u-s-cracking-down-militarization-local-police-n360381

Johnson, T. L., & Heilman, C. W. (2001). An embarrassment to all Minnesotans: Racial disparity in the criminal justice system. *Bench & Bar of Minnesota*, 58. Retrieved from: http://www.mnbar.org/benchandbar/2001/may-jun01/racial-disparity.htm

Kaste, M. (2015, May 29). As police body cameras increase, what about all that video? *National Public Radio*. Retrieved from http://www.npr.org/sections/alltechconsidered/2015/05/29/410572605/as-police-body-cameras-increase-what-about-all-that-video

Kleiman, M. (2009). *When brute force fails: How to have less crime and less punishment*. Princeton, NJ: Princeton University Press.

Kristoff, N. D. (2012, January 26). How pimps use the web to sell girls. *The New York Times*. Retrieved from http://www.nytimes.com/2012/01/26/opinion/how-pimps-use-the-web-to-sell-girls.html?_r=0

Lieberman, J., Koetzle, D., & Sakiyama, M. (2013). Police departments' use of facebook: Patterns and policy issues. *Police Quarterly*, 16, 438–462.

Lowry, R. (2015). #SomeBlackLivesDontMatter. *Politico Magazine*, May 27. Retrieved from http://www.politico.com/magazine/story/2015/05/ferguson-freddie-gray-policing-118348.html#.VWdY0rq1hUs

Lunden, I. (2015, February 25). Target says credit card data breach cost it $162M in 2013–2014. *Techcrunch*. Retrieved from http://techcrunch.com/2015/02/25/target-says-credit-card-data-breach-cost-it-162m-in-2013-14/

Lynch, M. (2012). Theorizing the role of the 'war on drugs' in US punishment. *Theoretical Criminology*, 16, 175–199.

Margolin, E. (2015, June 14). Clergy sex abuse scandal sees surge of activity. What's behind it? MSNBC. Retrieved from http://www.msnbc.com/msnbc/clergy-sex-abuse-scandal-sees-surge-activity-whats-behind-it

Mayer-Schönberger, V., & Cukier, K. (2014). *Big data: A revolution that will transform how we live, work, and think.* Boston, MA: Houghton Mifflin Harcourt.

McDonough, B. (2015, April 26). New program targets domestic abuse hot spots in Minneapolis. *KSTP News.* Retrieved from http://kstp.com/article/stories/s3778284.shtml

McKinney, M. (2014, August 19). Minneapolis police struggle to hire diverse force. *Star Tribune.* Retrieved from http://www.startribune.com/despite-wave-of-retirements-mpls-police-struggle-to-hire-diverse-force/271772331/

Minneapolis Police Department. (2014, December 12). Body Camera Pilot Program. Retrieved from http://www.minneapolismn.gov/www/groups/public/@communications/documents/webcontent/wcms1p-135024.pdf

Minnesota Coalition Against Sexual Violence. (2014). *Minnesota Child Victim Act.* Retrieved from http://www.mncasa.org/assets/PDFs/SVJI-Child%20Victim%20Act%20Fact%20Sheet.pdf

Minnesota Department of Health. (2015a). *General information about the Minnesota medical cannabis program.* Retrieved from http://www.health.state.mn.us/topics/cannabis/about/factsheet.html

Minnesota Department of Health. (2015b). *Safe Harbor in Minnesota.* Retrieved from http://www.health.state.mn.us/injury/topic/safeharbor/

Minnesota Human Trafficking Task Force. (2015). *Service providers and organizations.* Retrieved from http://mnhttf.org/human-trafficking/organizationsproviders/

Minnesota Office of Justice Programs. (2012). *Human trafficking in Minnesota.* Retrieved from https://dps.mn.gov/divisions/ojp/forms-documents/Documents/Human%20Trafficking%20Final%20Report.pdf

Minnesota Office of Justice Programs. (2014). *Human trafficking in Minnesota.* Retrieved from https://dps.mn.gov/divisions/ojp/forms-documents/Documents/2014%20Human%20Trafficking%20Report.pdf

Mohr, E. (2015, March 3). Five from St. Paul charged in sex trafficking ring. *Pioneer Press.* Retrieved from: http://www.twincities.com/localnews/ci_27632857/five-from-st-paul-charged-sex-trafficking-ring

Mueller, B., & Baker, A. (2014, December 20). Two N.Y.P.D. officers are killed in Brooklyn ambush; suspect commits suicide. *New York Times.* Retrieved from http://www.nytimes.com/2014/12/21/nyregion/two-police-officers-shot-in-their-patrol-car-in-brooklyn.html?_r=0

Nadeau, S. (2012, August 30). Columbia Heights Police Department receives 2012 International Association of Chiefs of Police Community Policing

Award. Press Release. Retrieved from http://www.ci.columbia-heights.mn.us/DocumentCenter/View/846

National Corporation of State Legislators. (2015). *Human trafficking overview.* Retrieved from http://www.ncsl.org/research/civil-and-criminal-justice/human-trafficking-overview.aspx

National Institute on Drug Abuse. (2014, December). *What is marijuana?* Retrieved from http://www.drugabuse.gov/publications/research-reports/marijuana/what-marijuana

National Institute of Justice. (2009). *MAPS: The history of mapping at NIJ.* Retrieved from http://www.nij.gov/topics/technology/maps/pages/history.aspx

National Network for Safe Communities. (2014). *National initiative for building community trust and justice announced.* Retrieved from http://nnscommunities.org/our-work/commentary/national-initiative-for-building-community-trust-and-justice-announced

Nelson, T. (2013, August 15). St. Paul police crime lab back up and running after scandal. *MPR News.* Retrieved from http://blogs.mprnews.org/cities/2013/08/st-paul-police-crime-lab-back-up-and-running-after-scandal/

Nienstedt, J. (2015, January 16). Letter from Archbishop John Nienstedt. Retrieved from http://www.archspm.org/archspm_news/letter-archbishop-john-nienstedt/

Norfleet, N., & Walsh, J. (2015, February 7). St. Paul police officers lead in rising use of deadly force. *Star Tribune.* Retrieved from http://www.startribune.com/st-paul-police-officers-lead-in-rising-use-of-deadly-force/291169771/

O'Connor, T. (2008). The criminology of terrorism: Theories and models. In K. Borgeson & Valeri, R. (eds.), *Terrorism in America* (pp. 17–46). Sudbury, MA: Jones & Bartlett.

PBS Newshour. (2013, September 23). Kenyan foreign minister says 'two or three' Americans involved in mall attack. Retrieved from http://www.pbs.org/newshour/bb/africa-july-dec13-kenyaminister_09-23/

Polaris Project. (2015). *Senate passes bipartisan anti-human trafficking legislation.* Retrieved from http://www.polarisproject.org/media-center/news-and-press/press-releases/1123-senate-passes-bipartisan-anti-human-trafficking-legislation

Police Foundation. (2014). Promoting officer integrity through early engagement and procedural justice. Retrieved from http://www.policefoundation.org/content/promoting-officer-integrity-through-early-engagement-and-procedural-justice

Police Foundation. (2015). *Unmanned aerial vehicles in policing.* Retrieved from http://www.policefoundation.org/content/unmanned-aerial-vehicles-policing

President's Task Force on 21st Century Policing. (2015). *Final report of the President's Task Force on 21st Century Policing.* Washington, DC: Office of Community Oriented Policing Services

Pyrooz, D., Sweeten, G., & Piquero, A. (2013). Continuity and change in gang membership and gang embeddedness. *Journal of Research in Crime and Delinquency,* 50, 239–71.

Ramsay, G., & Harteau, J. (2014, September 16). Counterpoint: Open up the police recruitment process. *Star Tribune.* Retrieved from http://www.startribune.com/opinion/commentaries/275216041.html

Roth, J. (1994, February). Psychoactive substances and violence. National Institute of Justice, Research in Brief NCJ 145534. Washington, DC: U.S. Department of Justice.

Sageman, M. (2008). *The leaderless Jihad.* Philadelphia, PA: University of Pennsylvania Press.

Scheck, T. (2015, June 28). Ad campaign to highlight Minnesota cops' good work. *MPR News.* Retrieved from http://www.mprnews.org/story/2015/06/28/police-union-ad-campaign

Scott, A. (2014, September 30). Should police need warrants to use drones? *US News.* Retrieved from http://www.usnews.com/opinion/articles/2014/09/30/should-police-in-california-need-warrants-to-use-drones

Sengupta, S. (2013, February 15). Rise of drones in U.S. drives efforts to limit police use. *New York Times.* Retrieved from http://www.nytimes.com/2013/02/16/technology/rise-of-drones-in-us-spurs-efforts-to-limit-uses.html?pagewanted=all&_r=0

Shaw, C., & McKay, H. (1942). *Juvenile delinquency in urban areas.* Chicago: University of Chicago Press.

Sherman, L., & Weisburd, D. (1995). General deterrent effects of police patrol in crime 'hot spots': A randomized, controlled trial. *Justice Quarterly,* 12, 625–48.

Simons, A. (2015, May 7). Body-cam rules pass as part of license reader bill in Minnesota Senate. *Star Tribune.* Retrieved from http://www.startribune.com/minnesota-senate-passes-police-body-cam-rules/303014731/

Stanek, R. (2012). *Testimony of Richard W. Stanek to the subcommittee on crime, terrorism, and homeland security.* Retrieved from http://judiciary.house.gov/_files/hearings/Hearings%202012/Stanek%2007252012.pdf

Stanley, J. (2015). Police body-mounted cameras. With right policies in place, a win for all. Version 2.0. *American Civil Liberties Union.* Retrieved from https://www.aclu.org/sites/default/files/assets/police_body-mounted_cameras-v2.pdf

Target Brands, Inc. (2015). *Data breach FAQ.* Retrieved from https://corporate.target.com/about/shopping-experience/payment-card-issue-faq

Tyler, T. (2004) Enhancing police legitimacy. *The ANNALS of the American Academy of Political and Social Science*, 593, 84–99.

United Nations Office of Drugs and Crime. (2015). *What is human trafficking*. Retrieved from http://www.unodc.org/unodc/en/human-trafficking/what-is-human-trafficking.html

United States Conference of Catholic Priests. (2011). *Charter for the Protection of Children and Young People*. Retrieved from http://www.usccb.org/issues-and-action/child-and-youth-protection/upload/Charter-for-the-Protection-of-Children-and-Young-People-revised-2011.pdf

United States Conference of Catholic Priests. (2015). *Report on the Implementation of the Charter for the Protection of Children and Young People*. Retrieved from http://www.usccb.org/issues-and-action/child-and-youth-protection/upload/2014-Annual-Report.pdf

United States Department of Homeland Security. (2014). *Definition of human trafficking*. Retrieved from http://www.dhs.gov/definition-human-trafficking

United States Department of Homeland Security. (2015). *Countering violent extremism*. Retrieved from http://www.dhs.gov/topic/countering-violent-extremism

United States Department of Justice. (2015). *Pilot programs are key to our countering violent extremism efforts*. Retrieved from http://www.justice.gov/opa/blog/pilot-programs-are-key-our-countering-violent-extremism-efforts

United States Department of State. (2004). *Intelligence Reform and Terrorism Prevention Act of 2004: Title VII—Implementation of 9/11 Commission Recommendations*. Retrieved from http://www.state.gov/m/ds/hstcenter/41449.htm

United States Department of State. (2006). *Fact sheet: Distinctions between human smuggling and human trafficking*. Washington, DC: Human Smuggling and Trafficking Center. Retrieved from http://www.state.gov/documents/organization/90541.pdf

Vatican. (2015, June 10). Pope approves "abuse of office" proposals for bishops in sex abuse cases. Retrieved from http://www.news.va/en/news/pope-approves-abuse-of-office-proposals-for-bishop

Vigil, D. (2002). *A rainbow of gangs: Street cultures in the mega-city*. Austin, TX: University of Texas Press.

Virginia Legislative Information System. (2013). *HB 2012 Drones; Moratorium on use of unmanned aircraft systems by state or local government department, etc.* Retrieved from http://lis.virginia.gov/cgi-bin/legp604.exe?131+sum+HB2012

West Coast Children's Clinic. (2015). *Matrix of screening tools to identify commercially sexually exploited youth*. Retrieved from http://www.cwda.org/downloads/tools/csec/WCC-Matrix.pdf

Wiktorowicz, Q., & Kaltenthaler, K. (2006). The rationality of radical Islam. *Political Science Quarterly*, 121, 295–319.

Wilder Foundation. (2013). 2012 Minnesota homeless study. Retrieved from http://www.wilder.org/Wilder-Research/Publications/HomelessStudyTables 2012/All-2012-Homeless-Counts-3-13.pdf

Women's Foundation of Minnesota. (2015). Minnesota girls are not for sale. Retrieved from http://www.wfmn.org/mn-girls-are-not-for-sale/about-us/ what-is-mn-girls-are-not-for-sale/

Xiong, B. (2015, March 12). Law enforcement program losing students. *KARE 11*. Retrieved from http://www.kare11.com/story/news/local/2015/03/12/ law-enforcement-program-losing-students/70234696/

Yuen, L., & Ibrahim, M. (2015, April 20). Feds charge six Minnesotans with trying to join ISIS. *MPR News*. Retrieved from http://www.mprnews.org/ story/2015/04/20/6-charged-with-trying-to-join-isis

Yuen, L., Ibrahim, M., & Aslanian, S. (2015, March 25). Called to fight: Minnesota's ISIS recruits. *MPR News*. Retrieved from http://www.mprnews.org/ story/2015/03/25/minnesota-isis

Xiong, C. (2015, February 27). Couple sentenced for prostituting 15-year-old in St. Paul home. *Star Tribune*. Retrieved from: http://www.startribune.com/ couple-sentenced-for-prostituting-15-year-old-in-st-paul-home/294409261/

About the Authors

Jeff Bumgarner, Ph.D., is Professor and Chair of the Department of Criminal Justice and Political Science at North Dakota State University. Dr. Bumgarner is a licensed Minnesota peace officer and has several years of law enforcement experience at the federal, county, and local levels. He formerly served on the Minnesota Board on Judicial Standards and the Training Committee for the Minnesota Chiefs of Police Association. He is the author or co-author of five books, including *Federal Law Enforcement: A Primer* (Carolina Academic Press) as well as several peer-reviewed articles and book chapters.

Susan Hilal, Ph.D., is Professor and Chair of the School of Law Enforcement and Criminal Justice at Metropolitan State University. She has published a variety of articles in both trade and peer-reviewed journals as it relates to the topics of police education, mass murder, and juvenile justice issues. Her publications appear in *Policing and Society, Critical Issues in Justice and Politics, the FBI Law Enforcement Bulletin, Homicide Studies, Group Processes & Intergroup Relations, Journal of Criminal Justice Education,* and *Police Chief Magazine.*

James Densley, D.Phil., is Associate Professor of Criminal Justice at Metropolitan State University and an Associate of the Extra-Legal Governance Institute at the University of Oxford. His teaching and research interests include street gangs, criminal networks, violence, and theoretical criminology. Densley is the author of *How Gangs Work* (Palgrave Macmillan, 2013) and articles in such outlets as *Journal of Research in Crime and Delinquency, Crime & Delinquency, Journal of Contemporary Criminal Justice, Policing & Society,* and *Social Problems.* He has also contributed to news outlets such as *CNN, The Sun,* and *Viceland.*

Index